BIOBEHAVIORAL
RESILIENCE
to STRESS

BIOBEHAVIORAL RESILIENCE to STRESS

Edited by Brian J. Lukey and Victoria Tepe

CRC Press
Taylor & Francis Group
Boca Raton London New York

CRC Press is an imprint of the
Taylor & Francis Group, an **informa** business

Cover: Photo courtesy of Spc. Leah R. Burton, U.S. Army.

CRC Press
Taylor & Francis Group
6000 Broken Sound Parkway NW, Suite 300
Boca Raton, FL 33487-2742

First issued in paperback 2019

ISBN-13: 978-1-4200-7177-1 (hbk)
ISBN-13: 978-0-367-86486-6 (pbk)

This book contains information obtained from authentic and highly regarded sources Reasonable efforts have been made to publish reliable data and information, but the author and publisher cannot assume responsibility for the validity of all materials or the consequences of their use. The Authors and Publishers have attempted to trace the copyright holders of all material reproduced in this publication and apologize to copyright holders if permission to publish in this form has not been obtained. If any copyright material has not been acknowledged please write and let us know so we may rectify in any future reprint

---

Library of Congress Cataloging-in-Publication Data

Biobehavioral resilience to stress / editors, Brian J. Lukey, Victoria Tepe.
    p. ; cm.
    Includes bibliographical references and index.
    ISBN 978-1-4200-7177-1 (hardback : alk. paper) 1. Post-traumatic stress disorder.
    2. Stress (Psychology) 3. Fortitude. 4. War neuroses. 5. Adaptability (Psychology) 6.
    Stress tolerance (Psychology) I. Lukey, Brian J. II. Tepe, Victoria.
    [DNLM: 1. Stress, Psychological--psychology. 2. Adaptation, Psychological.
    3. Behavioral Research--trends. 4. Combat Disorders--psychology. 5. Military
    Personnel--psychology. 6. Social Adjustment. WM 172 B6143 2008]

    RC552.P67B557 2008
    616.85'21--dc22   2007048872

Visit the Taylor & Francis Web site at
http://www.taylorandfrancis.com

and the CRC Press Web site at
http://www.crcpress.com

Contents

Foreword

Military service involves exposure to multiple sources of chronic, acute, and potentially traumatic stress, especially during deployment and combat. Such stress can affect not only short- and long-term health but also human performance and even survival. Military experience over the last two decades has focused significant attention on previously underemphasized health threats ranging from stress disorders to traumatic brain injury, a grouping of medical conditions that science may show is a continuum. This volume summarizes what recent research has determined about stress and brain injury, identifies questions still to be answered, and suggests priorities for scientific inquiry.

The desired outcome of increased understanding of stress and injuries affecting cognitive function is an enhanced ability to promote and build resilience in military personnel. This outcome will benefit the individual, the unit, the mission, and the national defense. Science related to stress resilience is militarily important to the extent that it offers practical applications in areas such as human performance optimization, health protection and readiness, operational risk management, and reduction of first-term attrition. It is ethically and militarily essential to promote psychological preparedness among active duty members and reservists whose service may involve stressors such as prolonged deployments in extreme environments, exposure to insurgent warfare, sleep deprivation, and general physiological stress. Research that supports a preventive strategy and tools or methods to improve personal resilience will reduce the human, organizational, and financial costs associated with military psychiatric casualties, mental health intervention, and the need for long-term care.

Key objectives of this volume are to advance understanding about factors that affect resilience in performance-critical military operations and to motivate progress toward what may be possible. We intend this volume to inform the design and focus of future research leading to enhanced stress protection and resilience among those who serve in the national defense, not only in the military but also in fields such as emergency management, law enforcement, and transportation. Science can help us to understand the psychosocial and biological basis of stress resilience, to recognize stress vulnerability among troops, and to identify and train "resilient" individuals who can withstand and perform in psychologically demanding occupations and settings.

A potentially important adjunct to increased understanding of factors relevant to stress is the ability to measure and assess resilience. Current knowledge provides an opportunity to expand existing instruments to include putative biomarkers of resilience. Improved measurement techniques would benefit the study of resilience as it is affected by stressors such as sleep deprivation, nutritional compromise, and weight loss. Since military personnel experience stress associated with the use of new military systems, we should consider human factors in designing training techniques that may help reduce such stress and thus improve operational performance. Research and testing can help determine whether direct training in specific attributes of resilience may be helpful to prevent or treat symptoms of stress-related disorders. This research and testing may require comprehensive analysis and review of existing experimental, occupational, and therapeutic resilience training techniques.

This volume was initiated by the Military Operational Medicine Research Directorate of the U.S. Army Medical Research and Materiel Command (USAMRMC) in response to recognized defense needs and was managed by the Department of Defense Survivability/Vulnerability Information Analysis Center (SURVIAC). Contributors to this book are uniquely qualified military and civilian experts from a variety of disciplines. Each chapter identifies important ideas for current practice and objectives for future research. Together, they underscore our need to understand individual differences as they relate to the neurobiological underpinnings of stress resilience. We hope that this volume will inspire and guide future research toward new discoveries and breakthroughs in our understanding of biobehavioral resilience to stress.

We thank the many experts and thinkers whose contributions and participation supported the development of a cohesive volume to demonstrate the broad relevance of stress resilience to military and civilian concerns. Also, we extend our thanks to Barbara Palmer and Dr. Victoria Tepe of SURVIAC for their painstaking editorial work and skilled management of this project.

Dr. Robert E. Foster
Director, BioSystems
Office of the Deputy Under Secretary of Defense (Science & Technology)

Ellen Embrey
Deputy Assistant Secretary of Defense for Force Health Protection
and Readiness

Editors

Brian J. Lukey, PhD, has served 22 years in the U.S. Army Medical Service Corps and is an international authority in medical defense research. He has served as the director of Military Operational Medicine, which focuses on research involving methods to better handle stressors in warfare, including excessive heat, cold, high altitude, and fatigue. Col. Lukey currently is the Commander of the U.S. Army Medical Materiel Development Activity, which manages advanced development of medical products for warfighters.

Victoria Tepe, PhD, is a behavioral neuroscientist with 23 years of professional research experience in academic, medical, and military settings. Her works are widely published in biobehavioral sciences, including cognitive neuropsychology and human performance. In addition to this book, Dr. Tepe has coedited *The Science and Simulation of Human Performance* (Elsevier, 2004) and *Warfighter's Guide to Psychology and Performance* (in preparation).

Contributors

Dewleen G. Baker
Department of Psychiatry
University of California San Diego
Veteran Affairs Center for Stress and
  Mental Health
San Diego, California

Paul T. Bartone
Center for Technology and
  National Security Policy
National Defense University
Washington, District of Columbia

David M. Benedek
Department of Psychiatry
  and Center for the Study of
  Traumatic Stress
Uniformed Services University
  School of Medicine
Bethesda, Maryland

Amy E. Bolton
Strategic Analysis Inc.
Arlington, Virginia

George A. Bonanno
Teachers College
Columbia University
Manhattan, New York

Lyle E. Bourne Jr.
University of Colorado
  at Boulder
Boulder, Colorado

John Bradley
Department of Psychiatry
Walter Reed Army Medical Center
Washington, District of Columbia

Donald Campbell
Department of Behavioral Sciences
  and Leadership
U.S. Military Academy
West Point, New York

Kathleen Campbell
Department of Behavioral Sciences
  and Leadership
U.S. Military Academy
West Point, New York

Dennis Charney
Mount Sinai School of Medicine
New York, New York

Jeff Cigrang
Wright-Patterson Medical Center
Wright Patterson Air Force Base
Dayton, Ohio

Ellen Embrey
Office of the Secretary of Defense
Deputy Assistant Secretary of Defense for
  Force Health Protection and Readiness
Falls Church, Virginia

Robert D. Forsten
U.S. Army Special Operations Command
Ft. Bragg, North Carolina

Robert E. Foster
Office of the Deputy under Secretary
  of Defense (Science & Technology)
Washington, District of Columbia

Barbara Fredrickson
Department of Psychology
University of North Carolina
  at Chapel Hill
Chapel Hill, North Carolina

Karl E. Friedl
U.S. Army Research Institute
  of Environmental Medicine
Natick, Massachusetts

Howard N. Garb
Wilford Hall Medical Center
Lackland Air Force Base
San Antonio, Texas

Brian J. Lukey
U.S. Army Medical Research
  and Materiel Command
Fort Detrick, Maryland

Thomas R. Mabry
United States Air Force Academy
Colorado Springs, Colorado

James A. Martin
Bryn Mawr College
Bryn Mawr, Pennsylvania

George R. Mastroianni
United States Air Force Academy
Colorado Springs, Colorado

Bruce S. McEwen
The Rockefeller University
New York, New York

James W. Ness
Department of Behavioral Sciences
  and Leadership
U.S. Military Academy
West Point, New York

Fatih Ozbay
Yale University School
  of Medicine
New Haven, Connecticut

Barbara Palmer
Survivability/Vulnerability
  Information Analysis Center
Dayton, Ohio

David M. Penetar
Behavioral Psychopharmacology
  Research Laboratory
McLean Hospital/Harvard Medical
  School
Belmont, Massachusetts

Victoria B. Risbrough
Department of Psychiatry
University of California San Diego
San Diego, California

Elspeth Cameron Ritchie
Office of the Surgeon General
United States Army

David E. Rohall
Western Illinois University
Macomb, Illinois

Brett Schneider
Department of Psychiatry
Walter Reed Army Medical Center
Washington, District of Columbia

Nicholas J. Schork
Scripps Genomic Medicine
The Scripps Research Institute
La Jolla, California

Steven M. Southwick
Yale University School of Medicine
National Center for PTSD
New Haven, Connecticut

Mark A. Staal
U.S. Air Force Special Operations
  Command
Hurlburt Field, Florida

Victoria Tepe
Survivability/Vulnerability Information
  Analysis Center (SURVIAC)
Dayton, Ohio

Michele Tugade
Vassar College
Poughkeepsie, New York

Robert J. Ursano
Department of Psychiatry and
  Center for the Study of Traumatic Stress
Uniformed Services University
  School of Medicine
Bethesda, Maryland

Christian Waugh
Stanford University
Stanford, California

Maren Westphal
Teachers College
Columbia University
Manhattan, New York

Rita A. Yaroush
University of Colorado at Boulder
Boulder, Colorado

Introduction

BARBARA PALMER AND VICTORIA TEPE
Survivability/Vulnerability Information Analysis Center (SURVIAC)

Mental health practitioners are frequently called upon to identify early signs of stress-related disorder in individuals who experience potentially traumatic stress as part of their work. Unfortunately, it remains difficult to predict or prevent stress-related disorder. Stress-related psychological, social, and behavioral problems are often subtle until they become extreme. Events that cause trauma reactions in some individuals are more easily tolerated by others. Individuals who withstand and overcome exposure to extreme stress in one instance may find it debilitating in another situation. The effort to understand resilience to stress is challenged by the variety and complexity of an individual and circumstantial differences, which influence how stress is perceived and processed by the human mind and body.

History of the Problem

Formal scientific research on the subject of resilience began in the 1970s when researcher Norman Garmezy (Garmezy, 1971, 1974), in an effort to better understand why some schizophrenic individuals were generally more competent than others, turned his attention to the study of children who were "manifestly competent" despite the stress of impoverishment (Garmezy & Streitman, 1974):

> What were the roots of their adaptation? The term "resilient" came in not as a simile for competence, but as an extension of their competencies despite their early background of very high stress experiences. ... I think that resilience is manifest competence despite exposure to significant stressors.
>
> **(From "Resilience: An Interview with Norman Garmezy,"**
> **Glantz and Johnson, 1999, p. 7)**

The observations reported by Garmezy and others (Cicchetti & Walker, 2001; Garmezy, Masten & Tellegen, 1984; Garmezy & Rutter, 1983; Luthar, Cicchetti & Becker, 2000; Luthar & Zigler, 1991; Masten, 2001; Masten, Best & Garmezy, 1990; Rutter, 1985) have challenged traditional assumptions

xiii

concerning the impact of severe adversity, poverty, trauma, or cumulative stress on psychosocial development of a child. What was once seen as a deterministic and unavoidable calculus for psychopathology is now considered, if not yet fully understood, to be a matter of adaptation. In her research to better understand regulatory processes associated with the development of human competency, Masten (2001) conceives of resilience as "ordinary magic" (see also Masten, 2004; Masten et al., 2004). Developmental researchers are now concerned with the need to identify specific adaptive (versus maladaptive) personality characteristics, processes, and strategies that promote competence, mastery, and growth in the face of adversity.

Scientific interest in resilience has also expanded well beyond the field of child development to include the study of risk versus resilience to stress in adult populations, with particular attention to resilience as a protective factor against the development of posttraumatic stress disorder (PTSD) (Agaibi & Wilson, 2005; Bonanno, 2004; Connor, 2006; Flach, 1990; Hoge, Austin & Pollack, 2007; King, King, Fairbank, Keane & Adams, 1998; King, King, Foy, Keane & Fairbank, 1999; King, Vogt & King, 2004; Voges & Romney, 2003; Yehuda, 2004). There seems to be little doubt that resilience can mitigate negative effects of exposure to extreme stress. The more pressing question now is by what mechanism(s) resilience exerts its benefit and, relatedly, how resilience can be promoted or optimized.

As yet, there is no clear consensus on the question of whether resilience is something we have (a unique or universal capacity), something we do (coping behavior), or something we do with what we have. Thus, it is not surprising that researchers differ in their conceptions of resilience as a set of characteristics (e.g., Rauh, 1989), a trait (e.g., Work, Parker & Cowen, 1990), an outcome (e.g., Rutter, 1985), or a process (e.g., Egeland, Carlson & Sroufe, 1993; Richardson, Neiger, Jensen & Kumpfer, 1990). Kaplan (1999) provides an extensive critical review of these differences and their implications for causal models of resilience. Although it is certainly desirable that researchers aspire to the development of a more consistent, well-defined, and scientifically grounded construct, it is also necessary to acknowledge the difficulty inherent in doing so. Currently, the presence or absence of resilience is inferred *post hoc* by the absence of psychological disorder when disorder might otherwise be expected (but cannot be predicted with certainty) in individuals who are presumed to be "at risk" for stress-related psychopathology. Thus, researchers are faced with the logically daunting and operationally convoluted task of devising testable hypotheses to explore the relationship between a poorly defined construct and its presumed impact, which in turn is defined by the absence of measurable change.

In this experimentally challenging context, investigators continue working to identify key and relevant factors of resilience as a phenomenon, capacity, or process that supports positive outcome in the face of adversity.

Researchers have identified some specific psychosocial characteristics (e.g., optimism, hardiness) and physical factors (e.g., fitness, nutrition) that appear as attributes in common among notably resilient individuals. The ongoing challenge is to determine what aspects of stress resilience are both necessary and sufficient to classify resilient (or nonresilient) individuals as such and to formulate a basis for predicting and enhancing human performance in high-stress situations and events. We propose that this effort should be guided by particular attention to factors that are observable and relatable across multiple disciplinary perspectives and methodologies. Of particular importance here are any and all explorations that elucidate relevant genetic variations and the underlying biological basis of resilience to stress as a physiologically observable phenomenon (Charney, 2004; Curtis & Cicchetti, 2003; Epel, McEwen & Ickovics, 1998). To the extent that psychosocial factors (e.g., personality characteristics, cognitive styles, cultural differences) can be related to known and reliable sources of physiological variance, there emerges a more valid basis for the development of more predictive theoretical, experimental, and applied frameworks.

Military Relevance

The need for resilience is felt more urgently nowhere than in military combat, where exposure to extreme and ongoing stress is all but unavoidable. From early basic training to assignment on or off the battlefield, modern war fighters must contend with a variety of intense physical and psychological demands. In particular, service members deployed to conflicts overseas must reckon with prolonged separation from loved ones, extreme climate, grueling physical load, cultural isolation, sleep deprivation, and, of course, a persistently heightened concern for their own safety and that of their fellow war fighters. Modern military leaders and war fighters are well aware that operational effectiveness and physical survival may at times quite literally depend upon the ability to withstand and overcome the effects of extreme, ongoing, and potentially cumulative sources of stress.

Interest in this question has been fueled by renewed awareness of exposure to stress and stress-related problems associated with unconventional (insurgent) warfare, terrorism, and natural disasters. It is essential for resilience research to keep pace with the needs of those who serve in the interest of national security and public safety. Just as war fighters confront exposure to extreme stress in combat, so do civilian "first responders" to violent, hazardous, tragic, and sometimes gruesome results of crime, terrorism, mass casualty accidents, and natural disasters. In each case, negative effects of stress on performance will tend to compromise professional readiness, effectiveness, and survivability. Effective training to promote or enhance resilience would offer a valuable opportunity for improved preparation and sustainability. However, this objective requires a better understanding of the specific psychosocial and biological factors that are most relevant to stress resilience in performance-critical operational settings.

Although the potential utility of resilience research extends well beyond the immediate needs and concerns of military professionals and first responders, it should be acknowledged that the military domain offers a uniquely inspiring and useful model of individual and group resilience. Military organizations and communities have many decades of experience in stress management and coping. Service members and their families confront and cope with the stresses of fear, upheaval, and loss on an ongoing and cumulative basis, which is unimaginable to most civilians. As such, the military community serves as a uniquely informative real-world "laboratory" for the study of individual, organization, and community resilience to stress. Concerning the broader scientific relevance of resilience to the study of human behavior, there may be no more informative setting than the military community and its members.

By the same token, military service members and their families mirror the general population to the extent that some individuals are more resilient to stress than others. Thus, it is of interest to the military to understand the basis for relevant individual differences, to identify those who are likely to be most susceptible to stress, and to develop programs that can be implemented to promote or enhance resilience before, during, or after deployment as needed. Anticipated benefits of resilience research and development include prediction and prevention of operational performance deficits, assessment and screening, modeling and decision support, training, design and development of countermeasures, improved operational effectiveness, increased survivability, fewer psychiatric casualties, and reduced intervention and compensation costs.

Volume Overview

The intent of this volume is to provide the reader with a useful and interdisciplinary state-of-the-art review of current knowledge as related to stress resilience, with practical emphasis on the need to identify and harness critical aspects of resilience. The reader is provided with a solid foundation of existing knowledge as the basis for practical consideration of how current knowledge and future research might be utilized to predict, prevent, or assess vulnerability versus resilience to stress. Drawing from the best and most current research in their respective fields, contributing authors identify factors that they believe are essential to a scientifically useful and behaviorally predictive understanding of resilience and offer practical recommendations on how current knowledge might be implemented to advance the state of the art toward the state of the possible.

We hope that this volume exemplifies the utility of collaborative interdisciplinary effort when put to the task of addressing a common interest. Contributors represent a relevant range of scholarly and applied experts from within the military and academia. Insights and examples are drawn from a variety of disciplinary perspectives and human operational contexts. Each chapter is grounded in rigorous research with emphasis on relevance to a variety of real-world operations and settings. The volume includes practical examples to illustrate a variety of conditions under which individuals may be exposed to severe stress or potentially traumatic events.

This volume is organized in to four sections. First, the reader is presented with relevant aspects of stress and its treatment in the specific context of military life. This section begins with a chapter by Howard Garb (Wilford Hall Medical Center) and Lt. Col. Jeff Cigrang (Wright-Patterson Medical Center), who describe psychological screening strategies and programs currently employed by the U.S. military. Military mental health experts Col. Elspeth Cameron Ritchie (U.S. Army Psychiatric Consultant to the Surgeon General), Lt. Col. Brett Schneider (Walter Reed Army Medical Center), Lt. Col. Robert Forsten (U.S. Army Special Operations Command), and Col. John Bradley (Walter Reed Army Medical Center) then present an overview of military psychiatry as it is currently practiced to identify and manage stress-related mental health issues in combat and at home. Together, these chapters offer the nonmilitary reader an overview of contemporary military priorities in the areas of stress management and intervention.

Psychologists George Mastroianni (U.S. Air Force Academy), Thomas Mabry (U.S. Air Force Academy), Lt. Col. David Benedek (Uniformed Services University School of Medicine), and Robert Ursano (Uniformed Services University School of Medicine) expand consideration of stress in military life to include stressors unique to modern warfare, including military transformation and systems changes, network centric warfare, and new technologies. Finally, in this section, behavioral and leadership science experts Donald Campbell (U.S. Military Academy), Kathleen Campbell (U.S. Military Academy), and Lt. Col. James Ness (U.S. Military Academy) consider the impact and importance of leadership upon individual and group performance and survival under stress.

The second section of this volume considers biological, physiological, and genetic factors related to stress and resilience. Neuroscientists Steven Southwick (Yale University School of Medicine), Fatih Ozbay (Yale University School of Medicine), Dennis Charney (Mount Sinai School of Medicine), and Bruce McEwen (Rockefeller University) explore the neurobiological basis for resilience to stress in terms of brain structures, processes, and mechanisms associated with the regulation of responses to stress. Psychophysiologists

Christian Waugh (Stanford University), Michele Tugade (Vassar College), and Barbara Fredrickson (University of North Carolina at Chapel Hill) consider the physiology of emotion, with specific attention to stress anticipation and recovery. Physiologists Col. Karl Friedl (U.S. Army Medical Research and Materiel Command) and David Penetar (McLean Hospital/Harvard Medical School) address the plasticity of human responsiveness to extreme environments, focusing on factors that moderate resilience (versus vulnerability) to stress and illness. Finally, biomedical researchers Dewleen Baker (University of California San Diego; Veterans Affairs Center for Stress and Mental Health), Victoria Risbrough (University of California San Diego), and Nicholas Schork (The Scripps Research Institute) identify known genetic and environmental risk factors for vulnerability to PTSD, with specific attention to factors that may account for resilience to the development of PTSD.

The third section of this volume is dedicated to the consideration of various psychosocial aspects of resilience. This section begins with a chapter by Maren Westphal (Columbia University Teachers College), George Bonanno (Columbia University Teachers College), and Col. Paul Bartone (National Defense University), who consider specific "resilient" dispositional coping styles and argue that resilience to trauma is both common and distinct from trauma recovery. Cognitive psychologists Maj. Mark Staal (U.S. Air Force Special Operations Command), Amy Bolton (Strategic Analysis, Inc.), Rita Yaroush (University of Colorado at Boulder), and Lyle Bourne Jr. (University of Colorado at Boulder) then review effects of stress on attention, memory, judgment, and decision making and address the specific moderating factors that promote resilience to stress-related performance decrements. Finally, sociologist David Rohall (Western Illinois University) and James Martin (Bryn Mawr College) consider various social structural conditions and "community capacity" variables that influence psychological responses to stressful events.

This volume concludes with an editorial overview of conclusions and recommendations offered by contributing authors, highlighting emergent themes and related issues to advance the science of resilience toward predictive research, theory, and application.

Conclusion

This volume has been assembled to provide multidisciplinary perspective on the meaning and relevance of human resilience to stress in performance-critical contexts. Our purpose is to document the state of the art in such a way that inspires progress toward the state of the possible. Contributors to this volume share the hope that behavioral, medical, and military scientists will recognize the importance of this and related efforts to the scientific community, in general, and to military science, in particular.

In closing, we wish to acknowledge the dedicated efforts of those who contributed directly and indirectly to this significant undertaking. We extend recognition and thanks to our contributing authors whose perseverance and patience have been appreciated. To our project sponsors at the U.S. Army Medical Research and Materiel Command, we owe our sincerest gratitude for supporting this project in every respect. Finally, we wish to acknowledge and thank the following individuals for their helpful recommendations, interest, and essential guidance as members of this project's Advisory Committee:

Stephen T. Ahlers (Naval Medical Research Center)
Kenneth Boff (Air Force Research Laboratory)
Robert E. Foster (Office of the Secretary of Defense)
Robert Gifford (Uniformed Services University of the Health Sciences)
Lt. Col. Carl Hover (U.S. Army Medical Research and Materiel Command)
Maj. Nathan H. Johnson (Air Force Research Laboratory)
Col. Breck Lebegue (Air Force Research Laboratory)
Capt. Michael G. Lilienthal (Office of the Deputy Assistant Secretary of the Navy)
Col. Brian J. Lukey (U.S. Army Medical Research and Materiel Command)
George Mastroianni (U.S. Air Force Academy)
Col. Michael Russo (U.S. Army Aeromedical Research Laboratory)
Maj. Tammy M. Savoie (Air Force Research Laboratory)
Cdr. Dylan Schmorrow (Office of Naval Research)
Cdr. Russell Shilling (Office of Naval Research)
James L. Spira (Naval Medical Center)
Maj. Melba Stetz (U.S. Army Aeromedical Research Laboratory)

References

Agaibi, C.E. & Wilson, J.P. (2005). Trauma, PTSD, and resilience: A review of the literature. *Trauma, Violence, & Abuse, 6*, 195–216.

Bonanno, G.A. (2004). Loss, trauma, and human resilience. Have we underestimated the human capacity to thrive after extremely aversive events? *American Psychologist, 59*, 20–28.

Charney, D.S. (2004). Psychobiological mechanisms of resilience and vulnerability: Implications for successful adaptation to extreme stress. *American Journal of Psychiatry, 161*, 195–216.

Cicchetti, D. & Walker, E.F. (2001). Stress and development: Biological and psychological consequences. *Development and Psychopathology, 13*, 413–418.

Connor, K.M. (2006). Assessment of resilience in the aftermath of trauma. *Journal of Clinical Psychiatry, 67*, 46–49.

Curtis, W.J. & Cicchetti, D. (2003). Moving research on resilience into the 21st century: Theoretical and methodological considerations in examining biological contributors to resilience. *Development and Psychopathology, 15,* 773–810.

Egeland, B., Carlson, E. & Sroufe, L.A. (1993). Resilience as process. *Development and Psychopathology, 5,* 517–528.

Epel, E.S., McEwen, B.S. & Ickovics, J.R. (1998). Embodying psychological thriving: Physical thriving in response to stress. *Journal of Social Issues, 54,* 301–322.

Flach, F. (1990). The resilience hypothesis and post traumatic stress disorder. In: Wolfe, M.E. & Mosnaim, A.D. (Eds.), *Post Traumatic Stress Disorder: Etiology, Phenomenology and Treatment.* Washington, D.C.: American Psychiatric Press.

Garmezy, N. (1971). Vulnerability research and the issue of primary prevention. *American Journal of Orthopsychiatry, 41,* 101–116.

Garmezy, N. (1974). Children at risk: The search for antecedents of schizophrenia. *Schizophrenia Bulletin, 8,* 14–90.

Garmezy, N., Masten, A.S. & Tellegen, A. (1984). The study of stress and competence in children: A building block for developmental psychopathology. *Child Development, 55,* 97–111.

Garmezy, N. & Rutter, M. (Eds.) (1983). *Stress, Coping and Development in Children.* New York: McGraw-Hill.

Garmezy, N. & Streitman, S. (1974). Children at risk: Conceptual models and research methods. *Schizophrenia Bulletin, 9,* 55–125.

Hoge, E.A., Austin, E.D. & Pollack, M.H. (2007). Resilience: Research evidence and conceptual considerations for posttraumatic stress disorder. *Depression and Anxiety, 24,* 139–152.

Kaplan, H.B. (1999). Toward an understanding of resilience: A critical review of definitions and models. In: Glantz, M.D. & Johnson, J.L. (Eds.), *Resilience and Development: Positive Life Adaptations* (pp. 17–83). New York: Kluwer Academic/Plenum Publishers.

King, D.W., King, L.A., Foy, D.W., Keane, T.M. & Fairbank, J.A. (1999). Posttraumatic stress disorder in a national sample of female and male Vietnam veterans: Risk factors, war-zone stressors, and resilience-recovery variables. *Journal of Abnormal Psychology, 108,* 164–170.

King, D.W., Vogt, D.S., & King, L.A. (2004). Risk and resilience factors in the etiology of chronic PTSD. In: Litz, B.T. (Ed.), *Early Interventions for Trauma and Traumatic Loss in Children and Adults: Evidence-Based Directions.* New York: Guilford Press.

King, L.A., King, D.W., Fairbank, J.A., Keane, T.M. & Adams, G.A. (1998). Resilience-recovery factors in post-traumatic stress disorder among female and male Vietnam veterans. *Journal of Personality and Social Psychology, 74,* 420–434.

Luthar, S.S., Cicchetti, D. & Becker, B. (2000). The construct of resilience: A critical evaluation and guidelines for future work. *Child Development, 71,* 543–562.

Luthar, S.S. & Zigler, E. (1991). Vulnerability and competence: A review of research on resilience in childhood. *American Journal of Orthopsychiatry, 61,* 6–22.

Masten, A.S. (2001). Ordinary magic: Resilience processes in development. *American Psychologist, 56,* 227–238.

Masten, A.S. (2004). Regulatory processes, risk and resilience in adolescent development. *Annals of the New York Academy of Sciences, 1021,* 310–319.

Masten, A.S., Best, K. & Garmezy, N. (1990). Resilience and development: Contributions from the study of children who overcome adversity. *Development and Psychopathology, 2*, 425–444.

Masten, A.S., Burt, K., Roisman, G.I., Obradović, J., Long, J.D. & Tellegen, A. (2004). Resources and resilience in the transition to adulthood: Continuity and change. *Development and Psychopathology, 16*, 1071–1094.

Rauh, H. (1989). The meaning of risk and protective factors in infancy. *European Journal of Psychology of Education IV, 2*, 161–173.

Richardson, G.E., Neiger, B.L., Jensen, S. & Kumpfer, K.L. (1990). The resiliency model. *Health Education, 21*, 33–39.

Rutter, M. (1985). Resilience in the face of adversity: Protective factors and resistance to psychiatric disorder. *British Journal of Psychiatry, 147*, 598–611.

Voges, M.A. & Romney, D.M. (2003). Risk and resiliency factors in posttraumatic stress disorder. *Annals of General Hospital Psychiatry, 2*, 4.

Work, W.C., Parker, G.R. & Cowen, E.L. (1990). The impact of life stressors on childhood adjustment: Multiple perspectives. *Journal of Community Psychology, 18*, 73–78.

Yehuda, R. (2004). Risk and resilience in posttraumatic stress disorder. *Journal of Clinical Psychiatry, 65*, 29–36.

Section I

Stress and Resilience in Military Life

Psychological Screening: Predicting Resilience to Stress*

1

HOWARD N. GARB

Lackland Air Force Base

JEFF CIGRANG

Wright Patterson Air Force Base

Contents

---

* The views expressed in this chapter are those of the authors and are not the official policy of the Department of Defense or the U.S. Air Force.

Psychological Screening: Predicting Resilience to Stress

Screening for emotional problems routinely occurs at recruitment and military enlistment stations. Nonetheless, even after preenlistment screening is conducted, large numbers of military personnel are separated from the military due to behavioral or mental health problems. For example, in the U.S. Air Force alone, 15.8% of first-term enlistments from 1994 to 1999 were later separated due to behavioral or mental health problems (Garb & Fiedler, 2006). This raises the question of how early screening might be improved to better identify individuals who are at risk or vulnerable to psychological disorder.

Research-based psychological screening questionnaires have been developed, but their use in the military is still limited. These measures do not directly address resilience to stress per se, but they do pose questions related to preservice adjustment history. As will be made clear in this chapter, there is a large body of research to indicate that individuals who have a history of serious mental illness or criminal behavior are less likely to deal with stress in a resilient manner.

This chapter begins with a review of the need for, and current practices associated with, early psychological screening in the military. Note that not all military psychological screening practices and specific contexts will be covered here. For instance, our review does not consider instruments specifically designed for pre- or postdeployment screening (e.g., Deployment Risk and Resilience Inventory; King, King & Vogt, 2003). Rather, our emphasis is on current practices, needs, and possibilities with respect to screening at the time of recruitment/enlistment and basic training. We also address research findings relevant to demographic, psychological, behavioral, and experiential factors that may be helpful in the assessment of risk versus resilience to stress. Finally, we consider how currently available information and knowledge might be applied to support the development of improved early screening instruments and procedures.

Why Is Psychological Screening Important?

Although it may seem obvious that the military should want to employ only the most stress-resilient personnel available, it can be difficult to generate consensus support on how best to implement this ideal as a practical matter. Commanders in charge of recruitment sometimes discourage the use of recruitment-level screening procedures that might significantly reduce the number of potential available recruits. Training commanders who welcome recruitment-level screening may frown upon subsequent procedures that tend to increase attrition from basic military training (BMT). Finally, field commanders would be pleased to see their attrition rates reduced by more effective screening at enlistment processing and during basic training.

Concerns about the impact of screening on recruitment and training can be addressed in the context of several other practical issues. First, there are currently in place strict limits on the number of non–high school graduates who can join the military. Given these limits, it is important to identify individuals who are most likely to perform well. Appropriate early screening could be very beneficial in this respect.* Second, an even more important benefit may be that of reduced first-term attrition, which for decades has been recorded at a level above 30%. This figure includes all separations, including those due to medical problems, but more often than not, attrition is related to emotional and behavioral difficulties. If first-term attrition could be reduced by even just a few percentage points, the U.S. military could save tens of millions of dollars each year and fewer new recruits would be needed (General Accounting Office, 1997). Last but not the least, effective early screening for resilience to stress would promote the development of a more resilient military force in general.

Current Practice

During the 1980s and 1990s, more than $10 million were invested to develop standardized screening instruments for military use. Workgroups and committees enlisted the help of top military and civilian psychologists. The instruments they developed gathered biodata relevant to preservice adjustment, including antisocial behavior and emotional distress (Adaptability Screening Profile [ASP], Barnes et al., 1989; Armed Services Applicant Profile [ASAP], Trent & Quenette, 1992; Assessment for Security Positions and Enlistment [ASPEN], Flyer, 2004). The intent of this effort was to assist applicant selection by screening prior to basic training. None of these tests ever became operational.

The National Research Council (NRC, 2006) issued a report that addressed current military enlistment standards and critiqued preenlistment psychological screening procedures that are currently employed by the U.S. military. Unfortunately, most screening instruments currently in use are not evidence-based. The NRC's report acknowledged the difficulty in conducting systematic research in this area, noting that opportunities for relevant statistical analyses are limited because "in some cases data are not entered into the system; in other cases, data accessibility is limited due to privacy concern; and in still other cases, relevant data on conditions and outcomes are not linked" (pp. 143–144).

Early screening begins at recruitment stations when each applicant completes a medical prescreen (Department of Defense [DoD] Form 2807-2).

---

* As preparation of this chapter neared completion, restraints were being adjusted to increase the number of nonhigh school graduates who can join the U.S. Army. This change would allow as many as 20% of new recruits to have a General Educational Development (GED).

At present, only one item in this form addresses the issue of psychiatric disorder, inquiring as to whether the applicant has ever seen a mental health professional for any reason. Although this is useful information, many individuals who have severe mental or behavioral problems have never received treatment and so would not be identified by an honest answer to this question.

At military enlistment processing stations, recruits complete a medical history questionnaire. Unfortunately, attrition data were not gathered to construct and evaluate this questionnaire. Thus, it is not clear which test items, if any, might be useful as a means to identify individuals who may be at increased risk for attrition based on a history of medical or psychiatric problems.

There is one instrument currently in use to screen non–high school graduate applicants prior to their induction. The Assessment of Individual Motivation (AIM) was developed by researchers at the U.S. Army Research Institute (White & Young, 1998). The AIM gathers information that relates to personality traits, such as the tendency to strive for excellence in the completion of work-related tasks, the tendency to have a positive outlook on life, and the tendency to interact with others in a pleasant manner. Early results obtained by researchers at the U.S. Army Research Institute suggested that higher scores on the AIM were associated with lower rates of first-term attrition (e.g., White & Young, 1998). Based in part on these positive results, the Army began using the AIM operationally with non–high school graduates in 2000 as part of the GED Plus program. However, the AIM was later also evaluated by the Human Resources Research Organization (HumRRO) and by independent consultants working directly for the Army Research Institute. These additional examinations of AIM's operational performance showed that "its validity as a predictor of attrition under the GED Plus program was much lower than it had demonstrated in previous work in a research setting" (Knapp, Heggestad & Young, 2004, p. v).

In response to these findings, Young, White, Heggestad, and Barnes (2004) explored several possible approaches to improving the AIM's scoring rules. By scoring a specific subset of AIM items, Young et al. obtained statistically significant results for the prediction of attrition ($r = 0.13$). Based on this result, the authors then constructed a new attrition screen, known as the Tier 2 Attrition Screen (TTAS), which consists of the (1) AIM with the new scoring system based on subset items, (2) Armed Services Vocational Aptitude Battery (ASVAB) math knowledge and word knowledge scores, and (3) gender-normed body mass index. Positive results have been reported for the TTAS (Young et al., 2004).* Despite the reported success of the TTAS

---

* As a result, in the 2007 fiscal year, the U.S. Army will be permitted to double (to 14,200) the number of non–high school graduates it was permitted to enlist during the previous year (Kennedy, 2006).

thus far, ongoing evaluations are needed. Follow-up data should be gathered over a number of years to adequately address the question of attrition from military service. Also, it is important to clarify if the addition of the AIM to the other components of the TTAS leads to an increment in validity.

An Early Psychiatric Screen (EPS) is still undergoing evaluation through research (Koltko-Rivera & Niebuhr, 2004). This test was designed and developed* for use prior to basic training, to identify psychiatric conditions such as anxiety, depression, mania, psychosis, and antisocial tendencies. However, because the EPS is still in the early stages of evaluation, conclusions cannot yet be drawn concerning its validity.†

Finally, a new biodata screening instrument, the Lackland Behavioral Questionnaire (Lackland BQ; Garb, 2005), has been designed for the screening of all U.S. Air Force recruits during basic training. The Lackland BQ is designed to gather biodata relevant to preservice adjustment, including antisocial behavior and behavior related to mental disorder and treatment. The decision to employ a biodata questionnaire was based in part on an examination of the results that were obtained by the study of earlier biodata tests such as the ASP, ASAP, and ASPEN. Because the Lackland BQ was only recently constructed, research data on its validity are still being collected.

Risk Factors for Stress and Attrition

In extreme or dangerous conditions, the ability to perform under stress may be nothing less than critical to psychological and physical survival. Adequate training is certainly necessary to improve survivability under stress, and the demands of military training are often an effective means to "weed out" individuals who lack the fortitude or commitment to endure the harsh and prolonged challenges of combat.

Although BMT is helpful as a means to de-select recruits who have low tolerance for the basic demands of military performance, it is not a perfect filter by which to identify all entrants who might eventually succumb to stress. Our most current perspective on first-term attrition emerges from a review published in 2004 by the U.S. Army Center for Health Promotion and Preventive Medicine at the request of the Center for Accessions Research (Knapik, Jones, Hauret, Darakjy & Piskator, 2004). Findings reported in this

---

* Development of the EPS was sponsored by the Accession Medical Standards Analysis and Research Activity (AMSARA), within the Division of Preventive Medicine at the Walter Reed Army Institute of Research.
† Results on convergent validity (but not discriminant validity) have been reported for a sample of college students (Koltko-Rivera & Niebuhr, 2004). Results have not yet been reported for data gathered from military personnel.

review are consistent with those of earlier reports (e.g., Trent & Laurence, 1993) as well as with ongoing research (Buddin, 2005), which concludes that more than one-third of all recruits will leave the military service before the end of their first enlisted term. About one-third of attrition occurs in the first 6 months of service, and about one-half occurs during the first year (Fischl & Blackwell, 2000; Flyer & Elster, 1983; Klein, Hawes-Dawson & Martin, 1991; Military personnel, 2000; Trent & Laurence, 1993). While early separations are commonly related to mental health issues, later separations are more often related to drug/alcohol problems or offenses such as violent behavior. Despite best efforts to develop effective screening strategies, attrition rates remain high and have not decreased during the past 20 years.

Another pressing concern for the military is that even the most thoroughly trained, stable, well-behaved, and apparently resilient war fighter can find himself or herself quite suddenly unable to perform very well-learned tasks under the uniquely stressful and sometimes traumatic conditions of real combat. Likewise, exposure to traumatic stress may bring about psychological difficulties such as posttraumatic stress disorder (PTSD).*

Clearly, it is in the military's interest to optimize the resilience of its fighting force, and one means of doing so is to improve and implement psychological screening methods that can identify resilient characteristics and behavior. Resilience is a complex phenomenon that involves multiple factors of psychosocial, experiential, behavioral, and physiological influence. In order to identify, measure, and screen for resilience, we need to develop a clear and useful understanding of what makes some individuals more resilient than others to particular types of stress, and why the same individual might be more or less resilient to different types of stress. To that end, we can consider specific factors that have already been linked to stress-related outcomes such as first-term attrition, PTSD, and violent or criminal behavior.

Demographic Factors

Specific demographic variables have been associated with first-term attrition as well as with PTSD (Brewin, Andrews & Valentine, 2000; Knapik et al., 2004). Although these relationships are correlative in nature, they are of unique interest for their consistency with stress-related outcome. In general,

---

* PTSD is a syndrome that can result from exposure to traumatic experiences, including those encountered in combat. Symptoms of PTSD include unwanted thoughts about the original trauma, nightmares, flashbacks, loss of interest, detachment, sleep disturbance, pronounced startle response, emotional numbing, and trouble concentrating. Research suggests that between 15% and 31% of Vietnam veterans have suffered from PTSD (Kulka et al., 1990; Centers for Disease Control, 1988; Rosen, 2004). Current estimates of the prevalence of PTSD among different groups of U.S. military personnel returning from the war in Iraq vary widely, but likely approximate 12–13% (Hoge et al., 2004).

the magnitude of demographic variable relationships tends to be more powerful for first-term attrition than for PTSD. This may be the case in part because while all trainees are exposed to roughly the same rigors of basic training and technical schooling, the severity of combat-related trauma is variable and plays a more determinant influence with respect to PTSD (Brewin et al., 2000).

Basic demographic variables such as gender, race, and age have demonstrated statistically significant relationships to attrition and oftentimes to PTSD as well. Although the relationships between demographic variables and PTSD are small in magnitude (r ranging from 0.05 to 0.14; Brewin et al., 2000), they are consistent with stronger correlations that point to higher attrition rates for females (versus males), black males (versus black females), and Native Americans (versus other recruits). Other findings are also important here. Significantly lower attrition rates are found among Asian/Pacific Islanders and among individuals 19–22 years of age (versus 17–18-year-olds and those over the age of 23). Some of these demographic findings may have broad implications for resilience and vulnerability to stress. For example, it is also the case that when compared with the general U.S. population, Native Americans have the highest rate of suicide and Asian/Pacific Islanders have the lowest rate of suicide (Gould, Greenberg, Velting & Shaffer, 2003).

Interestingly, level of education also appears to be related to both early attrition and PTSD (Brewin et al., 2000; Knapik et al., 2004). Attrition is dramatically higher among recruits who have not finished high school (50% attrition versus 25% overall attrition), even when comparison groups are controlled for aptitude. The relation between education and PTSD is consistent, though certainly less dramatic ($r = 0.10$), with poorly educated military personnel being more likely to develop PTSD. These results suggest that for whatever reason(s) not yet understood, there exists some relationship between education and resilience. Psychosocial and behavioral factors that may be relevant to this relationship are discussed in the next section.

Psychosocial and Behavioral Factors

Studies emerging from various behavioral subspecialties point to specific psychosocial factors and characteristics that may be relevant to resilience. Among these are aptitude and intelligence, criminal history, tobacco use, mental health history, childhood abuse, and specific personality traits.

Aptitude and Intelligence

Although recruits are seldom given tests that measure (or predict) mental health and behavioral problems, they are given tests that do an excellent job of evaluating aptitude (Campbell & Knapp, 2001; Knapik et al., 2004).

The ASVAB, consisting of a number of scales (or subtests), is given to all personnel entering the U.S. military. The Armed Forces Qualification Test (AFQT) is calculated from four scales of the ASVAB: (1) word knowledge, (2) paragraph comprehension, (3) arithmetic reasoning, and (4) mathematics knowledge. The AFQT is a good measure of intelligence, and, in fact, was used as a measure of intelligence by the Centers for Disease Control (CDC) for its Vietnam Experiences Study (1988).

Higher AFQT scores are modestly associated with lower attrition, meaning that those endowed with good intelligence are likely to do relatively well in the military (this assertion is based on the results from more than two dozen studies; see Knapik et al., 2004, p. 10). When high school graduate status is controlled for, AFQT is still a modestly successful predictor of attrition, suggesting that the reason intelligence is a relatively good predictor of attrition is not simply because recruits with more education do better on the AFQT. On the other hand, high school graduation status is a more powerful predictor of attrition than is the AFQT composite. This difference is probably due to the additional relevance of other psychosocial variables. Presumably, successful high school graduation represents some degree of perseverance, generally appropriate behavior, and ability to function cooperatively with teachers and peers (Knapik et al., 2004, pp. 6–7).

Several studies have reported higher rates and increased severity of PTSD symptoms among individuals with lower intelligence scores (Kaplan et al., 2002; Macklin et al., 1998; McNally & Shin, 1995; Silva et al., 2000; Vasterling et al., 2002). Among military personnel, this correlation ($r = -0.25$; McNally & Shin, 1995) remains significant even after adjustment for combat exposure and education level. Intelligence measures gathered before and after combat exposure (using the AFQT and a standardized intelligence test given at a Veterans Administration Medical Center) indicate that lower intelligence increases the likelihood of developing PTSD. These findings do not support the hypothesis that PTSD symptoms negatively affect performance on intelligence tests. Rather, intellectual ability may be a protective factor for several reasons. It may allow individuals to better (1) comprehend their symptoms, (2) express themselves when talking about their symptoms, and (3) engage in flexible and creative problem solving.

Criminal History

Preservice antisocial behavior has been identified as one possible predictor of military attrition (Knapik et al., 2004). Unfortunately, many recruits enter military service with a history of antisocial or criminal behavior. For example, in one survey of 1891 male U.S. Navy recruits, 15% reported that they had either attempted or completed a rape (Merrill et al., 1998). Among these individuals, 14.6% reported using force or the threat of force; 57.7% attempted or completed penetration when the woman was incapable of giving consent by virtue of intoxication; and 27.7% used both the threat of force or force as well as alcohol or drugs. In a larger study using two additional samples, 11.6% and 9.9% of male U.S. Navy recruits reported having committed rape, and 2–4% reported that they had attempted to commit rape (Merrill, Thomsen, Gold & Milner, 2001).

Flyer (1996) examined the legal backgrounds of 100,000 male recruits who had enlisted in the U.S. Army, Navy, Marine Corps, or Air Force between 1985 and 1989. This study included analysis of various records, including state (California) arrest and citation files, the California history database that includes juvenile records, and results from the Entrance National Agency Check (ENTNAC). (At the time of the study, the ENTNAC consisted of a limited background check conducted as part of the process for granting confidential/secret clearance.) Flyer found that more than one of four recruits (27%) had an arrest record and 7% had an unfavorable ENTNAC report. Recruits with a preservice arrest history were much more likely to be separated from military service due to unsuitability (36%) than were recruits who had no preservice arrests (21%). Even when controlling for education level, Flyer found that preservice arrest history was strongly related to separation from the military due to unsuitability.

Anecdotal evidence suggests that preservice criminal behavior may also be related to subsequent criminal activity while serving in the military. Although fortunately rare, criminal incidents involving members of the U.S. military sometimes do occur and may reveal preservice antisocial behavior as a relevant antecedent condition. For example, two incidents that occurred in Iraq were reported to have involved soldiers whose violent preservice criminal histories may have portended trouble (Carollo & Kaplow, 2005). Although anecdotal evidence of a link between preservice and in-service antisocial or criminal behavior is for now strictly anecdotal, it seems reasonable and obvious that individuals with a preservice history of criminal or violent behavior should be very closely and conservatively scrutinized prior to acceptance for service in the U.S. military.

The propensity for aggressive and impulsive behavior has also been linked to an increased risk for suicide (Apter, Plutchik & van Praag, 1993; McKeown et al., 1998; Sourander, Helstela, Haavisto & Bergroth, 2001). For example, in a Finnish longitudinal study (Sourander et al., 2001), aggressive 8-year-olds were more than twice as likely as other children to report 8 years later that they had considered or attempted suicide. Among the general population, disruptive disorders are common in male teenage suicide victims. Conduct disorder, often comorbid with mood, anxiety, or substance abuse disorder, has been documented in approximately one-third of suicides among male teenagers (Brent et al., 1993; Shaffer et al., 1996).

Smoking Behavior

In the literature review sponsored by the Center for Accessions Research, Knapik et al. (2004) cited six studies that revealed a statistically significant relationship between smoking behavior and attrition from the military (Booth-Kewley, Larson & Ryan, 2002; Knox, 1998; Larson, Booth-Kewley & Ryan, 2002; Quester, 1999; Snoddy & Henderson, 1994; Talcott, Haddock, Klesges, Lando & Fiedler, 1999). Other studies have reported similar results (e.g., Flyer, 2004; Hattiangadi, Lee & Quester, 2004; Klesges, Haddock, Chang, Talcott & Lando, 2001). For example, Klesges et al. (2001) observed that smokers in the U.S. Air Force were 1.8 times more likely than nonsmokers to be discharged during their first year of military enlistment. Remarkably, a history of smoking behavior is predictive of attrition even after smokers have stopped smoking.

In a study of U.S. Navy trainees who were tested during basic training, Flyer (2004) found that the rate of attrition for smokers was nearly twice (75%) that of nonsmokers (37.3%) among trainees who had a GED or were non–high school graduates. In fact, the rate of attrition among nongraduate nonsmokers was more closely comparable to that of all trainees who held a traditional high school diploma (31%).

It would be reasonable to think that higher rates of attrition among smokers might be related to the physical effects of smoking, but studies to date suggest otherwise. The aerobic capacity of smokers in basic training is similar to that of nonsmokers (Daniels et al., 1984; Knapik et al., 2001). Although individuals who are smokers may have more medical problems in basic training, two studies (Booth-Kewley et al., 2002; Talcott et al., 1999) report that the association between cigarette smoking and medical attrition is very weak and that cigarette smoking is primarily a risk factor for legal and behavioral discharges (e.g., discharges related to fraudulent entry, misconduct, the commission of a serious offense, substandard performance, personality disorder, drug/alcohol abuse). The working group sponsored by the Center for Accessions Research (Knapik et al., 2004, p. 25) concluded that "cigarette smoking may be a marker for some yet undefined psychosocial factors (e.g., risk taking) that is linked with attrition."

Recent findings also suggest that smoking may be linked not only to attrition, but also to other types of negative outcomes. For example, in a Finnish study of 10,943 adolescents, regular smoking at age 14 predicted later drunk driving (Riala, Hakko, Isohanni, Järvelin & Räsänen, 2004). In the U.S. military, a study of 6950 Navy recruits tested during basic training linked smoking to a history of antisocial behavior and subsequent difficulties during training (Flyer & Eitelberg, 2005). Heavy smokers (those who smoked a pack or more a day) were three times more likely than nonsmokers to have a record of truancy and multiple suspensions from high school. Almost one in five (19%) smokers reported having been in trouble with the police on two or more occasions (compared with only 6% of nonsmokers). Heavy smokers were more likely to have difficulty following orders, engage in alcohol and illicit drug use, find it difficult to sleep at night, and be in poor physical condition.

Some studies indicate that smoking behavior may be a marker for other types of psychopathology (Alvarado & Breslau, 2005). For example, smoking has been associated with a significantly increased risk for depression, suicidal ideation, and suicide attempts (e.g., Hallfors et al., 2004; Makikyro et al., 2004; Toros, Bilgin, Sasmaz, Bugdayci & Camdeviren, 2004). The results from these studies are correlative and thus may simply indicate that individuals who suffer psychological difficulties are more likely to smoke. However, data from an even more recent longitudinal study (Breslau et al., 2005) indicated that current daily smoking (but not past smoking) predicted the subsequent occurrence of suicidal thoughts and attempts. The effect of current smoking was significant even when controlled for the possible effects of prior depression and substance abuse disorders (adjusted odds ratio, 1.82). Current daily smoking was also predictive of suicidal thoughts and behavior when the investigators controlled for the effect of prior suicidality and prior psychiatric disorders (adjusted odds ratio, 1.74).

At least one recent study points to tobacco use (smoking) as a potential indicant of genetic predisposition to PTSD (Koenen et al., 2005). This study was based on an analysis of data taken from the Vietnam Era Twin Registry, which contains data on 6744 male–male twins who served in the military during the Vietnam War era. The authors found a statistically significant relationship between nicotine dependence (ND) and diagnosis of PTSD (odds ratio = 1.55, confidence interval 1.22–1.97) among twins who had experienced one or more traumatic events. The relationship between ND and PTSD was greater for monozygotic twins than for dizygotic twins. Approximately 62% (0.21/0.34) of the PTSD-ND covariance was accounted for by shared genetic effects (Koenen et al., 2005).

Although smoking behavior is a powerful predictor of attrition when paired with other information (e.g., whether someone is a non–high school graduate), cautious interpretation is appropriate. Most individuals who smoke will function capably and will not be separated from the military.

Mental Health History

Past and current mental health is predictive of future functioning. For example, more than 80% of individuals who experience a major depressive episode (a severe form of depression) will experience recurrent episodes (Kessler et al., 2003).

Screening questions that address mental health are predictive of attrition (Garb & Fiedler, 2006). When screening was done during basic training for the U.S. Air Force, 46% of trainees who endorsed the item, "I usually feel down," were separated from service in less than 4 years, compared with just 30% of those who responded "false" to the same question. When trainees were asked to respond to the statement, "I have seriously thought about taking my life more than once," attrition rates were 48% and 30% for those who answered "true" and "false," respectively.

Certainly, mental illness has known relevance to suicide and PTSD. Although relatively few young people with psychiatric disorders commit suicide, 90% of those who commit suicide have suffered at least one psychiatric disorder (see Gould et al., 2003). Similarly, previous psychiatric history is a predictor of PTSD in military populations (weighted average $r = 0.14$; Brewin et al., 2000).

Childhood Physical or Sexual Abuse

Numerous studies have demonstrated a relationship between childhood abuse and subsequent attrition from the military (Booth-Kewley et al., 2002; Carbone, Cigrang, Todd & Fiedler, 1999; Caulfield, 2000; Cigrang, Carbone, Todd & Fiedler, 1998; Crawford & Fiedler, 1992; Knapik et al., 2004; Merrill, Stander, Thomsen, Crouch & Milner, 2004; Smikle, Fiedler, Sorem, Spencer & Satin, 1996; Staal, Cigrang & Fiedler, 2000). For example, in a prospective study of 5491 U.S. Navy recruits (Merrill et al., 2004), 55% reported having been exposed or directly victimized by family violence, physical abuse, or sexual abuse. Merrill et al. found that attrition rates were significantly higher for these recruits. Rates of attrition for male and female recruits who had experienced all three types of abuse were 3.0 and 1.4 times greater than attrition rates for recruits who had not been exposed to family violence or abuse, respectively.

Although statistical relationships reported in the literature are generally small in magnitude, it appears that a history of child abuse may also relate to a range of psychiatric symptoms later in life. Child abuse has been linked to somatization (physical complaints without known physical basis), depression, anxiety, and hostility (Rosen & Martin, 1996). Longitudinal community studies have found that self-reports of childhood physical and sexual abuse are associated with an increased risk of suicidal behavior in adolescence (Fergusson, Horwood & Lynskey, 1996; Silverman, Reinherz & Giaconia, 1996). A review of the literature on PTSD (Brewin et al., 2000) identified one study that reported a correlative relationship ($r = 0.25$) between child abuse and PTSD in military populations. Two additional studies of military populations also point to a possible relationship between childhood abuse and the subsequent development of PTSD-related symptoms (Merrill, 2001; Merrill, Thomsen, Sinclair, Gold & Milner, 2001). That is, some individuals who enter the military already suffer from undiagnosed PTSD symptoms that may be exacerbated by exposure to combat-related stress.

Although it would be unfair to exclude applicants from the military based on whether they have been abused as children, the scientific literature on childhood and adolescent abuse may ultimately prove to be very helpful in our understanding of psychological resilience. The CDC and the DoD are now evaluating the feasibility of collaborative study to better understand the long-term effects of adverse childhood events (ACE). This effort could play an important part in clarifying the relevance of childhood abuse to specific psychological and medical problems later in life and to the erosion or development of psychological and physical resilience.

Personality Traits

Studies have shown consistent but modest relations between some personality traits and military attrition (e.g., Butters, Retzlaff & Gilbertini, 1986; Elsass, Fiedler, Skop & Hill, 2001; Fiedler, Oltmanns & Turkheimer, 2004; Lubin, Fiedler & Whitlock, 1996, 1999; McCraw, 1990; McCraw & Bearden, 1990; Quick, Joplin, Nelson, Mangelsdorff & Fiedler, 1996). In a study of U.S. Air Force trainees who were tested on their last day of basic training, an instrument known as the Schedule for Non-Adaptive and Adaptive Personality (SNAP; Clark, 1993) was used successfully to identify and predict 61% of the trainees who would separate from the Air Force within 2 years after testing and 57% of those who would remain on active duty (Fiedler et al., 2004). In the same study, peer ratings (Peer Inventory for Personality Disorders; see Thomas, Turkheimer & Oltmanns, 2003) identified 51% of the Airmen who separated within 2 years after basic training. Peer ratings were especially helpful as a means to assess antisocial personality traits, while self-report ratings were more helpful as a means to identify personality traits and personality disorders related to strong feelings of emotional distress.

The personality construct known as *hardiness* is thought to be a measure of resilience (Kobasa, Maddi & Kahn, 1982) and so may be an especially important variable for understanding how individuals react to stress. Individuals who score high on scales of hardiness are those who are generally committed to find a meaningful purpose in their lives, believe that they can influence their surroundings and the outcome of events, and believe that they can grow from both positive and negative life experiences. In a cross-sectional study (Bartone, 1999), U.S. Army personnel completed several measures and questionnaires in one sitting. Measures of hardiness were predictive of measures of level of functioning, and significant interactions were found between hardiness, combat stress exposure, and stressful life events.

Personality measures may ultimately prove to be valuable to military screening. For example, personality traits such as conscientiousness and persistence have obvious specific relevance to military performance and may also help us to improve our more general understanding of psychological resilience and its attributes.

Conclusions and Recommendations

Improvements in military screening would support the development of a military force whose members are optimally suited to handle the physical and psychological demands of military training, service, and combat. In addition, the U.S. General Accounting Office reports that tens of millions of federal dollars could be saved annually by the reduction of military attrition through improved screening (e.g., General Accounting Office, 1982, 1997). With these objectives in mind, we offer specific recommendations to promote relevant advancement in the areas of basic research, enlistment standards, psychological screening, and information sharing.

Basic Research

There is a clear and pressing need to identify and assess specific factors that influence psychological risk and resilience to stress. Current research already underway may be very helpful in this respect. As previously noted, a collaborative DoD–CDC research initiative has begun to examine the effects of childhood abuse on psychological and physical well-being in adulthood. This is an essential area of investigation whose results should inform the advancement of theory, experimentation, and application (e.g., psychological screening).

In addition, the DoD and Veterans Administration Medical Center are currently involved in a joint effort (Recruit Assessment Program [RAP]) that may eventually support routine collection of demographic, psychosocial, occupational, and health risk data from all new U.S. military personnel. Although the explicit focus of the RAP effort is to improve the quality of personnel medical records, the resulting data may also directly or indirectly support the identification of psychosocial and demographic risk factors for stress-related health problems.

Much additional basic research is needed. We know that a number of factors are related to military attrition and overall mental health, including demographic factors, education, intelligence, criminal history, smoking behavior, prior mental health history, childhood abuse, and personality. However, little is known about how these factors interact with one another. Similarly, little is known about the underlying mechanisms by which these factors exert their effects. For example, the occurrence of childhood abuse might have an effect on education level, criminal history, smoking behavior, prior mental health history, and personality. If so, this may help us to understand the observed correlation between child abuse and attrition. It is useful to study correlative relationships among specific factors and outcome, but in order to identify meaningful markers and predictors of resilience, we need to better understand how multiple factors might interrelate or interact.

Enlistment Standards

Enlistment standards should be directly informed by research findings related to performance and outcome. While this may seem noncontroversial as a point of principle, it is less straightforward in practical terms. Simply put, potentially useful raw data are too often and in too many ways left inaccessible to military researchers. To correct this problem, the National Research Council (2006) has identified the need to improve military data management such that data from military recruitment and enlistment processing stations can be linked with other datasets of interest (e.g., attrition, health, training, and promotion). This would, in effect, provide a database to support the identification of enlistment standards with demonstrable relevance to outcome. With this in mind, we recommend that updated processes be developed to support information collected at recruitment and military enlistment processing stations. Enlistment data currently recorded using paper and pencil forms should instead be gathered or entered by the use of computer-administered forms on a secure Web site.

Psychological Screening

The primary purpose of this chapter has been to call attention to the need for better military psychological screening to identify individuals who are vulnerable or resilient to stress. By the end of this year, the Lackland BQ will have been administered to approximately 32,000 U.S. Air Force recruits. The resulting data will then be assessed to determine their predictive value with respect to attrition. This will provide a timely context for updated cost–benefit analysis, review, and practical directives. We would recommend that these efforts be led by a joint services panel of subject matter experts and a newly convened National Research Council working group. Key objectives should include careful consideration of newly accrued data and analyses and the formulation of specific recommendations for the improvement of military psychological screening instruments and procedures.

It is reasonable to consider whether or how existing measures of resilience might be used for preenlistment or early enlistment screening. Because the Deployment Risk and Resilience Inventory (King et al., 2003) was designed specifically to evaluate personnel returning from deployment, it would likely be difficult to adapt to the context of early screening. However, other measures might be more useful. For example, it may be relatively easy and helpful to adapt and implement existing measures of hardiness (e.g., Bartone, 1999).

Information Sharing

Information about personnel preservice adjustment can be useful at various times and in various contexts throughout military service. This information should be made more widely available to military trainers and leaders. There are specific settings in which psychological screening and preservice adjustment data could be used to support improved performance and success of military personnel. For example, when military trainees perform poorly during basic training, their leaders must order interventions to address and resolve performance problems. Psychological screening data could help to ensure that interventions are as appropriate as possible to individual needs and issues. Likewise, military psychologists would probably find it helpful to have access to prior psychological screening information that might inform subsequent command-ordered evaluations to determine the need for intervention or disciplinary action. In some cases, it would be helpful to the psychologist to know if the individual had acknowledged a history of getting into trouble and whether previous trouble had occurred prior to enlistment. Psychological screening results could also be used as one component of prescreening for sensitive job positions. Individuals who acknowledged preservice antisocial behavior when they were originally screened at enlistment may be effectively ruled out for subsequent, more stringent and discriminating screening procedures that are required to qualify for certain job positions.

Taken together, the actions described here as recommendations would promote significant advancement toward improved information gathering, sharing, and usage. If gathered and applied effectively, psychological screening data could be used not only to reduce military attrition and its associated costs but also to improve the overall quality, strength, effectiveness, and survivability of U.S. military personnel.

References

Alvarado, G. F. & Breslau, N. (2005). Smoking and young people's mental health. *Current Opinion in Psychiatry, 18*, 397–400.

Apter, A., Plutchik, R. & van Praag, H. M. (1993). Anxiety, impulsivity and depressed mood in relation to suicidal and violent behavior. *Acta Psychiatrica Scandinavica, 87*, 1–5.

Barnes, J. D., Gaskins, R. C., III, Hansen, L. A., Laurence, J. H., Waters, B. K., Quenette, M. A. & Trent, T. (1989). *The Adaptability Screening Profile (ASP): Background and Pilot Test Results.* Alexandria, VA: Human Resources Research Organization.

Bartone, P. T. (1999). Hardiness protects against war-related stress in army reserve forces. *Consulting Psychology Journal: Practice and Research, 51*, 72–82.

Booth-Kewley, S., Larson, G. E. & Ryan, M. A. K. (2002). Predictions of naval attrition. I. Analysis of 1-year attrition. *Military Medicine, 167*, 760–769.

Brent, D. A., Perper, A. J., Moritz, G., Allman, C., Friend, A., Roth, C., et al. (1993). Psychiatric risk factors for adolescent suicide: A case-control study. *Journal of the American Academy of Child and Adolescent Psychiatry, 32,* 521–529.

Breslau, N., Schultz, L. R., Johnson, E. O., Peterson, E. L. & Davis, G. C. (2005). Smoking and the risk of suicidal behavior: A prospective study of a community sample. *Archives of General Psychiatry, 62,* 328–334.

Brewin, C. R., Andrews, B. & Valentine, J. D. (2000). Meta-analysis of risk factors for posttraumatic stress disorder in trauma-exposed adults. *Journal of Consulting and Clinical Psychology, 68,* 748–766.

Buddin, R. J. (2005). *Success of First-Term Soldiers: The Effects of Recruiting Practices and Recruit Characteristics.* Santa Monica, CA: Rand.

Butters, M., Retzlaff, P. & Gibertini, M. (1986). Non-adaptability to basic training and the millon clinical multiaxial inventory. *Military Medicine, 151,* 574–576.

Campbell, J. P. & Knapp, D. J. (Eds.) (2001). *Exploring the Limits in Personnel Selection and Classification.* Mahwah, NJ: Erlbaum.

Carbone, E. G., Cigrang, J. A., Todd, S. L. & Fiedler, E. R. (1999). Predicting outcome of military basic training for individuals referred for psychological evaluation. *Journal of Personality Assessment, 72,* 256–265.

Carollo, R. & Kaplow, L. (2005). Justice at war: Troops receive light sentences for violent crimes against Iraqis. *Dayton Daily News,* October 2, p. A1.

Caulfield, M. B. (2000). *Adaptation to First Term Enlistment among Women in the Marine Corps.* Boston, MA: VA Boston Healthcare System.

Centers for Disease Control. Vietnam Experiences Study (1988). Health status of Vietnam veterans: I. Psychosocial characteristics. *Journal of the American Medical Association, 259,* 2701–2707.

Cigrang, J. A., Carbone, E. G., Todd, S. & Fiedler, E. R. (1998). Mental health attrition from air force basic training. *Military Medicine, 163,* 834–838.

Clark, L. A. (1993). *Schedule for Non-Adaptive and Adaptive Personality* (SNAP). Minneapolis, MN: Regents of the University of Minnesota.

Crawford, S. L. & Fiedler, E. R. (1992). Childhood physical and sexual abuse and failure to complete military basic training. *Military Medicine, 157,* 645–648.

Daniels, W. L., Patton, J. F., Vogel, J. A., Jones, B. H., Zoltick, J. M. & Yancey, S. F. (1984). Aerobic fitness and smoking. *Medicine and Science in Sports and Exercise, 16,* 195–196.

Elsass, W. P., Fiedler, E., Skop, B. & Hill, H. (2001). Susceptibility to maladaptive responses to stress in basic military training based on variants of temperament and character. *Military Medicine, 166,* 884–888.

Fergusson, D. M., Horwood, L. J. & Lynskey, M. T. (1996). Childhood sexual abuse and psychiatric disorder in young adulthood. II. Psychiatric outcomes of childhood sexual abuse. *Journal of the American Academy of Child and Adolescent Psychiatry, 35,* 1365–1374.

Fiedler, E. R., Oltmanns, T. F. & Turkheimer, E. (2004). Traits associated with personality disorders and adjustment to military life: Predictive validity of self and peer reports. *Military Medicine, 169,* 207–211.

Fischl, M. A. & Blackwell, D. L. (2000). *Attrition in the Army from Signing of the Enlistment Contract Through 180 Days of Service* (Research Report No. 1750). Alexandria, VA: US Army Research Institute for the Behavioral and Social Sciences.

Flyer, E. S. (1996). *California Male Recruits with a Preservice Arrest History: Identification, Characteristics, and Behavior on Active Duty*. Monterey, CA: Naval Postgraduate School.

Flyer, E. S. (2004). *Development and Validation of a Biographical Questionnaire to Screen GED/Non-High School Graduate Applicants for Navy Service*. Monterey, CA: Naval Postgraduate School.

Flyer, E. S. & Eitelberg, M. (2005). *Preservice Cigarette Smoking and Behavioral Adjustment of Navy Recruits*. Monterey, CA: Naval Postgraduate School.

Flyer, E. S. & Elster, R. S. (1983). *First-Term Attrition among Non-Prior Service Enlisted Personnel: Loss Probabilities Based on Selected Entry Factors* (Report No. NPS54-83-007). Monterey, CA: Naval Postgraduate School.

Garb, H. N. (2005). *The Lackland Behavioral Questionnaire (Lackland BQ)*. Unpublished manuscript.

Garb, H. N. & Fiedler, E. (2007). *Strategies for Scale Construction*. Manuscript submitted for publication.

General Accounting Office (1997). *Military Attrition: DOD Could Save Millions by Better Screening Enlisted Personnel* (GAO/NSIAD-97-39). Washington, D.C.: Author.

General Accounting Office (1982). *Service Programs to Reduce Costly Attrition by Developing and Using Biodata Inventories* (FPCD-82-27). Washington, D.C.: Author.

Gould, M. S., Greenberg, T., Velting, D. M. & Shaffer, D. (2003). Youth suicide risk and preventive interventions: A review of the past 10 years. *Journal of the American Academy of Child and Adolescent Psychiatry, 42*, 386–405.

Hallfors, D. D., Waller, M. W., Ford, C. A., Halpern, C. T., Brodish, P. H. & Iritani, B. (2004). Adolescent depression and suicide risk: Association with sex and drug behavior. *American Journal of Preventive Medicine, 27*, 224–231.

Hattiangadi, A. U., Lee, G. & Quester, A. O. (2004). *Recruiting Hispanics: The Marine Corps Experience Final Report*. Alexandria, VA: Center for Naval Analyses.

Hoge, C. W., Castro, C. A., Messer, S. C., McGurk, D., Cotting, D. I. & Koffman, R. L. (2004). Combat duty in Iraq and Afghanistan, mental health problems, and barriers to care. *New England Journal of Medicine, 351*, 13–22.

Kaplan, Z., Weiser, M., Reichenberg, A., Rabinowitz, J., Caspi, A., Bodner, E., et al. (2002). Motivation to serve in the military influences vulnerability to future posttraumatic stress disorder. *Psychiatry Research, 109*, 45–49.

Kennedy, K. (2006). Finessing the dropout count: Thousands of recruits don't show up on the rolls of diploma-less. *Army Times*, August 14.

Kessler, R. C., Berglund, P., Demler, O., Jin, R., Koretz, D., Merikangas, K. R., et al. (2003). The epidemiology of major depressive disorder: Results from the National Comorbidity Survey Replication (NCS-R). *JAMA, 289*, 3095–3105.

King, D. W., King, L. A. & Vogt, D. S. (2003). *Manual for the Deployment Risk and Resilience Inventory (DRRI): A Collection of Measures for Studying Deployment-Related Experiences in Military Veterans*. Boston, MA: National Center for PTSD.

Klein, S., Hawes-Dawson, J. & Martin, T. (1991). *Why Recruits Separate Early* (Report No. R-3980-FMP). Santa Monica, CA: The RAND Corporation.

Klesges, R. C., Haddock, C. K., Chang, C. F., Talcott, G. W. & Lando, H. A. (2001). The association of smoking and the cost of military training. *Tobacco Control, 10*, 43–47.

Knapik, J. J., Jones, B. H., Hauret, K., Darakjy, S. & Piskator, E. (2004). *A Review of the Literature on Attrition from the Military Services: Risk Factors for Attrition and Strategies to Reduce Attrition.* Aberdeen Proving Ground, MD: US Army Center for Health Promotion and Preventive Medicine.

Knapik, J. J., Sharp, M. A., Canham-Chervak, M., Hauret, K., Patton, J. F. & Jones, B. H. (2001). Risk factors for training-related injuries among men and women in basic combat training. *Medicine and Science in Sports and Exercise, 33,* 946–954.

Knapp, D. J., Heggestad, E. D. & Young, M. C. (2004). *Understanding and Improving the Assessment of Individual Motivation (AIM) in the Army's GED Plus Program.* Alexandria, VA: United States Army Research Institute for the Behavioral and Social Sciences.

Knox, B. W. (1998). *Analysis of Navy Delayed Entry Program and Recruit Training Center Attrition.* Monterey, CA: Naval Postgraduate School. Thesis.

Koenen, K. C., Hitsman, B., Lyons, M. J., Niatura, R., McCaffery, J., Goldberg, J., et al. (2005). A twin registry study of the relationship between posttraumatic stress disorder and nicotine dependence in men. *Archives of General Psychiatry, 62,* 1258–1265.

Koltko-Rivera, M. E. & Niebuhr, D. W. (2004). *The Entry Psychiatric Screen (EPS): A Psychiatric Screening Procedure for Applicants for Military Service.* Winter Park, FL: Professional Services Group Inc.

Kulka, R. A., Schlenger, W. E., Fairbank, J. A., Hough, R. L., Jordan, B. K., Marmar, C. R. & Weiss, D. S. (1990). *Trauma and the Vietnam War Generation.* New York: Brunner/Mazel.

Larson, G. E., Booth-Kewley, S. & Ryan, A. K. (2002). Predictors of naval attrition. II. A demonstration of potential usefulness for screening. *Military Medicine, 167,* 770–776.

Lubin, B., Fiedler, E. R. & Whitlock, R. V. (1996). Mood as a predictor of discharge from air force basic training. *Journal of Clinical Psychology, 52,* 145–151.

Lubin, B., Fiedler, E. R. & Whitlock, R. V. (1999). Predicting discharge from airforce basic training by pattern of affect. *Journal of Clinical Psychology, 55,* 71–78.

Macklin, M. L., Metzger, L. J., Litz, B. T., McNally, R. J., Lasko, N. B., Orr, S. P. & Pittman, R. K. (1998). Lower precombat intelligence is a risk factor for posttraumatic stress disorder. *Journal of Consulting and Clinical Psychology, 66,* 323–326.

Makikyro, T. H., Hakko, H. H., Timonen, M. J., Lappalainen, J. A., Ilomaki, R. S., Marttunen, M. J., Laksy, K. & Rasanen, P. K. (2004). Smoking and suicidality among adolescent psychiatric patients. *Journal of Adolescent Health, 34,* 250–253.

McCraw, R. K. (1990). Personality factors in failure to adapt to the military. *Military Medicine, 155,* 127–130.

McCraw, R. K. & Bearden, D. L. (1990). Personality factors in failure to adapt to the military. *Military Medicine, 155,* 127–130.

McKeown, R. E., Garrison, C. Z., Cuffe, S. P., Waller, J. L., Jackson, K. L. & Addy, C. L. (1998). Incidence and predictors of suicidal behaviors in a longitudinal sample of young adolescents. *Journal of the American Academy of Child and Adolescent Psychiatry, 37,* 612–619.

McNally, R. J. & Shin, L. M. (1995). Association of intelligence with severity of post-traumatic stress disorder symptoms in Vietnam combat veterans. *American Journal of Psychiatry, 152,* 936–938.

Merrill, L. L. (2001). Trauma symptomatology among female U.S. Navy recruits. *Military Medicine, 166,* 621–624.

Merrill, L. L., Newell, C. E., Milner, J. S., Koss, M. P., Hervig, L. K., Gold, S. R., et al. (1998). Prevalence of premilitary adult sexual victimization and aggression in a Navy recruit sample. *Military Medicine, 163,* 209–212.

Merrill, L. L., Stander, V. A., Thomsen, C. J., Crouch, J. L. & Milner, J. S. (2004). Childhood exposure to family violence and attrition in the Navy. *Military Medicine, 169,* 465–469.

Merrill, L. L., Thomsen, C. J., Gold, S. R. & Milner, J. S. (2001). Childhood abuse and premilitary sexual assault in male Navy recruits. *Journal of Consulting and Clinical Psychology, 69,* 252–261.

Merrill, L. L., Thomsen, C. J., Sinclair, B. B., Gold, S. R. & Milner, J. S. (2001). Predicting the impact of child sexual abuse on women: The role of abuse severity, parental support, and coping strategies. *Journal of Consulting and Clinical Psychology, 69,* 992–1006.

Military personnel (2000). *Services Need to Assess Efforts to Meet Recruiting Goals and Cut Attrition* (Report No. GAO/NSIAD-00-146). Washington, D.C.: General Accounting Office.

National Research Council (2006). *Assessing Fitness for Military Enlistment: Physical, Medical, and Mental Health Standards.* Committee on the Youth Population and Military Recruitment: Physical, Medical, and Mental Health Standards, P. R. Sackett & A. S. Mavor (Eds.). Board on Behavioral, Cognitive, and Sensory Sciences, Division of Behavioral and Social Sciences and Education. Washington, D.C.: The National Academies Press.

Quester, A. O. (1999). *Bootcamp Attrition Rates: Predictions for FY 1999* (Report No. CAB 99-57). Alexandria, VA: Center for Naval Analysis.

Quick, J. C., Joplin, J. R., Nelson, D. L., Mangelsdorff, A. D. & Fiedler, E. (1996). Self-reliance and military service training outcomes. *Military Psychology, 8,* 279–293.

Riala, K., Hakko, H., Isohanni, M., Järvelin, M. R. & Räsänen, P. (2004). Teenage smoking and substance use as predictors of severe alcohol problems in late adolescence and in young adulthood. *Journal of Adolescent Health, 35,* 245–254.

Rosen, L. N. & Martin, L. (1996). Impact of childhood abuse history on psychological symptoms among male and female soldiers in the U.S. Army. *Childhood Abuse & Neglect, 20,* 1149–1160.

Shaffer, D., Gould, M., Fisher, P., Trautman, P., Moreau, D., Kleinman, M., et al. (1996). Psychiatric diagnosis in child and adolescent suicide. *Archives of General Psychiatry, 53,* 339–348.

Silva, R. R., Alpert, M., Munoz, D. M., Singh, S. M., Matzner, F. & Dummitt, S. (2000). Stress and vulnerability to posttraumatic stress disorder in children and adolescents. *American Journal of Psychiatry, 157,* 1229–1235.

Silverman, A. B., Reinherz, H. Z. & Giaconia, R. M. (1996). The long-term sequelae of child and adolescent abuse: A longitudinal community study. *Child Abuse & Neglect, 20,* 709–723.

Smikle, C. B., Fiedler, E. R., Sorem, K. A., Spencer, D. K. & Satin, A. J. (1996). The impact of sexual abuse on job attrition in military recruits. *Military Medicine, 161*, 146–148.

Snoddy, R. O. & Henderson, J. M. (1994). Predictors of basic infantry success. *Military Medicine, 159*, 616–622.

Sourander, A., Helstela, L., Haavisto, A. & Bergroth, L. (2001). Suicidal thoughts and attempts among adolescents: A longitudinal 8 year follow-up study. *Journal of Affective Disorders, 63*, 59–66.

Staal, M. A., Cigrang, J. A. & Fiedler, E. R. (2000). Disposition decisions in U.S. Air Force basic trainees assessed during mental health evaluations. *Military Psychology, 12*, 187–203.

Talcott, G. W., Haddock, C. K., Klesges, R. C., Lando, H. & Fiedler, E. (1999). Prevalence and predictors of discharge in United States Air Force basic military training. *Military Medicine, 164*, 269–274.

Thomas, C., Turkheimer, E. & Oltmanns, T. F. (2003). Factorial structure of pathological personality as evaluated by peers. *Journal of Abnormal Psychology, 112*, 81–91.

Toros, F., Bilgin, N. G., Sasmaz, T., Bugdayci, R. & Camdeviren, H. (2004). Suicide attempts and risk factors among children and adolescents. *Yonsei Medical Journal, 45*, 367–374.

Trent, T. & Laurence, J. H. (Eds.) (1993). *Adaptability Screening for the Armed Forces.* Washington, D.C.: Office of Assistant Secretary of Defense.

Trent, T. & Quenette, M. A. (1992). *Armed Services Applicant Profile (ASAP): Development and Validation of Operational Forms* (TR-92-9). San Diego, CA: Navy Personnel Research and Development Center.

White, L. A. & Young, M. C. (1998). Development and validation of the Assessment of Individual Motivation (AIM). Paper presented at the annual meeting of the American Psychological Association, San Francisco, CA.

Young, M. C., White, L. A., Heggestad, E. D. & Barnes, J. D. (2004). Operational validation of the Army's new pre-enlistment attrition screening measure. Paper presented at the annual meeting of the American Psychological Association, Honolulu, HI.

Resilience and Military Psychiatry

2

ELSPETH CAMERON RITCHIE
Office of the Surgeon General
United States Army

BRETT SCHNEIDER AND JOHN BRADLEY
Walter Reed Army Medical Center

ROBERT D. FORSTEN
U.S. Army Special Operations Command

Contents

It seems clear that people can behave with great resilience, even heroism, in circumstances when experts beforehand had predicted mass panic and civil breakdown. One reason may be that people can see a wider purpose to accepting these risks, and also become active participants in the process.

—Simon Wessely (*Risk, Psychiatry, and the Military*, 2005)

Introduction

The goal of this chapter is to address the current status and practice of military psychiatry to identify and manage mental health issues in the military. In particular, we consider the strengths and the limitations of current practice as they relate specifically to vulnerability or resilience to stress. Here, we define resilience as the ability to adjust easily to stress or to recover quickly and effectively from exposure to stress. It is important to note, however, that formal military doctrine does not refer to "resilience" per se but rather emphasizes the importance of "enhancing adaptive stress reactions" and "preventing maladaptive stress reactions" (Department of the Army, 2006).

The explicit goal of current military mental and behavioral health policy and practice is to maintain individual and unit readiness (i.e., the ability to fight effectively in the near term and on short notice). By design, current strategies focus on prevention as well as management of stress reactions that could have a negative impact upon behavior or performance. For example, when stress interferes with concentration and attention, service members may find it difficult or impossible to perform any of the military mission–relevant tasks. Military mental health providers often measure success by tracking "return to duty" rates for service members who present as potential casualties of combat-related stress.

Individual readiness is determined by the commander's or the doctor's assessment of each combatant's ability to perform basic and specific job-related tasks. An entire military unit may be deemed "combat ineffective" if less than 85% of its member personnel are unavailable for active duty due to death, injury, or debilitating reactions to stress. Many reactions to stress are potentially preventable or treatable. In order to ensure combat effectiveness for military units, it is important for commanders and clinicians to recognize and address any circumstances or difficulties that might cause or increase casualties of combat-related stress.

We begin this chapter with a brief history of combat psychiatry. Our purpose is to provide historical context for the emergence and development of current interventions. We then consider the current issues relevant to the prevention, management, and treatment of combat stress throughout the cycle of military deployment. Then the management of stress-related disorders in the theater of operations is discussed, and this chapter is concluded with a brief discussion of treatment strategies if soldiers are evacuated for psychiatric reasons. The overall topic of military psychiatry is a large one, and many topics are covered in more detail elsewhere (Jones, 1995; Jones & Fong, 1994; Ritchie & Owens, 2004).

A Brief History of Combat Psychiatry

All wars produce stress reactions. The documented history of military psychiatry dates at least as far back as World War I, when psychological casualties were diagnosed as victims of "shell shock." This diagnosis reflected an underlying notion that behavioral changes were the direct result of organic damage from exposure to artillery blasts. Early in World War II, service members who demonstrated psychological or behavioral symptoms were classified as "not yet diagnosed, nervous." Later in World War II, such symptoms were attributed instead to "battle fatigue." This term was helpful in that it suggested the potential for recovery by rest and replenishment. However, few psychological casualties who were evacuated out of theater were able to return to the combat environment. Neither hospital treatment (during World War I) nor psychoanalysis (during World War II) relieved the symptoms commonly suffered by psychological casualties of war. In contrast, when service members were treated for psychological or behavioral symptoms in theater (at "forward" locations) with brief supportive therapy and the expectation of return to duty, most (60–80%) were able to continue performing their duties as service members in combat (Jones, 1995; Shepard, 2001).

During the early months of the Korean War (July–September 1950), American military psychological casualties occurred at a rate of 250 per 1000, principally within the U.S. Army and Marine Corps. These numbers overwhelmed resources that had been assigned to manage psychological casualties at forward locations. Casualties were thus evacuated to Japan or the United States, and very few returned to duty. When the principles of early and far-forward treatment were eventually reinstituted in October 1950, as many as 80% of neuropsychiatry casualties were again able to return to duty after early intervention and treatment in theater (Glass, 1973; Ritchie, 2002).

Thus it is by direct experience that the U.S. military has come to recognize the value of simple and immediate psychological intervention on the battlefield. Basic principles for the early management of psychological casualties would later be codified as "proximity, immediacy, expectancy, and simplicity" (PIES), which directed simple immediate treatment, without evacuation, and with the expectation of return to duty (Artiss, 1963; Glass, 1973; Salmon, 1929).

The principles of PIES were followed throughout the Vietnam War, during which time relatively few combat stress–related casualties were reported. Although the principles of PIES were applied to great benefit in Vietnam, it is difficult to know how much of the apparently dramatic reduction in combat stress casualties in theater may have been due to the use of drugs or alcohol as self-initiated strategies to cope with the stress of combat. Most substance users in Vietnam discontinued substance abuse after the war. However, some may have suffered more long-term psychological morbidity as a result (Jones, 1995). There are few good statistics available to address the overall incidence of psychological morbidity during the Vietnam War itself, but Vietnam veterans were studied extensively many years after the war ended. In fact, the long-term consequences of extreme stress first gained the attention of researchers and the public shortly after the Vietnam War, when it became clear that many service members were suffering lasting effects of trauma. Their symptoms often included flashbacks, hypervigilance, night terrors, social isolation, amnesia, panic, and emotional numbing. Clinicians described the syndrome as "posttraumatic stress disorder" (PTSD).

In 1980, PTSD was added to the American Psychiatric Association's *Diagnostic Statistical Manual of Mental Disorders* (DSM). Serious research into the cause and treatment of PTSD began in the late 1980s. It eventually became apparent that as many as 30% of all Vietnam veterans had experienced at least some symptoms of PTSD since their return from the war (Kulka et al., 1990a,b). Considerable amounts of money have since been invested in PTSD research and treatment (Shepard, 2001), the findings of which are well-represented in military and civilian scientific literature alike.

During the first Persian Gulf War (Operation Desert Shield/Storm, 1990–1991), immediate psychological casualties reported were few. However, in subsequent years, veterans of the first Gulf War have exhibited a constellation of physical, psychological, and neuropsychological symptoms, which is now most commonly described as "Gulf War syndrome." It is not yet known to what extent psychological trauma and exposure to chronic stress may contribute to Gulf War syndrome (Riddle et al., 2003).

Medical planners for the current wars in Afghanistan and Iraq have applied lessons learned from this past experience. In addition, psychiatric epidemiologic principles are employed in an effort to quantify the psychological impact of war. Mental Health Advisory Teams (MHATs) are now sent to each combat zone to survey service members and mental health providers. The first MHAT team survey (performed in Iraq in the fall of 2003 and published in the summer of 2004) documented that 77% of deployed service members reported no stress or mild stress, 16% moderate stress, and 7% severe stress. Surveys for specific diagnostic categories indicated that 7.3% of respondents screened positive for anxiety, 6.9% for depression, and 15.2% for traumatic stress. The overwhelming majority (83%) of those surveyed did not meet screening criteria for behavioral health functional impairment. Behavioral health units in the combat zone reported that more than 95% of service members who presented for psychological evaluation were subsequently returned to duty (Medical Health Advisory Team, 2003).

The second MHAT team (MHAT-II) evaluated service members deployed during the second year of the Iraq War (2004) and found that the percentage of service members who screened positive for a mental health–related problem had decreased from 18% to 13%. Ten percentage (10%) of service members then screened positive for symptoms of acute or posttraumatic stress. The U.S. Army National Guard and reserve units whose members performed transportation and nonmedical combat service support demonstrated higher rates of mental health problems and held less positive perceptions of combat readiness and training than did service members in other units (Mental Health Advisory Team, 2005). Reports for Operation Enduring Freedom (Afghanistan) and a 1995 follow-up survey (Iraq) are pending.

Combat and Operational Stress Control

Military behavioral and mental health care includes intervention and treatment of stress symptoms, maladaptive behavioral responses to extreme environments, and mental illnesses that can affect mission capability and individual function. Military mental health personnel are trained in the principles of combat and operational stress control (COSC), which emphasize the goal of preventing maladaptive operational and combat stress reactions. Each branch of military service has adopted its own doctrine and programmatic effort by which these principles are applied as well as any service-specific organizational or cultural issues that might relate to their implementation. For example, the U.S. Navy and Marine Corps currently apply the same principles under the program heading, operational stress control and readiness (OSCAR). For the purpose of maintaining consistency throughout this chapter, we focus primarily on U.S. Army doctrine and practice. The Department of Defense (2001) has determined a need to update this doctrine across the services. An updated directive for COSC is currently under development.

Combat and Operational Stress Reactions

The purpose of COSC doctrine is to promote service member and unit readiness by enhancing adaptive stress reactions, preventing maladaptive stress reactions, assisting service members to control combat and operational stress reactions, and assisting service members who present with behavioral or psychiatric disorders (Department of Defense, 2001). Simply put, stress control is intended to promote the ability of service members to cope with the potentially damaging effects of combat.

As part of COSC doctrine, the U.S. Army has developed a system to classify combat and operational stress reactions (COSRs). Under this system, stress reactions are classified as either adaptive or maladaptive. *Adaptive stress reactions* are characterized as reactions that enhance individual and unit performance. Benefits might include improved cohesiveness, morale, responsibility, courage, and strength. In effect, adaptive reactions are those that demonstrate resilience to stress at the individual or unit level. They are attributed as the result of "physiological stress response, together with other individual factors (such as personality and training) and social/environmental factors (such as good leadership and peer relationships)" (Department of the Army, 2006).

Maladaptive stress reactions, which may be transient or persistent, include misconduct or behavioral disorders (e.g., depression or anxiety) that develop or are exacerbated as the result of deployment or combat stress. Stress-related misconduct is usually characterized by rule breaking or criminal behavior and may include behavior such as mutilating enemy dead, killing enemy prisoners, killing noncombatants, torture, alcohol and drug abuse, recklessness, indiscipline, looting, malingering, self-inflicted injury, killing their own leaders ("fragging"), or desertion (Department of the Army, 2006).

Prevention and Preparation through Training

COSC doctrinal objectives are now also addressed explicitly or implicitly as part of basic military training, as personnel are presented with new challenges and must learn to accommodate and adapt to stress. Basic training emphasizes the need for physical, technical, and situational readiness, and psychological resilience can be seen as a positive collateral outcome of these objectives. Basic and other military training also fosters a strong sense of unit cohesion, mental and physical toughness, leadership development, and rapid situation assessment skills, all of which are encapsulated in the construct known as "warrior ethos" (Department of the Army, 1999).

The process of training an individual to become a military service member, and to serve as part of a working team, inculcates a set of beliefs and values that form the basis for a cohesive sense of the self, an appreciation for the meaning of one's work, and knowledge of one's purpose in the context of a larger organization. This training promotes a strong sense of *esprit de corps*, which is at least anecdotally correlated with adaptability and, ultimately, survivability (Department of the Army, 2006). Moreover, the military correlates of social support (morale, cohesion) and individual hardiness—factors commonly recognized as important to individual and group resilience—appear to affect emotionally sustaining behavior in context of military service (Manning, 1991).

Prevention is a key objective in fostering resilience to stress among deployed service members. By emphasizing preparation and prevention, the U.S. military also promotes the view that each individual service member and each military unit can (and should) claim at least some level of control over responses and reactions to stresses that are unavoidably associated with deployment and combat.

COSC on the Battlefield

Despite all the best efforts to prepare and train for the stress of combat, inevitably some individuals will suffer stress-related difficulties and disorders that interfere with their effective performance on the battlefield. In recognition of this reality, the U.S. Army deploys mental health providers to combat zones as members of combat units, medical units, and units specifically designed to provide combat stress control intervention and treatment. Traditionally, each U.S. Army combat division has included division mental health (DMH) personnel assigned directly to a unit consisting of three behavioral health officers (one psychiatrist, one psychologist, and one social worker) and as many as seven enlisted service members with specialized training as paraprofessional mental health technicians. Recently, however, the army unit organization has changed such that mental health personnel are now assigned at the brigade combat team (BCT) level. Medical units such as combat support hospitals and area support medical battalions also have mental health personnel assigned to them, usually including two or three behavioral health officers and several technicians.

The U.S. Army also trains dedicated combat stress control (CSC) units whose mission is to provide specific mental health interventions as needed in the theater of military operation. CSC units are "stand-alone" units that include a unit commander and unit-assigned vehicles. CSC units may be configured as a detachment (20–40 active duty personnel) or as a company (approximately 80 reservist personnel).

Military psychiatry defines interventions as universal, selective, indicated, or treatment (Department of the Army, 2006). These four categories are analogous to the concepts of primary, secondary, and tertiary prevention of disease and dysfunction in the field of public health. Universal interventions are preventive in nature, targeting the general military population at the unit level. For example, combat stress personnel provide psychoeducational briefings, which they deliver at the unit level to educate unit members about stress management strategies and resources. These briefings also help to identify mental health providers as present, available, and approachable. Other examples of universal interventions include command consultations, unit surveys, or "sensing" sessions (similar to focus groups). These initiatives provide commanders with opportunities to identify and begin to address unit issues or areas of dysfunction.

Selective interventions are targeted at units or at individual service members who have already been identified as being at higher-than-average risk for stress-related problems. This risk category would include units whose members have been exposed to a traumatic incident and engaged in protracted operations. In situations of this type, combat stress and trauma specialists are assigned to provide affected units with targeted service known as traumatic event management (TEM). This service involves the evaluation and selection of intervention techniques as warranted by the unit's specific situation. The TEM approach draws upon the civilian model of critical incident stress management (CISM) (see Everly & Mitchell, 1997; Mitchell & Everly, 1997).

The TEM doctrine has been modified in response to recent findings that call into question the effectiveness of critical event debriefing as a strategy to prevent traumatic reactions. For example, some studies have cautioned that critical event debriefing may be ineffective as a means to prevent PTSD and may even increase the risk of PTSD in some individuals (see NIMH, 2002; Ritchie, Friedman & Watson, 2006). TEM instead emphasizes the need for a more flexible approach, which includes "psychological first aid" as needed and as appropriate to each specific or unique situation. TEM specialists may conclude that formal critical event debriefing is not indicated, but rather there is a need for other proactive interventions such as personnel rotations (i.e., to control or limit individual exposure to traumatic stress).

Indicated interventions target individual service members who have demonstrated behavior that suggests the need for mental health intervention or treatment. These individuals may be identified by their leaders, colleagues, mental health or other health care providers, or by self-referral. Indicated interventions may also target entire units whose performance has been compromised. Indicated interventions recognize and apply the traditional military forward psychiatry concepts of PIES, including simple restorative interventions such as "three hots and a cot" (food and rest).

Service members who display symptoms of stress-related dysfunction or disorder should be treated as soon as the problem is recognized and should receive the necessary support as close as possible in proximity to their assigned unit (support system). These individuals are reassured that their symptoms are usually "a normal response to an abnormal situation," and that with the help of some brief, simple, and often very practical restorative interventions (sleep, nutrition, hygiene), they will soon return to their prior level of functioning and will be able to return to their original units. Although it is recognized on the basis of historical and recent experience that evacuated combat stress casualties rarely return to their units, those who experience significant difficulties are evacuated when military mental health care professionals recognize that it is necessary and appropriate to do so.

Treatment interventions are targeted exclusively at military personnel who demonstrate symptoms of behavioral disorders, poor coping skills, or a history of exposure to trauma, family or social dysfunction, or other difficulties that make it difficult to handle stress. Treatment interventions may include medication management, individual therapy, or group therapy. When adequate treatment can be provided at the "outpatient" level, clinicians must determine what type and extent of intervention can be safely and effectively administered in the field within the member's unit. Certainly, the need for "inpatient" care generally necessitates evacuation from the field of combat.

Deployment Cycle Support

Predeployment Support

Prior to deployment, service members and their families partake in a comprehensive program that aims to foster resilience to the stress of separation. U.S. soldiers are monitored annually for their readiness to deploy. Predeployment screening for readiness (soldier readiness process [SRP]) reviews the status of the service member's financial, legal, medical, dental, and family affairs with respect to deployment readiness. It is considered critical to identify and resolve early any issues that may serve as stressors or impediments during deployment.

Deployable units are typically supported by a family readiness group (FRG), which serves as an ongoing, formalized support network for the families of unit personnel. FRGs are often structured around a "chain of concern" in that more experienced spouses provide leadership to support younger, less experienced military families. The FRG is a critical resource because it fosters a sense of hardiness and independence during some prolonged periods of time when service members are unavailable to their families. FRGs frequently establish childcare networks, support groups, workshops, and newsletters to share information about their unit's deployment and to make families aware of opportunities and events that may promote an ongoing sense of connectedness and involvement while service members are away from home.

Service members themselves also receive information and support aimed at helping them to cope with separation from loved ones. CSC units at the brigade, division, and corps levels provide numerous services designed to counter the negative effects of operational stress and thereby improve unit readiness. For example, CSC units offer deployment cycle support briefings, which provide consultation and education about stresses associated with deployment. These briefings also offer helpful guidance about how to cope with specific types of stress associated with current operations (e.g., civilian casualties, improvised explosive devices [IEDs]).

Predeployment Mental Health Screening

Predeployment mental health screening is utilized primarily to identify at-risk personnel who should be monitored and supported as needed. Individuals with identified mental health problems are evaluated to determine whether their mental health status is adequately controlled and, if necessary, whether ongoing treatment (e.g., psychotherapy or medication) can be safely supported during deployment.

Full-time active duty military personnel also enjoy the benefits of free military medical care and readiness screening (see above). However, medical care and readiness screening procedures are less consistent with respect to personnel who have been activated from the U.S. Army Reserve or Army National Guard. Reservists are activated to a mobilization site where they undergo predeployment preparation, screening, and certification. There, a reserve augmentation unit administers the medical SRP, which is designed to screen for various conditions that might impair individual or collective hardiness for the mission at hand.

Deployment Support

Throughout deployment, CSC units and personnel provide services and support as needed for prevention as well as treatment. These medical and mental health personnel conduct a variety of outreach programs, including unit risk assessments, psychoeducational briefings on stress management and suicide prevention, and leader training to identify and reduce operational stress. These preventive measures empower leaders to actively manage the stress and the morale of their service members. They also serve to familiarize service members with CSC personnel and services so that they will be more likely to request consultation or clinical intervention when needed.

Redeployment/Postdeployment Support

Individual rotation of service members to and from the battlefield is now believed to have caused or exacerbated many of the stress-related problems experienced by service members and units in serving in Vietnam. Based on the lessons learned from the Vietnam War, the U.S. Army now employs a functional team approach to deployment and redeployment. Every effort is made to keep original units intact through deployment and redeployment.

This approach helps to foster unit cohesion and also provides a forum for dealing with the shared experience of deployment as a group.

When service members return to their home station after experience in combat, they are confronted by many challenges. Those who have been exposed to traumatic experiences must find some way to frame and assimilate their experiences as a cohesive, meaningful narrative that is understandable within the more general context of civilian life. Often, this challenge is overcome by understanding difficult experiences as having occurred in the service of a greater purpose or ideal. However, some service members may still find it quite difficult to reintegrate into their families and society. Battlefield survival skills such as extreme vigilance may be difficult to turn off, even when they have maladaptive effects in the context of ordinary civilian life.

The U.S. Army attempts to facilitate its members' transition from the battlefield to the home front by utilizing a construct and program now known as "battlemind" (http://www.battlemind.org/). Battlemind refers to the soldier's inner strength to face fear and adversity in combat with courage. Soldiers receive battlemind briefings after they return home. This briefing and others describe and normalize emotional and cognitive changes experienced by those who have served in combat and forecast the gradual resolution of resulting emotions. The purpose of this approach is to depathologize emotional difficulties and thereby diminish the resulting anxiety. End-of-tour training also encourages service members to recognize difficulties and to seek help early when problems occur.

Immediately after returning home from combat, there is a high potential for risky thrill-seeking behavior. Service members returning from combat may drive too fast, purchase new "toys" (e.g., motorcycles or weapons), become physically aggressive, or test their physical and psychological limits in other ways. Some become sexually promiscuous in an effort to make up for lost time or to rebound from a failed or failing relationship. Occasionally, returning service members turn to heavy drinking as a way to relieve psychological or emotional pain or to test and demonstrate a "hard-living tough guy" persona. Whether or not returning service members appear to be suffering from symptoms of stress—in fact, some may think of themselves as "bulletproof" to stress—dysfunctional behavior is problematic for family members and colleagues.

The postdeployment period may also require service members to reckon with losses they have suffered in combat. Memorial services are routinely held, both in theater and upon return. It is important for service members to have an opportunity for closure in the form of ritual to recognize and grieve the loss of fellow warriors. Even when individual memorial services have been held in theater, it can be extremely helpful to hold a remembrance service for an entire unit, including the families of those who lost their lives in combat. This type of service provides an opportunity for survivors to mark the contributions and sacrifices of others and thus also to recognize and reinforce their own sense of individual and unit pride in dedication to purpose.

In the redeployment phase, individual service members are formally screened for symptoms of trauma, depression, and stress. Each service member is required to complete a postdeployment health assessment (DD Form 2796) prior to leaving the theater of operations. This screening instrument is designed to identify individuals who may be at risk for stress-related problems and, if indicated, to provide referral for mental health evaluation and treatment, as needed, before the affected service member returns home.

The postdeployment health assessment screening procedure does not guarantee that all symptomatic service members will be identified prior to returning home. To the contrary, it is reasonable to assume that some individuals may respond to screening questions dishonestly simply to avoid delay returning home due to evaluation and treatment. It is also understood that some symptoms may not be noticeable or problematic for many weeks or months after returning home from combat. Therefore, service members are reassessed 3–6 months after their return from combat.

The postdeployment health reassessment (DD 2900) screening procedure is designed to identify service members who are experiencing difficulty in managing reintegration or who have developed medical or psychiatric illness since their return from deployment. As service members complete each deployment cycle and begin preparations for subsequent tours of deployment, these screening, prevention, and treatment procedures occur in cyclical fashion and help to ensure optimal readiness in an at-risk population.

Managing Stress-Related Disorders in Theater

This section addresses interventions and strategies applied to support service members' ability to function adequately when confronted by stress-related disorders or symptoms that may be provoked or exacerbated by service in combat or in other deployed settings. This discussion will focus on three categories of stress-related and mood disorders—depression, anxiety, and sleep disorders—which are the three psychiatric problems most commonly diagnosed and managed in the military theater of operations.

Depression

Depression is a complex psychological phenomenon whose symptoms include physical, emotional, and cognitive difficulties. Any or all of these symptoms can have a direct negative impact on an individual's ability to confront and manage stress. The Walter Reed Army Institute of Research has conducted numerous survey studies to assess the mental health of soldiers during and after deployment. Consistently these surveys show that about 13% of soldiers experience symptoms of PTSD, anxiety, and depression while they are deployed, and about 17% experience symptoms after they return home (Hoge et al., 2004).

Clinicians deployed in Iraq have observed that a common chief complaint among service members who have been diagnosed with depression is the need for increased dosage of antidepressant medication after recurrence or exacerbation of symptoms due to the stress of deployment. Antidepressant medications are extremely useful to correct the neurochemical imbalance associated with depression. However, most antidepressants currently available must be taken for several weeks before they begin to demonstrate beneficial effect. When pharmaceutical intervention is indicated, clinicians frequently prescribe selective serotonin reuptake inhibitors (SSRIs). Non-SSRI antidepressants are also available and may be especially useful for individuals who have comorbid problems such as attention deficit disorder (ADD), nicotine dependence, or anxiety.

Numerous other types of therapies have also been demonstrated effective in treating depressive disorders in structured or community mental health settings. The realities of combat can make it difficult for military clinicians to offer behavioral therapy in a classical clinical setting. Nevertheless, military mental health professionals offer variant forms of supportive therapy, relaxation training, cognitive behavioral therapy, psychodynamically oriented therapy, and social skills/coping strategies education to treat depressive and anxiety disorders in theater. In each case, the goal is to identify and correct behavioral or cognitive impediments to effective and healthy performance.

Anxiety

Anxiety disorders are the most common and treatable form of psychiatric illness. Anxiety can be treated by psychological therapy, pharmaceutical intervention, or a combination of both. Anxiety disorders include generalized anxiety disorder (GAD), obsessive compulsive disorder (OCD), panic disorder, phobias, PTSD, and acute stress disorder (ASD). In each case, anxiety is sufficiently severe that it interferes with functioning by causing panic, avoidance, or hypervigilant behavior.

Not surprisingly, a wide variety of data sources identify an increase in the prevalence of PTSD during and after exposure to combat in Iraq and Afghanistan. Hoge et al. (2004) observed a "strong relationship between combat experiences, such as being shot, handling dead bodies, knowing someone who was killed, or killing enemy combatants, and the prevalence of PTSD." Their findings pointed to a direct relationship between the extent of exposure to combat and likelihood of developing PTSD symptoms. Specifically, PTSD prevalence ranged from as low as 4.5% among service members who were never involved in a firefight to as high as 19.3% among those who had been involved in at least five firefights.

Anxiety disorders may be treated by clinical therapies such as cognitive behavioral therapy, exposure therapy, and eye movement desensitization and reprocessing (EMDR) therapy. These methods are particularly effective in treating ASD and PTSD but may be difficult to perform in a combat zone as mission or travel requirements may interfere with the need for weekly therapeutic sessions over a sustained period of time. For service members who must be treated while serving in the theater of operations, therapy usually focuses on alleviating specific symptoms that interfere with performance in the field.

Interestingly, symptoms such as hypervigilance can be seen as highly adaptive and even essential to survival while in combat and thus may not indicate the need for intervention or treatment until the postdeployment phase. If medical intervention is indicated for anxiety disorder, SSRIs are usually the preferred pharmaceutical approach (APA Practice Guidelines, 2004; Ball, Kuhn, Wall, Shekhar & Goddard, 2005; Stahl, 2000). Benzodiazepines may also be helpful in the treatment of panic disorder. However, caution is warranted in light of recent findings, which suggest that benzodiazepines can actually increase the severity of PTSD, especially if used for a long period of time (APA Practice Guidelines, 2004). Venlafaxine (Effexor XR) may be useful in treating GAD with depression (Howland & Thase, 2005; Thase, Entsuah & Rudolph, 2001).

Sleep Disorders

Insomnia has been the most commonly reported symptom of combat-related stress among service members deployed in Iraq. Since prolonged sleep deprivation can have a potentially critical effect on performance (see Belenky et al., 1994), it is a common focus for treatment in a combat zone. In the absence of other symptoms indicative of underlying medical issues, insomnia can be treated first by behavioral intervention (e.g., sleep hygiene education). If pharmaceutical intervention becomes necessary, drug selection must take into account possible side effects (e.g., drowsiness), personnel occupation and current duties, comorbid symptoms if any, history of substance abuse if any, and individual limitations or difficulties that might interfere with effective self-administration of medication according to instructions. Deployment formulary medications for the treatment of insomnia include trazodone, zolpidem, lorazepam, clonazepam, prazosin, and quetiapine. As an adjunct in the treatment of ASD and PTSD, alpha- or beta-blocker medications can be used to target autonomic symptoms and nightmares.

In our experience, trauma-related nightmares are common but often are initially unreported. The relationship between trauma nightmares and subsequent other symptoms is currently unknown. The antihypertensive prazosin (Minipress) may be helpful in treating trauma-related nightmares (Raskind et al., 2003). Other pharmacologic approaches such as adrenergic blockade and the serotonergic antagonistic effects of quetiapine also show promise but require further study.

Chronic Combat Stress Reactions: Treatment Issues

What the U.S. Army refers to as chronic combat stress reaction is essentially synonymous with PTSD. It may be treated in theater as described under anxiety disorders. However, if a soldier is unable to perform effectively after a trial period of treatment or if a soldier is deemed dangerous to self or others, then evacuation from the field may be necessary.

When service members are identified as a psychiatric casualty in need of evacuation, they are first evacuated from the theater of operations to an inpatient medical unit such as Landstuhl Army Medical Center in Germany. Very few who are evacuated to Germany will later return to service. Between 2001 and 2004, only 5% of service members who were evacuated to Germany for psychiatric care were able to return to service in Iraq or Afghanistan (Rundell, 2006). If service members require more than a standard few days of treatment in Germany, they are transferred to Walter Reed Army Medical Center (Washington, District of Columbia) or to other hospitals closer to their homes. There most will spend another week or two receiving inpatient psychiatric care before they are being transferred to the psychiatric continuity service.

The psychiatric continuity service was developed to serve the needs of veterans who return from Iraq and Afghanistan suffering psychiatric disorders or symptoms. The mission of this service is to provide specialty outpatient care in an interdisciplinary, multimodal, and multilevel setting designed to address the needs of service members who no longer need inpatient care but do require intensive outpatient care. The treatment model employed by the psychiatric continuity service attempts to enhance resilience as a means to improve individual coping and prevent attrition. Service members' difficulties are managed until an appropriate and effective disposition can be determined. In some cases, disposition might mean returning to duty. In most cases, service members may be granted medical retirement from active or reserve duty.

Because service members who undergo medical evaluation board review must remain at Walter Reed Army Medical Center for extended periods of time, the psychiatric continuity service has developed three levels of care within a tier system of care originally developed by Walter Reed Army

Medical Center psychiatrists, Colonel (Ret) Douglas Waldrep and Colonel (Ret) Raymond Lande. The first and most intensive stage of treatment is administered as day hospitalization (6 h of treatment per day). This level of treatment normally continues for 2 weeks but can be extended indefinitely if indicated. Service members who demonstrate improvement are transitioned to an intensive outpatient program, where they continue to meet with a therapist 1–4 times each week and with a team psychiatrist 1–4 times each month. Service members can be treated at this level for an extended period of time while they wait for a determination concerning their future disposition (return to duty versus separation). Eventually, they transition to a less intensive model of care, with the option to transition back to a higher level of care if needed.

Conclusions and Recommendations

This chapter has reviewed and described techniques that are currently employed by military commanders and behavioral health personnel to identify and manage stress-related mental and behavioral health problems among members of the U.S. military. Where possible, we have identified relationships between current practice and the goal of promoting psychological resilience to stress. The U.S. military presently has a robust approach to preparing its service members and their families for the realities of deployment and to supporting them through the many challenges of the deployment cycle itself. This approach includes prevention as well as treatment and concludes by facilitating adaptive return to military or civilian life after deployment.

Although military policy and doctrine do not at present make explicit reference to "resilience" per se, it is certainly a primary and implied concern of many programs and practices that target service members' ability to confront and overcome negative effects of combat-related stress. As our theoretical and scientific understanding of resilience improves, U.S. military combat stress control programs will undoubtedly recognize its explicit relevance and applicability to mental health in the context of military service. Further rigorous research in this area would be helpful but is notoriously difficult to achieve even without the challenges of continuous combat. In the meantime, military psychiatrists are continually assessing preparation and intervention strategies that may be helpful to service members.

Although resilience may be a difficult construct to define and test, it is clear that military personnel possess very high levels of physical and psychological resilience. Many of our nation's soldiers are currently serving in their second or third deployments to Iraq. They and their families demonstrate essential resilience every day and so may provide a uniquely informative and inspiring basis by which to identify and assess resilient personal attributes and coping strategies. We hope that future research in this area will recognize the broader relevance of the military experience as a model of individual, organizational, and community-based resilience.

References

American Psychiatric Association (2004). *American Psychiatric Association Practice Guidelines for the Treatment of Psychiatric Disorders. Compendium 2004*. Arlington, VA: American Psychiatric Association.

Artiss, K.L. (1963). Human behavior under stress: from combat to social psychiatry. *Military Medicine*, 128 (10), 1011–1015.

Ball, S.G., Kuhn, A., Wall, D., Shekhar, A. & Goddard, A.W. (2005). First-line treatment for generalized anxiety disorder. *Journal of Clinical Psychiatry*, 66 (1), 94–99.

Belenky, G., Penetar, D., Thorne, D., Popp, K., Leu, J., Thomas, M., et al. (1994). The effects of sleep deprivation on performance during continuous combat operations. In: Marriott, B.M. (Ed.), *Food Components to Enhance Performance* (pp. 127–136). Washington, D.C.: National Academy Press.

Department of Defense (February 2001). *Combat Stress Control*. Department of Defense Directive 6490.5.

Department of the Army (August 1999). *Army Leadership*. FM 22-100.

Department of the Army (June 2006). *Combat and Operational Stress Control*. FM 4-02.51.

Everly, G.S. & Mitchell, J.T. (1997). *Critical Incident Stress Management (CISM): A New Era and Standard of Care in Crisis Intervention*. Ellicott City, MD: Chevron.

Glass, A.J. (1973). Lessons learned. In: Glass, A.J. (Ed.), *Overseas Theaters. Vol 2. Neuropsychiatry in World War II* (pp. 989–1027). Washington, D.C.: Office of the Surgeon General, U.S. Army.

Hoge, C.W., Castro, C.A., Messer, S.C., McGurk, D., Cotting, D.I. & Koffman, R.L. (2004). Combat duty in Iraq and Afghanistan, mental health problems, and barriers to care. *New England Journal of Medicine*, 351 (1), 13–22.

Howland, R.H. & Thase, M.E. (2005). Comorbid depression and anxiety: when and how to treat. *Journal of Psychiatry*, 329 (11), 891–1047.

Jones, F.D. (1995). Psychiatric lessons of war. In: Jones, F.D., Sparacino, L.R., Wilcox, V.L., Rothberg, J.M. & Stokes, J.W. (Eds.), *Textbook of Military Medicine, Part I: War Psychiatry* (pp. 3–33). Washington, D.C.: Office of the Surgeon General, U.S. Army.

Jones, F.D. & Fong, Y.H. (1994). Military psychiatry and terrorism. In: Jones, F.D., Sparacino, L.R., Wilcox, V.L. & Rothberg, J.M. (Eds.), *Military Psychiatry: Preparing in Peace for War* (pp. 263–269). Washington, D.C.: Office of the Surgeon General, Walter Reed Army Institute of Research.

Kulka, R.A., Schlenger, W.E., Fairbank, J.A., Hough, R.L., Jordan, B.K. & Marmar, C.R., et al. (1990a). *The National Vietnam Veterans Readjustment Study: Tables of Findings and Technical Appendices*. New York: Brunner/Mazel.

Kulka, R.A., Schlenger, W.E., Fairbank, J.A., Hough, R.L., Jordan, B.K., Marmar, C.R., et al. (1990b). *Trauma and the Vietnam War Generation: Report of Findings from the National Vietnam Veterans Readjustment Study*. New York: Brunner/Mazel.

Manning, F.J. (1991). Morale, cohesion and *esprit de corps*. In: Reuven, G. & Mangelsdorff, D.A. (Eds.), *Handbook of Military Psychology* (pp. 453–454). Chichester, England: John Wiley & Sons.

Mental Health Advisory Team (December 2003). *Operation Iraqi Freedom (OIF). Mental Health Advisory Team (MHAT) Report*. U.S. Army Surgeon General & HQDA G-1. http://www.armymedicine.army.mil/news/mhat/mhat.cfm

Mental Health Advisory Team—II (January 2005). *Operation Iraqi Freedom (OIF-II) Mental Health Advisory Team (MHAT-II) Report*. U.S. Army Surgeon General. http://www.armymedicine.army.mil/news/mhat_ii/mhat.cfm

Mitchell, J.T. & Everly, G.S. (1997). The scientific evidence for critical incident stress management. *Journal of Emergency Medical Services*, 22 (1), 86–93.

National Institute of Mental Health (2002). *Mental Health and Mass Violence— Evidence Based Early Psychological Intervention for Victims/Survivors of Mass Violence: A Workshop to Reach Consensus on Best Practices*. Washington, D.C.: Government Printing Office.

Raskind, M.A., Peskind, E.R., Kanter, E.D., Petrie, E.C., Radant, A., Thompson, C.E., et al. (2003). Reduction of nightmares and other PTSD symptoms in combat veterans by prazosin: a placebo-controlled study. *American Journal of Psychiatry*, 160 (2), 371–373.

Riddle, J., Brown, M., Smith, T., Ritchie, E.C., Brix, K.A. & Romano, J. (2003). Chemical warfare and the Gulf War: the threat and its impact on Gulf veterans' health. *Military Medicine*, 168 (8), 606–613.

Ritchie, E.C. (2002). Psychiatry in the Korean War: perils, PIES and prisoners of war. *Military Medicine*, 167 (11), 898–903.

Ritchie, E.C., Friedman, M. & Watson, P. (2006). *Interventions Following Mass Violence and Disasters: Strategies for Mental Health Practice*. New York: Guilford Press.

Ritchie, E.C. & Owens, M. (2004). Military issues. *Psychiatric Clinics North America*, 27, 459–471.

Rundell, J.R. (2006). Demographics of and diagnoses in Operation Enduring Freedom and Operation Iraqi Freedom personnel who were psychiatrically evacuated from the theater of operations. *General Hospital Psychiatry*, 28 (4), 3526.

Salmon, T.W. (1929). The care and treatment of mental diseases and war neurosis ("shell shock") in the British Army. In: Bailey, P., Williams, F.E., Komora, P.A., Salmon, T.W. & Fenton, N. (Eds.), *Neuropsychiatry. Vol 10. The U.S. Medical Department of the United States Army in the World War* (pp. 497–523). Washington, D.C.: Office of the Surgeon General, U.S. Army.

Shepard, B. (2001). *A War of Nerves: Soldiers and Psychiatrists in the Twentieth Century*. Cambridge, MA: Harvard University Press.

Stahl, S.M. (2000). *Essential Psychopharmacology: Neuroscientific Basis and Practical Applications*. 2nd ed. New York: Cambridge University Press.

Thase, M.E., Entsuah, A.R., Rudolph, R.L. (2001). Remission rates during treatment with venlafaxine or selective serotonin reuptake inhibitors. *The British Journal of Psychiatry*, 178 (3), 234–241.

Wessely, S. (2005). Risk, psychiatry, and the military. *British Journal of Psychiatry*, 186, 459–466.

The Stresses of Modern War

3

GEORGE R. MASTROIANNI AND THOMAS R. MABRY
United States Air Force Academy

DAVID M. BENEDEK AND ROBERT J. URSANO
Uniformed Services University

Contents

Resilience has proven to be a useful construct in the study of human adaptation to stress and adversity (Bonnano, 2004). However, because human beings are complex creatures embedded in dynamic social and cultural environments, it is understandably difficult to define the concept of resilience in a way that enables researchers to identify, measure, or manipulate its essential features. Other behavioral scientific concepts such as stress (Cannon, 1953; McCarty, 1989; Selye, 1980), situation awareness (Endsley, 1995), and mental workload (Eggemeier, 1988) have posed similar difficulties. Like resilience, these constructs attempt to describe essential but empirically elusive human characteristics and capacities. Such complex constructs can often produce valuable insights and interventions in their respective areas of concern only after many years of challenging research and confusing or contradictory findings.

Here, we take the position that resilience is neither simply a trait nor simply an outcome. Rather, resilience is described as the interaction between individuals and their environment that leads to the achievement and maintenance of effective health and performance under stress. Currently available evidence indicates that multiple factors conspire to affect resilience. These factors include personal attributes, task requirements, environmental variables, social and cultural factors, and organizational context. In particular, resilience to the stresses of war depends upon the complex, dynamic, and interactive influences of individual, environmental, and social variables.

Prior to the current war in Iraq, our most recent experience with protracted military conflict occurred in Vietnam. The shattering consequences of that experience have led to fundamental changes in the U.S. military force development and personnel policies. Not the least of these changes was the transition to an all-volunteer force (AVF). Our military establishment has changed dramatically since the end of the Vietnam era, and these changes must condition our understanding of the performance of our military under current and future conditions. Today's AVF is composed of both active and reserve components whose members include more women, more married service members, and generally well-educated service members due to higher standards in recruitment (Huffman & Payne, 2006; Kelley, 2006). In general, members of the AVF military also tend to be more socially and politically conservative than their civilian counterparts (Segal & Segal, 2004).

For the purpose of this chapter, it is important to consider that the types and effects of stress associated with military service will to some degree depend upon the specific characteristics of military personnel themselves, the resulting overall composition of the military force, and the interactive effects of force composition and contemporary demands on individual and team performance. For example, service members who are married and have children may be differently or more profoundly affected by the stress of deployment than their unmarried counterparts. If the majority of personnel in a particular unit are uniquely vulnerable to a particular source of stress, the performance of the unit as a whole may deteriorate more rapidly or more severely than a unit whose members are less vulnerable. Changes in the composition of the AVF can occur gradually, for example, as an effect of long-term national demographic or socioeconomic trends, or more suddenly as a result of policies that affect recruitment and retention. Such changes are important to our understanding of stress and resilience in the context of individual and group military performance.

A presumed advantage of a voluntary military force is that its members are motivated by commitment to military life and mission. This motivation, in turn, should promote the development and maintenance of greater resilience to stress among service members and their families. Individuals who have been exposed to extreme stress or trauma generally demonstrate a better emotional outcome if they believe their experience served a "higher purpose" (Brewin, Andrews & Valentine, 2000; Watson & Shalev, 2005). It has also been shown that mental health outcomes in the aftermath of the war are mediated by the extent to which a nation endorses military mission and how positively it receives and welcomes war fighters on their return from war (Bolton, Litz & Glenn, 2002; Johnson et al., 1997). The choice to volunteer for military service inspires public expression of support, recognition, and gratitude, which may have similar positive effects on those war fighters returning from combat.

Other significant changes in modern military personnel and force management policies have led to significant improvements in cohesion, morale, and commitment among the U.S. service members (Marlowe, 2001). These improvements can promote enhanced resilience to stress and reduce stress casualties (Bliese, 2006; Bliese & Castro, 2003; Britt, Davison, Bliese & Castro, 2004; Britt & Dickinson, 2006; Helmus & Glenn, 2004; Thomas & Castro, 2003).

Resilience is needed when an individual experiences stress in a particular environment or in response to a particular event. Dramatic changes in the demographic profiles of the military services have occurred in the last several decades and can be expected to continue. Current members of the U.S. military have been selected differently, trained and treated differently, and now serve differently than their predecessors. Explicating the relationship between these differences (including personal variables) and resilience to stress is a major goal of this volume. The environment in which our service members currently operate has also changed dramatically over recent decades. Moreover, it appears that the current process of change and transformation in the U.S. military will continue for decades to come. A way to prepare for the changes that lie ahead is to consider what lessons have been learned in the past. In the next section, we consider the modern history of military service and what can be learned from it.

Demands and Expectations of Military Service: A Modern Historical Overview

During World War II and through the Korean War, a largely conscripted military fought with the expectation of service for "the duration." Conscripted service members were trained quickly and sent directly into combat. For most American service members, World War II and the Korean War were experienced as difficult but temporary interruptions of civilian life. As soon as hostilities ceased, vast numbers of service members were rapidly demobilized and reintegrated back into the civilian sector (Stouffer, Suchman, DeVinney, Star & Williams, 1949). For veterans of World War II and the Korean War, the primary risk factor for stress-related psychiatric disorder and dysfunction was direct exposure to intense combat. Marlowe (2001) noted that during World War II, "… the United States suffered an average of one diagnosed psychological casualty for every four wounded" (p. 49).

Higher incident rates were reported especially during intense opera-
tions. Rosner (1944) reported that 40% of the casualties evacuated from
Guadalcanal "suffered from disabling neuromental disease" (as cited in
Marlowe, 2001, p. 49).

The Vietnam War was exceptional for many reasons; the notable fact is
that it yielded a higher rate of psychiatric casualties among those who had
been engaged in the conflict after the period of most intense combat, which
occurred in 1968–1969 (Hyams, Wignall & Roswell, 1996; Marlowe, 2001).
Post–Vietnam War scholarship is marked by an ongoing effort to identify
and understand what specific economic, sociopolitical, and psychological
factors may have contributed to this phenomenon. For example, Hiley-Young
and colleagues examined data on 207 consecutively admitted veterans with
and without posttraumatic stress disorder (PTSD) and found that childhood
victimization, degree of combat exposure, and participation in war zone
abusive violence (specifically, mutilation) predicted subsequent development
of PTSD (Hiley-Young, Blake, Abueg, Rozynko & Gusman, 1995).

For most of the last half of the twentieth century, the oppressive but
comparatively stable conditions of the Cold War made it possible to maintain military personnel and rotation policies that fostered a fairly predictable career pattern for most American service members. Within reasonable
limits, personal and family concerns could be anticipated, planned, and
managed in the context of a military career that would probably not require
extended deployment or combat. With the exception of the Vietnam War,
contingencies involving combat deployment were quite brief. Early epidemiologic studies of PTSD focused primarily on civilians but also included a
small percentage of Vietnam veterans. These studies found a 4% lifetime rate
of PTSD in nonwounded veterans but a 20% lifetime prevalence of PTSD
in veterans who had been wounded in combat (Helzer, Robins & McElvoy,
1987). Rates of psychiatric illness for nondeployed veterans have not otherwise been extensively studied.

After the Cold War, there came a period of force reductions. From 1989
to 1999, the end-strength dropped from 2.1 to 1.4 million (Bruner, 2004).
Against this background of instability and turbulence in the force structure,
the United States deployed the largest military force since Vietnam War in
the first Persian Gulf War (1990–1991). The Gulf War period of high-intensity
combat lasted just 3 months, involving relatively low rates of stress-related
morbidity during the conflict itself. After Vietnam War, and as distinct from
World War II, postdeployment problems were significant among Gulf War
veterans. Controversy surrounding "Gulf War syndrome" led to the development of elaborate military physical and mental health screening programs,
which are currently in place (Marlowe, 2001). Researchers have identified
several factors that likely contribute to the stress of modern military service,
including unpredictability of "tour" length (deployment period), limited

time spent in garrison (home base), and instability of garrison location (Bell, Bartone, Bartone, Schumm & Gade, 1997).

Current conflicts in Iraq and Afghanistan have been unexpectedly stressful for many members of the U.S. military. After a relatively brief period of intense combat, the current war in Iraq has evolved into the most extended conflict since the Vietnam War. The nature, scope, and duration of current military operations in Iraq have forced American war fighters to confront and endure uniquely stressful conditions, conflicting demands, and, sometimes, ambiguous expectations. Combat-related risks and exposure to extreme stress and trauma are now experienced as actual or potential threats to all service members, regardless of their occupational training or operational duties. There is no clearly defined "front line" in Iraq. The methods employed by a determined insurgent militia—sudden, frequent, and inherently unpredictable roadside attacks—are more similar in kind and effect to those of terrorism than those of traditional warfare. For American and coalition war fighters who have been trained to oppose more traditional enemies, this context is uniquely stressful (Hoge et al., 2004; Holloway & Benedek, 1999; Maguen, Suvak & Litz, 2006).

In addition to the unique character of current military conflicts, war fighters whose roles were once recognized as noncombative in nature are now fully vulnerable to direct or observed violence. For example, service members who are assigned to specialties such as administration, maintenance, and logistics are now at an increased risk for negative health and mental health outcomes because they are often exposed to dead bodies (e.g., recently killed combatants or human remains from mass grave sites) (Ursano, Fullerton, Kao & Bhartiya, 1995; Ursano & McCarroll, 1990). Although conventional combat usually provides temporally distinct separation between expected periods of high-stress combat operations versus less stressful periods of service at lower intensity or operational tempo, current conflicts largely erase this distinction. Service members in Iraq are constantly vulnerable to insurgent attacks such as roadside bombs and kidnapping. Although their level of exposure and resulting stress may vary from day-to-day, military personnel know that no matter where they are assigned or engaged in Iraq, they are on the "front line" and may be targeted by insurgents. Thus, the U.S. military personnel rarely have an opportunity to fully "decompress" or recover from combat-related stress. Even those who have not been deployed to the operational zone of conflict know that they may be vulnerable. Incidents such as the bombing of Khobar Towers and the attack on the USS *Cole* underscore the essentially permanent vulnerability of modern American military personnel.

As noted recently by Maguen et al. (2006), few large-scale studies have yet been conducted to assess the incident rates of stress-related or psychological casualties from Iraq and Afghanistan. Using anonymous

surveys, Hoge et al. (2004) studied the members of four U.S. combat infantry units before or 3–4 months after their return from combat duty in Iraq
or Afghanistan. The results of this survey study indicated significant risk
for mental health problems, especially among those who had been deployed
to Iraq.

Stresses of Modern Military Service in War

While it may be the case that resilience to stress represents a set of capacities
or characteristics that can be developed or encouraged to generate positive
effect, it might also be worthwhile to consider specific strategies to enhance
resilience to stressors that war fighters are especially likely to confront as part
of modern warfare (Bonanno, 2004). At every level, soldiers and leaders can
take positive steps to enhance resilience. Individuals can develop and sustain
positive expectations about their deployment and service. Appraising experiences in a positive light, even when expectations may not be met, is crucial in
resisting the destructive effects of stress. Accepting that negative and painful
experiences can still be an occasion for positive personal growth is a way to
make meaning of even difficult and disturbing experiences. Leaders can help
prepare their units for stressful experiences by fostering open and honest
communication and maintaining a positive and supportive organizational
climate.

The scope of the current conflict in Iraq has necessitated an unprecedented
use of reservists and members of the U.S. Army National Guard. Part-time
service members are now forced to consider and accept a very different model
of service in which they are more likely to experience overseas deployment
and its associated risks (Wisher & Freeman, 2006). The demography and the
training of these forces overlap only partially with that of their full-time,
active duty counterparts (Pickell, 2001). On an average, reservists are older
and their training is more variable. Part-time military personnel are thus
subject to specific types of stress that active duty service members do not
routinely confront, particularly in the areas of employment, income, and
family support services (Dunning, 1996). For example, because reservists
and National Guard members and their families maintain civilian lives that
are often geographically more remote from their assigned military units or
formal military installations, support services are in many cases less available and less accessible.

Repetitive and lengthy deployments to Iraq or Afghanistan have also
challenged the full-time military force, especially the U.S. Army and Marine
Corps. Members of these organizations have had to revise their expectations
of military life to anticipate that a military career may now involve several
lengthy periods of dangerous overseas service, punctuated by comparatively

brief interludes of garrison service near their families. This change may significantly alter the cost–benefit calculus involved in considering the military as a career option.

Many difficulties currently faced by the U.S. war fighters in Iraq are related to the fact that the "military we have" was not designed, trained, equipped, or maintained with current operations in mind. New threats associated with technologically advanced and insidious weaponry have forced the creation and training of highly specialized service members whose skill sets are unique and difficult to replace. The possibility that these unique personnel might be injured or killed in battle is a new and unique source of stress for those whose survival may at some point depend upon the expertise of a few designated specialists (Benedek et al., 2001; Norwood & Ursano, 1996). Meanwhile, war fighters must reckon with the perceived threat of exposure to indiscriminate weapons of mass casualty. Although such weapons have not been used as predicted at the onset of the Iraq War, there persists an apparently reasonable belief that the enemy has both the capability and willingness to employ such weapons. Media and intelligence bulletins, images of protective suits, "threat level" assessments, and early warning system alarms likely contribute to the perception that exposure is an imminent or inevitable threat. Certainly, there is chronic stress associated with the persistent fear of exposure to insidiously harmful agents that may be difficult or impossible to detect, identify, or avoid (Stuart, Ursano, Fullerton, Norwood & Murray, 2003).

Perhaps the most significant and far-reaching development among the new developments in the day-to-day experience of the warfare is that service members now have fairly routine access to advanced communication tools such as e-mail and satellite telephony through which they can maintain ongoing close contact with loved ones. Although this communication is certainly a positive development in many ways, it is also something of a mixed blessing with respect to stress. Real-time awareness of the "mundane" stresses of home life may prove as stressful for the war fighter as the first-hand accounts of war are for their family members and friends at home. Resulting stress may be compounded by the service member's sense of helplessness or inability to "fix" various problems (financial difficulties, health problems, parenting or marital issues) often confronted by those left behind.

Greater access to communication, information, and media coverage also provides service members with unprecedented awareness of the political aspect of war and the extent to which the fellow citizens support, oppose, or debate the worthiness of its objectives. Such information may be good or bad for morale. News of controversy surrounding the war effort may be troubling and may even erode the war fighter's own sense of confidence, purpose, mission, and achievement (Dauber, 2006).

Our Modern Military into the Future

Virtually every critical aspect of military policy and practice—force structure, doctrine, equipment, and budget—is influenced by expectations and predictions concerning the nature of future armed conflict. Today's competing visions differ largely by the degree to which future conflicts are foreseen as likely to resemble the Cold War (past) or as focusing primarily upon operations designed to preserve regional stability (present). In either case, we must try to anticipate accurately the resulting needs for continued positive development and maintenance of an effective military force and for adequate support and service to its members.

Some policy makers and military planners believe that it is only a matter of time before China emerges as a global economic and regional military competitor to the United States. If this scenario dominates the thinking of defense planners, the likely result is that the U.S. military will once again be transformed as a technologically updated version of the pre–Iraq War military (Hammes, 2004). Such a force would likely be designed and employed to engage in infrequent, high-intensity, and short-duration combat. The initial few weeks of the Iraq War might be seen as a useful model for the employment of such a force. In such a scenario, the stress associated with military service would resemble that experienced by the service members during the Cold War era, that is, periods of combat would be limited in scope and duration only as needed to prevent a much larger catastrophic conflict. Ironically, during the Cold War, military conflicts and resulting stressors were limited by the need to avoid mishaps, misunderstandings, or escalation that might raise the threat of global annihilation.

An alternative vision of future conflict emphasizes stability and support operations of the sort that are now intended in Iraq. Although this scenario clearly is not the sort of conflict we might prefer as a nation, some (e.g., Hammes, 2004) have argued that this may very well be the sort of ongoing struggle that is forced upon us. This scenario implies persistent endurance of current conditions, which include repetitive and lengthy deployments and ongoing exposure of nearly all deployed service members to intense combat-related stress. Any considerable reduction of stress and its effects would require that our current military force be redesigned or reorganized in ways that better support such ongoing operations with less strain on service members (Ullman, 2004).

Although the threat of nuclear war with the Soviet Union no longer provides a damper to limit military conflict, the overwhelming military superiority of the United States exerts essentially the same dampening effect on the willingness of other nations to engage in conventional warfare against American military forces. Although it is true that the expanding economy and growing military capabilities of China may eventually alter this dynamic, it is unlikely that the United States will face a credible challenge from a peer or near-peer enemy nation in the near future. On the contrary, the power of the United States has been successfully confronted in the past by nonpeer nations (e.g., Vietnam and Somalia) and is now challenged in Iraq by opponents who employ rudimentary technology to fight in unconventional ways that challenge our high-technology force. As a result, American war fighters must endure the multiple unique stresses associated with an unfamiliar type of warfare against an enemy whose followers are quite willing to defy conventional rules of war.

A potentially useful vision of the future has been aptly described as the "three-block war" (General Charles Krulak, USMC; Krulak, 1999). In this scenario, the U.S. military forces continue to be engaged in operations similar to the current war in Iraq and are trained and well-prepared to engage flexibly and as needed in conventional high-intensity combat, peacekeeping and stability operations, and humanitarian or nation-building projects. In Iraq, the boundaries between these activities frequently blur or shift with the passage of mere moments or with the taking of a few steps between zones of operation. Consequently, there is a clear and pressing need for flexibility and adaptability that must now be emphasized and integrated as a key aspect of military training and preparation. In his commentary on the three-block war scenario, General Krulak emphasizes that under the real-time glare of constant news coverage, strategic success may well depend upon the actions of very junior service members. Decentralized by design, the three-block war would moot traditional distinctions among strategic, operational, and tactical levels. In conventional conflict, great ends require great means (i.e., military power on a grand scale) whereas in the three-block war, these same great ends might be achieved by seemingly trivial means. For example, a dusty, remote checkpoint that is manned by just a few low-ranking soldiers could very well be the stage for a military drama whose strategic consequences are broad and significant. For example, television images showing U.S. soldiers mistakenly opening fire on a car full of unarmed civilians who did not understand their order to stop could trigger widespread protests and undermine efforts to win the cooperation of the general population necessary to establish long-term security and stability.

The three-block war scenario tends to push power "down" the traditional hierarchy. It requires that leadership, initiative, judgment, and courage be exercised by virtually everyone, at all times, anywhere and everywhere within the broad zone of combat. This pervasive and profound extension of responsibility implies a host of concomitant potential and actual stresses, resilience to which will necessitate training and preparation. If service members are properly prepared and oriented to cope with the demands and expectations of military service, they may be better able to regard their experiences in a more positive light as challenges that are empowering and ennobling.

The potentially stressful effects of intense media coverage noted above are not limited to combat practices. The increasing attention paid by news media and international agencies to the handling and care of persons who are captured on the battlefield is also noteworthy. While medical personnel have historically confronted moral and ethical issues related to caring for wounded enemy combatants, there is more recently some lack of certainty regarding the extent to which international law affords protection to enemy noncombatants and other persons who are detained but not held formally as prisoners of war. These issues pose a challenge for military police, guards, and others who are charged with caring for the health and safety of mixed populations. Moreover, media analyses critical of military practices and policies related to the handling of captured personnel may raise questions in the minds of the public and may even diminish their sense of commitment to military objectives. This altered perspective on the righteousness or justifiability of the mission may make it more difficult for some people to express or demonstrate support for deployed service members and for veterans upon homecoming. The relevance of poor homecoming reception to the development of PTSD has been noted in several studies (Johnson et al., 1997; Solomon & Oppenheimer, 1986).

War affects war fighters, their families, their communities, and the entire nation. Even the initial anticipation of military action and the buildup of forces can cause stress. Stress persists and becomes more intense with deployment, transportation to distant theaters of operation, adaptation to extreme and dangerous environments, and finally combat. Return and reunion, along with the anticipation of possible redeployment, contribute additional stress to the overall "cycle of deployment" in modern war. During and after the war, the emotional, behavioral, and health-related outcomes of stress may be mitigated to some extent by the support of comrades, health-related services, and positive social reception and homecoming experiences. These are the case points to the necessity of understanding the stresses of modern war as multidimensional (sociocultural, psychological, biological) and as deserving additional multidisciplinary research to promote resilience among those who sacrifice so much in service to their nation.

As we face the uncertain challenges of a new century, members of the U.S. armed forces will surely confront many additional changes and demands associated with military service. We cannot foresee the precise nature, timing, or results of these changes. However, it is crucial to consider the circumstances, conditions, expectations, and demands of modern military service as best we can and to clarify how these factors affect war fighters and how the U.S. military might best reduce stress and promote resilience among its members.

References

Bell, D.B., Bartone, J., Bartone, B.T., Schumm, W.R. & Gade, P.A. (1997). *USAREUR Family Support During Operation Joint Endeavor: Summary Report.* Alexandria, VA: U.S. Army Research Institute for the Behavioral and Social Sciences.

Benedek, D.M., Ursano, R.J., Holloway, H.C., Norwood, N.E., Grieger, T.A., Engel, C.C., et al. (2001). Military and disaster psychiatry. In N.J. Smelser & P.B. Baltes (Eds.), *The International Encyclopedia of the Social and Behavioral Sciences* (Vol. 14), (pp. 9850–9857). Oxford, England: Elsevier Press.

Bliese, P.D. (2006). Social climates: drivers of soldier well-being and resilience. In T.W. Britt, A.B. Adler & C.A. Castro (Eds.), *Military Life: The Psychology of Serving in Peace and Combat: Vol. 2. Operational Stressors* (pp. 213–234). Westport, CT: Praeger Security International.

Bliese, P.D. & Castro, C.A. (2003). The soldier adaptation model (SAM): applications to peacekeeping research. In T.W. Britt & A.B. Adler (Eds.), *The Psychology of the Peacekeeper: Lessons from the Field* (pp. 185–203). Westport, CT: Praeger Security International.

Bolton, E.E., Litz, B.T. & Glenn, D.M. (2002). The impact of homecoming reception on the adaptation of peacekeepers following deployment. *Military Psychology, 14,* 241–251.

Bonnano, G. (2004). Loss, trauma, and human resilience. *American Psychologist, 59(1),* 20–28.

Brewin, C.R., Andrews, B. & Valentine, J.D. (2000). Meta-analysis of risk factors for post-traumatic stress disorder in trauma-exposed adults. *Journal of Consulting and Clinical Psychology, 68,* 748–766.

Britt, T.W., Davison, J., Bliese, P.D. & Castro, C.A. (2004). How leaders can influence the impact that stressors have on soldiers. *Military Medicine, 169(7),* 541–545.

Britt, T.W. & Dickinson, J.M. (2006). Morale during military operations: a positive psychology approach. In T.W. Britt, A.B. Adler & C.A. Castro (Eds.), *Military Life: The Psychology of Serving in Peace and Combat: Vol. 1. Military Performance* (pp. 157–184). Westport, CT: Praeger Security International.

Bruner, E.F. (2004). Military Forces: What Is the Appropriate Size for the United States? (Congressional Research Services RS21754). Retrieved September 14, 2006, from http://fpc.state.gov/documents/organization/60575.pdf

Cannon, W.B. (1953). *Bodily Changes in Pain, Hunger, Fear and Rage* (2nd ed.). Boston, MA: Charles T. Branford Company.

Dauber, C.E. (2006). Life in wartime: real-time news, real-time critique, fighting in the new media environment. In T.W. Britt, A.B. Adler & C.A. Castro (Eds.), *Military Life: The Psychology of Serving in Peace and Combat: Vol. 4. Military Culture* (pp. 180–210). Westport, CT: Praeger Security International.

Dunning, C.M. (1996). From citizen to soldier. In R.J. Ursano & A.E. Norwood (Eds.), *Emotional Aftermath of the Persion Gulf War: Veterans, Families, Communities, and Nations* (pp. 197–226). Washington, D.C.: American Psychiatric Press, Inc.

Eggemeier, F.T. (1988). Properties of workload assessment techniques. In P. Hancock & N. Meshkati (Eds.), *Human Mental Workload.* Amsterdam: North-Holland.

Endsley, M.R. (1995). Toward a theory of situation awareness in dynamic systems. *Human Factors, 37*, 85–104.

Hammes, T.X. (2004). *The Sling and the Stone*. St. Paul, MN: Zenith Press.

Helmus, T.C. & Glenn, R.W. (2004). *Steeling the Mind: Combat Stress Reactions and Their Implications for Urban Warfare* (RAND MG-191-A). Santa Monica, CA: RAND Corporation.

Helzer, J.E., Robins, L.N. & McElvoy, L. (1987). Post-traumatic stress disorder in the general population. Findings of the epidemiologic catchment area survey. *New England Journal of Medicine, 317(26)*, 1630–1634.

Hiley-Young, B., Blake, D.D., Abueg, F.R., Rozynko, V. & Gusman, F.D. (1995). War zone violence in Vietnam: an examination of premilitary, military, and post-military factors in PTSD in-patients. *Journal of Traumatic Stress, 8(1)*, 125–141.

Hoge, C.W., Castro, C.A., Messer, S.C., McGurk, D., Cotting, D.I. & Koffman, R.L. (2004). Combat duty in Iraq and Afghanistan, mental health problems, and barriers to care. *The New England Journal of Medicine, 351(1)*, 13–22.

Holloway, H. & Benedek, D.M. (1999). The changing face of terrorism and military psychiatry. *Psychiatric Annals, 29(6)*, 364–375.

Huffman, A.H. & Payne, S.C. (2006). The challenges and benefits of dual-military marriages. In T.W. Britt, A.B. Adler & C.A. Castro (Eds.), *Military Life: The Psychology of Serving in Peace and Combat: Vol. 3. The Military Family* (pp. 115–137). Westport, CT: Praeger Security International.

Hyams, K.C., Wignall, F.S. & Roswell, R. (1996). War syndromes and their evaluations: from the U.S. civil war to the Persian Gulf War. *Annals of Internal Medicine, 125(5)*, 398–405.

Johnson, D.R., Lubin, H., Rosenheck, R., Fontana, A., Southwick, S. & Charney, D. (1997). The impact of homecoming reception on the development of posttraumatic stress disorder: the West Haven Homecoming Stress Scale (WHHSS). *Journal of Traumatic Stress, 10*, 269–277.

Kelley, M.L. (2006). Single military parents in the new millennium. In T.W. Britt, A.B. Adler & C.A. Castro (Eds.), *Military Life: The Psychology of Serving in Peace and Combat: Vol. 3. The Military Family* (pp. 91–114). Westport, CT: Praeger Security International.

Krulak, C. (1999). Strategic corporal: leadership in the three-block war. *Marine Corps Gazette, 83(1)*, 18–22.

Maguen, S., Suvak, M. & Litz, B.T. (2006). Predictors and prevalence of posttraumatic stress disorder among military veterans. In T.W. Britt, A.B. Adler & C.A. Castro (Eds.), *Military Life: The Psychology of Serving in Peace and Combat: Vol. 2. Operational Stress* (pp. 141–169). Westport, CT: Praeger Security International.

Marlowe, D.H. (2001). *Psychological and Psychosocial Consequences of Combat and Deployment with Special Emphasis on the Gulf War* (RAND MR-1018/11-OSD). Santa Monica, CA: RAND Corporation.

McCarty, R. (1989). Stress research: principles, problems, and prospects. In G.R. Van Loon, R. Kvetnansky, R. McCarty & J. Axelrod (Eds.), *Stress: Neurochemical and Humoral Mechanisms* (pp. 3–13). New York: Gordon and Breach.

Norwood, A.E. & Ursano, R.J. (1996). The Gulf War. In R.J. Ursano & A.E. Norwood (Eds.), *Emotional Aftermath of the Persion Gulf War: Veterans, Families, Communities and Nations* (pp. 3–21). Washington, D.C.: American Psychiatric Press.

Pickell, G. (2001). Taking center stage: the reserve components and their growing role in the national military strategy. In D.E. Vandergriff (Ed.), *Spirit, Blood, and Treasure* (pp. 255–277). Novato, CA: Presidio Press.

Rosner, A.A. (1944). Neuropsychiatric casualties from Guadalcanal. *American Journal of Medical Science, 207.*

Segal, D.R. & Segal, M.W. (2004). America's military population. *Population Bulletin, 59(4),* 3–40.

Selye, H. (Ed.). (1980). *Selye's Guide to Stress Research (Vol. 1).* New York: Van Nostrand Reinhold.

Solomon, Z. & Oppenheimer, B. (1986). Social network variables and stress reaction lessons from the 1973 Yom Kippur war. *Military Medicine, 151(1),* 12–15.

Stouffer, S.A., Suchman, E.A., DeVinney, L.C., Star, S.A. & Williams, R.M. (1949). *The American Soldier: Adjustment During Army Life.* Princeton, NJ: Princeton University Press.

Stuart, J.S., Ursano, R.U., Fullerton, C.S., Norwood, A.E. & Murray, K. (2003). Belief in exposure to terrorist agents: reported exposure to nerve or mustard gas by Gulf War veterans. *Journal of Nervous and Mental Disease, 191(7),* 431–436.

Thomas, J.L. & Castro, C.A. (2003). Organizational behavior and the U.S. peacekeeper. In T.W. Britt & A.B. Adler (Eds.). *The Psychology of the Peacekeeper, Lessons from the Field.* Westport, CT: Praeger Security International.

Ullman, H. (2004). *Finishing Business.* Annapolis, MD: Naval Institute Press.

Ursano, R.J., Fullerton, C.S., Kao, T.C. & Bhartiya, V.R. (1995). Longitudinal assessment of posttraumatic stress disorder and depression after exposure to traumatic death. *Journal of Nervous and Mental Disease, 183(1),* 36–42.

Ursano, R.J. & McCarroll, J.E. (1990). The nature of the traumatic stressor: handling dead bodies. *Journal of Nervous and Mental Disease, 178,* 396–398.

Watson, P. & Shalev, A.Y. (2005). Early intervention in patients with acute stress. *CNS Spectrums, 10(2),* 123–131.

Wisher, R.A. & Freeman, M.W. (2006). The U.S. reserve component: training strategies for adapting to deployment. In T.W. Britt, A.B. Adler & C.A. Castro (Eds.), *Military Life: The Psychology of Serving in Peace and Combat: Vol. 4. Military Culture* (pp. 81–96). Westport, CT: Praeger Security International.

Resilience through Leadership

4

DONALD CAMPBELL, KATHLEEN
CAMPBELL, AND JAMES W. NESS

*Department of Behavioral Sciences and
Leadership, U.S. Military Academy*

Contents

> In 1914, explorer Ernest Shackleton led a 28-men expedition through frigid
> seas and across icy wastelands to the South Pole. His expedition would be
> plagued by extreme misfortune, relentless hardship, and prolonged suffer-
> ing. Shackleton and his team never reached the South Pole. More remarkably,
> they survived their journey. Their story serves as testimony to the combined
> power of leadership and resilience in the face of adversity.

This chapter will examine and answer questions concerning leadership and
its impact on human resilience. First, we will explore a number of essential
ideas relating to the general nature of leadership, the personal characteristics
and behavior of effective leaders, and the broad processes by which leaders
reach out and influence the mind-set, and the behavior of their followers.
We will also explore the concept of "resilience" by considering theoretical
linkages between resilience and current notions regarding stress, stressors,
and stress episodes (acute events that produce short-term strain). These
foundational ideas will support an integrated conceptual structure to explicate the potential effects of leadership on resilience. Finally, we will consider
the "state of the possible" regarding the potential power of leadership to
increase individual and team resilience in stressor-filled and stress-inducing
work environments.

Leadership: Basic Considerations

To understand the effect(s) of leadership on resilience, we must first examine
the nature of leadership itself. A review of the relevant literature turns up
almost as many definitions of "leadership" as there are researchers interested
in it (e.g., Antonakis, Cianciolo & Sternberg, 2004; Bass, 1990; Daft, 2005; Yukl,
2005). Rather than attempting to wrestle with or reconcile many different con-
ceptualizations of leadership, we choose instead to highlight commonalities
that can be found among them. These commonalities capture the essential
characteristics of leadership and thus reveal the core nature of the construct.

Eliciting Willing Acceptance of Influence

Contained in virtually every definition of leadership is the notion that
leadership is a process of social influence. An effective leader must inspire
individuals to do willingly what they might not otherwise be inclined to do.

Leadership, then, is a special case of a much broader construct, interpersonal power. The distinguishing characteristic and theoretical significance of leadership is that it requires the unforced, voluntary acceptance of influence (see Katz & Kahn, 1978).

A complicating factor is that responsiveness to influence can also occur as a key aspect in interpersonal interactions that may or may not involve leadership per se. For example, influence can be exerted simply by exercising positional authority such as that held by a parent or a boss. To overcome this conceptual obstacle, some leadership researchers (i.e., Katz & Kahn, 1978) suggest that true leadership is an "incremental" influence, that is, an influence over and above the influence that stems simply from a person's positional authority or the rewards and the sanctions that can be issued from it. In this view, leaders are individuals who can access and exert an extra reservoir of influence over and above the influence that is purely positional, particularly in the form of charisma and personal (referent) power.

Other investigators (e.g., French & Raven, 1968) simply acknowledge that social influence may derive from several sources (e.g., expertise, legitimate authority, power to reward or punish, referent power) and that leaders distinguish themselves as such by tapping into more sources of influence or by using a more effective combination of them. The U.S. Army's approach to leadership embodies this philosophy. The Army defines leadership as "influencing people—by providing purpose, direction and motivation—while operating to accomplish the mission and improving the organization" (FM 22–100, 1999: 1–4). The Army expects its leaders to use all available bases of social power—formal authority, expertise, rewards, punishments, and charisma—in leading subordinates to achieve mission and organizational goals.

Personal and Inherent Qualities

Another notion common among many views of leadership is that something inherent or intrinsic to the nature or character of an individual plays an essential role in effective leadership. There is widespread agreement that certain personal qualities of a leader will tend to exert a significant effect upon the willing compliance of others. Frameworks that emphasize personal charisma (e.g., Burns, 1978; House, 1977) or the ability to inspire and transform followers (e.g., Bass & Riggio, 2006) are noteworthy examples of this view. Likewise, there are many popular "trait" formulations of leadership (e.g., Stogdill, 1974; Yukl, 2005). In each case, the fundamental assertion is that influence resides in some special configuration of personal qualities that only true leaders possess.

Although no specific leadership trait combination has yet been identified, formal efforts to develop leadership typically assume that individuals are sensitive to leadership attributes and values such as confidence and competence, integrity, trustworthiness, loyalty, and honor. For example, U.S. Army leadership doctrine emphasizes character-based leadership and presumes that leadership characteristics will directly or indirectly influence soldiers' behavior. Specific values and attributes such as integrity and honor are thus regarded as crucial elements of effective leadership, warranting careful cultivation in the leader development process (Campbell & Dardis, 2004).

Action and Behavior

Finally, all theories of leadership recognize the importance of leader action. Leaders influence followers not only through their observable personal characteristics (who they are) but also through their behavior (what they do). Virtually all researchers have concluded that effective leaders act in ways that (1) reinforce and strengthen group processes and (2) aid followers in achieving organizational as well as personal goals.

Investigators have long recognized two essential styles of behavior as critical to effective leadership. These have been described by different researchers as task-oriented and people-oriented behavior (Blake & Mouton, 1964; Fiedler, 1971), initiation of structure and consideration (Stogdill, 1974), directive/ achievement-oriented style and supportive/participative style (House & Mitchell, 1975), and telling/selling style and participative/delegating style (Hersey & Blanchard, 1993). Whatever its stylistic label, effective leadership requires that an individual employ influence to help the group accomplish its objectives and simultaneously maintain or enhance interpersonal relationships and group cohesiveness. For example, even before Ernest Shackleton's ill-fated expedition began, tensions among members of his team threatened to disrupt group performance. Animosity had developed between the highly educated, mostly upper-class scientists and the working-class crew of sailors, carpenters, and ship's hands. Shackleton intervened and was able to shape his diverse group of explorers into a tight, cohesive team. Several sophisticated theoretical models (Fiedler & Garcia, 1987; Hersey & Blanchard, 1993; House & Mitchell, 1975; Vroom & Yetton, 1973) have been put forth to address the question of what situational variables shape the actions of effective leaders. Although these models differ in their details, we find consensus between the two most compelling and elaborate. These models (Hersey & Blanchard, 1993; House & Mitchell, 1975) agree that maximum influence and willing compliance occur when leaders provide followers with what they need when they need it, that is, effective leaders provide direction and guidance when purpose is obscure; encouragement and support when morale is low or commitment is weak; involvement and participation when cohesion is absent; and so forth.

Implications

If our basic notions regarding leadership are correct, Shackleton had an opportunity to employ two primary strategies to influence his men's reactions to the extreme dangers they faced in the Antarctic. He could influence them by making obvious his personal qualities and leadership characteristics, and he could influence them by his actions and behavior. Clearly, by his character as well as his behavior, Shackleton performed as an effective leader. He was able to exert a substantial degree of influence over his fellow explorers, who willingly accepted his influence and followed his leadership. Somehow, then, through this dynamic or the processes essential to it, resilience helped Shackleton and his men endure the relentless physical and extreme psychological demands of a seemingly hopeless situation in an extraordinarily harsh environment. This raises the question of how effective leadership can inure the leader and his or her followers to extreme stress. Before we can address this issue, we must first explore the nature of resilience itself.

Concepts of Biobehavioral Resilience

The term "resilience" has its roots in material science, where it refers to the capacity of a strained body to recover its size and shape after compressive stress deformation. As a behavioral scientific construct, resilience is defined in different ways by different researchers who view resilience as a trait, as a capacity, or as an outcome. Here, we adopt the view that resilience is the capacity to cope with or adapt to significant risk and adversity and to recover quickly from stressful change or misfortune.

There is great interest in the characteristics and processes that enable individuals and groups to "bounce back" after experiencing substantial reverses of fortune. Consequently, resilience has been studied by researchers in a number of different disciplines and reported in various literatures, including business and organizational psychology (e.g., Maddi, 2002; Maddi & Khoshaba, 2005; Youssef & Luthans, 2005), family counseling (e.g., Walsh, 1998, 2002), and child development (e.g., Luthar, Cicchetti & Becker, 2000). Among these various fields of interest, there is general agreement concerning specific experiences and characteristics that make some individuals, units, or organizations more or less resilient to stress than others. Taken together, these factors suggest that resilience is not so much a trait (something a person has) as it is a process (something a person does; cf. Siebert, 2002). Thus, although physiology and genetics certainly play an important role in resilience (see Baker, Risbrough & Schork, this volume; Friedl & Penetar, this volume), evidence indicates that people can also learn to be resilient through experience and by developing qualities that facilitate coping, adaptation, and recovery from stress (e.g., Luthans, Vogelgesang & Lester, 2006; Maddi & Khoshaba, 2005).

In the effort to identify qualities and characteristics essential to resilience, different investigators have adopted different approaches and have employed different terminology. For example, academic scholars such as Maddi and Khoshaba (2005) examined resilience under the rubric of hardiness and concluded that three factors form the basis of psychological resilience: commitment, control, and challenge. Coutu (2002) approached resilience from a managerial and practitioner perspective, concluding that psychological resilience to stress requires (1) a staunch acceptance of reality, (2) a deep belief that life is meaningful, and (3) an uncanny ability to improvise. Walsh (2002) studied resilience from a family and group dynamics perspective and identified four processes essential to group resilience: (1) the group's belief system, (2) its organizational pattern, (3) its specific communication process, and (4) its broader interaction pattern. In the sections that follow, we draw on all three approaches but for the sake of organizational convenience, we use Coutu's general framework to examine resilience characteristics in detail.

Facing Reality with Determination

Coutu (2002) has argued that in extreme stressor-filled environments, resilient individuals are able to generate an accurate and very realistic picture of their circumstance and its difficulties. In the face of adversity, optimism may also be helpful, provided it does not distort reality or mask denial (cf. Seligman, 1998). Resilience entails a capacity to gauge obstacles and problems accurately while maintaining a strong determination to prevail.

The capacity to face unvarnished reality while remaining resolute is similar to Maddi and Khoshaba's (2005) notion that stress-hardy individuals possess a "control" orientation. This refers to an individual's determination to try to influence outcomes—by the exercise of knowledge, skill, imagination, and choice—even under very difficult circumstances (Kobasa, Maddi & Kahn, 1982). In addition, this orientation apparently promotes the development of a broad array of functional responses to stress, which can then be drawn upon even in the most threatening environments (Bartone, Ursano, Wright & Ingraham, 1989).

Likewise, Walsh's (2002) analysis indicates that resilient families (and presumably other groups) have the capacity to analyze and contextualize obstacles and possess a "can-do" spirit that supports initiative-taking and perseverance. By focusing on their strengths and potential for effectiveness, resilient groups nurture confidence in their members' abilities to overcome the odds. In summary, it is a distinguishing characteristic of resilient individuals and groups that they possess a determination to control their own destiny, even as they acknowledge and confront inimical forces and dire circumstances beyond their control.

Imposing Meaning on Hardship

Another hallmark characteristic of resilient people is their capacity to see or create meaning in the face of misfortune, adversity, and suffering. This propensity enables resilient individuals to envision progress forward from current hardships toward a better anticipated future. Rather than seeing themselves as victims of a terrible and mindless fate, resilient people and groups devise ways to frame their misfortune in a more personally understandable way, and this serves to protect them from being overwhelmed by difficulties in the present (Coutu, 2002). This capacity is apparently bolstered by strong value systems or frameworks, which promote an orientation toward survival and may indirectly suggest strategies for perseverance (cf. Frankl, 1963).

Similarly, Maddi, and Khoshaba (2005) emphasize the importance of an orientation toward commitment. In this context, commitment refers to active involvement. Rather than take false protection in withdrawal or apathy, resilient individuals involve themselves in life events, including those that may be very stressful. Such commitment and continuing involvement promotes an ability to view present sufferings and hardships as just one part of an individual's broader life experience.

Walsh (2002) also underscores the importance of finding meaning in the face of adversity. Her analysis at the family level suggests that shared ideas or beliefs enable group members to recast a crisis as a challenge that is both manageable and meaningful. Like Coutu (2002), Walsh also notes that transcendent or spiritual values often play a significant role in the effort to find purpose in suffering.

Not all investigators agree that meaning-making is an essential component of resilience. For example, Siebert (1996, 2002) argues that survivors (e.g., POWs and Holocaust victims) rely not upon their ability to make meaning of hardship, but rather upon their grim determination to keep going and to demonstrate that their spirits have remained intact even as their bodies have suffered. Certainly, it may be difficult or impossible for even the most resilient person to make meaning of some circumstances. However, it is reasonable to argue that basic survival-oriented defiance is, at its core, very much about imposing purpose (meaning) upon an otherwise intolerable situation.

Willingness to Improvise

Coutu's (2002) research suggests that a third critical characteristic of resilient people is their capacity to improvise solutions to problems even when they may not have the appropriate resources or proper tools. Resilient individuals make the most of whatever resources are available to them. They imagine possibilities and see connections in situations where less resilient individuals would likely become stymied and discouraged. Coutu (2002) further argues that the capacity to improvise can be found in organizations. In resilient organizations, improvisation is treated as a core skill, and organizational culture empowers employees to exercise judgment to do whatever it takes to get the job done right and on time (e.g., see Campbell, 2000). This may help to explain why some companies are able to survive and recover after major business calamities, while others succumb to lesser misfortune.

In a similar vein, Walsh (2002) emphasizes that resilient groups are resourceful and are inclined to engage in creative brainstorming. They rise to challenges, often because adversity draws out resources and strengths that previously lay dormant. Adaptive processes such as willingness to change, reorganize, and engage in collaborative problem-solving play a significant role in allowing resilient groups to buffer stress and to manage a threatening environment effectively. Resilient groups might already possess improvisational flexibility or might develop the capacity over time in response to stressful circumstances. Maddi and his colleagues (e.g., Maddi & Kobasha, 2005) describe this aspect of resilience as challenge orientation, referring to the personal view that stress and change are inherent to life and should not be seen as fearsome, but rather as opportunities for learning and growth. Individuals who hold this orientation typically react to change and stress with innovation and flexibility (Turnipseed, 1999).

Leadership as a "Resilience Reserve"

In a general way, we can now offer a potentially useful answer to the question of how leaders can employ their influence to build and encourage resilience in their followers, teams, or units. If resilience requires the willingness to face reality with determination, the ability to impose meaning on hardship, and the capacity to improvise and be flexible, then leaders can bolster individual and group resilience by demonstrating, shaping, and encouraging these essential skills. In effect, effective leadership can be seen as a "resilience reservoir," supplying and promoting resilience through the leader's own qualities and characteristics and demonstrating resilience by the leader's own behavior and action.

Shackleton's leadership on the Antarctic expedition effectively illustrates his critical role as a resilience reservoir for his fellow explorers. For example, when ice first trapped the *Endurance* and Shackleton's group was in despair, Shackleton improvised and convinced his team that the ship could serve effectively as a winter shelter (see Alexander, 1998). When that failed, Shackleton improvised further by using salvage to create a base camp on the ice. When cracks and leads in the ice hinted at the unsoundness of the decision to await rescue, Shackleton forced the group to face reality and devised several alternative survival strategies. Through his actions and through his strength of character, Shackleton's leadership demonstrated and encouraged every essential component of resilience, even when group resilience itself was at dangerously low ebb. Eventually, Shackleton and his team were able to navigate several small whaleboats through frigid currents to reach Elephant Island. Though uninhabited and inhospitable, Elephant Island provided relative safety from the sea.

Having found a place of temporary safety for his team, Shackleton then chose five of his most skillful men to chart the way another 800 miles across the sea to South Georgia Island. Before he departed Elephant Island, Shackleton exhorted the rest of his team not to give up and assured the 22 men left behind that he would bring rescue. After weeks at sea, Shackleton and his remaining companions finally landed on South Georgia Island. Incredibly, they then made their way over and through the ice-covered passes of a snow-covered mountain range to the shelter of a permanent whaling station. There, they organized the rescue of their fellow team members left behind on Elephant Island. Remarkably, all had survived.

If correct, the notion of a resilience reservoir suggests that effective leadership can facilitate and reinforce group resilience and, speculatively, that an effective leader's individual resilient character and behavior might even partially substitute for group resilience. We will revisit this line of reasoning later in the chapter. First, we will examine resilience within a broader theoretical framework, as one component of a complex of variables highlighted by two models of human stress.

Resilience and Models of Stress

Thus far, we have considered individual and unit resilience within a common-sense context of adversity and misfortune. In this context, resilience serves to buffer an individual or group against psychological and physical strains exerted by hostile environments or threatening circumstances. More specifically, we might say that resilience serves to moderate or mediate the relationship between external stressors and internal stress (perceived strain). For example, resilience might directly moderate psychological or behavioral components of the stressor–strain relationship. Alternatively, a more resilient individual might experience a lower level of internal stress (perceived strain) than a less resilient cohort.

Stress researchers have long been interested in variables and processes that moderate or mediate stressor–strain relationships (e.g., see Barling, Kelloway & Frone, 2005; Brief, Schuler & Van Sell, 1981; Cooper, Dewe & O'Driscoll, 2001; Ivancevich & Matteson, 1980). Numerous theoretical models have been put forth to address specific processes and variables involved in biochemical stress (e.g., Selye, 1956), psychosomatic stress (e.g., Lachman, 1972), adaptation stress (Mechanic, 1962), occupational stress (e.g., House, 1974), and social environment stress (e.g., French & Kahn, 1962). For the purpose of understanding the relation between leadership and resilience, we find especially useful two models of stress that focus on the "fit" between person and environment. These are McGrath's (1976) Four Processes model and Karasek's (1979) demand–control–support (D–C–S) model.

Four Processes Stress Model

McGrath (1976) conceptualizes stress as a four-stage cycle that involves appraisal, decision-making, performance, and outcome. When confronted by a stressful situation, the individual must first cognitively appraise (correctly or incorrectly) the situation as one that will lead to undesirable results if left unchecked. Next, the individual must choose or decide upon a course of action that is intended to mitigate the detrimental aspects of the situation. The individual then executes the selected course of action. Finally, the individual must evaluate the extent to which his or her behavior and actions are successful in changing the situation. Successful change depends both upon the extent to which selected behavior can have a realistic effect on the situation and upon the individual's ability to perform the selected behavior or action.

Like virtually all stress models, the Four Processes model employs what is essentially a stimulus (S)–organism (O)–response (R) framework to understand human response to stress. This approach presumes that individuals (Os) interpret and evaluate various stressors (Ss) as demands, which must be met by action (Rs). In Figure 4.1, we present the Four Processes model in the context of an S–O–R framework to illustrate various ways in which resilience might moderate stressor–strain connections. As Figure 4.1 indicates,

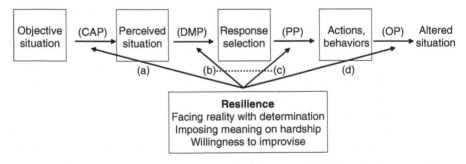

Figure 4.1 Possible moderator influences of resilience within the four processes stress model. CAP, cognitive appraisal process; DMP, decision-making process; PP, performance process; OP, outcome process.

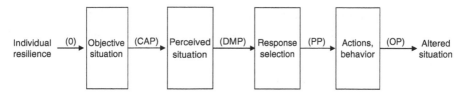

Figure 4.2 Resilience as a possible mediator within the four processes stress model. O, differential exposure; CAP, cognitive appraisal process; DMP, decision-making process; PP, performance process; OP, outcome process.

resilience could somehow influence the way an individual sees and evaluates stressors in the objective environment. For example, (1) resilience might facilitate an efficient, determined, or realistic assessment and grant the individual more advance time to plan and deal with the threat; (2) alternatively, resilience might affect the decision-making process by increasing or decreasing the number of responses considered as potentially useful, improving task focus, or promoting increased creativity and improvisation; (3) resilience might also influence performance processes such that the individual is better able to continue applying and improvising relevant skills and abilities with a sense of purpose (meaning), rather than surrendering to fear or apathy; and (4) finally, resilience could affect outcome by promoting goal-directed and realistic judgments concerning the efficacy of action and performance.

It is possible that resilient people are simply more successful in avoiding stressful situations or that they do not cognitively frame stressors as such or in the same way that less resilient individuals do. In this case, resilience may serve a mediating role by determining whether individuals will place themselves in situations where they might reasonably expect to confront common stressors (cf. Cooper et al., 2001: 118–120). Figure 4.2 depicts resilience as a mediator of exposure to stress.

At present, there is virtually no empirical evidence available to address or test the conceptual relationships we have outlined in Figures 4.1 and 4.2. Although it may seem intuitively appealing to consider that resilience moderates stress reactivity (Figure 4.1), it remains possible that resilience exerts a mediating influence upon stress exposure itself (Figure 4.2). Both lines of reasoning warrant attention and investigation. Thus, it is reasonable to conclude that if the relationships we hypothesize here are correct, it is likely that effective leadership can promote resilience through interactions with each of the Four Processes theorized by McGrath.

Demand–Control–Support Stress Model

Karasek (1979) and Karasek and Theorell (1990) developed a second and particularly useful model for understanding resilience and stress.

This model relates specifically to work-related stress and holds that individuals are most likely to experience strain from high job demands (D) when they feel unable to control (C) their work-related tasks or influence their work procedures (i.e., when they have little decision latitude). The reasoning behind this argument is that high work demands create anxiety about performance, which in turn can be reduced or offset only by the perception of control over significant aspects of the work environment (Cooper et al., 2001: 135–136). Other researchers (e.g., Johnson & Hall, 1988) have expanded upon Karasek's original model to argue that social support (S) may also reduce the strain of high work-related demands. For example, colleagues and supervisors can provide social support in the form of help and feedback (e.g., instrumental, emotional, informational, and appraisal support; see also House, 1981).

In the context of the D–C–S model, resilience might be understood as potentially helpful to the perception of control or use of social support. Specific characteristics of resilience (e.g., willingness to improvise and determination) bear obvious relevance to control and thus may facilitate experience and perception of control. A similar effect is implied in our analysis of the Four Process model with respect to cognitive reactions to stress. The second contribution of the D–C–S model is its proposition that social support serves to buffer the expected effects of extreme demands. If this idea is correct, it suggests an additional avenue by which resilient individuals might benefit. Guided by their determination to make use of all potential resources, resilient people may be more willing and more active in seeking social support (e.g., Walsh, 2002). In fact, the proposition that social support can play a significant role in buffering against strain suggests the need to recognize an additional and potentially important marker of resilience itself. As individuals seek social support, they may strengthen and reinforce their own and others' (e.g., family or unit) capacity for resilience.

Although not every study has demonstrated that social support serves to buffer stress (e.g., Schaubroeck & Fink, 1998), many studies have (see Cooper et al., 2001: 140–149 for a brief review). Walsh's (2002) work in the area of family resilience certainly supports the idea that social support may play a significant role in buffering against stress. The potential beneficial effect of social support introduces the need to expand our consideration of how an effective leader might increase the resilience of his or her followers. Certainly, extraordinary personal qualities and behavior are important and perhaps even essential under demanding or hostile conditions. However, the D–C–S model suggests that leaders might increase or reinforce followers' resistance on a daily basis simply by performing conventional interactions effectively. By engaging fully in various ordinary, daily interactions with followers who seek resources and support, an effective leader may help to build the basis for improved resilience to the chronic stressors of everyday life and work.

Resilience: Trait versus State

As implied by the discussion above, practical treatments of resilience often reflect a dual orientation. Sometimes resilience is presented as a relatively fixed individual characteristic, such as a personality trait. For example, Norlander, Von Schedvin, and Archer (2005) described resilience as "thriving," which they related in turn to affective personality traits. They found that the most resilient subjects were those who had both high positive affect and high negative affect. By contrast, their least resilient subjects were characterized as having low positive affect and high negative affect.

In other instances, resilience has been conceived as a dynamic, developable, and interactive state (e.g., Luthans et al., 2006), the purpose of which is to develop strategies for coping with environmental demands. It is certainly possible, even likely, that resilience may reveal itself as a consistent personality attribute (or combination of traits), as a state response to situational demands, or as an interaction of trait and state variables. In our consideration of how leadership may affect individual or group resilience, we consider both trait and state aspects of the construct. The resulting implications for the role of leadership are different, but in each case interesting and important.

If we view resilience as a trait (sometimes termed "ego-resiliency"; see Luthar et al., 2000), we anticipate that an effective leader could serve to encourage or reinforce behavioral expression of resiliency that is already resident in the character of others. Success in doing so would likely depend primarily upon the leader's own characteristics (creativity, perceptivity, resourcefulness, inspirational ability, etc.). Relatedly, poor leadership might serve to discourage the expression of resilient behavior. By contrast, if we view resilience as a state (the outcome of situational and individual factors), then it is something that can be developed (Luthans et al., 2006). In this case, an effective leader might be able to create or improve resilience in others, whereas an ineffective leader might inhibit the development of resilience. Researchers in the field of leadership have just begun to examine specific questions relating to the potential positive and negative effects leaders can have upon resilience in their followers. Conclusions regarding these and related conceptually important ideas await the results of stringent empirical tests. Britt, Davison, Bliese, and Castro (2004) have discussed resilience as a state in terms of military leaders and their soldiers. They have observed the leader as helpful and are currently examining the role of leadership as a factor that may serve to "predict stress, act as a buffer against the negative effects of stress and . . . enable variables that have been found to decrease the

adverse effects of stress (e.g., role clarity, self-efficacy, and job engagement)"
(Britt et al., 2004, 541).

Stressors in Military Environments

Before we address the role of leadership and resilience in military settings,
we must first consider what types of stressors are typically found in military environments. For the purpose of organization and clarity, we will
separately address the stressors that are typical in routine (nondeployed)
and deployed settings. Although there is certainly some degree of overlap
between these two conditions of military service, each involves some unique
stressors.

In each case, we apply a classification system (see Campbell & Noble,
2005) to identify three different types of stressors: (1) incompatibility stressors, (2) incapacity stressors, and (3) distraction stressors. This system is
based on the notion that, while all stressors may potentially interfere with
job performance, different types of stressors do so in different ways. Specifically, incompatibility stressors cause strain and threaten performance
because they create questions or conflicts regarding job-related tasks or roles.
Incapacity stressors directly constrict the individual's capacity to perform
required tasks, for example, for lack of personal skills or absence of essential
resources. Finally, distraction stressors shift attention away from required
tasks and direct it instead toward physically or psychologically significant
corollary matters and concerns (e.g., harsh climate, boredom, loneliness).
We hypothesize that the impact of leadership on resilience and perhaps even
the very nature of resilience itself may depend upon what type(s) of stressors
are confronted in a given situation.

Stressors in Routine, Nondeployed Environments

Work-related stressors in nondeployed military environments are similar
to those encountered in civilian work settings. Investigators have examined
various types of stressors related to job role (Dobreva-Martinova, Villeneuve,
Strickland & Matheson, 2002; Bliese & Castro, 2000; Barling & MacIntyre,
1993; Day & Livingstone, 2001), work relationships (Planz & Sonnek, 2002;
Jex & Thomas, 2003; Carbone & Cigrang, 2001), time and workload (Bliese
& Halverson, 1996; Gold & Friedman, 2000), and change and transition
(Planz & Sonnek, 2002). Researchers have also studied the effects of physical
work demands (e.g., Bowles, Holger & Picano, 2000), sleep deprivation (e.g.,
Britt, Stetz & Bliese, 2004), and job-related environmental stressors such as
extreme climates, toxic agents, and normal but inherently hazardous work
conditions (e.g., handling explosives; cf. Norwood, 1997).

Table 4.1   Typical Stressors in Routine, Nondeployed Military Environments

Stressors	Examples
Incompatibility Stressors	
Within role conflicts	Individual achievement versus group success
Between role conflicts	Family obligations versus soldier obligations
Person role conflicts	Personal values versus military values
Incapacity Stressors	
Role overloads	Excessive demands, time pressures, work pace, long hours
Role ambiguity	Unfamiliar or new assignment
Responsibility for others	Squad leader, company commander
Physically taxing demands	Forced marches in full gear
Difficulties with supervisor	Unable to achieve performance expectations
Distraction Stressors	
Physical conditions	Hard environment, harsh climate, fatigue, sleep deprivation
Psychological conditions	Boredom, confusion, feelings of isolation, loneliness
Difficulties with peers	Conflicts, unaccepted, untrustworthy
Difficulties with family	Excessive separations, absence during times of crises
Fear of injuries	Ordnance accidents, aviation accidents
Anxiety about future	Changes in responsibilities, work hours, location

Table 4.1 presents various job-related stressors within the classification scheme described earlier. One limitation of this system is that classification categories are not mutually exclusive. Thus, judgment must be exercised in the assignment of some stressors to one or another category. In some cases, appropriate assignment may depend largely upon job context or the expected severity of the potential consequences of a given stressor in a particular context. Nonetheless, by underscoring broad qualitative differences among types of stressors, the classification system applied here and in Table 4.1 is helpful as a means to appreciate the fact that different stressors may produce different types or levels of strain (e.g., Jex & Crossley, 2005). For instance, certain stressors might cause primarily psychological strain (e.g., anxiety or depression), while the effects of others are largely physical (e.g., fatigue, pain) or behavioral (e.g., excessive risk-taking, substance abuse). An interest in leadership, resilience, or both introduces the need to accommodate such differences and to distinguish between psychological and physical resilience (e.g., Tugade, Fredrickson & Barrett, 2004).

Although the key characteristics that define resilience might be consistent in each case, we would expect their relative significance to vary depending upon the type of stressor(s) encountered and whether the resulting strain is primarily psychological or primarily physical. For example, the ability to impose meaning on hardship may be very important for coping with fear, but not particularly helpful in overcoming the effects of sleep deprivation. The ability to improvise and adapt to a harsh environment may be essential to coping with extreme weather, but may offer little or no relief from depression. While such distinctions may seem to have little practical impact in situations that require psychological as well as physical resilience and perhaps also an interplay among all relevant characteristics and variables, leaders might function more effectively if they understand which of their own characteristics or behavior might have the most direct or dramatic beneficial impact on specific types of strain.

Stressors in Deployed Environments

Work-related stressors in deployed environments overlap with those encountered in more routine conditions, but the stressors associated with deployed military service are distinct in two ways. First, specific stressors are likely to occupy a more central position in the individual's work experience. For example, within-role conflicts (Table 4.1) may be more common for those who are deployed to operations other than war (e.g., peacekeeping operations). Individuals who are engaged in such operations often experience strain as they attempt to reconcile their identity as warfighters with their duty to exercise impartiality, restraint, and minimal involvement (cf. Weerts et al., 2002). This type of strain is often exacerbated by rules of engagement that incongruously restrict options for protection or require soldier-peacekeepers to remain passive even when they encounter clear threats to themselves and to others (e.g., Bartone & Vatikus, 1998; Litz, Orsillo, Friedman & Ehlich, 1997; Shigemura & Nomura, 2002).

Similarly, incapacity stressors and distraction stressors may take on greater significance in deployed environments. For example, difficult living conditions and lack of privacy may have more dramatic effects as stressors in the context of deployment (Bliese & Britt, 2001; Yerks, 1993). Extreme physical and professional workloads, long duty days, and little time off may cause notable strain in deployed settings (Nisenbaum, Barett, Reyes & Reeves, 2000; Britt & Bliese, 2003). Relationships with civilian peers and multinational colleagues assume special importance and thus potentially unique strains arise from unfamiliarity, suspicion, or miscommunication (e.g., Downie, 2002). During deployment, soldiers may experience critical distraction stressors related to separation from family and concerns about the family's ability to cope (MacDonald et al., 1998). Finally, deployment often brings about significant changes in work responsibilities, which in turn may create anxiety about meeting new role expectations and performing unfamiliar tasks (incapacity stressors). This type of anxiety may be more severe in deployed (vs. nondeployed) environments because deployed personnel understand that the consequences of poor performance may be injury or death.

Military personnel in deployed environments also confront a variety of stressors unique to combat, mission requirements, leadership, climate,

Table 4.2   Stressors Unique to Deployed Military Environments

Stressors	Examples
Mission Stressors	
Incompatibility	Overlapping areas of responsibility
Incapacity	Responsibility without clear authority
Distraction	Evolving objectives and contradictory goals
Cultural Stressors	
Incompatibility	Different values and unfamiliar ways
Incapacity	Uncertainty about how to act/react
Distraction	Relating to unfamiliar conditions
Leadership Climate Stressors	
Incompatibility	Contradictory expectations
Incapacity	Unmet physical/environmental needs
Distraction	Information oversights/communication failures
Combat Stressors	
Incompatibility	Killing and injuring others
Incapacity	Active fighting, dealing with loss of comrades
Distraction	Witnessing civilian suffering

and cultural differences (see Table 4.2). Because these unique stressors are inherently complex and because the consequences of resulting performance breakdown are potentially severe, associated strain effects might be attributable to all of the three stressor categories identified earlier (incompatibility demands, incapacity, and distraction).

Combat-related stressors occur most predictably in the context of war, but also in other situations and operations where survival is uncertain (Dekel, Solomon, Ginzburg & Neria, 2003). Obvious stressors are combat-related injuries and the threat of injury or death. Deployed personnel may also witness injury, suffering, and death of others (e.g., combatants, civilians, children) or experience the loss of comrades (Rosebush, 1998; Weerts et al., 2002). They might be forced to observe the gruesome results of atrocities (Hotopf et al., 2003) or retrieval and disposal of human remains (MacDonald et al., 1998). All of these stressors are unique to deployment and are potentially severe in their effects.

Deployment can also introduce cognitive stressors related to the nature of the undertaking itself. Peacekeeping operations are especially prone to confusion and ambiguity regarding the mission goals and long-term value (Ballone et al., 2000). Confusion and uncertainty may be exacerbated by poor understanding of history and social context and by the fact that mission objectives often change or evolve in response to shifting political realities. Related stressors, common among multinational units, may involve lack of clarity with respect to organizational relationships and overlapping areas of authority and responsibility (Shigemura & Nomura, 2002).

Cultural issues and differences also present a host of potential stressors. These are a common source of stress for those involved in multinational peacekeeping efforts. Deployed personnel may be uncertain about how to relate to foreign soldiers (Bartone & Vatikus, 1998) and how to deal with a local population whose language and culture are unfamiliar (Downie, 2002). They may also confront stressors associated with the navigation of strange and potentially dangerous surroundings, assignments to locate unfamiliar but important resources, and, frequently, the determination of appropriate ways to relate to a population of civilian combatants (Litz et al., 1997).

Finally, even as deployment makes obvious the importance of good leadership, it is often the case that leadership changes hands in deployed environments. Troops may feel uncertain about the competency and commitment of a newly assigned and unfamiliar leader (Bartone & Vatikus, 1998). Faith in leadership may also be compromised by inconsiderate commanders who might neglect soldiers' physical needs and well-being, including their desire for regular briefings and up-to-date information about the operation in which they are engaged (Downie, 2002; Yerks, 1993).

Leadership, Resilience, and Adverse Environments

How might military leaders exercise their influence to encourage or improve resilience and buffer their troops from the wide variety of stressors they may encounter in deployed and nondeployed settings? To address this question now, we must rely heavily upon concepts, constructs, and relationships hypothesized throughout this chapter and suggested by what is currently a very limited body of empirical evidence. It is hoped that this effort might provide a helpful early guidance to researchers.

To determine the potential impact of leadership on resilience, we must first attend to the specific nature of the adverse environment or situation in which resilience is needed. For example, some situations require resilience to chronic strain (due to routine stressors) while others require resilience to acute, episodic strain (due to extreme but temporary stressors). How might effective leadership differ with respect to promoting resilience in each case? In typical at-risk environments, the leader who wants to foster resilience will focus on buffering and protecting followers from the stressors they encounter on a regular, perhaps even daily basis (see Luthar et al., 2000). This might require the leader to do little or nothing more than what an effective leader would strive to do in any event, that is, to engage in normal leadership.

Drawing on ideas put forth by Hersey and Blanchard (1993), we can say that the effective leader normally attempts to provide followers with help in clarifying their roles and reconciling task incompatibilities. The effective leader would make resources and time available for followers to acquire the skills and capacities necessary to fulfill their job responsibilities and meet their performance demands. The effective leader would normally seek and support organizational initiatives to minimize strain that may be the predictable result of harsh conditions, strenuous schedules, family worries, and the like. In effect, when normal leadership is properly executed, it should facilitate the expression of natural resilience skills or traits (meaning-making, determination, and improvisation) among those who follow or serve (cf. Luthans et al., 2006).

Resilience Creation

In extraordinarily adverse conditions, normal leadership may not be sufficient to overcome the effects of acute, extreme stressors. Confronted by extreme stress, the effective leader may also have to create new or additional resilience among followers. In this situation, resilience is better construed as a "state," that is, as an outcome of leadership directly interacting with the existing characteristics of followers. We hypothesize that this type of effect will occur when a leader draws on his or her resilient characteristics (situational assessments as identified in the Four Processes model) and uses these cognitive and behavioral assessments to much more forcefully guide and shape the cognitive and behavioral assessments of followers. In effect, the successful leader will inspire and encourage followers to adopt his or her (resilient) perception of the situation.

In Table 4.3, we outline how this type of resilience creation might occur. As the table indicates, leaders can influence how their followers react to and evaluate a stress cycle. Leader qualities and actions can affect

Table 4.3   Resilience as an Interaction Outcome of Leader Characteristics and Follower Characteristics: An Illustration

Followers' Stress Episode Processes	Leader Qualities	Leader Actions	Interactive Outcome	Resilience Characteristics
Cognitive appraisal	Credibility, insight	Persuasive analysis	"This is a threat but we can prevail."	Determination, meaning-making
Decision-making	Expertise, confidence	Direction/ guidance	"Here are some actions we might take."	Improvisation of a strategy
Performance	Judgment, innovation	Direction/ encouragement	"Here's how we might implement our plan."	Improvisation of a method
Outcome	Judgment, flexibility	Persuasive analysis	"Here's what we need to do now."	Determination; meaning-making

how followers appraise the situation in which they find themselves, the choices they consider making in response, the way they implement their decisions, and the way they evaluate the effectiveness of their actions. Table 4.3 suggests that leader qualities (e.g., credibility and insightfulness) and leader actions (e.g., persuasive explanation) can direct followers' own assessments (e.g., their cognitive appraisal, decision-making, etc.), onto paths that are identical to that of the leader. This ensures that followers see the situation as the leader does, perhaps to better appreciate the seriousness of the group's position, while also offering hope that a successful resolution is possible.

Similarly, the leader can help followers to identify new courses of action (obvious to the leader) by directing their decision-making processes. Line 3 of Table 4.3 continues this idea of followers' respect for the leader's judgment and direction permitting the leader to influence followers' performance processes (improvised methods and means considered). Finally, line 4 of the table brings the resilience creation process of one stress cycle to a close and conceivably starts another. Of course, the process of resilience creation remains highly similar to the process of resilience facilitation, with the exception that when a leader creates resilience, his or her assessments and evaluations are much more directive and, especially, pivotal to group functioning.

Specific Issues

In the following sections, we examine several specific and more narrowly focused issues in the area of leadership and resilience. One of these is the relationship between style of leadership and its likely impact on followers' mental health and, by implication, upon followers' resilience. Another concern is the leader's potential to create or foster resilience through training. Finally, we consider the leader's ability to encourage broad use of specific coping mechanisms associated with resilience.

Leadership Style, Social Support, and Mental Health

Several recent studies and reports (e.g., NATO RTO, 2007) highlight the importance of leadership style as an influence on resilience and mental health outcome. Leaders who empower and provide support for their workforce enhance their employees' sense of personal control and prevent alienation (e.g., Burke et al., 2006). This is important to the extent that factors such as control and alienation may affect mental health outcome after exposure to stress. Regeka, Hill, and Glancy (2000) studied firefighters who had been exposed to tragic events on the job and found that those who perceived they had low personal control and felt alienated from others were more likely to experience depression and to be diagnosed as suffering from post traumatic stress disorder (PTSD) than those who felt they were in control and who reported good social support.

Similarly, Solomon and Berger (2005) studied Zaka* body handlers who gather up the body parts, blood, and tissue of Israelis who have died violently (e.g., in suicide bombings or violent accidents). Fewer than 3% of these Zaka volunteers demonstrated symptoms of PTSD. Instead, they reported feeling a low sense of danger and a high sense of self-efficacy. The researchers suggest that a high degree of resilience among the Zaka body handlers is derived from a sense of meaning (work is altruistic and spiritual) and from social support (they receive a great deal of respect and admiration from their supervisors and from the Israeli people). As noted earlier, these factors are crucial components of resilience. They are also factors that person-oriented leaders can strive to foster, even in enormously stressful work environments. Leaders may be able to increase the psychological resilience of others by helping them to appreciate the meaningfulness of their work (Bartone, 2006).

Rosen et al. (1999) observed that although certain hardiness scores (measured through the use of surveys) were relatively equivalent for male and female service members deployed to combat areas during the first Persian Gulf War, female service members reported more stress. This difference was explained in terms of different levels of bonding between female (vs. male) service members and their leaders and colleagues. Rosen et al. concluded that leaders should emphasize bonding and ensure that female soldiers receive adequate support from leaders and peers.

Other researchers (e.g., Adler & Dolan, 2006; Bartone, 1999) have reported evidence that hardiness protects Army Reserve forces from the effects of war-related stress due to the disruption of their civilian jobs and separation from family. Specifically, hardy soldiers were found less likely to suffer from depression or PTSD than their nonhardy counterparts. Thus, leaders may be able to foster resilience to stress by providing support that encourages or promotes hardiness. For example, leaders can reinforce subordinates' sense of self-efficacy and help them to find meaning in their work. Cole, Bruch, and Vogel (2006) examined workers during times of organizational crisis and found that supervisor support positively related to employee hardiness and negatively related to employee cynicism. In this case, supervisor support took the form of stressing the significance of the work in which the employees were involved and ensuring them of their ability to achieve success.

Vogt, Pless, King, and King (2005) evaluated adjustment outcomes for male and female service members upon their return from deployment to

* ZAKA is an abbreviation for "Identifying Victims of Disaster" (in Hebrew: Zihuy Korbanot Asson). The ZAKA organization is a community emergency response team that is officially recognized by the government of the state of Israel.

the first Persian Gulf War. These returning soldiers had been exposed to mission-related stressors as well as interpersonal stressors. Female service members reported experiencing more interpersonal strain than did their male colleagues, and this type of stress also had a greater negative impact upon female soldiers' postdeployment mental health. Much of the female soldiers' stress was related to separation from family and the guilt they felt because they were unable to fulfill their roles as wives, mothers, and daughters. Other researchers have observed that among female victims of sexual abuse, those who are more resilient report less self-blame and fewer feelings of stigmatization (Dufour & Nadeau, 2001). By extension, leaders may be able to foster greater resilience among women by helping them to understand that they are not abandoning their families when their jobs require separation.

Bliese (2006) reports on a series of studies carried out at the Walter Reed Army Institute of Research from the early 1990s through 2005. Researchers studied soldiers' psychological well-being as a driver of resilience and job performance in combat. Bliese and his colleagues define well-being as a construct that includes, but is not limited to, factors such as depression, morale, job satisfaction, and physical health. Based on research conducted at Walter Reed, they observe that a positive social climate established by unit leadership is the most significant contributor to soldiers' well-being. This finding reinforces the ideas of Johnson and Hall (1998), who argue that social support serves to reduce stress. While it is possible that resilient individuals may be more likely to seek social support on their own initiative, leaders can facilitate this tendency by ensuring that social support is available when needed.

Resilience, Leadership, and Training

Recently, it has been reported that many U.S. service members have experienced significant mental health problems after serving in Afghanistan or Iraq. Hoge, Auchterlonie, and Milliken (2006) studied warfighters who experienced combat in these overseas operations in 2003 and 2004. The authors found that 19.1% of those who served in Iraq, 11.3% of those who served in Afghanistan, and 8.5% of those who served in other deployment areas reported mental health problems upon their return from deployment. The use of mental health services or resignation from the military was significantly and positively correlated with combat experience. These findings have led researchers, policy makers, and military leaders to propose that troops should receive resilience training prior to their deployment and further that there is a need for researchers to identify new ways of imparting coping strategies to troops during deployment (Munsey, 2006; see also NATO RTO, 2007).

Numerous studies suggest that resilience can be enhanced by training. For example, Sadow and Hopkins (1993) reported that resiliency training improved levels of perceived self-efficacy and sense of personal control among homeless, substance-abusing veterans. Maddi, Kahn, and Maddi (1998) report beneficial effects of hardiness training as a means to promote resilience to illness. Waite and Richardson (2004) employed resilience training in an occupational context and found that workers who received resilience training demonstrated significant improvements in self-esteem, increased personal feelings of control, a belief in the purpose of their lives and work, and enhanced interpersonal relations.

Lloyd and Foster (2006) cite their experience in training athletes to improve performance and inoculate against stress, observing that such training may be helpful in high-conflict work groups or in occupations where stress is an integral part of the work. Taking an indirect approach, other studies have focused on leaders' behavior in the area of self-fulfilling prophecy (Dov, 1992; Davidson & Eden, 2000). In each case, leaders were trained to foster a culture of high expectations, to fight negative stereotypes, and to provide strong, positive support for all their employees. Subordinates to these leaders were found to benefit by enhanced feelings of personal control, deep appreciation for the meaning of their work, and intense desire to meet challenges. Research involving U.S. soldiers indicates that individuals who see themselves engaged in meaningful work and recognize the benefits of hardship are less likely to experience negative effects of stress (Britt, Adler & Bartone, 2001). Thus, it is likely that resilience can be enhanced by leaders who encourage and reinforce positive perceptions of meaningful service, duty, and sacrifice.

Other research efforts indicate that resilience training may be useful as a means to prepare individuals for new or potentially stressful experiences. Goldstein and Smith (1999) report the benefits of cross-cultural training as a means to enhance adaptability and emotional resilience in students preparing for study abroad. Van Breda (1999) developed a resilience training program for individuals who experience recurring separations from their families. The program was effective in training business executives, sales representatives, and military personnel and their family members to employ coping mechanisms designed to help with frequent separations.

There is evidence to indicate that resilience to stress depends to some extent upon the use of coping strategies that emphasize problem-solving, communications, and control. It remains to be seen whether or to what extent resilient coping strategies can be imparted, but it is certainly possible that resilience may be enhanced by learning to frame stress realistically and with an orientation to challenge (vs. threat). Maddi (2005) recently observed that resilient individuals have the courage and the willingness to face stressors rather than denying or "awfulizing" them. This orientation inspires resilient individuals to approach stressors as challenges to be met and to interact with others who can provide assistance and encouragement. Sharkansky et al. (2000) have reported that the most psychologically healthy soldiers are those who cope with stress by employing approach-based coping strategies, that is, thinking about problems, devising plans and sticking to them, and talking to others about problems and plans. By contrast, soldiers who use avoidance-based coping strategies (ignore the problem) are more likely to suffer nega-tive effects of stress. Similarly, a study by Berk (1998) found that UNICEF employees and the children they served (in Bosnia) were more resilient to trauma when they employed coping strategies that involved acceptance of social support and thought-stopping techniques to distance themselves from circumstances beyond their control.

Support for Soldiers

In recognition of the need for psychological support, the U.S. Army now pro-vides a 48 h reprieve to soldiers who are overwhelmed by the strain of combat. These soldiers are permitted to move to a safer area where they can shower, sleep, eat hot meals, and talk with mental health professionals if desired. The Army now also provides predeployment training aimed at improving soldier resilience and has improved the availability and the accessibility of mental health professionals to deployed troops. Finally, soldiers and their families receive psychological and social support when military personnel return home from deployment (e.g., NATO RTO, 2007). The American Psychologi-cal Association offers additional informative support materials, such as its brochure entitled "Homecoming: Resilience after Wartime."

The U.S. Navy provides dedicated mental health services to Marines. Navy psychologists are matched with Marine regiments months prior to their deployment, during deployment, and back at home. Mental health professionals assigned to support U.S. troops in Iraq work to foster psycho-logical resilience so that troops will be better able to capitalize on individual and unit strengths. Thus, it certainly appears that military policymakers and military organizational leaders are implicitly aware of the need for psycho-logical resilience as a matter of operational performance and survivability and that the modern U.S. military is taking steps to build resilience in its troops before and throughout the deployment cycle. We expect and certainly hope that the benefits of these efforts will be evident in future analyses of long-term mental health and well-being among U.S. military personnel.

Conclusions and Recommendations

Although effective leadership can certainly have a potentially substantial impact upon psychological resilience, we remain limited in our ability to transform current knowledge into formalized and applied leadership train-ing and development programs. This difficulty is due in large part to the problem of conceptual ambiguity in our current understanding of resilience. As long as conceptual ambiguity persists, researchers may be understandably reluctant to propose comprehensive theoretical frameworks to guide additional research and development. New research should attend to the need for improved definition and specificity concerning essential factors, criteria, and measures of resilience. Meanwhile, we would encourage investigators who are interested in leadership and resilience, to adopt (as we have done in this chapter) an intuitively useful working definition of resilience, and to carefully consider associated findings and implications with respect to other frameworks and disciplinary perspectives.

Researchers in this area must also consider what type(s) of leadership influence they wish to consider or evaluate. Our review suggests that effects of leadership on subordinates' resilience may occur and perhaps occur differently within the context of at least three distinct types of leadership (i.e., normal leadership, inspirational leadership, and institutional leadership). Investigative orientation should reflect these distinct leadership types as well as their potentially unique forms of influence upon psychological resilience. Below, we briefly consider and offer suggestions for future research in each case.

Normal Leadership Effects

Because even ordinary work environments involve routine stressors, many individuals and work units often experience ongoing, chronic strain. In such circumstances, effective leadership that helps to increase a workers' resilience is both valuable and appropriate. Programs that help leaders to identify and engage in actions that promote resilience should be of interest to policy makers. As noted earlier, currently available research suggests that leader actions that buffer and protect against routine stressors also tend to promote factors and benefits associated with stress resilience. For example, leaders can emphasize work meaningfulness, help to build and facilitate group cohesion, offer social support when needed, and empower subordinates toward a greater sense of control in the workplace.

Future studies should be designed to focus, as specifically as possible, upon the relationship between leadership and resilience. For example, there is a need to address the full range of leader behavior that may potentially facilitate (or impede) resilience in individuals and working groups. Such studies will require careful thought, not only to identify potentially relevant leader actions, but also to define and measure resilience in a manner that is both meaningful and useful. Researchers should seek to avoid confounding the relationship between leadership and resilience with other, presumably separable effects of effective leadership (or management) upon other aspects of subordinate performance such as productivity, job satisfaction, or professionalism.

Inspirational Leadership Effects

In the case of inspirational leadership, it appears that leader characteristics may interact with subordinates' characteristics. The notion that a leader might create or call forth resilience is an intriguing theoretical possibility, with significant practical implications. Although we are able to outline in conceptual terms how such an effect or interplay might occur (see Table 4.3), current research on the question remains uncomfortably anecdotal. There is a need for specific research to address and test processes such as those we have proposed in Table 4.3. Such studies should be designed to directly test the impact of inspirational leadership on a team's ability to demonstrate resilience in the face of hardship. Here again, resilience should be operationally defined such that observed differences are both measurable and distinct from other parameters of group performance. Environments that demand inspirational leadership and resilience are typically extreme and often dangerous. It is neither feasible nor ethical to conduct laboratory research in such settings. Rather, researchers must turn their attention to field situations (e.g., combat) from which data can be derived. For example, investigators might consider joint cooperative studies of leadership and resilience as may occur during the rigorous and often extreme training of elite military units (e.g., U.S. Navy Seals and U.S. Army Rangers). Such studies, if designed to focus specifically upon inspirational leadership and group resilience and conducted in accord with normal training evaluations and after-action reviews, could offer a wealth of substantive data and insight.

Institutional Leadership Effects

Finally, there is the question of how high-level institutional leadership might affect the resilience of all who work within the organization. As our earlier analysis indicates, psychological resilience to stress may be enhanced or reduced not only by the behavior of leaders immediately above the individuals and working groups of interest, but also by the actions taken (or not taken) by those at even higher organizational levels. Early and obvious support for effective coping may help to set the tone for successful stress management. For example, organizational leadership may promote resilience by providing resilience training programs that are adequate and appropriate to the types of stressors associated with job performance. Evidence from the study of hardiness training indicates that such programs may be particularly beneficial for individuals in "at-risk" populations (e.g., former drug users and laid-off workers). There is a need for additional research to address how such programs might be modified to address the needs of other populations, such as those who work in uniquely stressful, at-risk occupations (e.g., soldiers, firefighters, police officers).

Institutional leaders can also indirectly foster resilience by encouraging and funding studies aimed at identifying new strategies and techniques for resiliency training. Coping strategies that improve individuals' problem-solving and communication abilities appear to be related to increased resilience, and institutional leaders can emphasize the importance of these examinations by continuing to encourage such research and by making available the necessary resources.

As we have observed throughout this chapter, the understood and practical impacts of leadership on resilience will undoubtedly vary depending upon how the constructs of leadership and resilience are operationally defined, measured, and applied. Nonetheless, based upon the evidence that is currently available, we are persuaded that future investigations will provide significant conceptual insights concerning resilience and the manner in which leaders can apply their skills and authority to promote resilience in all work environments. We hope that future research will recognize the need for practical benefit, including the design and the application of leadership training programs and resilience development initiatives.

References

Adler, A. & Dolan, C. (2006). Military hardiness as a buffer of psychological health on return from deployment. *Military Medicine, 171*, 93–98.

Alexander, C. (1998). *The Endurance: Shackleton's Legendary Antarctic expedition.* New York: Alfred A. Knopf.

Antonakis, J., Cianciolo, A. & Sternberg, R. (Eds.) (2004). *The Nature of Leadership.* Thousand Oaks, CA: Sage Publications.

Barling, J., Kelloway, K. & Frone, M. (Eds.) (2005). *Handbook of Work Stress.* Thousand Oaks, CA: Sage Publications.

Barling, J. & MacIntyre, A. (1993). Daily work stressors, mood and emotional exhaustion. *Work & Stress, 7(4)*, 315–325.

Bartone, P. (1999). Hardiness protects against war-related stress in Army Reserve forces. *Consulting Psychology Journal: Practice and Research, 51*, 72–82.

Bartone, P.T. (2006). Resilience under military operational stress: can leaders influence hardiness? *Military Psychology, 19 (Suppl.)*, S131–S148.

Bartone, P., Ursano, R., Wright, K. & Ingraham, L. (1989). The impact of a military air disaster on the health of assistance workers: a prospective study. *Journal of Nervous and Mental Disease, 177*, 317–328.

Bartone, P. & Vatikus, M. (1998). Dimensions of psychological stress in peacekeeping operations. *Military Medicine, 163(9)*, 587–592.

Bass, B. (1990). *Bass & Stogdill's Handbook of Leadership.* New York: Free Press.

Bass, B. & Riggio, R. (2006). *Transformational Leadership.* Mahwah, NJ: Lawrence Erlbaum Associates.

Berk, J. (1998). Trauma and resiliency during war: a look at the children and humanitarian aid workers of Bosnia. *Psychoanalytic Review, 85*, 639–658.

Blake, R. & Mouton, J. (1964). *The Managerial Grid.* Houston, TX: Gulf Publishing.

Bliese, P. (2006). Social climates of soldiers' well-being and resilience. In: Adler, A., Castro, C. & Britt, T. (Eds.), *Military Life: The Psychology of Serving in Peace and Combat (Vol. 2): Operational Stress* (pp. 213–234). Westport, CN: Praeger Security International.

Bliese, P. & Britt, T. (2001). Social support, group consensus and stressor-stress relationship: social context matters. *Journal of Organizational Behavior, 22,* 425–436.

Bliese, P. & Castro, C. (2000). Role clarity, work overload and organizational support: multilevel evidence of the importance of support. *Work & Stress, 14,* 65–74.

Bliese, P. & Halverson, R. (1996). Individual and nomothetic models of job stress: an examination of work hours, cohesion, and well being. *Journal of Applied Social Psychology, 26,* 1171–1189.

Bowles, S., Holger, U. & Picano, J. (2000). Aircrew perceived stress: examining crew performance, crew position and captain personality. *Aviation, Space, and Environmental Medicine, 71(11),* 1093–1097.

Brief, A., Schuler, R. & Van Sell, M. (1981). *Managing Job Stress.* Boston, MA: Little, Brown.

Britt, T., Adler, A. & Bartone, P. (2001). Deriving benefits from stressful events: the role of engagement in meaningful work and hardiness. *Journal of Occupational Health Psychology, 6,* 53–63.

Britt, T. & Bliese, P. (2003). Testing the stress-buffering effects of self-engagement among soldiers on military operations. *Journal of Personality, 71,* 245–265.

Britt, T., Davison, J., Bliese, D. & Castro, C. (2004). How leaders can influence the impact that stressors have on soldiers. *Military Medicine, 69,* 541–545.

Britt, T., Stetz, M. & Bliese, P. (2004). Work-relevant values strengthen the stressor-strain relation in elite Army units. *Military Psychology, 16,* 1–17.

Burke, C., Stagle, K., Klein, C., Goodwin, G., Salas, E. & Halpin, S. (2006). What types of leadership behaviors are functional in teams? A meta-analysis. *Leadership Quarterly, 17,* 288–307.

Burns, J. (1978). *Leadership.* New York: Harper & Row.

Campbell, D. (2000). The proactive employee: managing workplace initiative. *Academy of Management Executive, 14,* 52–66.

Campbell, D. & Dardis, G. (2004). The "Be, Know, Do" model of leader development. *Human Resource Planning, 27(2),* 26–39.

Campbell, D. & Nobel, O. (2005). Occupational stressors in military service: a review and classification. Department of Behavioral Sciences and Leadership Working Paper, U.S. Military Academy, West Point, NY.

Carbone, E. & Cigrang, J. (2001). Job satisfaction, occupational stress, and personality characteristics of Air Force military training instructors. *Military Medicine, 166,* 800–802.

Cole, M., Bruch, H. & Vogel, B. (2006). Emotions as mediators between perceived supervisor support and psychological hardiness on employee cynicism. *Journal of Organizational Behavior, 27,* 463–484.

Cooper, C., Dewe, P. & O'Driscoll, M. (2001). *Organizational Stress.* Thousand Oaks, CA: Sage Publications.

Coutu, D. (2002). How resilience works. *Harvard Business Review,* May, 46–55.

Daft, R. (2005). *The Leadership Experience.* Mason, OH: Thomson South-Western.

Davidson, O. & Eden, D. (2000). Remedial self-fulfilling prophecy: two field experiments to prevent Golem effects among disadvantaged women. *Journal of Applied Psychology, 85,* 386–398.

Day, A. & Livingstone, H. (2001). Chronic and acute stressors among military personnel: do coping styles buffer their negative impact on health? *Journal of Occupational Health Psychology, 6,* 348–360.

Dobreva-Martinova, T., Villeneuve, M., Strickland, L. & Matheson, K. (2002). Occupational role stress in the Canadian forces: its association with individual and organizational well-being. *Canadian Journal of Behavioral Science, 34,* 111–121.

Dov, E. (1992). Leadership and expectations: Pygmalion effects and other self-fulfilling prophecies in organizations. *Leadership Quarterly, 3,* 271–305.

Downie, S. (2002). Peacekeepers and peace—builders under stress. In: Yael, D. (Ed.), *Sharing the Front Line and the Back Hills: International Protectors and Provincial Peacekeepers, Humanitarian Aid Workers and the Media in the Midst of Crisis.* Amityville, NY: Baywood Publishing.

Dufour, M. & Nadeau, L. (2001). Sexual abuse: a comparison between resilient victims and drug-addicted victims. *Violence and Victims, 16,* 655–672.

Fiedler, F. (1971). Validation and extension of the contingency model of leadership effectiveness: a review of empirical findings. *Psychological Bulletin, 76,* 128–148.

Fiedler, F. & Garcia, J. (1987). *New Approaches to Effective Leadership: Cognitive Resources and Organizational Performance.* New York: John Wiley.

FM 22–100 (1999). *Army Leadership: Be, Know, Do.* Washington, D.C.: Department of the Army.

Frankl, V. (1963). *Man's Search for Meaning.* New York: Washington Square Press.

French, J. & Kahn, R. (1962). A programmatic approach to studying the industrial environment and mental health. *Journal of Social Issues, 18,* 1–47.

French, J. & Raven, B. (1968). The bases of social power. In: Cartwright, D. & Zander, A. (Eds.), *Group Dynamics: Research and Theory* (pp. 259–269). New York: Harper & Row.

Gold, M. & Friedman, S. (2000). Cadet basic training: an ethnographic study of stress and coping. *Military Medicine, 165,* 147–152.

Goldstein, D. & Smith, D. (1999). The analysis of the effects of experiential training on sojourners' cross-cultural adaptability. *International Journal of Intercultural Relations, 23,* 157–173.

Hersey, P. & Blanchard, K. (1993). *Management of Organizational Behavior.* Englewood Cliffs, NJ: Prentice Hall.

Hoge, C., Auchterlonie, J. & Milliken, C. (2006). Mental health problems, use of mental health services, and attrition from military service after returning from deployment to Iraq or Afghanistan. *Journal of the American Medical Association, 295,* 1023–1032.

House, J. (1981). *Work Stress and Social Support.* Reading, MA: Addison-Wesley.

House, J. (1974). Occupational stress and coronary heart disease: a review and theoretical integration. *Journal of Health and Social Behavior, 15,* 12–27.

House, R. (1977). A theory of charismatic leadership. In: Hunt, J. & Larson, L. (Eds.), *Leadership: The Cutting Edge* (pp. 189–207). Carbondale, IL: Southern Illinois University Press.

House, R. & Mitchell, T. (1975). Path-goal theory of leadership. In: Steers, R. & Porter, L. (Eds.), *Motivation and Work Behavior* (pp. 383–394). New York: McGraw-Hill.

Ivancevich, J. & Matteson, M. (1980). *Stress and Work*. Glenview, IL: Scott, Foresman.

Jex, S. & Crossley, C. (2005). Organizational consequences. In: Barling, J., Kelloway, K. & Frone, M. (Eds.), *Handbook of Work Stress* (pp. 575–578). Thousand Oaks, CA: Sage Publications.

Jex, S. & Thomas, J. (2003). Relations between stressors and group perceptions: main and mediating effects. *Work & Stress, 17*, 158–169.

Johnson, J. & Hall, E. (1988). Job strain, work place social support, and cardiovascular disease: a cross-sectional study of a random sample of the working population. *American Journal of Public Health, 78*, 1336–1342.

Karasek, R. (1979). Job demands, job decision latitude, and mental strain: implications for job redesign. *Administrative Science Quarterly, 24*, 285–308.

Karasek, R. & Theorell, T. (1990). *Health Work: Stress, Productivity, and the Reconstruction of Working Life*. New York: Basic Books.

Katz, D. & Kahn, R. (1978). *The Social Psychology of Organizations*. New York: Wiley.

Kobasa, S., Maddi, S. & Kahn, S. (1982). Hardiness and health: a prospective study. *Journal of Personality and Social Psychology, 42*, 168–177.

Lachman, S. (1972). *Psychosomatic Disorders: A Behavioral Interpretation*. New York: John Wiley.

Litz, B., Orsillo, S., Friedman, M. & Ehlich, P. (1997). Posttraumatic stress disorder associated with peacekeeping duty in Somalia for U.S. military personnel. *American Journal of Psychiatry, 15*, 178–184.

Lloyd, P. & Foster, S. (2006). Creating healthy, high-performance workplaces: strategies from health and sport psychology. *Consulting Psychology Journal: Practice and Research, 58*, 23–29.

Luthans, F., Vogelgesang, G.R. & Lester, P. (2006). Developing the psychological capital of resiliency. *Human Resource Development Review, 5*, 25–44.

Luthar, S., Cicchetti, D. & Becher, B. (2000). The construct of resilience: a critical evaluation and guidelines for future work. *Child Development, 71*, 543–562.

MacDonald, C., Chamberlain, K., Long, N., Pereira-Laird, J. & Mirfin, K. (1998). Mental health, physical health, and stressors reported by New Zealand Defense Forces peacekeepers: a longitudinal study. *Military Medicine, 163*, 477–481.

Maddi, S. (2002). The story of hardiness: twenty years of theorizing, research, and practice. *Consulting Psychology Journal, 54*, 173–185.

Maddi, S. (2005). On hardiness and other pathways to resilience. *American Psychologist, 60*, 261–262.

Maddi, S., Kahn, S. & Maddi, K. (1998). The effectiveness of hardiness training compared to relaxation training and social support training. *Consulting Psychology Journal: Practice and Research, 50*, 78–86.

Maddi, S. & Khosaba, D. (2005). *Resilience at Work: How to Succeed No Matter What Life Throws at You*. New York: Amacom.

McGrath, J. (1976). Stress and behavior in organizations. In: Dunnette, M.D. (Ed.), *Handbook of Industrial and Organizational Psychology* (pp. 1351–1395). Chicago, IL: Rand McNally.

Mechanic, D. (1962). *Students Under Stress*. Glencoe, IL: The Free Press.

Munsey, C. (2006). Soldier support: psychologists help troops handle the stresses of combat in Iraq and the anxieties of coming home. *Monitor on Psychology, 37*, 36–37.

NATO Research and Technology Organisation (2007). *A Leader's Guide to Psychological Support across the Deployment Cycle* (RTO-TR-HFM-081). Retrieved 26 April 2007, from the NATO RTO website: http://www.rta.nato.int/pubs/rdp. asp?RDP=RTO-TR-HFM-081

Nisenbaum, R., Barett, D., Reyes, M. & Reeves, W. (2000). Deployment stressors and a chronic multi-symptom illness among Gulf War veterans. *Journal of Nervous and Mental Diseases, 188*, 259–266.

Norwood, A. (1997). Joining forces: psychiatry and readiness. *Military Medicine, 162*, 225–228.

Planz, S. & Sonnek, S. (2002). Work stress in the military: prevalence, causes, and relationship to emotional health. *Military Medicine, 167*, 877–882.

Regeka, C., Hill, J. & Glancy, G.D. (2000). Individual predictors of traumatic reactions in firefighters. *Journal of Nervous and Mental Diseases, 188*, 333–339.

Rosen, L. et al. (1999). Gender differences in subjective distress attributable to anticipation of combat among U.S. Army soldiers deployed to the Persian Gulf during Operation Desert Storm. *Military Medicine, 164*, 753–757.

Sadow, D. & Hopkins, B. (1993). Resiliency training and empowerment among homeless, substance-abusing veterans: increasing a sense of self-efficacy and control as a result of resiliency training. *Research Communications in Psychology, Psychiatry and Behavior, 18*, 121–134.

Schaubroeck, J. & Fink, L. (1998). Facilitating and inhibiting effects of job control and social support on stress outcomes and role behaviors: a contingency model. *Journal of Organizational Behavior, 19*, 167–195.

Selye, H. (1956). *The Stress of Life*. New York: McGraw-Hill.

Sharkansky, E. et al. (2000). Coping with Gulf War combat stress: mediating and moderating effects. *Journal of Abnormal Psychology, 109*, 188–197.

Shigemura, J. & Nomura, S. (2002). Mental health of peacekeeping workers. *Psychiatry and Clinical Neurosciences, 56*, 483–491.

Siebert, A. (1996). *The Survivor Personality*. New York: Perigee Books.

Siebert, A. (2002). How resilience works. Letter to editor. *Harvard Business Review*, July, 121.

Solomon, Z. & Berger, R. (2005). Coping with the aftermath of terror: resilience of ZAKA body handlers. *Journal of Aggression, Maltreatment & Trauma, 10*, 593–604.

Stogdill, R. (1974). *Handbook of Leadership: Survey of Theory and Research*. New York: Free Press.

Tugade, M., Fredrickson, B. & Barrett, L. (2004). Psychological resilience and positive emotional granularity: examining the benefits of positive emotions on coping and health. *Journal of Personality, 72*, 1162–1190.

Turnipseed, D. (1999). An analysis of the influence of work environment variables and moderators of the burnout syndrome. *Journal of Applied Social Psychology, 25*, 782–800.

Van Breda, A. (1999). Developing resilience to routine separations: an occupational social work intervention. *Families in Society, 80*, 597–605.

Vogt, D., Pless, A., King, L. & King, D. (2005). Deployment stressors, gender and mental health outcomes among Gulf War I veterans. *Journal of Traumatic Stress, 18,* 115–127.

Vroom, V. & Yetton, P. (1973). *Leadership and Decision-Making.* Pittsburgh, PA: University of Pittsburgh Press.

Waite, P. & Richardson, G. (2004). Determining the efficacy of resilience training in the work site. *Journal of Allied Health, 33,* 178–183.

Walsh, F. (1998). *Strengthening Family Resilience.* New York: Guilford Press.

Walsh, F. (2002). A family resilience framework: innovative practice applications. *Family Relations, 51,* 130–139.

Weerts, J. et al. (2002). Studies on military peacekeepers. In: Yael, D. (Ed.), *Sharing the Front Line and the Back Hills: International Protectors and Provincial Peacekeepers, Humanitarian Aid Workers and the Media in the Midst of Crisis.* Amityville, NY: Baywood Publishing.

Yerks, S. (1993). The "uncomfortable": making sense of adaptation to war zone. *Military Medicine, 158,* 421–423.

Youssef, C.M. & Luthans, F. (2005). Resiliency development of organizations, leaders & employees: multi-level theory building for sustained performance. In: Gardner, W., Avolio, B.J. & Walumbwa, F.O. (Eds.), *Authentic Leadership Theory and Practice. Origins, Effects, and Development.* Oxford, U.K.: Elsevier.

Yukl, G. (2005). *Leadership in Organizations.* Englewood Cliffs, NJ: Prentice Hall.

Section II

Physiology of Stress
and Resilience

Adaptation to Stress and Psychobiological Mechanisms of Resilience

5

STEVEN M. SOUTHWICK
Yale University School of Medicine
National Center for PTSD

FATIH OZBAY
Yale University School of Medicine

DENNIS CHARNEY
Mount Sinai School of Medicine

BRUCE S. McEWEN
The Rockefeller University

Contents

The human biobehavioral stress response consists of behavioral and physiological reactions to "stressors" (events or situations) that are perceived as difficult, threatening, challenging, or dangerous. Challenges that are exhilarating and manageable are sometimes described as "good" (i.e., motivating) stress, whereas those that imply threat and danger, or are persistent and irritating, are usually seen as "bad" (unhealthy) stress. The frequency and the duration of stress may determine whether its ultimate effects are positive or negative. Also important is whether and to what extent an individual feels a sense of control or mastery over a challenging situation or its outcome.

Stress-related trauma may result from exposure to extreme stress or violence such as experience in combat or a natural disaster, or it may occur as the result of physical or psychological abuse. Less extreme but more pervasive are a variety of relatively ordinary and sometimes chronic stressors encountered in the course of daily life. These might include persistent financial burdens and everyday hassles at work and at home as well as less frequent but unavoidable life events such as job loss, relocation, divorce, or the death of a loved one. Stress-related health problems may result from chronic physical stress due to heat, cold, hunger, injury, substance abuse, and vigorous physical activity beyond one's capacity. Quality and quantity of sleep, diet, and exercise also play an important role in determining how the human body and brain will handle stress.

In this chapter, we consider the neurobiological basis for resilience to stress in terms of brain structures, processes, and mechanisms associated with the regulation of factors and phenomena related to resilience. It is important to note that because these mechanisms are highly complex and involve a host of neurotransmitters, peptides, and hormones that interact with multiple neural circuits—including those involved in the regulation of fear, reward, learning, and social behavior—they are not yet fully understood. Nor is the psychological construct of resilience yet well-defined. Thus, our consideration is constrained by limitations common to the discussion of relationships between brain and behavior. Our observations are offered as a model to guide future theory and research in this area.

The Stress Response

Systemic stress mediators are produced by the autonomic, neuroendocrine, and immune systems. These mediators interact in a nonlinear manner, as illustrated in Figure 5.1. Regulated by endogenous biological clocks found in each cell and coordinated by a central pacemaker located in the suprachiasmatic nucleus of the brain, these mediators also perform "housekeeping" functions. In contrast to the notion of general adaptation syndrome (Selye, 1998), each type of mediator responds to different types of challenges in somewhat different ways.

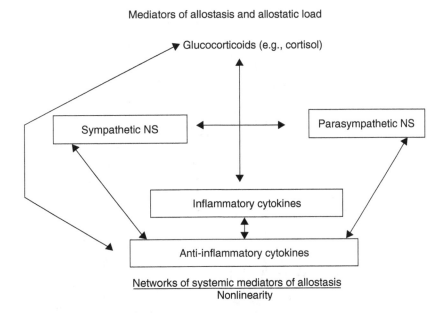

Figure 5.1 Interacting mediators of stress response. Each mediator affects the activity of other mediators in positive and negative ways. The result is a nonlinear network of effects on sympathetic and parasympathetic nervous system functions.

Adaptation to Stress

Initial responses to stress are primitive but effective means to improve the odds of survival. The classic fight-or-flight response involves activation of immune function, energy mobilization, and memory enhancement to recognize and avoid similar dangers in the future (McEwen, 2006). To emphasize the importance of adaptive function and to clarify ambiguities associated with stress as a general term, McEwen coined the term "allostasis" (McEwen, 1998; McEwen & Stellar, 1993). Allostasis refers to the process of achieving stability (i.e., homeostasis) through change. This process involves each of the stress response mediators shown in Figure 5.1. The activities of these mediators ensure maintenance of specific parameters (pH values, oxygen tension, and body temperature) within a narrow range as necessary for survival.

Allostatic overload.   Chronic stress can lead to fatigue, anxiety, anger, frustration, and a feeling of lacking control. People sometimes describe this experience as feeling "stressed out." The consequences and the symptoms of chronic stress may include sleep deprivation, overeating, alcohol abuse, smoking, and other types of unhealthy or dangerous behavior that, if continued over days, weeks, months, or years, can cause dysregulation of critical stress response mediators and thus interfere with allostasis. The consequence of chronic stress is described as allostatic overload (McEwen & Wingfield, 2003) (Figure 5.2).

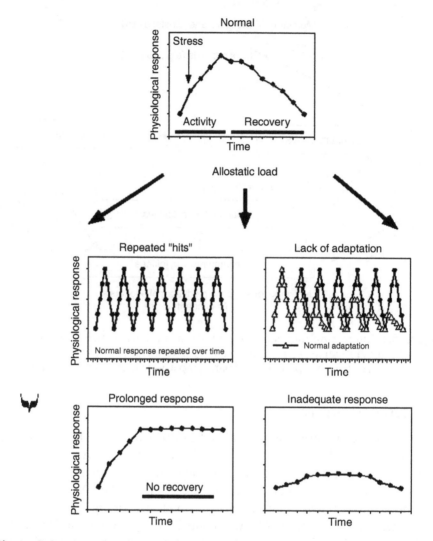

Figure 5.2 Allostatic overload. Top panel shows a normal stress response that is turned on by the stressor and shut off when the stressor is removed. The repetition of many stressful events (upper left panel) and the lack of adaptation (upper right panel) illustrate two types of chronicity leading to allostatic overload. Individual stress responses may be prolonged (lower left panel) or inadequate to the situation (lower right panel). When there is excess or insufficiency of one mediator (e.g., cortisol), other mediators are also affected (e.g., elevated inflammation associated with low cortisol; reduced inflammation associated with high cortisol). (From McEwen, B.S., *New Engl. J. Med.*, 338, 171–179, 1998. With permission.)

Allostatic overload is an essentially unhealthy outcome of chronic stress. Initially, many predisease indicators are made worse by chronic stress. Such indicators may include hypertension, obesity, metabolic alterations (e.g., elevated cholesterol and proinflammatory cytokines), loss of bone mineral and muscle protein, shortening of telomeres and reduced telomerase activity, memory impairment, and increased anxiety. Over longer periods of time, overt disease becomes more likely. Certainly, individuals vary in their genetic and psychological vulnerability to disease. It is not yet known precisely to what extent chronic stress increases vulnerability to specific types of illness, but the well-known multiple biochemical effects of stress make it reasonable to consider the potentially broad effects of chronic stress on multiple body systems and disease-related processes.

Stress and the Brain

The brain is the gatekeeper to the social and physical environment (see Figure 5.3). When an event is perceived as threatening, associated behavioral and physiological responses are determined by processes in specific brain structures. Stress alters the chemistry of the brain and can also effect changes in brain circuitry. Evidence of neuroanatomical and neurochemical changes indicate that the brain itself is sensitive to both acute and chronic stress. The functional effects of these changes may include anxiety, memory impairment, altered judgment, and increased sensitivity to drugs and alcohol. The biochemical mechanisms for these effects are complex, involving circulating hormones as well as endogenous mediators such as neurotransmitters and neurotrophins. In general, these effects can be attributed to stress-related changes that occur in structures of the brain limbic system (hypothalamus, amygdala, and hippocampus) and in the prefrontal cortex.

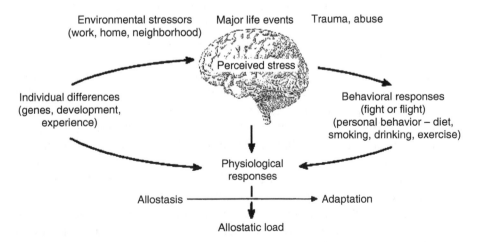

Figure 5.3 The brain as gatekeeper for stress perception and behavioral and physiological stress responses. (From McEwen, B.S., *New Engl. J. Med.*, 338, 171–179, 1998. With permission.)

The hypothalamus is a nexus for inputs from the rest of the brain, and serves as a regulatory center for many physical processes and systems, including responses to emotional stimuli and stress. The amygdala plays a critical role in mediating fear and aggression. The amygdala also sends signals that activate autonomic and hormonal responses to stress. These signals are associated with behavioral responses to stress, including "freezing" in response to danger (LeDoux, 1996). Cells in the amygdala undergo physical changes (remodeling of dendrites and synaptic connections) in response to repeated stress. In addition, there is recent evidence to indicate that a single exposure to traumatic stress may provoke new synapse formation or retraction in the amygdala and that such changes are accompanied by aggressive and anxious behavior (McEwen & Chattarji, 2004). For example, exposure to a single acute immobilization stress for the first time in a rat's life causes increased anxiety that can be measured 10 days later, along with increased density of spine synapses in the amygdala (Vyas, Mitra, Shankaranarayana Rao & Chattarji, 2002). Similar effects have been observed to last for weeks in rats after exposure to a natural predator such as a cat (Adamec, Burton, Shallow & Budgell, 1998; Mesches, Fleshner, Heman, Rose & Diamond, 1999), and there is evidence for lasting effects of such exposure on autonomic, neuroendocrine, and behavioral indices (Korte, Koolhaas, Wingfield & McEwen, 2005).

The hippocampus is a brain structure that is essential to memory. The hippocampus works together with the amygdala to store information about "where we were and what we were doing" at the time of an emotionally charged event. The hippocampus also plays a key role in spatial navigation and memories of events in daily life. When exposed to chronic stress, the hippocampus itself undergoes structural remodeling; hippocampal cells demonstrate changes in spine synapse density, dendrite branching, and length (McEwen, 1999). These changes are accompanied by deficits in hippocampal-dependent memory (Conrad, LeDoux, Magariños & McEwen, 1999).

The prefrontal cortex acts as a master control region for both autonomic and neuroendocrine responses to stress. Prefrontal cortical processes also serve to limit impulsive behavior and support executive functions such as decision-making and the shifting of attention to newly relevant stimuli that predict reward or punishment (Damasio, 1997). Repeated stress causes remodeling of prefrontal neuronal dendrites and synaptic connections; these changes are accompanied by impairment in tests of mental flexibility and attention shifting (Liston et al., 2006; Radley et al., 2005; Wellman, 2001). Although the predominant effect of repeated stress is retraction of dendrites and spines, there is also evidence for stress-induced expansion of dendrites in the orbitofrontal cortex. Dendrites and spines in the prefrontal cortex may respond rapidly to acute stressors (Izquierdo, Wellman & Holmes, 2006).

Repeated exposure to unavoidable stress can lead to "learned helplessness," which can be understood as a learned sense of futility (versus control). Learned helplessness is associated with specific brain chemical and structural alterations. For example, recent work has highlighted the importance of downstream inhibitory control of the serotonin system in the midbrain, over-activity of which is a key feature of learned helplessness. Specifically, lesions of the rat medial prefrontal cortex cause serotonin hyperactivity and learned helplessness behavior even when rats are given the option to control the stressor stimulus (Amat et al., 2005). Research in this area suggests that the prefrontal cortex plays an important role in mediating sense of control, which in turn appears to be a critical feature of resilience to stress. In the following section, we consider this and other findings relevant to the neurobiological basis of resilience to stress.

Neurochemistry of Resilience to Stress

The mediators of allostasis (e.g., cortisol and adrenalin) act in the short run to promote adaptation to acute stress, leading, for example, to enhanced immune defense, memory for places that are dangerous, replenishment of depleted energy resources, and more efficient cardiovascular function (e.g., to enable flight from danger). However, when these same mediators become over-active or when the network of allostasis depicted in Figure 5.1 becomes dysregulated, potentially deleterious consequences include impaired immune function, impaired memory, increased anxiety, and other changes associated with allostatic load (see earlier discussion). In this context, resilience can be conceived as the ability to minimize allostatic load, for example, by switching off the allostatic stress response when the stimulus threat or danger has ended.

Autonomic Nervous System Responses to Stress

The autonomic nervous system (ANS) regulates involuntary functions such as heart rate, blood pressure, and digestion. Its two subsystems—the sympathetic nervous system (SNS) and the parasympathetic nervous system (PNS) —exert opposing effects to maintain a balance in the functioning of these vital bodily systems. The SNS responds to stress by increasing heart rate, constricting blood vessels, increasing blood pressure, and slowing down digestion. However, there is significant individual variability in the extent of these responses. Some people overreact to stress by demonstrating an unusually robust SNS response to stress. If left unchecked, persistent SNS hyperresponsiveness can contribute to depression, chronic anxiety, posttraumatic stress disorder (PTSD), and increased risk for a host of medical conditions, including hypertension, cardiovascular disease, and disorders of immune function.

Conversely, it appears that individuals who are resilient to stress are able to maintain SNS activation within a more conservative window of effective but adaptive responsiveness. It has been proposed that such individuals are activated to an extent that is strong enough to respond effectively to danger but moderate enough to avoid incapacitation, depression, anxiety, and debilitating fear (Charney, 2004; Morgan III et al., 2002; Southwick, Vythilingam & Charney, 2005). Dienstbier (1991), summarizing data from multiple studies, has proposed that performance is enhanced during optimal SNS activation: relatively low levels of baseline epinephrine with robust increases in epinephrine and norepinephrine (NE) in response to challenges, followed by relatively rapid return to baseline levels.

Neuropeptide Y (NPY), an amino acid that is released with NE when the SNS is strongly activated, is one of the neurochemicals that helps to maintain SNS activity within an optimal activation range (reviewed by Southwick et al., 1999). One effect of NPY is to inhibit the continued release of NE so that the SNS does not overshoot. Preliminary studies of highly resilient special operations soldiers (special forces) have shown that during extremely stressful training scenarios, high levels of NPY are associated with better performance (Morgan III et al., 2000, 2002). It is possible that rapid and marked increases in NE among these soldiers are held in check by robust increases in NPY.

By contrast, researchers have observed reduced levels of NPY among combat veterans diagnosed with PTSD (Rasmusson et al., 2000). When the SNS is stressed or provoked, these individuals demonstrate an associated increase in NE, but the accompanying release of NPY may be inadequate to hold the rising levels of NE in check. Numerous neurobiological studies strongly suggest that an increase in NE can contribute to an exaggerated increase in heart rate, blood pressure, respiratory rate, anxiety, panic, vigilance, and intrusive trauma-related memories (reviewed in Southwick et al., 1999). Thus, it appears that NPY plays a role in mediating resilience to stress.

Galanin, a peptide that is involved in neuroendocrine control, cardiovascular regulation, food intake, pain control, learning and memory, and anxiety may also be associated with resilience to stress. Like NPY, galanin is coexpressed in a high percentage of noradrenergic neurons and tends to be released when NE activity is high. In rats, central administration of galanin reduces the firing rate of the locus coeruleus, which contains more than half of the brain's noradrenergic neurons, and when injected into the amygdala blocks the anxiogenic effects of stress (Bing, Moller, Engel, Soderpalm & Heilig, 1993; Möller, Sommer, Thorsell & Heilig, 1999). The overall net effect of NE hyperactivity may thus depend on the balance between NE, NPY, and galanin. This supports the notion that resilience to stress is associated with the regulation of noradrenergic activity within an optimal window.

Hypothalamic-Pituitary-Adrenal Axis Responses to Stress

In response to acute and chronic stresses, the hypothalamus secretes corticotropin-releasing factor (CRF), which in turn stimulates the anterior pituitary gland to synthesize and release adrenocorticotropin hormone (ACTH). ACTH stimulates the synthesis and release of adrenal cortisol and dehydroepiandrosterone (DHEA). In the short run, cortisol mobilizes and replenishes energy stores, inhibits growth and reproductive systems, contains the immune response, and affects behavior through actions on multiple neurotransmitter systems and brain regions (Yehuda, 2002). However, animal studies have shown that if stress remains chronic, prolonged elevations of glucocorticoid may cause damage to CA3 pyramidal neurons of the hippocampus; changes include reductions in dendritic branching, a loss of dendritic spines, and a reduction in the growth of new granule cell neurons in the dentate gyrus (Sapolsky, 2003). Damage to the hippocampus may impair its normal capacity to inhibit the HPA axis, resulting in even greater glucocorticoid levels and possible additional damage to the hippocampus.

Corticotropin-releasing hormone (CRH) initiates the neuroendocrine response to stress by stimulating the pituitary gland to release ACTH and the locus coeruleus to release NE (Grammatopoulos & Chrousos, 2002). When CRF is administered centrally, it causes increased heart rate, increased blood pressure, decreased appetite, decreased sexual activity, increased arousal, and a reduction in reward expectations (Owens & Nemeroff, 1991). These changes and symptoms are commonly seen in depression and anxiety. The activation of CRH-1 receptors is associated with anxiety-like responses, while the stimulation of CRH-2 receptors is associated with anxiolytic-like responses (Bale et al., 2000, 2002). It has been proposed that regulation of these two CRH receptor types influences psychological and physiological responses to stress. The capacity to restrain or regulate the initial CRH response to acute stress and the prolonged CRH response to chronic stress may facilitate psychobiological resilience to stress-induced disorders such as PTSD and depression.

DHEA helps to modulate the effects of cortisol. In the brain, DHEA's antiglucocorticoid and antiglutamatergic activity may confer neuroprotection (reviewed in Charney, 2004). The administration of DHEA has been shown to exert antidepressant effects in patients diagnosed with major depression (Wolkowitz et al., 1999). Various studies of DHEA effects suggest that DHEA plays a role in neurobiological resilience to stress. Findings include a negative correlation between plasma DHEA levels and depression (Goodyer, Herbert & Altham, 1998); a negative relationship between

DHEA/cortisol ratio and dissociation (Morgan III et al., 2004); a negative correlation between DHEA reactivity (in response to ACTH administration) and severity of PTSD symptoms (Rasmusson et al., 2004); and a positive correlation between DHEA/cortisol ratio and performance among elite special forces soldiers during intensive survival training (Morgan III et al., 2004).

Allopregnanolone, another neuroactive steroid, may play a role in determining vulnerability versus resilience to stress. Allopregnanolone has anxiolytic effects when it is released by the adrenal gland during stress. It is believed that allopregnanolone exerts negative feedback inhibition to the HPA axis. In a recent study of premenopausal women during the follicular phase of their menstrual cycles, cerebrospinal fluid levels of allopregnanolone were significantly lower in those diagnosed with PTSD compared with controls (Rasmusson et al., 2006). It is possible that DHEA and allopregnanolone may confer resilience to stress by helping to terminate and protect against the damage effects of prolonged HPA axis activation.

Genetic Factors Associated with SNS and HPA Responses to Stress

Genetic factors contribute to an individual's capacity to cope with stressful experiences by interacting with environmental factors. In the field of statistical genetics, heritability refers to the proportion of variation in a trait that is directly explained by genetic factors. Responses to traumatic experiences may be influenced by heritable factors linked to the variability of personality traits, trauma exposure history, and psychophysiological reactivity. For example, in a study of 100 healthy twin female pairs, investigators showed that heart rate, skin conductance, and blood pressure responses to socially stressful films were moderately heritable (Lensvelt-Mulders & Hettema, 2001). Several twin studies of Vietnam War veterans have also shown that genetic factors play a significant role in PTSD (see Baker, Risbrough & Schork, this volume; True et al., 1993).

Of primary relevance here is the question of genetic influence upon nervous system activity, in particular SNS and HPA responses involved in moderating adaptation to stress. One recent example for a genetically mediated variation in SNS activity was reported by Finley et al. (2004), who found that a polymorphism in the alpha adrenergic-2 receptor gene was associated with autonomic hyper-responsiveness in healthy subjects. Similarly, NPY levels during stress exposure have been shown to be affected by polymorphism in the gene that encodes the NPY molecule (Kallio et al., 2001). The relationship between life stress, noradrenergic systems, and depression appears to be mediated, in part, by alpha-2 adrenergic receptor subtypes. Studies employing knockout mice suggest that the alpha-2a adrenergic receptor is stress protective, while the alpha-2c adrenergic receptor contributes to stress susceptibility. Additionally, prolonged stress has been shown to decrease alpha-2 adrenergic receptor density in limbic brain structures (Jimenez-Rivera et al., 1996).

The HPA system is dependent on the expression of multiple genes, each containing several polymorphisms that may modify an individual's response to stress. For example, the μ-opioid receptor gene (Hernandez-Avila, Wand, Luo, Gelernter & Kranzler, 2003), the angiotensin I-converting enzyme (ACE-I) gene (Baghai et al., 2002), and the ACTH gene (Slawik et al., 2004) are all known to harbor mutations that affect the release of cortisol and ACTH in response to stress. An interesting study by Wust et al. (2004) demonstrated that a particular glucocorticoid receptor gene variant can reduce cortisol release in response to psychosocial stress. Additional studies are needed to elucidate the association between the neurosteroid response to stress and the heritable variation within HPA system genes.

Other than the preliminary studies identified above, it is largely unknown which specific genes confer resilience via specific mechanisms in humans. Researchers in the field of molecular genetics have only recently begun to investigate gene–environment interactions as they relate to various psychiatric disorders. For example, it is established that polymorphism in the serotonin transporter (5-HTT) attenuates vulnerability to major depression and suicidal response to stressful life events (Caspi et al., 2003). This is the first genetic variant that has been identified as a possible inherited resilience factor. The same genetic polymorphism has also been linked to reduced vulnerability to social stressors in women (Grabe et al., 2005). Very recently, Kaufman et al. (2006) reported that the brain-derived neurotrophic-factor (BDNF) gene and 5-HTT genes, in conjunction with low social support, cumulatively increase the risk for depression in maltreated children.

These preliminary findings are consistent with the stress-diathesis theory, which proposes that psychiatric symptoms are caused by environmental stressors only when there is genetic or developmental vulnerability. Individuals who inherit and carry certain alleles may thus be resilient to specific effects of stress and associated psychological sequelae. If so, inherited biological resilience may serve as a first-line defense against the effects of stress and trauma. With the identification of additional resilience-related genes and a better understanding of the mechanisms by which they counter environmental stress, we may be able to conceptualize new biological interventions to administer as a means to promote resilience in the immediate aftermath of trauma. Future genetic studies focusing on intermediate or endophenotypes of pathology and resilience may elucidate additional relevant gene–environment interactions.

Developmental Influences on SNS, HPA, and Resilience

Early stress in the form of prolonged and variable postnatal maternal separation has repeatedly been shown to promote long-term changes in brain
regions and neurotransmitter systems that have been implicated in the
pathophysiology of depression, PTSD, and resilience. For example, chronic
hyper-responsiveness of the HPA axis, the locus coeruleus/noradrenergic
system, and exaggerated emotional reactivity to stress all have been associated with prolonged and variable maternal separation (Bremner & Vermetten,
2001). It is likely that such exaggerated reactivity increases reactivity and vulnerability to the later development of stress-related disorders such as depression and PTSD (Kaufman, Plotsky, Nemeroff & Charney, 2000).

On the other hand, there exists a body of animal studies whose results
suggest that early exposure to mild to moderate stress that can be managed
may actually enhance the capacity to cope with stress in the future (see review
by Dienstbier, 1989). Controlled exposure to stress, as a means to enhance
resilience to stress, is known as stress inoculation. In studies of squirrel
monkeys, Parker, Buckmaster, Schatzberg, and Lyons (2004) found that stress
inoculation via brief intermittent maternal separation during postnatal weeks
17–27 led to diminished anxiety responses on subsequent exposure to a novel
environment. Stress-inoculated monkeys were also found to have lower basal
plasma ACTH and cortisol levels, and lower stress-induced cortisol levels. At
18 months of age, these monkeys were administered a response inhibition test
and were found to have superior prefrontal cortex function compared with
non-stress inoculated monkeys (Parker, Buckmaster, Justus, Schatzberg &
Lyons, 2005). These results suggest that early, mild, and controlled stress may
alter key neurobiological systems and thus serve to reduce allostatic load upon
future exposure to stress.

Rats reared in a nurturing environment have also been found to demonstrate enhanced tolerance to stress in adulthood. Rat pups that receive
15 min of handling per day during the first 3 weeks of life are less reactive to stress and less fearful in novel environments as adults compared
with rat pups that are not handled (Ladd, Thrivikraman, Huot & Plotsky,
2005). They also demonstrate reduced ACTH and corticosterone responses
to stress as well as a more rapid return of corticosterone levels to baseline
after exposure to stress. It appears that early environments influence and
shape the development of stress-related neurobiological systems with early
deprivation and uncontrollable stress promoting future exaggerated neurobiological stress reactivity (stress sensitization) and early nurturing or mild
to moderate stress having a positive effect on future stress reactivity (stress
inoculation). Of note, animal "adoption" studies have shown that even after
stress-induced neurobiological and behavioral alterations occur, it may be

possible to modify these alterations by subsequent supportive maternal care giving and pharmacological interventions (Caldji et al., 1998; Kuhn & Schanberg, 1998).

Far less is known about the effects of early environment on later neurobiological stress reactivity in human beings. In one study, pediatric inpatients with previous positive separation experiences (i.e., staying with grandparents for short periods of time) experienced less stress during their hospital stays (Stacey, 1970). Childhood exposure to mild stress has also been associated with reduced heart rate and blood pressure responses to distressing laboratory tests in adolescents (Boyce & Chesterman, 1990). Further, better psychiatric outcomes have been reported among adult natural disaster and torture survivors who had experienced similarly traumatic events earlier in their lives (Basoglu et al., 1997; Knight, Gatz, Heller & Bengtson, 2000; Norris & Murrell, 1988).

The notion that manageable and controlled doses of stress can have steeling or stress-inoculating effects has been incorporated into a number of clinical therapeutic approaches for the treatment and/or prevention of trauma. Using a stress inoculation-based intervention, Wells, Howard, Nowlin, and Vargas (1986) demonstrated that surgical patients who underwent preoperative stress inoculation experienced less postoperative pain and anxiety. Similarly, stress-inoculation training has been found to be an effective treatment for chronically stressed community residents (Long, 1985). The neurobiological basis for stress-inoculation effects in human subjects is not yet well understood.

Psychosocial Factors of Allostatic Load and Resilience

Psychological resilience to stress has been considered for its relationship to numerous psychosocial variables, many of which are discussed throughout this volume. Here, we address four psychosocial factors of particular relevance to the neurobiological systems considered in the present chapter. Although our current understanding of these factors remains incomplete, the existing body of literature is sufficient to suggest relationships of interest.

Dispositional Optimism

Dispositional optimism is thought to be an important psychosocial factor in the moderation of stress. Defined as generalized positive expectations for the future, optimism has been associated with reduced psychiatric symptoms upon exposure to stressful life events (Carver et al., 1999); better self-reported physical health (Scheier et al., 1989); lower blood pressure and reduced rehospitalization risk following coronary vascular surgery (Scheier et al., 1999); buffering blood pressure responses to violence exposure (Clark, Benkert & Flack, 2006); higher natural killer cell cytotoxicity (NKCC) in HIV+ women (Byrnes et al., 1998) and men with prostate cancer (Penedo et al., 2006); lower HIV viral load among gay men (Milam, Richardson, Marks, Kemper & McCutchan, 2004); and lower mortality in patients with head and neck cancers (Allison, Guichard, Fung & Gilain, 2003). On the other hand, different investigators have failed to find an association between optimism and reduced mortality in lung cancer patients (Schofield et al., 2004) and CD4 count among HIV+ gay men (Tomakowsky, Lumley, Markowitz & Frank, 2001).

To delineate the differential effects of optimism on coping with brief versus long-term stress, Cohen et al. (1999) followed a cohort of 39 women for 3 months and measured their NKCC, CD4, and CD8 T cell sublets. Using an autoregressive linear model, the authors found that optimism moderated immune outcomes differentially in response to acute versus persistent stressors. Specifically, while optimism buffered immune response parameters following exposure to acute stress, optimists also had more immune decrements than pessimists upon exposure to chronic stress (Cohen et al., 1999). Sieber et al. (1992) studied changes in NKCC in adult males after exposure to controllable and uncontrollable stresses (noise) and found that subjects who perceived that they had control over the stressor did not show any reduction in NKCC. However, optimism amplified the detrimental effects of uncontrollable stress on NK activity. Segerstrom, Taylor, Kemeny, and Fahey (1998) argued that negative effects of optimism on the immune system might be explained by "the engagement hypothesis," which asserts that optimistic (versus pessimistic) people remain engaged with stressful conditions for longer periods of time. For example, when highly difficult research subjects are given or impossible anagrams are to be solved, optimism serves to increase their task engagement time and skin conductance, and recovery levels of salivary cortisol (Nes, Segerstrom & Sephton, 2005). Segerstrom, Taylor, Kemeny, and Fahey (1998) speculated that optimism may enhance immunity by enabling early termination of response to relatively easy or straightforward stress via problem-solving, but that immune dysfunction occurs as the result of prolonged exposure to persistent, chronic, or complex stress. In other words, optimism may facilitate allostasis when the stressors are brief and simple, but may increase allostatic load when stressors are chronic and complex.

Additional support for the moderating effects of optimism can be found in studies of baseline and stress-induced cortisol levels. Lai et al. (2005) found that subjects with higher optimism scores also had lower cortisol secretion in the mornings. Creswell et al. (2005) have observed that the affirmation of personal values prior to stress exposure is associated with lower subsequent cortisol responses to stress and that optimism appeared to be an important moderating factor for this effect.

Exercise

Many scientific studies have demonstrated that moderate exercise leads to improved physical and mental health. Good physical fitness has been shown to delay death, particularly from causes such as cardiovascular disease and cancer, while poor physical fitness is associated with early death by numerous medical conditions (Blair et al., 1989). Moderate exercise also tends to improve emotional well-being. In a large study of subjects from 15 member states of the European Union, subjects who were physically active reported better mental health than those who were sedentary (Abu-Omar, Rutten & Robine, 2004). Exercise has also been shown to be effective as a means to improve mild depressive symptoms among otherwise healthy individuals and as a means to reduce the severity of depression in young adult, middle-aged, and older subjects diagnosed with major depressive disorder. A meta-analysis has found that exercise is as effective as cognitive behavioral therapy for reducing mood-related symptoms in patients suffering from depression (Manber, Allen & Morris, 2002). In a randomized controlled treatment study of middle-aged men with major depression, 16 weeks of aerobic exercise was as effective in reducing the symptoms of depression as was either 16 weeks of treatment with the antidepressant sertraline or 16 weeks of exercise plus sertraline (Babyak et al., 2000).

Aerobic exercise also appears to decrease anxiety in healthy individuals and in patients with anxiety disorders (Broman-Fulks, Berman, Rabian & Webster, 2004; Fremont & Wilcoxon Craighead, 1987; McAuley, Mihalko & Bane, 1996; Salmon, 2001), particularly those who misinterpret and catastrophize anxiety-related physical symptoms (e.g., rapid heart rate, sweating). When "anxiety sensitive" individuals exercise regularly and vigorously, they can learn that physical signs of physiological activation and arousal are not dangerous. Regular exercise has also been shown to improve cognition and memory and to exert a protective effect in elderly individuals with and without Alzheimer's disease (Colcombe et al., 2004; Friedland et al., 2001; Laurin, Verreault, Lindsay, MacPherson & Rockwood, 2001). Although there are relatively few well-controlled studies of exercise and mental health, on the whole it appears that moderate exercise is associated with both physical and psychological well-being (Paluska & Schwenk, 2000). In formerly sedentary elderly adults, daily exercise such as 30 minutes of walking for just 6 months leads to improved executive function and attention and also increases associated activation of prefrontal and parietal cortices.

The positive effects of exercise on physical and mental health are likely due to its impact upon the stress response, allostasis, and allostatic load.

For example, physical exertion and mental stress are known to cause robust activation of the HPA axis. However, this response tends to be dampened in exercise-trained, aerobically fit individuals. The result is reduced cortisol release, less brain exposure to cortisol, and possibly less neuronal damage. Additionally, it is well known that aerobically fit individuals tend to have reduced heart rate and blood pressure and that these parameters return more rapidly to baseline after physical exertion in individuals who are aerobically fit (Dienstbier, 1991).

Exercise also appears to reduce allostatic load by enhancing neurogenesis and increasing a number of nerve growth factors such as BDNF. BDNF is a protein that is known to enhance the growth of brain cells, cell survival (Barde, 1994), formation of connections between neurons based on activation patterns, and learning and repair of damaged nerve cells (Cotman & Berchtold, 2002). Unlike chronic stress, which reduces the effectiveness of neurotrophic factors, aerobic exercise increases the production of these factors by "turning on" relevant genes. Increased levels of neurotrophic factors (e.g., BDNF) have been detected in rodent brains after several days to several weeks of wheel running. It is also likely that chronic stress impairs neurogenesis in human subjects, which may, in turn, contribute to depression and poor cognitive functioning. Further, it is likely that vigorous aerobic exercise increases neurogenesis in human subjects, which may help to improve cognition and reduce symptoms of depression (Smith, Makino, Kvetnansky & Post, 1995).

Finally, aerobic exercise may serve to protect against the negative effects of future stress. Rats that are kept stationary for a week prior to severe experimentally induced stress experience greater reductions in hippocampal BDNF and tolerate stress well lesser than do rats that have engaged in voluntary wheel running for the same 1-week period prior to induced stress (Russo-Neustadt, Alejandre, Garcia, Ivy & Chen, 2004). Analogously, in a prospective study of adult human subjects, Harris and colleagues found that exercise predicted less concurrent depression over a period of 10 years (Harris, Cronkite & Moos, 2006). It is important to note, however, that not all studies have observed that physical activity confers protective effects. For additional consideration of exercise and protective effects against stress and trauma, see Friedl and Penetar (this volume).

Social Support

Social support has been extensively studied in relation to stress and resilience. Clinical studies of traumatic stress clearly demonstrate the beneficial effects of social support on mental health. For example, Boscarino (1995) found that after controlling for trauma exposure, military veterans with high levels of social support were 180% less likely to develop PTSD compared with those with low levels of social support.

Oxytocin and vasopressin are two neuropeptides that have been strongly implicated in the regulation of social attachment and the promotion of positive social interactions (Bartz & Hollander, 2006) as well as in the mediation of the anxiolytic effects of social support. Differential oxytocin and vasopressin receptor expression patterns in specific areas of the brain (ventral pallidum and medial amygdala) have been shown to influence the type and the duration of social attachments formed by voles. For example, montane voles typically avoid social contact except while mating; they have lower levels of oxytocin receptors in the nucleus accumbens compared with prairie voles, which are highly social and typically monogamous (Insel & Shapiro, 1992). Oxytocin is critical for learning social cues and has been shown to enhance maternal care in rats (Francis, Champagne & Meaney, 2000). Oxytocin also exerts anxiolytic effects that are associated with attenuated secretion of corticosterone in lactating rodents (Neumann, Torner & Wigger, 2000). One recent study showed that oxytocin served to increase the calming effects of social support among healthy men undergoing the Trier Social Stress Test (Heinrichs, Baumgartner, Kirschbaum & Ehlert, 2003).

Preclinical studies suggest that social isolation is associated with elevated heart rate and blood pressure, hypercortisolemia, and atherosclerosis (Rozanski, Blumenthal & Kaplan, 1999). Results from human studies are consistent in that low social support is associated with increased blood pressure (Uchino, Cacioppo & Kiecolt-Glaser, 1996) and exaggerated cardiovascular and neuroendocrine responses to laboratory stressors (Steptoe, Owen, Kunz-Ebrecht & Brydon, 2004). There is also a vast animal literature to suggest that social support plays a critical role in normal development and responses to early life stressors (for a thorough review, see Kaufman, Plotsky, Nemeroff & Charney, 2000).

In short, the available literature suggests that neurobiological factors play a role in forming social attachments and in mediating the beneficial behavioral and neuroendocrine effects of social support. These findings suggest that it may be possible to intervene and enhance resilience in at-risk individuals by providing them with nurturing environments and social support.

Possible Interventions

The findings and relationships reviewed in this chapter have implications for the prevention and reversal of stress-induced alterations in neurobiological systems and associated behavior and psychiatric symptoms. For example, it may be possible to enhance stress resilience by providing social support, improving aerobic fitness, learning cognitive strategies that promote optimism, and incorporating training principles that serve to "inoculate" against future stress or trauma. In the context of military readiness, these objectives might take the form of refined or additional group training and education (improve unit cohesion), physical fitness (cardiovascular health), stress management techniques (meditation, relaxation), and cognitive behavioral training (orientation to optimism and cognitive reframing). Ideally, such training should be accompanied by efforts to reduce allostatic load by discouraging unhealthy lifestyle choices (smoking, alcohol consumption, sleep deprivation, poor nutrition).

The information considered in this chapter also suggests that it may be useful to consider new pharmacological approaches to the treatment or prevention of traumatic stress effects. Of particular interest would be the development of agents that can effectively stabilize HPA function and reduce SNS reactivity. For example, CRF antagonists could exert anxiolytic, antidepressant, and preventive effects against the development of stress-induced mood and anxiety-related disorders. Additionally, it would be reasonable to predict that agents that help to contain stress-related SNS activation (e.g., agents that modulate NPY and NE release) would thereby enhance resilience to stress. Pharmacologic intervention may prove a useful complement to relaxation techniques and cognitive behavioral therapies that bolster capacity to modulate limbic activity.

Because military life and service can be demanding, stressful, and sometimes traumatizing, it is important to pursue research and applications toward reducing allostatic load and thus promoting the psychological and physical resilience of service members.

References

Abu-Omar, K., Rutten, A. & Robine, J. M. (2004). Self-rated health and physical activity in the European Union. *Sozial- und Praventivmedizin, 49*(4), 235–242.

Adamec, R. E., Burton, P., Shallow, T. & Budgell, J. (1998). NMDA receptors mediate lasting increases in anxiety-like behavior produced by the stress of predator exposure—implications for anxiety associated with posttraumatic stress disorder. *Physiology and Behavior, 65*(4–5), 723–737.

Allison, P. J., Guichard, C., Fung, K. & Gilain, L. (2003). Dispositional optimism predicts survival status 1 year after diagnosis in head and neck cancer patients. *Journal of Clinical Oncology, 21*(3), 543–548.

Amat, J., Baratta, M. V., Paul, E., Bland, S. T., Watkins, L. R. & Maier, S. F. (2005). Medial prefrontal cortex determines how stressor controllability affects behavior and dorsal raphe nucleus. *Nature Neuroscience, 8*(3), 365–371.

Babyak, M., Blumenthal, J. A., Herman, S., Khatri, P., Doraiswamy, M., Moore, K. et al. (2000). Exercise treatment for major depression: maintenance of therapeutic benefit at 10 months. *Psychosomatic Medicine, 62*(5), 633–638.

Baghai, T. C., Schule, C., Zwanzger, P., Minov, C., Zill, P., Ella, R. et al. (2002). Hypothalamic-pituitary-adrenocortical axis dysregulation in patients with major depression is influenced by the insertion/deletion polymorphism in the angiotensin I-converting enzyme gene. *Neuroscience Letters, 328*(3), 299–303.

Bale, T. L., Contarino, A., Smith, G. W., Chan, R., Gold, L. H., Sawchenko, P. E. et al. (2000). Mice deficient for corticotropin-releasing hormone receptor-2 display anxiety-like behaviour and are hypersensitive to stress. *Nature Genetics, 24*(4), 410–414.

Bale, T. L., Picetti, R., Contarino, A., Koob, G. F., Vale, W. W. & Lee, K. (2002). Mice deficient for both corticotropin-releasing factor receptor 1 (CRFR1) and CRFR2 have an impaired stress response and display sexually dichotomous anxiety-like behavior. *Journal of Neuroscience, 22*(1), 193–199.

Barde, Y. A. (1994). Neurotrophins: a family of proteins supporting the survival of neurons. *Progress in Clinical and Biological Research, 390*, 45–56.

Bartz, J. A. & Hollander, E. (2006). The neuroscience of affiliation: forging links between basic and clinical research on neuropeptides and social behavior. *Hormones and Behavior, 50*(4), 518–528.

Basoglu, M., Mineka, S., Paker, M., Aker, T., Livanou, M. & Gok, S. (1997). Psychological preparedness for trauma as a protective factor in survivors of torture. *Psychological Medicine, 27*(6), 1421–1433.

Bing, O., Moller, C., Engel, J. A., Soderpalm, B. & Heilig, M. (1993). Anxiolytic-like action of centrally administered galanin. *Neuroscience Letters, 164*(1-2), 17–20.

Blair, S. N., Kohl, H. W., III, Paffenbarger, R. S., Jr, Clark, D. G., Cooper, K. H. & Gibbons, L. W. (1989). Physical fitness and all-cause mortality. A prospective study of healthy men and women. *Journal of the American Medical Association, 262*(17), 2395–2401.

Boscarino, J. A. (1995). Post-traumatic stress and associated disorders among Vietnam veterans: the significance of combat exposure and social support. *Journal of Traumatic Stress, 8*(2), 317–336.

Boyce, W. T. & Chesterman, E. (1990). Life events, social support, and cardiovascular reactivity in adolescence. *Journal of Developmental and Behavioral Pediatrics, 11*(3), 105–111.

Bremner, J. D. & Vermetten, E. (2001). Stress and development: behavioral and biological consequences. *Development and Psychopathology, 13*(3), 473–489.

Broman-Fulks, J. J., Berman, M. E., Rabian, B. A. & Webster, M. J. (2004). Effects of aerobic exercise on anxiety sensitivity. *Behaviour Research and Therapy, 42*(2), 125–136.

Byrnes, D. M., Antoni, M. H., Goodkin, K., Efantis-Potter, J., Asthana, D., Simon, T. et al. (1998). Stressful events, pessimism, natural killer cell cytotoxicity, and cytotoxic/suppressor T cells in HIV+ black women at risk for cervical cancer. *Psychosomatic Medicine, 60*(6), 714–722.

Caldji, C., Tannenbaum, B., Sharma, S., Francis, D., Plotsky, P. M. & Meaney, M. J. (1998). Maternal care during infancy regulates the development of neural systems mediating the expression of fearfulness in the rat. *Proceedings of the National Academy of Sciences of the United States of America, 95*(9), 5335–5340.

Carver, C. S., Pozo, C., Harris, S. D., Noriega, V., Scheier, M. F., Robinson, D. S. et al. (1999). How coping mediates the effect of optimism on distress: a study of women with early stage breast cancer [references]. Suinn, R. M. VandenBos & Gary, R. (Eds), APA.

Caspi, A., Sugden, K., Moffitt, T. E., Taylor, A., Craig, I. W., Harrington, H. et al. (2003). Influence of life stress on depression: moderation by a polymorphism in the 5-HTT gene. *Science, 301*(5631), 386–389.

Charney, D. S. (2004). Psychobiological mechanism of resilience and vulnerability: implications for successful adaptation to extreme stress. *American Journal of Psychiatry, 161*(2), 195–216.

Clark, R., Benkert, R. A. & Flack, J. M. (2006). Violence exposure and optimism predict task-induced changes in blood pressure and pulse rate in a normotensive sample of inner-city black youth. *Psychosomatic Medicine, 68*(1), 73–79.

Cohen, F., Kearney, K. A., Zegans, L. S., Kemeny, M. E., Neuhaus, J. M. & Stites, D. P. (1999). Differential immune system changes with acute and persistent stress for optimists vs pessimists. *Brain, Behavior, and Immunity, 13*(2), 155–174.

Colcombe, S. J., Kramer, A. F., Erickson, K. I., Scalf, P., McAuley, E., Cohen, N. J. et al. (2004). Cardiovascular fitness, cortical plasticity, and aging. *Proceedings of the National Academy of Sciences of the United States of America, 101*(9), 3316–3321.

Conrad, C. D., LeDoux, J. E., Magariños, A. M. & McEwen, B. S. (1999). Repeated restraint stress facilitates fear conditioning independently of causing hippocampal CA3 dendritic atrophy. *Behavioral Neuroscience, 113*(5), 902–913.

Cotman, C. W. & Berchtold, N. C. (2002). Exercise: a behavioral intervention to enhance brain health and plasticity. *Trends in Neurosciences, 25*(6), 295–301.

Creswell, J. D., Welch, W. T., Taylor, S. E., Sherman, D. K., Gruenewald, T. L. & Mann, T. (2005). Affirmation of personal values buffers neuroendocrine and psychological stress responses. *Psychological Science, 16*(11), 846–851.

Damasio, A. R. (1997). Towards a neuropathology of emotion and mood. *Nature, 386*(6627), 769–770.

Dienstbier, R. A. (1989). Arousal and physiological toughness: implications for mental and physical health. *Psychological Review, 96*(1), 84–100.

Dienstbier, R. A. (1991). Behavioral correlates of sympathoadrenal reactivity: the toughness model. *Medicine and Science in Sports and Exercise, 23*(7), 846–852.

Finley, J. C., Jr, O'Leary, M., Wester, D., MacKenzie, S., Shepard, N., Farrow, S. et al. (2004). A genetic polymorphism of the alpha2-adrenergic receptor increases autonomic responses to stress. *Journal of Applied Physiology: Respiratory, Environmental and Exercise Physiology, 96*(6), 2231–2239.

Francis, D. D., Champagne, F. C. & Meaney, M. J. (2000). Variations in maternal behaviour are associated with differences in oxytocin receptor levels in the rat. *Journal of Neuroendocrinology, 12*(12), 1145–1148.

Fremont, J. & Wilcoxon C. L. (1987). Aerobic exercise and cognitive therapy in the treatment of dysphoric moods. *Cognitive Therapy and Research, 11*(2), 241–251.

Friedland, R. P., Fritsch, T., Smyth, K. A., Koss, E., Lerner, A. J., Chien, H. C. et al. (2001). Patients with Alzheimer's disease have reduced activities in midlife compared with healthy control-group members. *Proceedings of the National Academy of Sciences of the United States of America, 98*(6), 3440–3445.

Goodyer, I. M., Herbert, J. & Altham, P. M. E. (1998). Adrenal steroid secretion and major depression in 8- to 16-year-olds, III. Influence of cortisol/DHEA ratio at presentation on subsequent rates of disappointing life events and persistent major depression. *Psychological Medicine, 28*(2), 265–273.

Grabe, H. J., Lange, M., Wolff, B., Volzke, H., Lucht, M., Freyberger, H. J. et al. (2005). Mental and physical distress is modulated by a polymorphism in the 5-HT transporter gene interacting with social stressors and chronic disease burden. *Molecular Psychiatry, 10*(2), 220–224.

Grammatopoulos, D. K. & Chrousos, G. P. (2002). Functional characteristics of CRH receptors and potential clinical applications of CRH-receptor antagonists. *Trends in Endocrinology and Metabolism, 13*(10), 436–444.

Harris, A. H., Cronkite, R. & Moos, R. (2006). Physical activity, exercise coping, and depression in a 10-year cohort study of depressed patients. *Journal of Affective Disorders, 93*(1–3), 79–85.

Heinrichs, M., Baumgartner, T., Kirschbaum, C. & Ehlert, U. (2003). Social support and oxytocin interact to suppress cortisol and subjective responses to psychosocial stress. *Biological Psychiatry, 54*(12), 1389–1398.

Hernandez-Avila, C. A., Wand, G., Luo, X., Gelernter, J. & Kranzler, H. R. (2003). Association between the cortisol response to opioid blockade and the Asn40Asp polymorphism at the mu-opioid receptor locus (OPRM1). *American Journal of Medical Genetics, Part B, Neuropsychiatric Genetics : The Official Publication of the International Society of Psychiatric Genetics, 118*(1), 60–65.

Insel, T. R. & Shapiro, L. E. (1992). Oxytocin receptor distribution reflects social organization in monogamous and polygamous voles. *Proceedings of the National Academy of Sciences of the United States of America, 89*(13), 5981–5985.

Izquierdo, A., Wellman, C. L. & Holmes, A. (2006). Brief uncontrollable stress causes dendritic retraction in infralimbic cortex and resistance to fear extinction in mice. *Journal of Neuroscience, 26*(21), 5733–5738.

Jimenez-Rivera, C. A., Segarra, O., Santacana, G., Hoffman, T., Savage, D. D. & Weiss, G. K. (1996). Chronic imipramine treatment induces downregulation of alpha-2 receptors in rat's locus coeruleus and A2 region of the tractus solitarius. *Life Sciences, 58*(4), 287–294.

Kallio, J., Pesonen, U., Kaipio, K., Karvonen, M. K., Jaakkola, U., Heinonen, O. J. et al. (2001). Altered intracellular processing and release of neuropeptide Y due to leucine 7 to proline 7 polymorphism in the signal peptide of preproneuropeptide Y in humans. *The FASEB Journal, 15*(7), 1242–1244.

Kaufman, J., Plotsky, P. M., Nemeroff, C. B. & Charney, D. S. (2000). Effects of early adverse experiences on brain structure and function: clinical implications. *Biological Psychiatry, 48*(8), 778–790.

Kaufman, J., Yang, B. Z., Douglas-Palumberi, H., Grasso, D., Lipschitz, D., Houshyar, S. et al. (2006). Brain-derived neurotrophic factor-5-HTTLPR gene interactions and environmental modifiers of depression in children. *Biological Psychiatry, 59*(8), 673–680.

Knight, B. G., Gatz, M., Heller, K. & Bengtson, V. L. (2000). Age and emotional response to the Northridge earthquake: a longitudinal analysis. *Psychology and Aging, 15*(4), 627–634.

Korte, S. M., Koolhaas, J. M., Wingfield, J. C. & McEwen, B. S. (2005). The Darwinian concept of stress: benefits of allostasis and costs of allostatic load and the trade-offs in health and disease. *Neuroscience and Biobehavioral Reviews, 29*(1 special issue), 3–38.

Kuhn, C. M. & Schanberg, S. M. (1998). Responses to maternal separation: mechanisms and mediators. *International Journal of Developmental Neuroscience,* *16*(3–4), 261–270.

Ladd, C. O., Thrivikraman, K. V., Huot, R. L. & Plotsky, P. M. (2005). Differential neuroendocrine responses to chronic variable stress in adult Long Evans rats exposed to handling-maternal separation as neonates. *Psychoneuroendocrinology,* *30*(6), 520–533.

Lai, J. C., Evans, P. D., Ng, S. H., Chong, A. M., Siu, O. T., Chan, C. L. et al. (2005). Optimism, positive affectivity, and salivary cortisol. *British Journal of Health Psychology,* *10*(Pt 4), 467–484.

Laurin, D., Verreault, R., Lindsay, J., MacPherson, K. & Rockwood, K. (2001). Physical activity and risk of cognitive impairment and dementia in elderly persons. *Archives of Neurology,* *58*(3), 498–504.

LeDoux, J. E. (1996). *The Emotional Brain: The Mysterious Underpinnings of Emotional Life.* New York: Simon & Schuster.

Lensvelt-Mulders, G. & Hettema, J. (2001). Genetic analysis of autonomic reactivity to psychologically stressful situations. *Biological Psychology,* *58*(1), 25–40.

Liston, C., Miller, M. M., Goldwater, D. S., Radley, J. J., Rocher, A. B., Hof, P. R. et al. (2006). Stress-induced alterations in prefrontal cortical dendritic morphology predict selective impairments in perceptual attentional set-shifting. *Journal of Neuroscience,* *26*(30), 7870–7874.

Long, B. C. (1985). Stress-management interventions: a 15-month follow-up of aerobic conditioning and stress-inoculation training. *Cognitive Therapy and Research,* *9*(4), 471–478.

Manber, R., Allen, J. J. B. & Morris, M. M. (2002). Alternative treatments for depression: empirical support and relevance to women. *Journal of Clinical Psychiatry,* *63*(7), 628–640.

McAuley, E., Mihalko, S. L. & Bane, S. M. (1996). Acute exercise and anxiety reduction: does the environment matter? *Journal of Sport and Exercise Psychology,* *18*(4), 408–419.

McEwen, B. S. (1998). Seminars in medicine of the Beth Israel Deaconess Medical Center: protective and damaging effects of stress mediators. *New England Journal of Medicine,* *338*(3), 171–179.

McEwen, B. S. (1999). Stress and hippocampal plasticity. *Annual Review of Neuroscience,* *22*, 105–122.

McEwen, B. S. (2006). Protective and damaging effects of stress mediators: central role of the brain. *Dialogues in Clinical Neuroscience,* *8*(4), 367–381.

McEwen, B. S. & Chattarji, S. (2004). Molecular mechanisms of neuroplasticity and pharmacological implications: the example of tianeptine. *European Neuropsychopharmacology,* *14*(Suppl. 5), S497–S502.

McEwen, B. S. & Stellar, E. (1993). Stress and the individual: mechanisms leading to disease. *Archives of Internal Medicine,* *153*(18), 2093–2101.

McEwen, B. S. & Wingfield, J. C. (2003). The concept of allostasis in biology and biomedicine. *Hormones and Behavior,* *43*(1), 2–15.

Mesches, M. H., Fleshner, M., Heman, K. L., Rose, G. M. & Diamond, D. M. (1999). Exposing rats to a predator blocks primed burst potentiation in the hippocampus *in vitro. The Journal of Neuroscience,* *19*(14), RC18 1–5.

Milam, J. E., Richardson, J. L., Marks, G., Kemper, C. A. & McCutchan, A. J. (2004). The roles of dispositional optimism and pessimism in HIV disease progression. *Psychology & Health, 19*(2), 167–181.

Möller, C., Sommer, W., Thorsell, A. & Heilig, M. (1999). Anxiogenic-like action of galanin after intra-amygdala administration in the rat. *Neuropsychopharmacology, 21*(4), 507–512.

Morgan, C. A., III, Rasmusson, A. M., Wang, S., Hoyt, G., Hauger, R. L. & Hazlett, G. (2002). Neuropeptide-Y, cortisol, and subjective distress in humans exposed to acute stress: replication and extension of previous report. *Biological Psychiatry, 52*(2), 136–142.

Morgan, C. A., III, Southwick, S., Hazlett, G., Rasmusson, A., Hoyt, G., Zimolo, Z. et al. (2004). Relationships among plasma dehydroepiandrosterone sulfate and cortisol levels, symptoms of dissociation, and objective performance in humans exposed to acute stress. *Archives of General Psychiatry, 61*(8), 819–825.

Morgan, C. A., III, Wang, S., Southwick, S. M., Rasmusson, A., Hazlett, G., Hauger, R. L. et al. (2000). Plasma neuropeptide-Y concentrations in humans exposed to military survival training. *Biological Psychiatry, 47*(10), 902–909.

Nes, L. S., Segerstrom, S. C. & Sephton, S. E. (2005). Engagement and arousal: optimism's effects during a brief stressor. *Personality and Social Psychology Bulletin, 31*(1), 111–120.

Neumann, I. D., Torner, L. & Wigger, A. (2000). Brain oxytocin: differential inhibition of neuroendocrine stress responses and anxiety-related behaviour in virgin, pregnant and lactating rats. *Neuroscience, 95*(2), 567–575.

Norris, F. H. & Murrell, S. A. (1988). Prior experience as a moderator of disaster impact on anxiety symptoms in older adults. *American Journal of Community Psychology, 16*(5), 665–683.

Owens, M. J. & Nemeroff, C. B. (1991). Physiology and pharmacology of corticotropin-releasing factor. *Pharmacological Reviews, 43*(4), 425–473.

Paluska, S. A. & Schwenk, T. L. (2000). Physical activity and mental health: current concepts. *Sports Medicine (Auckland, N.Z.), 29*(3), 167–180.

Parker, K. J., Buckmaster, C. L., Justus, K. R., Schatzberg, A. F. & Lyons, D. M. (2005). Mild early life stress enhances prefrontal-dependent response inhibition in monkeys. *Biological Psychiatry, 57*(8), 848–855.

Parker, K. J., Buckmaster, C. L., Schatzberg, A. F. & Lyons, D. M. (2004). Prospective investigation of stress inoculation in young monkeys. *Archives of General Psychiatry, 61*(9), 933–941.

Penedo, F. J., Dahn, J. R., Kinsinger, D., Antoni, M. H., Molton, I., Gonzalez, J. S. et al. (2006). Anger suppression mediates the relationship between optimism and natural killer cell cytotoxicity in men treated for localized prostate cancer. *Journal of Psychosomatic Research, 60*(4), 423–427.

Radley, J. J., Rocher, A. B., Janssen, W. G. M., Hof, P. R., McEwen, B. S. & Morrison, J. H. (2005). Reversibility of apical dendritic retraction in the rat medial prefrontal cortex following repeated stress. *Experimental Neurology, 196*(1), 199–203.

Rasmusson, A. M., Hauger, R. L., Morgan, C. A., Bremner, J. D., Charney, D. S. & Southwick, S. M. (2000). Low baseline and yohimbine-stimulated plasma neuropeptide Y (NPY) levels in combat-related PTSD. *Biological Psychiatry, 47*(6), 526–539.

Rasmusson, A. M., Pinna, G., Paliwal, P., Weisman, D., Gottschalk, C., Charney, D. et al. (2006). Decreased cerebrospinal fluid allopregnanolone levels in women with posttraumatic stress disorder. *Biological Psychiatry, 60*(7), 704–713.

Rasmusson, A. M., Vasek, J., Lipschitz, D. S., Vojvoda, D., Mustone, M. E., Shi, Q. et al. (2004). An increased capacity for adrenal DHEA release is associated with decreased avoidance and negative mood symptoms in women with PTSD. *Neuropsychopharmacology, 29,* 1546–1547.

Rozanski, A., Blumenthal, J. A. & Kaplan, J. (1999). Impact of psychological factors on the pathogenesis of cardiovascular disease and implications for therapy. *Circulation, 99*(16), 2192–2217.

Russo-Neustadt, A. A., Alejandre, H., Garcia, C., Ivy, A. S. & Chen, M. J. (2004). Hippocampal brain-derived neurotrophic factor expression following treatment with reboxetine, citalopram, and physical exercise. *Neuropsychopharmacology, 29*(12), 2189–2199.

Salmon, P. (2001). Effects of physical exercise on anxiety, depression, and sensitivity to stress: a unifying theory. *Clinical Psychology Review, 21*(1), 33–61.

Sapolsky, R. M. (2003). Stress and plasticity in the limbic system. *Neurochemical Research, 28*(11), 1735–1742.

Scheier, M. F., Matthews, K. A., Owens, J. F., Magovern, G. J., Sr., Lefebvre, R. C., Abbott, R. A. et al. (1989). Dispositional optimism and recovery from coronary artery bypass surgery: the beneficial effects on physical and psychological well-being. *Journal of Personality and Social Psychology, 57*(6), 1024–1040.

Scheier, M. F., Matthews, K. A., Owens, J. F., Schulz, R., Bridges, M. W., Magovern, G. J., et al. (1999). Optimism and rehospitalization after coronary artery bypass graft surgery. *Archives of Internal Medicine, 159*(8), 829–835.

Schofield, P., Ball, D., Smith, J. G., Borland, R., O'Brien, P., Davis, S. et al. (2004). Optimism and survival in lung carcinoma patients. *Cancer, 100*(6), 1276–1282.

Segerstrom, S. C., Taylor, S. E., Kemeny, M. E. & Fahey, J. L. (1998). Optimism is associated with mood, coping, and immune change in response to stress. *Journal of Personality and Social Psychology, 74*(6), 1646–1655.

Selye, H. (1998). A syndrome produced by diverse nocuous agents. *The Journal of Neuropsychiatry and Clinical Neurosciences, 10*(2), 230–231.

Sieber, W. J., Rodin, J., Larson, L., Ortega, S., Cummings, N., Levy, S. et al. (1992). Modulation of human natural killer cell activity by exposure to uncontrollable stress. *Brain, Behavior, and Immunity, 6*(2), 141–156.

Slawik, M., Reisch, N., Zwermann, O., Maser-Gluth, C., Stahl, M., Klink, A. et al. (2004). Characterization of an adrenocorticotropin (ACTH) receptor promoter polymorphism leading to decreased adrenal responsiveness to ACTH. *The Journal of Clinical Endocrinology and Metabolism, 89*(7), 3131–3137.

Smith, M. A., Makino, S., Kvetnansky, R. & Post, R. M. (1995). Effects of stress on neurotrophic factor expression in the rat brain. Chrousos, G. P., McCarty, R., Pacak, K., Cizza, G., Sternberg, E., et al. New York: Academy of Sciences.

Southwick, S. M., Bremner, J. D., Rasmusson, A., Morgan III, C. A., Arnsten, A. & Charney, D. S. (1999). Role of norepinephrine in the pathophysiology and treatment of posttraumatic stress disorder. *Biological Psychiatry, 46*(9), 1192–1204.

Southwick, S. M., Vythilingam, M. & Charney, D. S. (2005). The psychobiology of depression and resilience to stress: implications for prevention and treatment. *Annual Review of Clinical Psychology, 1*, 255–291.

Stacey, M. (1970). *Hospitals, Children and Their Families: The Report of a Pilot Study.* London: Routledge & K. Paul.

Steptoe, A., Owen, N., Kunz-Ebrecht, S. R. & Brydon, L. (2004). Loneliness and neuroendocrine, cardiovascular, and inflammatory stress responses in middle-aged men and women. *Psychoneuroendocrinology, 29*(5), 593–611.

Tomakowsky, J., Lumley, M. A., Markowitz, N. & Frank, C. (2001). Optimistic explanatory style and dispositional optimism in HIV-infected men. *Journal of Psychosomatic Research, 51*(4), 577–587.

True, W. R., Rice, J., Eisen, S. A., Heath, A. C., Goldberg, J., Lyons, M. J. et al. (1993). A twin study of genetic and environmental contributions to liability for post-traumatic stress symptoms [see comment]. *Archives of General Psychiatry, 50*(4), 257–264.

Uchino, B. N., Cacioppo, J. T. & Kiecolt-Glaser, J. K. (1996). The relationship between social support and physiological processes: a review with emphasis on underlying mechanisms and implications for health. *Psychological Bulletin, 119*(3), 488–531.

Vyas, A., Mitra, R., Shankaranarayana, R. B. S. & Chattarji, S. (2002). Chronic stress induces contrasting patterns of dendritic remodeling in hippocampal and amygdaloid neurons. *The Journal of Neuroscience, 22*(15), 6810–6818.

Wellman, C. L. (2001). Dendritic reorganization in pyramidal neurons in medial prefrontal cortex after chronic corticosterone administration. *Journal of Neurobiology, 49*(3), 245–253.

Wells, J. K., Howard, G. S., Nowlin, W. F. & Vargas, M. J. (1986). Presurgical anxiety and postsurgical pain and adjustment: effects of a stress inoculation procedure. *Journal of Consulting and Clinical Psychology, 54*(6), 831–835.

Wolkowitz, O. M., Reus, V. I., Keebler, A., Nelson, N., Friedland, M., Brizendine, L. et al. (1999). Double-blind treatment of major depression with dehydroepiandrosterone. *American Journal of Psychiatry, 156*(4), 646–649.

Wust, S., Van Rossum, E. F., Federenko, I. S., Koper, J. W., Kumsta, R. & Hellhammer, D. H. (2004). Common polymorphisms in the glucocorticoid receptor gene are associated with adrenocortical responses to psychosocial stress. *Journal of Clinical Endocrinology and Metabolism, 89*(2), 565–573.

Yehuda, R. (2002). Current status of cortisol findings in post-traumatic stress disorder. *Psychiatric Clinics of North America, 25*(2), 341–368.

Psychophysiology of Resilience to Stress

6

CHRISTIAN WAUGH

Stanford University

MICHELE TUGADE

Vassar College

BARBARA FREDRICKSON

University of North Carolina at Chapel Hill

Contents

Psychophysiology of Resilience to Stress

Several years ago, researchers began to consider why some people were better able to endure and overcome the stress associated with potentially traumatic events than others. The ability to confront and adapt to stress and adversity is now commonly referred to as resilience (Block & Kremen, 1996). Although the construct of resilience is not yet well-defined in terms of its essential contributing factors, it is clear that resilience promotes effective adjustment to adversity. As such, it may help us to better understand key characteristics and coping strategies that enable some individuals to avoid the potentially debilitating effects of extreme stress and trauma. For example, in a study that examined postbereavement responses, resilient people were those who were characterized as experiencing less enduring grief symptoms after the loss of a loved one (Bonanno et al., 2002). After controlling other predictors such as subjective well-being, researchers found that resilient individuals also scored higher on indexes of global adjustment, work and social adjustment, and psychological and physical health adjustment (Klohnen, 1996). Fredrickson, Tugade, Waugh, and Larkin (2003) found that after the September 11, 2001, terrorist attack on the World Trade Center, self-reported resilient people felt more positive emotions in response to the event (but nearly the same negative emotions), and these positive emotions were associated with a reduced incidence of depression (Fredrickson et al., 2003). Certainly, resilience also plays a role in confronting the daily stresses of ordinary life. Although the everyday stresses of life, work, relationships, and finances may not qualify as severe or potentially traumatic, the cumulative physiological effects of chronic daily stress can produce adverse consequences for physical and mental health (Kohn, Lafreniere & Gurevich, 1991).

In this chapter, we focus on two phenomena that have broad relevance to stress in general: anticipation and recovery. Specifically, we show how stress anticipation relates to stress recovery. To the extent that the specific anticipative strategies may promote (versus hinder) recovery from exposure to stress, they may be considered as important to resilience (versus vulnerability). Anticipation of stress is common with respect to daily stressors, which are sometimes stressful in large part because they are foreseen. Examples include anticipation of a final exam in school, difficult conversations with loved ones, or a job interview. By contrast, severely stressful events may be traumatic precisely because they are shocking, that is, they occur without warning and allow little or no time or opportunity for anticipation or preparation. Nonetheless, some severely stressful experiences may be anticipated, such as job loss due to lay-offs, the decision to file for divorce, the loss of a loved one due to lengthy illness, or, in the case of military service members, deployment to combat.

Much of the existing literature on resilience to stress considers resilience in response to stressful events that have already occurred, that is, subjects of study are selected on the basis of having already experienced severe stress or trauma. Indeed, resilience researchers tend to define resilience as demonstrated coping in the face of an already-experienced trauma (Bonanno, 2004; Luthar & Cicchetti, 2000). Such studies have been informative in many ways but are limited to the extent that identification of potentially relevant pretrauma factors can only be done retrospectively, after the impact of traumatic experience itself. Many factors, such as anticipation in particular, may be difficult or impossible to identify, recall, or quantify after the fact. Thus, it is necessary to extend our consideration to include basic laboratory research paradigms that allow direct manipulation and measurement of stress anticipation as a means to observe related changes in adaptation and recovery.

In this chapter, we argue that the manner in which people anticipate stressful events can exert a large influence on how they recover. Here, we define recovery as an effective and efficient return to physiological (cardiovascular, neuroendocrinological) and psychological (mental health and well-being) homeostasis following a disruptive event (defined here as anticipation of or exposure to a stressful event). We address individual differences in key cognitive components of anticipation, such as perception and tolerance of uncertainty, confidence in coping, making positive meaning, and efficient learning. We suggest that resilient people are less likely to perceive uncertainty, high in their tolerance of uncertainty, confident in their coping resources, more likely to make positive meaning of adversity, and more efficient in their learning. Finally, we demonstrate how these resilient characteristics and strategies might be applied in the context of military training where anticipation may have significant consequences for subsequent resilience to the stress of deployment or combat.

Anticipation of Stress

In order to understand emotional or psychological response to an expected or foreseen source of stress, it is important to consider the role of prior expectancy. For example, it feels worse to fail a test that one expects to pass than to fail a test that one expects to fail (Shepperd & McNulty, 2002). In this section, we consider multiple factors that can reasonably be supposed to play a determinant role in anticipation of stress. These factors include perceived certainty, controllability, and confidence in coping. We further examine whether these factors are subject to individual differences in resilience.

Certainty

There is a growing body of evidence to suggest that the anticipation of a negative event leads to anticipative emotional responses, and further that anticipatory emotional responses predict subsequent emotional responses to the negative event itself. Grillon, Ameli, Merikangas, and Woods (1993)

first used a startle blink reflex* paradigm to demonstrate the effect of anticipation on emotional responses to an aversive stimulus. Specifically, Grillon
et al. (1993) demonstrated that the magnitude of the startle blink reflex is
greater when subjects anticipate a negative event (shock) than when they
anticipate a neutral event (no shocks). Nitschke et al. (2002) replicated this
finding using negative pictures as an aversive stimuli and observed in addition that state anxiety did not moderate the effect. However, in a separate
neuroimaging study, participants who anticipated aversive shock also demonstrated increased brain activation in the left insula, where activation is
associated with emotional response to aversive stimulation and was found to
correlate with state anxiety (Chua, Krams, Toni, Passingham & Dolan, 1999).
Although it remains unclear what role state anxiety may play in anticipatory
emotion, these findings clearly support the contention that anticipation plays
a key role in influencing emotional response prior to expected stress and
further that the anticipatory emotional response may be predictive of subsequent emotional response to the anticipated stressor itself.

The results of a recent neuroimaging study (Nitschke, Sarinopoulos,
Mackiewicz, Schaefer & Davidson, 2006) are consistent with earlier observations and provide additional support for the argument that anticipation
generates predictive emotional responses. In this study, participants were
given warning cues that signaled upcoming picture stimuli as either aversive or neutral. Participants' brain activity was recorded during anticipation and viewing of the picture stimuli. Interestingly, several areas of the
brain previously shown to be associated with emotion (anterior cingulate,
dorsolateral prefrontal cortex, orbitofrontal cortex) were activated during
anticipation as well as during actual viewing of the aversive or neutral picture stimuli. There was greater activation across these regions for aversive
than for neutral stimuli. These findings suggest that anticipation of a negative event may generate a preemptory emotional response, which mimics
subsequent emotional response to the event itself (Nitschke, Sarinopoulos,
Mackiewicz, Schaefer & Davidson, 2006). The investigators also reported a
correlation between self-reported state and trait negative affect as measured
by the positive and negative affectivity schedule (PANAS; Watson, Clark &
Tellegen, 1988) and increased activation in the right dorsolateral prefrontal
cortex during anticipation (Nitschke et al., 2006). This finding is consistent
with the previous research, indicating that people who are high in negative
affect also exhibit greater right-to-left hemisphere asymmetrical brain activity (Davidson, 1992).

---

* The startle blink response is measured by the magnitude of constriction of muscles
  around the eye in response to a startling stimulus (usually a loud noise or puff of air in
  the eye). The startle blink reflex tends to be greater in magnitude when people are viewing negative (versus neutral or positive) pictures (Lang, Bradley & Cuthbert, 1990).

It is not yet clear to what extent individual personality differences may affect anticipatory response to negative events. Anxiety is correlated with some physiological measures during anticipation, but findings in this area of inquiry are mixed. In a study that directly examined the personality traits of resilience (as measured by the ego-resiliency scale, ER89; Block & Kremen, 1996) and anticipatory anxiety, trait resilience did not correlate with physiological arousal or with expression of negative emotions during anticipation (Tugade & Fredrickson, 2004). This study employed a "recovery paradigm" (Fredrickson & Levenson, 1998) in which participants anticipated delivering a speech, which they believed would be evaluated by their peers. While study participants prepared their speeches, experimenters measured their cardiovascular reactivity as represented by heart rate, diastolic/systolic blood pressure, finger pulse amplitude, and pulse transmit time to the finger and the ear. They found that trait resilience did not correlate with cardiovascular reactivity or with reports of anxiety as documented during speech preparation (Tugade & Fredrickson, 2004). In summation, these findings suggest that trait resilience and, more generally, anxiety may not play a significant role in emotional arousal that occurs during anticipation of a negative event that is certain to occur.

It may be the case that personality variables play a more significant role when anticipating uncertain events. For example, it is well known that when faced with uncertainty, optimistic individuals tend to expect good things to occur (Scheier & Carver, 1985), whereas individuals who tend toward defensive pessimism expect the worst (Norem & Cantor, 1986). Individuals who score high on resilience measures also tend to be optimistic (Block & Kremen, 1996). Thus, it is reasonable to expect that when faced with the uncertain prospect of a negative event, resilient individuals may be more inclined to consider that the negative event may not occur. A neuroimaging study directly tested the effect of trait resilience during anticipation of an uncertain event (Waugh, Wager, Fredrickson, Noll & Taylor, 2007). Participants were first identified and grouped as high resilient (upper quartile) or low resilient (lower quartile) based on their scores on the ER89 (Block & Kremen, 1996). They were then shown one of the two cues. One cue was a safety cue, which indicated that a neutral picture would always follow. The other cue was a threat cue, which indicated that either a negative or a neutral picture would follow. The true probability (0.50) of neutral versus negative stimulus presentation was unknown to the study participants. The results showed that in response to the threat cue, low-resilient participants experienced much greater activation of the lateral orbitofrontal cortex (LOFC) than did their high-resilient counterparts (Waugh, Wager et al., 2007). Activation of the orbitofrontal cortex has previously been reported during anticipation of punishment (O'Doherty, Kringelbach, Rolls, Hornak & Andrews, 2001) and is also correlated with degree of uncertainty regarding the occurrence of anticipated events (Critchley, Mathias & Dolan, 2001). Hence, the findings reported by Waugh, Wager et al. (2007) suggest that when faced with uncertainty, low-resilient individuals tend to expect the worst outcome and experience physiological responses accordingly.

Controllability

The second important consideration in anticipation of stress is perceived control of outcome. A high level of confidence may support a sense of control and thus affect emotional response during anticipation of stress. In a meta-analysis of the relationship between acute psychological stress and cortisol, a hormone associated with preparing the body for stress, Dickerson and Kemeny (2004) found that for tasks requiring motivated performance, low-controllability tasks were associated with the most consistent and persistent cortisol responses. An effect of cortisol is its tendency to depress the body's immune system, which allows metabolic redirection to vital organs. This effect is adaptive in the short term, but chronically high levels of cortisol can lead to chronic immune depression and resulting deleterious health defects (Sapolsky, Romero & Munck, 2000). Therefore, chronic low perceived controllability may have serious implications for long-term coping and health (Dickerson & Kemeny, 2004).

Some researchers have also found that cardiovascular reactivity varies with the level of perceived control. In some studies of perceived control and cardiovascular reactivity, high levels of perceived control have been associated with increases in cardiovascular reactivity (Bongard, 1995; Manuck, Harvey, Lechleiter & Neal, 1978). However, experimental tasks in these studies tend to confound effort and control, and so observed effects on cardiovascular reactivity may not have been related to perceived controllability, but rather to level of effort in the attempt to avoid aversive stimulation (Obrist, Webb, Sutterer & Howard, 1970). Other studies have shown that when the level of effort is kept constant across all task conditions, higher perceived control is associated with decreased cardiovascular reactivity (Gerin, Litt, Deich & Pickering, 1995; Gerin, Pieper, Marchese & Pickering, 1992; Weinstein, Quigley & Mordkoff, 2002). A possible explanation for this effect is that perceived control supports adequate cardiovascular reactivity to engage in the task but not so much as to hinder task performance. Effects of this type are consistent with the well-documented "inverted U-curve" relationship between arousal and performance (Yerkes & Dodson, 1908).

Physiological responses to anticipation and stress can be related specifically to emotional experience and resilience. A recent study by Lerner, Gonzalez, Dahl, Hariri, and Taylor (2005) attempted to disentangle the influences of various specific emotional experiences and personality variables on cortisol and cardiovascular reactivity. Participants performed stressful tasks (e.g., counting backward while being urged to go faster by the experimenter) while experimenters recorded their facial expressions, cardio-vascular reactivity (blood pressure, arterial pulse, heart rate), and cortisol reactivity. The experimenters then coded the participants' facial expressions for signs of anger, disgust, and fear. Although these facial expressions are all related to negative emotion, anger and disgust tend to occur more specifi-cally in association with certainty and control, whereas fear is more specifi-cally related to appraisals of uncertainty and no control (Smith & Ellsworth, 1985). Lerner et al. (2005) observed that expressions of fear were positively correlated with cardiovascular and cortisol reactivity whereas expressions of anger and disgust were negatively correlated with cardiovascular and corti-sol reactivity. These findings suggest that the level of perceived control exerts a direct influence upon emotional response to stress, which in turn affects physiological reactivity.

Lerner et al. (2005) further reported that trait optimism (associated with high perceived control and resilience) mediated all of the observed relationships between facial expressions and physiology. Specifically, trait optimism predicted reduced cardiovascular and cortisol reactivity to task-related stress. This finding is consistent with the studies of hardiness as a personality component of resilience. Hardiness has been defined as being related to three major factors—commitment, control, and challenge (Kobasa, Maddi & Kahn, 1982)—and has further been shown to exert an influence upon physical as well as mental health (Florian, Mikulincer & Taubman, 1995; Kobasa, Maddi & Kahn, 1982). In a study of Israeli army recruits who were assessed for hardiness and mental health before and after a 4-month combat training period, soldiers who had higher levels of perceived control at the outset of training were found to have less mental distress and more positive signs of good mental health at the end of the training period (Florian, Mikulincer & Taubman, 1995).

Confidence in Coping

Similar to perceived control is confidence in an individual's own ability to cope with stress. Studies of resilience indicate that individuals who are resil-ient to stress tend to possess a strong sense of control as well as a high level of confidence or competence (Cowen, Wyman & Work, 1996; Florian et al., 1995; Masten et al., 1999). However, we believe that it is important to under-stand and approach perceived control (of a stressful event and its outcome) and confidence (in the ability to cope with stress and its outcome) as sepa-rable constructs. In situations where perceived control is low, that is, where it is apparently not possible to prevent or modify an expected stressor, a high degree of confidence in an individual's ability to cope with stress may serve to mediate emotional reactivity to anticipation of the expected stressor. For example, anticipating the certain impending death of a terminally ill family member may be quite stressful due to low perceived control. However, individuals' emotional reaction during the anticipation phase may be less severe if they have confidence in their own ability to cope with the unavoidable loss.

Reported effects of confidence upon emotional and physiological responses are best explained by the biopsychosocial theory of arousal regulation (Blascovich, 1992; Blascovich, Tomaka & Zanna, 1996; Tomaka, Blascovich, Kelsey & Leitten, 1993; Tomaka, Blascovich, Kibler & Ernst, 1997). This theory holds that when faced with a demanding task or situation, human beings perform two appraisals, the comparative results of which will influence their psychological orientation to the task. First, they appraise the perceived demand of the task as conceptualized in terms of the amount of effort it will require, its inherent uncertainty, and its associated risks or costs. Second, human beings appraise their own perceived coping resources. If perceived coping resources match or exceed the perceived demands of the task or situation, the human subject will orient to the task as a challenge. If perceived coping resources are inadequate to the perceived demand, the human subject will orient to the task or situation as a threat (Blascovich, 1992).

Resulting orientation to a demanding task will, in turn, predict physiological response as indexed by four measures of cardiovascular reactivity (heart rate, ventricular muscle contractility, cardiac output, peripheral resistance). Heart rate reflects the human operator's level of task engagement but does not typically differentiate challenge versus threat orientation to the task. Ventricular contractility (the degree to which the muscles in the heart are contracting) is typically increased in response to challenge, which also coincides with increased cardiac output and reduced total peripheral resistance. Taken together, these data suggest that when people feel challenged, their body responds by increasing sympathetic-adrenomedullary (SAM) activity, which is typically associated with improved cardiac performance and decreased feelings of stress (Tomaka et al., 1993). By contrast, when people feel threatened, they experience increased pituitary-adrenocortical (PAC) activity, which is associated with reduced cardiac performance and increased feelings of stress (Tomaka et al., 1993).

To address the question of causality, Tomaka et al. (1997) independently manipulated appraisal or orientation and physiological response patterns. They provided participants with explicit instructions to manipulate their orientation to the task and found that participants' cardiovascular response patterns were consistent with those described above. However, when the investigators independently manipulated cardiovascular response patterns by having participants pedal (versus sit) on a stationary ergometer (Study 2) or immerse their hand into cold (versus warm) water (Study 3), participants' orientation to the task was unaffected. Thus, it appears that cognitive appraisals that generate threat versus challenge orientations to demanding tasks also produce subsequent cardiovascular reactivity patterns (Tomaka et al., 1997).

This study is important because it indicates that confidence in coping is not merely a reflection or secondary effect of current physiological resources, but rather a psychological perspective or strategy that can be employed to improve coping with anticipation of stress.

An important effect of confidence in coping ability is that it promotes improved coping in response to the anticipated stressor (Taylor & Brown, 1988). In the previously described Israeli army recruits study (Florian et al., 1995), high perceived control predicted fewer symptoms of mental distress. Interestingly, the recruits' confidence in their ability to cope with combat training also mediated the relationship between perceived control and mental health (Florian et al., 1995). That is, soldiers who were identified as resilient at the outset of combat training also had a greater sense of control, which in turn was associated with greater confidence in coping ability and subsequently fewer symptoms of mental distress after training. These findings provide additional support for the notion that anticipatory confidence in coping can, indeed, lead to improved coping with stress when it occurs.

Conclusions

In this section, we have argued that the anticipation of stress is an important phenomenon to consider in the more general context of resilience to stress and further that the effects of anticipation are influenced by specific individual personality traits and situational variables. When stress is certain to occur, preemptory emotional reactions tend to mimic (predict) those that will subsequently occur in response to the expected stressor (Nitschke et al., 2006).

A possible explanation for this phenomenon is that preemptory emotional reactions are a means to enhance coping by preparing for or limiting the potentially damaging emotional impact of stress. Another possibility is that by promoting early physiological response, preemptory emotional reactions represent an effort to "prime" or otherwise prepare the body for action, performance, and physiological deprivation under demanding circumstances. The available evidence suggests that these explanations may not be mutually exclusive, but rather that they represent different phenomena associated with confidence in ability to cope with stress. That is, greater confidence will tend to promote an orientation to challenge (versus threat), which is in turn associated with physiological reactivity patterns that are associated with high performance and low stress (Tomaka et al., 1993). Thus, an orientation toward challenge may correspond to physical preparation for an action. By contrast, low confidence in coping ability leads to threat (versus challenge) orientation and subsequent physiological reactivity associated with poor performance and more pronounced feelings of stress (Tomaka et al., 1993). Thus, it may be the case that when threatened, people generate preemptory emotional responses as an effort to manage the emotional effects of stress rather than trying to reckon more directly with the underlying cause of those effects by taking action to thwart or control the stressor itself (Lazarus, 1993).

When stress is uncertain, individual differences play a significant role in emotional and physiological response to the anticipation of stress. Optimistic individuals (Scheier & Carver, 1985) tend to expect best possible outcome, while those who are defensively pessimistic (Norem & Cantor, 1986) tend to expect the worst. If an individual is wary that stress may occur but is willing to embrace the possibility that it may not, that individual may have less of a preemptive emotional response to the anticipation of stress. By contrast, if an individual expects stress and does not consider a positive alternative, that individual may experience a larger preemptive emotional response to the anticipation of its occurrence (Waugh, Wager et al., 2007).

Different expectations may stem from different levels of perceived control and confidence in coping. It is reasonable to consider that a high degree of perceived control tends to encourage focus upon action (i.e., prevention or manipulation of the anticipated stressor), as we would expect to see represented by physiological patterns that are associated with high levels of effort (Manuck et al., 1978). When task effort is controlled as an experimental variable, individuals who have a high level of perceived control tend to produce less cardiovascular reactivity (Manuck et al., 1978). Consistent with this point is the finding that resilient individuals—who are also characterized by high levels of perceived control and confidence—have less of an emotional response to the anticipation of an uncertain aversive stimulus. Thus, it may be that resilience to stress promotes conservation of physiological and emotional resources in situations where stress is possible but uncertain and uncontrollable. Over time, resource conservation may also enable resilient individuals to endure and cope with chronic or repeated uncontrollable stressors more effectively and at less physiological cost (Block & Kremen, 1996; McEwen, 2003).

Recovery

In this section, we consider how the anticipation of stress may affect recovery from stress. First, we address the question of how to define recovery with respect to physiology, resilience, and psychopathology. We then review available evidence with respect to a coping strategy termed "positive reappraisal," and we consider its implications for recovery from stress. Finally, we discuss how anticipation may influence recovery when an anticipated stressor fails to occur.

Defining Recovery

It is important to distinguish between resilience and recovery (e.g., Bonanno, 2004). Recovery can be understood as the process by which individuals who have experienced negative effects of stress or adversity gradually and eventually return to their original (prestress) levels of psychologically functional* and emotional well-being (Fredrickson et al., 2003). By contrast, resilience is more commonly viewed as an active maintenance of homeostasis and healthy function over time. When confronted by stress, resilient individuals exhibit a more stable "trajectory" of psychological functioning in response. Thus, resilience to stress tends to minimize the need for recovery from stress. Indeed, resilient individuals may not need to recover at all because they often thrive during times of adversity and enjoy the rewards of psychological growth (Carver, 1998). This perspective on resilience versus recovery is helpful because it allows the researcher to account for a broad range of negative and positive psychological outcomes in response to stress.

However, this same broad range of psychological outcome can be more difficult to map at the physiological level, where resilience and recovery may be somewhat more difficult to differentiate. In physiology, the concept of "allostasis" refers to the maintenance of stability through change (McEwen, 2003; Sterling & Eyer, 1988). Physiological systems that involve glucocorticoids (e.g., cortisol; Sapolsky et al., 2000), adrenaline, and cytokines can produce physiological changes, which are adaptive in the short run. However, if these processes are not turned off, they can produce allostatic load, whereby tissues can become damaged by chronic hormonal activation (McEwen, 1998). Thus, physiological resilience can be viewed as maintenance of stability such that allostatic load and resulting tissue damage are avoided. In this case, however, recovery (to homeostasis) is, by definition, an essential component of resilience. That is, maintenance of physiological stability cannot be accomplished if physiological systems do not recover from effects of stress to tolerable limits of their prestress levels. This definition does not imply that physiological recovery is the only factor important to physiological resilience or that the two constructs are indistinct. Nor does it imply that physiological recovery and resilience necessarily promote psychological growth. Rather, it is simply important to recognize that successful physiological recovery from the effects of stress is an essential aspect of physiological resilience. By extension, it is reasonable to suppose that unsuccessful physiological recovery would likely make it more difficult to achieve or sustain psychologically resilient processes, strategies, and outcomes.

Positive Reappraisal

There is a vast literature detailing the multitude of coping strategies that people employ to recover from stressful experiences (see review by Skinner,

---

* Individuals in "recovery" from stress may still experience subthreshold psychopathological symptoms (Bonanno, 2004).

Edge, Altman & Sherwood, 2003). Here, we focus specifically on positive reappraisal, which has direct implications for physiological recovery. Reappraisal refers to the act of revising individuals' appraisal of a situation in a way that is usually less negative than they had originally conceived it (Gross, 1998). By thinking about a situation in some new way, individuals can change their view to perceive a new and a more positive meaning (Park & Folkman, 1997). A common example of positive reappraisal can be found in the experience of grief. Those who experience the loss of a loved one are often encouraged to cope by focusing on the positive impact of a life well-lived, memories of shared experiences, joy, and love. Similarly, very stressful experiences can be reappraised as cherished opportunities to develop personal strengths, achieve new insights, or serve others in need.

A change in emotional response typically follows positive reappraisal (Gross, 1998). It is important therefore to note that the process of reappraisal is distinct from that of suppression; the latter describes an effort to change or hide emotional response directly, irrespective of cognitive appraisal. Laboratory studies suggest that reappraisal is the more successful of these two emotional regulation strategies. In a study by Gross (1998), experimental participants who were given instructions to reappraise emotionally disturbing information by focusing on technical details experienced less emotional reactivity as well as a less sympathetic arousal (skin conductance, finger temperature, finger pulse transit time) than those who were instructed simply to mask their emotions. Other studies have gone further to suggest that rather than detachment or distraction, a more powerful type of reappraisal in naturalistic situations may be able to reappraise aversive events in a positive light. Folkman and Moskowitz (2000) reviewed the coping literature and found that the co-occurrence of positive affect with negative affect can be very adaptive as a means of coping with chronic stress. In one study, care-giving partners of men suffering from AIDS experienced high levels of dysphoric mood, but also had levels of positive affect that were comparable with the general population (Folkman, Chesney & Christopher-Richards, 1994). The authors posited that experiencing positive affect in the midst of a negative life experience can have beneficial outcomes for psychological well-being. In another study, individuals assessed as having been resilient to stress prior to the terrorist attacks of 9/11 reported levels of negative emotion similar to those experienced by their nonresilient peers after the attacks but differing from that they also reported higher levels of positive emotion (Fredrickson et al., 2003). In addition, these positive emotions apparently served to buffer resilient individuals against depressive symptoms.

There is little question that positive reappraisal is beneficial to psychological recovery from stress. There is also evidence to suggest that the positive emotions that result from positive reappraisal may contribute to physiological recovery. The results of at least two studies indicate that induced positive emotion promotes recovery from the cardiovascular effects of negative emotion (Fredrickson & Levenson, 1998; Fredrickson, Mancuso, Branigan & Tugade, 2000). In each case, researchers recorded participants' cardiovascular activity before, during, and after speech preparation (stress anticipation "recovery paradigm"). After speech preparation, participants were signaled that they would not have to give their speech. This signal was delivered by the onset of a film clip designed to induce positive emotion (contentment, joy), neutral affect, or negative emotion (sadness). Physiological recovery was then observed as a measure of time necessary for cardiovascular activity to return to baseline (preanticipation) level. In each case during the experimental session, it was observed that physiological recovery occurred more quickly in study participants who had been induced to feel positive (versus neutral or negative) emotion (Fredrickson & Levenson, 1998; Fredrickson et al., 2000). The effects of positive emotion on recovery from stress can also be observed in relation to personality differences, specifically introversion versus extraversion. Extroversion is typically associated with positive affect (Watson & Clark, 1992). In a study of recovery from negative affect, extroverts (versus introverts) demonstrated quicker emotional recovery (Hemenover, 2003). In another study, subjects who were shown to have greater asymmetry of left-brain baseline activation—a characteristic which has been associated with well-being (Urry et al., 2004) and positive affectivity (Davidson, 1992)—demonstrated faster recovery as measured by reduced startle blink magnitude after exposure to an aversive picture (Jackson et al., 2003).

The relationship among positive emotion, recovery, and resilience is not yet well-defined but may reflect the tendency of resilient individuals to engage in positive reappraisal during anticipation of stress. For example, although resilient and nonresilient individuals demonstrated similar levels of cardiovascular reactivity during a speech preparation task, resilient individuals experienced faster recovery of cardiovascular reactivity (return to preanticipation baseline) (Tugade & Fredrickson, 2004). Whereas all study participants reported similar levels of negative emotion during stress anticipation, only resilient participants also reported having positive emotion. Thus, it appears that quicker physiological recovery is mediated by positive emotion, which only resilient individuals are inclined to consider or experience while anticipating a stressful event. Tugade and Fredrickson (2004) examined this relationship further by instructing all study participants to view the upcoming stressor (speech) as a challenge rather than as a threat. After receiving this instruction, nonresilient participants who were induced to view the task as a challenge (versus threat) reported experiencing more positive emotions while giving their speech and further demonstrated quicker physiological recovery after the speech (Tugade & Fredrickson, 2004).

Positive reappraisal is an important coping strategy that has been found to decrease the negative emotion and physiological reactivity that can be associated with stressful or aversive stimuli in the laboratory research setting (Gross, 1998). Although positive reappraisal may not extinguish negative emotion or physiological reactivity associated with the anticipation of stress, it may instead serve to temper the physiological costs that would otherwise occur in response to negative emotion. Hence, we conclude that positive reappraisal promotes resilience by facilitating recovery of physiological systems to a viable state within normal limits of baseline. This recovery, in turn, promotes adaptive physiological recovery from stress and helps to prevent allostatic load (McEwen, 1998).

Recovery from Anticipation of Stress

The various psychological and physiological consequences of anticipating stress have been addressed previously in this chapter. Many real-life situations involve anticipation of stress that may or may not occur. Obvious examples include waiting for significant medical test results, legal decisions, college admissions, or job interview results. In each case, anticipation involves a high level of uncertainty and provides opportunity to consider negative or positive outcome, that is, the awaited information may be bad news (stressor) or good news (no stressor). In this section, we examine how anticipatory processes may affect emotional response and physiological recovery when the resulting news is good news, that is, when the anticipated stressor does not occur. For the purpose of discussion, we consider here a specific example of real-life anticipated stress. If a woman discovers a suspicious lump in her breast, she will likely report it to her physician, who will in turn order tests to determine whether the lump is malignant (cancer) or benign (e.g., cyst). While the woman waits for the results of these tests, she endures a high level of uncertainty and naturally anticipates the possibility of bad news (stressor). Her full recovery from this period of anticipated stress cannot occur until she is given information (a safety signal) to assure her with certainty that her lump is benign (i.e., the anticipated stressor will not occur). It is important to differentiate this scenario and experience with that of vague, free-floating anxiety for which there is no clear information to terminate the stress of anticipation itself. For example, if the woman discovered her breast lump and did not report it to her physician, she would be left to endure indefinite anxiety with no clear resolution (no safety signal). It is our contention here that true "recovery" cannot ensue unless triggered by an apparently definitive (although potentially subjective) safety signal to convey that the anticipated stressor will not occur.

In a review of neurobiological systems that can be mapped to stress resilience versus vulnerability, Charney (2004) addressed the conditioning system whereby resilient individuals appear better able to learn environmental contingencies. Charney suggests that this enhanced ability makes resilient individuals less likely to generalize negative outcomes and thus better able to differentiate among safety signals, innocuous cues, and real threats (Charney, 2004). The ability to quickly and efficiently recognize the absence or nonoccurrence of an anticipated stressor may depend heavily on how the stressor was anticipated in the first place. We contend that the more certain an individual is about the occurrence of an anticipated stressor, the more time that the individual will need to recognize the safety signal as such and then to recover. Perceived certainty can be influenced by two factors. First, there may be information concerning statistical probability of the stressor's occurrence. For example, in the case of breast cancer, a physician might tell the patient that there is a 25% chance of malignancy. However, it is important to note that the effect of the understood statistical likelihood that the stressor will occur will be greatly affected by the severity of the stressor itself. If the stressor is understood to be life-threatening (e.g., cancer), even a relatively small percentage of its occurrence may generate a significant negative emotional anticipatory response (Baumeister, Bratslavsky, Finkenauer & Vohs, 2001).

The second influence on perceived certainty stems from the individual personality differences. Some people tolerate high levels of uncertainty (Freeston, Rheaume & Letarte, 1994) with fewer negative effects than people who are more sensitive to uncertainty. Individuals who are able to tolerate high levels of uncertainty may also be more optimistic (Scheier & Carver, 1985) and more inclined to embrace the possibility of a positive outcome (Norem & Cantor, 1986). Thus, if two individuals anticipate the same stressor with the same real probability of occurrence, they may experience very different emotional reactions due to their individual levels of tolerance.

In general, the greater the perceived probability of any given stressor's actual occurrence, the more similar will be its anticipatory effects to those of a stressor that is certain to occur (Paterson & Neufield, 1987; Waugh, Fredrickson & Taylor, 2006). An explanation for this point is that when the perceived certainty of stress is high, the intuitive response is to orient to its probable occurrence as a need to be "better safe than sorry" and thus to prepare psychologically and physiologically for the worst (i.e., expect that stress will occur). Individuals who adopt this approach and are wrong— that is, stress does not occur—will have to adjust more dramatically to a subsequent (unexpected, unprepared-for) presentation of a safety signal. Thus, we would expect the "better safe than sorry" approach to be associated with slower physiological recovery to baseline. By contrast, individuals who adopt a "wait and see" approach by focusing on the possibility that the stressor may not occur may achieve better conservation of physiological and emotional energy prior to observing the safety signal. In theory, the "wait and see" approach would avoid the impact of surprise and thus promote quicker identification of the safety signal and speedier subsequent recovery from stress anticipation.

There is now preliminary neuroimaging and behavioral evidence to suggest that nonresilient individuals are more likely to adopt the "better safe than sorry" orientation in anticipation of an uncertain stressor, whereas resilient individuals are more likely to adopt the "wait and see" orientation. Waugh, Wager et al. (2007) reported that when anticipating a possible (0.50) negative stimulus, nonresilient participants exhibited greater activation of the LOFC, a brain region associated with the anticipation of punishment (O'Doherty et al., 2001). When presented with the neutral picture that could have been aversive, nonresilient participants also demonstrated increased duration of activation in the insula, a region of the brain associated with core negative affect. In addition, LOFC activity during the anticipation period predicted the insula response to these 'relief' neutral pictures. These results suggest that nonresilient people generate a preemptive emotional response (LOFC)—"better safe than sorry"—which then affects their ability to recover from the threat (longer affective response to neutral pictures after threat). Resilient participants, on the other hand, exhibit minimal activity—"wait and see"—during anticipation and thus are better able to recover (neutral picture, the threat is gone).

In summary, differential recovery when an anticipated stressor does not occur depends to some extent on individual differences in anticipatory emotion and physiology. If an anticipated stressor is perceived to be very likely to occur—whether as determined by objective statistics or by individual bias toward worst outcome certainty—anticipatory stress will be associated with preemptive emotional and physiological reactivity that serves to prepare the body for action (Waugh, Wager et al., 2007). If the anticipated stressor then fails to occur, the heightened anticipatory response will likely require extra time and energy to downregulate and recover. Alternatively, if an anticipated stressor is viewed by actual or perceived probability to be unlikely to occur, emotional and physiological anticipatory responses will be less dramatic, reflecting a "wait and see" strategy that conserves energy and facilitates faster recovery.

An interesting question for the future research is how the ability to learn environmental contingencies (Charney, 2004) is related to anticipation and recovery from stress. It may be that an enhanced ability to learn and thus assess environmental contingencies supports more appropriate or effective strategy selection. Alternatively, strategy selection may affect learning or assessment. We propose that the causal relationship between learning and strategy selection is generally reciprocal, beginning as an initial emphasis on strategy selection in novel or unfamiliar situations (new environmental contingencies to be learned) and followed by reference to previously learned contingencies in the course of subsequent strategy selections.

Summary and Applications

In this chapter, we have reviewed and considered psychological and physiological evidence to address the question of how resilient individuals anticipate and recover from stressful events. This book emphasizes the need to understand how resilience applies to military life and service and particularly to service members' experiences and performance in combat. Here, we consider how the observations and relationships reviewed in this chapter might be put to use in the contexts of military training and selection. The purpose of this section is to provide a general guideline for consideration of future research.

Based on our current understanding of resilience and how it might best be applied to performance benefit, it seems clear that members of the armed services should be trained to appraise the possibility of combat duty as a positive challenge rather than as a threat. Challenge orientation is associated with greater perceived sense of control and confidence in coping, both of which are psychological factors previously shown to buffer war fighters from combat-related mental distress (Florian et al., 1995) and posttraumatic stress disorder (PTSD) symptoms (Sharkansky et al., 2000). For the purpose of research and development of new training programs, service members could be screened pre- and posttraining to assess challenge orientation, resilience, sense of control, and confidence in coping. Subsequent psychological, medical, and performance measures (e.g., before, during, and after combat exposure) could then be considered in specific relationship to these psychological principles.

Physiologically, challenge is manifested as a SAM response (increased heart rate, peripheral resistance, and cardiac output) associated with the body's preparation for engagement or action. The physiological profile associated with challenge predicts better performance in competitive situations (e.g., college sports; Blascovich, Seery, Mugridge, Norris & Weisbuch, 2004). By contrast, threat orientation is associated with a PAC response (Tomaka et al., 1993), which includes increased blood pressure, cortisol reactivity, and delayed cortisol recovery (Dickerson & Kemeny, 2004). It may be informative to conduct comprehensive physiological assessments among service members to identify profile tendencies during anticipation of combat (e.g., while discussing or otherwise preparing for deployment) and immediately after exposure to combat training scenarios (resilience to stress is associated with speedier cardiovascular recovery; Tugade & Fredrickson, 2004). Likewise, training regimens could be tested for their effectiveness in producing physiological patterns associated with challenge and action. Physiological challenge versus threat profiles may also be informative as additional data to support the identification of personnel who are best suited physiologically to cope with especially stressful job duties or dangerous missions.

The ability to experience positive emotion in the face of stress may also be a significant predictor of coping and resilience to the anticipated stress of combat (Folkman & Moskowitz, 2000; Fredrickson & Levenson, 1998; Fredrickson et al., 2000). The presence of positive emotion may also reflect challenge orientation as it is more typical of resilient individuals (Tugade & Fredrickson, 2004). From a research perspective, it is quite easy to measure emotional state with proper attention to two caveats. First, the researcher should consider and query daily open reports of general emotional state (i.e., "how do you feel right now?") as well as probe emotional state with respect to specific upcoming event of interest (e.g., "what do you think about your upcoming deployment to Iraq, how do you feel?"). These two types of reports will have different implications for assessing general well-being versus the day-to-day experience of positive emotion (Diener, 1994). Second, it is important to consider the frequency of positive and negative emotional experiences. Recent theory recognizes that one of the best indicators of psychological well-being, thriving, and resilience is a high ratio of positive to negative emotions felt within a given period of time (Fredrickson & Losada, 2005). A well-validated method of assessing positive and negative emotion frequencies is the day reconstruction method by which respondents summarize each day by noting all the day's activities and associated emotional reactions (Kahneman, Krueger, Schkade, Schwar, & Stone, 2004).

Conclusion

It is increasingly clear that in order to fully understand resilience to stress and trauma, it is important to understand stress anticipation and recovery. In this chapter, we have proposed that resilient individuals anticipate stress with a greater sense of perceived control, high confidence in their ability to cope, a positive orientation to challenge, and an ability to experience at least some positive emotional experience. This psychological profile is complemented by a physiological profile, which also reflects an orientation toward challenge and preparation for action. Importantly, the apparent cumulative effect of psychological and physiological resilience is a tendency toward quicker affective and physiological recovery, which in turn buffers against physical or mental illness. Additional research to clarify relevant mechanisms and their relationships and interactions would be particularly helpful to the development of techniques and strategies for improving performance and survival in high-stress and potentially life-threatening environments such as military combat.

References

Baumeister, R. F., Bratslavsky, E., Finkenauer, C. & Vohs, K. D. (2001). Bad is stronger than good. *Review of General Psychology, 5*(4), 323–370.

Blascovich, J. (1992). A biopsychosocial approach to arousal regulation. *Journal of Social and Clinical Psychology, 11*(3), 213–237.

Blascovich, J., Seery, M. D., Mugridge, C. A., Norris, R. K. & Weisbuch, M. (2004). Predicting athletic performance from cardiovascular indexes of challenge and threat. *Journal of Experimental Social Psychology, 40*(5), 683–688.

Blascovich, J., Tomaka, J. & Zanna, M. P. (1996). The biopsychosocial model of arousal regulation. In *Advances in Experimental Social Psychology. Vol. 28.* (p. 1), San Diego, CA, US: Academic Press.

Block, J. & Kremen, A. M. (1996). IQ and ego-resiliency: Conceptual and empirical connections and separateness. *Journal of Personality and Social Psychology, 70*(2), 349–361.

Bonanno, G. A. (2004). Loss, trauma, and human resilience: Have we underestimated the human capacity to thrive after extremely aversive events? *American Psychologist, 59*(1), 20–28.

Bonanno, G. A., Wortman, C. B., Lehman, D. R., Tweed, R. G., Haring, M., Sonnega, J., et al. (2002). Resilience to loss and chronic grief: A prospective study from preloss to 18-months postloss. *Journal of Personality and Social Psychology, 83*(5), 1150–1164.

Bongard, S. (1995). Mental effort during active and passive coping: A dual task analysis. *Psychophysiology, 32*, 242–248.

Charney, D. S. (2004). Psychobiological mechanisms of resilience and vulnerability: Implications for successful adaptation to extreme stress. *American Journal of Psychiatry, 161*(2), 195–216.

Chua, P., Krams, M., Toni, I., Passingham, R. & Dolan, R. (1999). A functional anatomy of anticipatory anxiety. *Neuroimage, 9*(6 Pt 1), 563–571.

Cowen, E. L., Wyman, P. A. & Work, W. C. (1996). Resilience in highly stressed urban children: Concepts and findings. *Bulletin of the New York Academy of Medicine, 73*(2), 267–284.

Critchley, H. D., Mathias, C. J. & Dolan, R. J. (2001). Neural activity in the human brain relating to uncertainty and arousal during anticipation. *Neuron, 29*(2), 537–545.

Davidson, R. J. (1992). Emotion and affective style: Hemispheric substrates. *Psychological Science, 3*(1), 39–43.

Dickerson, S. S. & Kemeny, M. E. (2004). Acute stressors and cortisol responses: A theoretical integration and synthesis of laboratory research. *Psychological Bulletin, 130*(3), 355–391.

Diener, E. (1994). Assessing subjective well-being: Progress and opportunities. *Social Indicators Research, 31*(2), 103–157.

Florian, V., Mikulincer, M. & Taubman, O. (1995). Does hardiness contribute to mental health during a stressful real-life situation? The roles of appraisal and coping. *Journal of Personality and Social Psychology, 68*(4), 687.

Folkman, S., Chesney, M. A. & Christopher-Richards, A. (1994). Stress and coping in caregiving partners of men with aids. *Psychiatric Clinics of North America, 17*(1), 35–53.

Folkman, S. & Moskowitz, J. T. (2000). Positive affect and the other side of coping. *American Psychologist, 55*(6), 647–654.

Fredrickson, B. L. & Levenson, R. W. (1998). Positive emotions speed recovery from the cardiovascular sequelae of negative emotions. *Cognition and Emotion, 12*(2), 191–220.

Fredrickson, B. L. & Losada, M. F. (2005). Positive affect and the complex dynamics of human flourishing. *American Psychologist, 60*(7), 678–686.

Fredrickson, B. L., Mancuso, R. A., Branigan, C. & Tugade, M. M. (2000). The undoing effect of positive emotions. *Motivation and Emotion, 24*(4), 237–258.

Fredrickson, B. L., Tugade, M. M., Waugh, C. E. & Larkin, G. R. (2003). What good are positive emotions in crisis? A prospective study of resilience and emotions following the terrorist attacks on the united states on September 11th, 2001. *Journal of Personality and Social Psychology, 84*(2), 365–376.

Freeston, M. H., Rheaume, J. & Letarte, H. (1994). Why do people worry? *Personality and Individual Differences, 17*(6), 791–802.

Gerin, W., Litt, M. D., Deich, J. & Pickering, T. G. (1995). Self-efficacy as a moderator of perceived control effects on cardiovascular reactivity: Is enhanced control always beneficial. *Psychosomatic Medicine, 57*, 390–397.

Gerin, W., Pieper, C., Marchese, L. & Pickering, T. G. (1992). The multidimensional nature of active coping: Differential effects of effort and enhanced control on cardiovascular reactivity. *Psychosomatic Medicine, 54*, 707–719.

Grillon, C., Ameli, R., Merikangas, K. R. & Woods, S. W. (1993). Measuring the time course of anticipatory anxiety using the fear-potentiated startle reflex. *Psychophysiology, 30*(4), 340–346.

Gross, J. J. (1998). Antecedent and response-focused emotion regulation: Divergent consequences for experience, expression, and physiology. *Journal of Personality and Social Psychology, 74*, 224–237.

Hemenover, S. H. (2003). Individual differences in rate of affect change: Studies in affective chronometry. *Journal of Personality and Social Psychology, 85*(1), 121–131.

Jackson, D. C., Mueller, C. J., Dolski, I., Dalton, K. M., Nitschke, J. B., Urry, H. L., et al. (2003). Now you feel it, now you don't: Frontal brain electrical asymmetry and individual differences in emotion regulation. *Psychological Science, 14*(6), 612–617.

Kahneman, D., Krueger, A. B., Schkade, D. A., Schwarz, N. & Stone, A. A. (2004). A survey method for characterizing daily life experience: The day reconstruction method. *Science, 306*(5702), 1776–1780.

Klohnen, E. C. (1996). Conceptual analysis and measurement of the construct of ego-resiliency. *Journal of Personality and Social Psychology, 70*(5), 1067–1079.

Kobasa, S. C., Maddi, S. R. & Kahn, S. (1982). Hardiness and health: A prospective study. *Journal of Personality and Social Psychology, 42*(1), 168–177.

Kohn, P. M., Lafreniere, K. & Gurevich, M. (1991). Hassles, health, and personality. *Journal of Personality and Social Psychology, 61*(3), 478–482.

Lang, P. J., Bradley, M. M. & Cuthbert, B. N. (1990). Emotion, attention, and the startle reflex. *Psychological Review, 97*, 377–395.

Lazarus, R. S. (1993). From psychological stress to the emotions: A history of changing outlooks. *Annual Review of Psychology, 44*, 1–15.

Lerner, J. S., Gonzalez, R. M., Dahl, R. E., Hariri, A. R. & Taylor, S. E. (2005). Facial expressions of emotion reveal neuroendocrine and cardiovascular stress responses. *Biological Psychiatry, 58*, 743–750.

Luthar, S. S. & Cicchetti, D. (2000). The construct of resilience: Implications for interventions and social policies. *Development and Psychopathology, 12*(4), 857–885.

Manuck, S. B., Harvey, A. H., Lechleiter, S. L. & Neal, K. S. (1978). Effects of coping on blood pressure responses to threat of aversive stimulation. *Psychophysiology, 15*(6), 544–549.

Masten, A. S., Hubbard, J. J., Gest, S. D., Tellegen, A., Garmezy, N. & Ramirez, M. (1999). Competence in the context of adversity: Pathways to resilience and maladaptation from childhood to late adolescence. *Development and Psychopathology, 11*(1), 143–169.

McEwen, B. S. (2003). Interacting mediators of allostasis and allostatic load: Towards an understanding of resilience in aging. *Metabolism, 52*(10 Suppl 2), 10–16.

McEwen, B. S. (1998). Stress, adaptation, and disease. Allostasis and allostatic load. *Annals of the New York Academy of Sciences, 840*, 33–44.

Nitschke, J. B., Larson, C. L., Smoller, M. J., Navin, S. D., Pederson, A. J. C., Ruffalo, D., et al. (2002). Startle potentiation in aversive anticipation: Evidence for state but not trait effects. *Psychophysiology, 39*(2), 254–258.

Nitschke, J. B., Sarinopoulos, I., Mackiewicz, K. L., Schaefer, H. S. & Davidson, R. J. (2006). Functional neuroanatomy of aversion and its anticipation. *NeuroImage, 29*(1), 106–116.

Norem, J. K. & Cantor, N. (1986). Defensive pessimism: Harnessing anxiety as motivation. *Journal of Personality and Social Psychology, 51*(6), 1208–1217.

Obrist, P. A., Webb, R. A., Sutterer, J. R. & Howard, J. L. (1970). The cardiac-somatic relationship: Some reformations. *Psychophysiology, 5*, 569–587.

O'Doherty, J., Kringelbach, M. L., Rolls, E. T., Hornak, J. & Andrews, C. (2001). Abstract reward and punishment representations in the human orbitofrontal cortex. *Nature Neuroscience, 4*(1), 95–102.

Park, C. L. & Folkman, S. (1997). Meaning in the context of stress and coping. *Review of General Psychology, 1*(2), 115–144.

Paterson, R. J. & Neufield, R. W. J. (1987). Clear danger: Situational determinants of the appraisal of threat. *Psychological Bulletin, 101*(3), 404–416.

Reis, H. T. & Gable, S. L. (2000). Event sampling and other methods for studying daily experience. In H. T. Reis & C. M. Judd (Eds.), *Handbook of Research Methods in Social and Personality Psychology* (pp. 190–222), New York, NY, US: Cambridge University Press.

Sapolsky, R. M., Romero, L. M. & Munck, A. U. (2000). How do glucocorticoids influence stress responses? Integrating permissive, suppressive, stimulatory, and preparative actions. *Endocrine Reviews, 21*(1), 55–89.

Scheier, M. F. & Carver, C. S. (1985). Optimism, coping, and health: Assessment and implications of generalized outcome expectancies. *Health Psychology, 4*(3), 219–247.

Sharkansky, E. J., King, D. W., King, L. A., Wolfe, J., Erickson, D. J. & Stokes, L. R. (2000). Coping with gulf war combat stress: Mediating and moderating effects. *Journal of Abnormal Psychology, 109*(2), 188–197.

Shepperd, J. A. & McNulty, J. K. (2002). The affective consequences of expected and unexpected outcomes. *Psychological Science, 13*(1), 85–88.

Skinner, E. A., Edge, K., Altman, J. & Sherwood, H. (2003). Searching for the structure of coping: A review and critique of category systems for classifying ways of coping. *Psychological Bulletin, 129*(2), 216–269.

Smith, C. A. & Ellsworth, P. C. (1985). Patterns of cognitive appraisal in emotion. *Journal of Personality and Social Psychology, 48*(4), 813–838.

Sterling, P. & Eyer, J. (1988). Allostasis: A new paradigm to explain arousal pathology. In S. Fisher & J. Reason (Eds.), *Handbook of Life Stress, Cognition, and Health* (pp. 629–649). New York: Wiley.

Taylor, S. E. & Brown, J. D. (1988). Illusion and well-being: A social psychological perspective on mental health. *Psychological Bulletin, 103*(2), 193–210.

Tomaka, J., Blascovich, J., Kelsey, R. M. & Leitten, C. L. (1993). Subjective, physiological, and behavioral effects of threat and challenge appraisal. *Journal of Personality and Social Psychology, 65*(2), 248–260.

Tomaka, J., Blascovich, J., Kibler, J. & Ernst, J. M. (1997). Cognitive and physiological antecedents of threat and challenge appraisal. *Journal of Personality and Social Psychology, 73*(1), 63–72.

Tugade, M. M. & Fredrickson, B. L. (2004). Resilient individuals use positive emotions to bounce back from negative emotional experiences. *Journal of Personality and Social Psychology, 86*(2), 320–333.

Urry, H. L., Nitschke, J. B., Dolski, I., Jackson, D. C., Dalton, K. M., Mueller, C. J., et al. (2004). Making a life worth living: Neural correlates of well-being. *Psychological Science, 15*(6), 367–372.

Watson, D. & Clark, L. A. (1992). On traits and temperament: General and specific factors of emotional experience and their relation to the five-factor model. *Journal of Personality, 60*, 441–476.

Watson, D., Clark, L. A. & Tellegen, A. (1988). Development and validation of brief measures of positive and negative affect: The PANAS scales. *Journal of Personality and Social Psychology, 54*(6), 1063–1070.

Waugh, C. E., Fredrickson, B. L. & Taylor, S. F. (2006). Adapting to life's slings and arrows: Individual differences in resilience when recovering from an anticipated threat. Unpublished Manuscript.

Waugh, C. E., Wager, T. D., Fredrickson, B. L., Noll, D. C. & Taylor, S. F. (2007). The neural correlates of trait resilience when anticipating and recovering from threat.

Weinstein, S. E., Quigley, K. S. & Mordkoff, J. T. (2002). Influence of control and physical effort on cardiovascular reactivity to a video game task. *Psychophysiology, 39*(5), 591–598.

Yerkes, R. M. & Dodson, J. D. (1908). The relation of strength of stimulus to rapidity of habit formation. *Journal of Comparative Neurological Psychology, 18*, 459–482.

Resilience and Survival in Extreme Environments

KARL E. FRIEDL

U.S. Army Research Institute of Environmental Medicine

DAVID M. PENETAR

McLean Hospital/Harvard Medical School

Contents

> In appreciation for whatever it is that makes men accomplish the impossible.
> —Alfred Lansing, *Endurance, Shackleton's Incredible Voyage*, 1959

Introduction

Human physical survival under harsh environmental conditions is fairly well understood and somewhat predictable as a function of known physiological mechanisms. These essential mechanisms can be seen as analogous to the factors that support or limit machine performance (e.g., fuel levels—energy availability; combustion requirements—oxygen availability, temperature; physical strain—biomechanical stress; oxidation and rust—oxidative stress from reactive oxygen species). Less well understood is the uniquely human plasticity of responsiveness to environmental challenge that permits exceptional performance in some individuals but not in others who share the same essential physiological attributes. This flexibility of response (resilience) to environmental challenge is moderated by factors such as training, acclimatization, behavior, and psychosocial cues.

Common environmental stressors include thermal strain, hypoxia, inadequate rest, high levels of physical work, and a variety of psychological factors such as traumatic exposure, overcrowding, or isolation. When environmental stressors persist without relief, human operators may experience lapses in mental performance and motivation, fatigue or collapse, injury, illness, or, in extreme cases, death. Cortical brain processes (psychological resilience) play a critical role both in mitigating the effects of environmental stress and in determining how human operators respond to it.

Coutu (2002) has identified specific abilities associated with resilience and success in business organizational structures. These include the ability to face reality, to find meaning in life, and to improvise (Coutu, 2002). These same abilities are important for survival in harsh environments such as prisoners of war (POW) camps, concentration camps, mountainous terrain, cold environments, arid environments, and settings that require high-endurance performance with sustained workload and extreme fatigue. Resilience to environmental adversity is thus a combined effect of psychological factors (outlook, flexibility, personality) and underlying physiological phenotype. The champion marathoner possesses innate and trained physiological advantages but probably cannot succeed without also having a high degree of psychological resilience.

The relative and interactive effects of behavior and physiology on human performance and survival are not yet well understood. It is particularly difficult to evaluate such potentially complex effects in terms of their impact upon performance in settings that are moderately stressful but not sufficiently challenging to press human functional capacity beyond tolerable limits. Thus, we have organized this chapter around several unique examples of extreme performance or survival. In each case, we will consider specific physiological mechanisms known to promote survival, mechanisms that may link psychological factors to physiological outcomes, and current efforts to expand the understanding of such effects and relationships.

Extremes of Human Endurance

Ernest Shackleton's last adventure to the Antarctic is widely used as a model of leadership, supported by a long list of teachable skills that can be used to overcome serious adversity (Morrell & Capparell, 2001; Perkins, Holtman & Kessler, 2000). In 1916, Shackleton was stranded with 27 fellow Antarctic explorers after their ship had been crushed in the ice pack. Against all odds, Shackleton successfully led his men to a safe refuge on Elephant Island, from where he precisely navigated a small boat across 800 miles of ocean waters to an inhabited island and then traveled over difficult mountainous terrain to reach a whaling station on the opposite side. Through his determined effort, Shackleton was finally able to bring help and rescue every one of his men. He demonstrated extraordinary performance despite extreme cold, fatigue, hunger, danger, and the apparent hopelessness of his plight. Certainly, Shackleton's success can be attributed to a large degree of skill acquired through training, experience, and preparation. However, it is also possible that an explorer of equivalent training and preparation may have failed to survive, or led his men to survive, such a journey. In addition to possessing myriad necessary skills, Shackleton brought to bear a uniquely sufficient ability to lead, motivate, and inspire. He promised his men that he would "bring them all back alive," and they believed he would do so. Shackleton's leadership, and its impact upon others, illustrates the importance of psychologically mediated resilience.

Four years before Shackleton's most difficult adventure, British explorer Robert Falcon Scott made an unsuccessful bid to be the first explorer to reach the South Pole. Scott's story illustrates a very different approach to challenge, and an apparent lack of resilience to the challenges of the journey. When Scott and his team arrived at the South Pole to discover the Norwegian flag had already been posted there just a few days earlier, Scott described it as "a horrible day." A photograph of Scott's team depicted them standing well apart from one another, looking obviously dejected (Huntford, 2000). Scott and his team began their return trip with severe disappointment. Within a few weeks, the men began to die. Three months into their journey home, Scott and his remaining team members succumbed to fatigue, frostbite, and malnourishment. They died in their sleeping bags at the site of their last camp, just 11 miles from a food and fuel depot. Certainly, the psychological orientation of Scott's team was not helped by Scott's own negative response to defeat. What should have been a survivable event was instead a tragedy, resulting from multiple failures in judgment and stamina.

Throughout history, the quest to extend the physical barriers of human endurance has inspired many remarkable examples of psychological resilience. In each case, extraordinary individuals have been able to push themselves beyond ordinary limits, in some cases risking their health and life in the process. The marathon celebrates the feat achieved by the Greek courier hero, Phidippides (490 BC), who himself died of exhaustion after pushing himself past the limits of human endurance to assist the Athenian Army in resisting invasion by the Persian Empire.* Modern day marathoners also sometimes push themselves beyond safe limits (Maron & Horvath, 1978). After winning the Boston marathon in 1982, Alberto Salazar slipped into unconsciousness due to extreme dehydration and heat exhaustion; it was determined that during competitive runs, Salazar's sweat rates approached an astounding 4 L/h (Armstrong, Hubbard, Jones & Daniels, 1986). Such highly motivated individuals often push themselves beyond physiologically tolerable heat and dehydration limits while training for the demands of performance in sports, the military, public safety, and emergency services. How is it possible to achieve or sustain extraordinary performance under extreme conditions? David Costill, who has made a lifetime study of predictors of distance running performance, concluded at a national meeting of the American College of Sports Medicine in 2001 that ultimately the winners in any group of elite performers are determined by psychological factors. Simply put, individuals who distinguish themselves are those who have the greatest confidence in their own capabilities and a genuine belief that they "are the best." These athletes and performers have in common their commitment to a single-minded purpose (e.g., quest for "the race that will break me") and self-confidence (Morgan & Costill, 1972, 1996).

Similar examples have been recorded involving mountaineers who push themselves to the limits of hypoxia. In 1978, Reinhold Messner and Peter Habeler became the first team of individuals to summit Mount Everest without the benefit of supplemental oxygen. This achievement was an incredible feat of individual psychological and physical resilience. At the summit of Mount Everest, maximal oxygen uptake is reduced to less than one-fourth of that at sea level. Physiologist John West estimates that if Mount Everest were even just a few meters higher, or if Messner and Habeler had encountered weather conditions with reduced barometric pressure, their achievement would not have been possible (West, 1989). The climbers collapsed repeatedly in the snow, moving at a rate of only 1 m/min as they approached the summit. Their success can only be attributed to the combined positive influence of genetics, training, and intense psychological motivation. Recounting the experience, Messner described a feeling of apathy (common at high altitude) mixed with defiance (Messner, 1979). This latter response is consistent with the winning attitude of elite runners.

---

* Phidippides ran a 280-mile course over rugged terrain from Athens to Sparta and back again, requesting support for the impending Battle of Marathon. After returning from this extraordinary run, Phidippides then marched and fought in battle, wearing heavy armor. Finally, he ran back to Athens (26 miles) to deliver news of victory. Shortly thereafter, Phidippides died of exhaustion.

In some instances, survival in extreme conditions may be explained by physiological reserve. For example, extreme energy deprivation can be explained fairly simply in terms of body fat reserves, which serve to protect against starvation and cold injury. For example, compared to their Indian counterparts, larger and better fed British soldiers were better able to survive the Siege of Kut-al-Amara in 1915 (Hehir, 1922). Similarly, women were more likely than men to survive the Siege of Stalingrad during World War II (Brozek, Wells & Keys, 1946). Fat stores and perhaps also fat energy utilization (Hoyt & Friedl, 2006) were probably key contributors to greater physical "resilience" in each case. There are numerous considerations in nutritional status (e.g., body fat/energy stores, antioxidant intake, iron and zinc balance, etc.) that may exert an important or determinant influence on mental and physical performance in extreme environments (Committee on Military Nutrition Research [CMNR], 2006).

Although psychological factors associated with survival are certainly less well-defined, there is little doubt that psychological factors are essential for survival in extreme environments. Several authors have proposed that one important aspect or component of resilience is a personality trait known as *hardiness* (King, King, Fairbank, Keane & Adams, 1998; Maddi, 1999). Hardy individuals tend to view difficult situations as positive challenges, and are guided by a strong sense of control and commitment (Kobasa, 1979). Likewise, individuals who employ psychological strategies to maintain hope, even in seemingly hopeless situations, appear more likely to survive in situations that involve psychological stress and energy deficit; these individuals seem to benefit by enhanced defense against infectious disease, as well as improved recovery from injury and illness (Friedl, 2003). The long-term consequences of extreme stress are more difficult to explain. For example, POW camp survivors have an increased risk of developing neurodegenerative disease (Page & Tanner, 2000). Those who succumb to these health consequences may reflect diminished resilience as a consequence of coping behaviors, the damaging effects of specific nutritional deficiencies and other stressors, or more susceptible genotypes.

For each anecdotal example of resilience to extreme environmental stress, there is a plausible mechanistic basis that expands upon general stress mechanisms as originally described by Walter Cannon and Hans Selye (Cannon, 1914; Selye, 1950). Clearly, the function and effects of the human mind, brain, and body are complex and interactive, providing multiple important opportunities and avenues to mediate human physiological and psychological responses to extreme environments. By pursuing an improved understanding of these mechanisms and their potential impact upon human resilience, we can maximize opportunities for survival and sustained effective performance.

The Physiological Basis of Performance Limits and Injury

Hochachka, Gunga, and Kirsch (1998) have suggested that the human ancestral phenotype arose under conditions that favored endurance performance under increasingly cold, hypoxic, and arid conditions. In their analysis, Hochachka et al. proposed that physiological responses, which developed originally through oxygen sensing to mitigate hypobaric hypoxia in Andean and Tibetan natives (Figure 7.1), are now common to an up-regulated version of the human phenotype that enhances endurance performance. For example, vascular endothelial growth factor (VEGF) stimulates angiogenesis to better accommodate the need for oxygen transport at altitude. Intramuscular VEGF response to the demands of physical training must also be important to the angiogenic responses that occur in endurance-trained athletes. Ultimately, the key physiological predictor of human performance is mitochondrial activity, which reflects all other critical functions (Hochachka et al., 1998; Hoyt & Friedl, 2006). In practical terms, sustained endurance activity in land-living mammals is limited by mitochondrial/respiratory function to approximately five times resting energy expenditure.*

High Altitude

As elevation increases, the partial pressure of oxygen decreases. In functional terms, reduced oxygen pressure makes less oxygen available to the body. This has profound consequences for the human body at altitudes of 8000 ft. and above. Hypobaric hypoxia is detrimental to physical and cognitive functions. However, hundreds of studies have demonstrated that the human body can acclimatize quite well to hypobaric hypoxia. Initial ascent to high altitude provokes a series of physiological changes that reflect an effort by the body to maintain maximum oxygen saturation to bodily tissues. These changes are observable as increases in heart rate, cardiac output, and ventilation rate.[†] Following acclimatization, heart rate and cardiac output return gradually to their near baseline (sea level) values, and stroke volume decreases. Respiration rate remains elevated, however. Neuroendocrine and metabolic processes support acclimatization to high altitude. During the first 4 days of exposure to altitude, norepinephrine (NE) levels (found in urine) rise, and

---

* This is quite different than factors that determine performance and survival limits for diving mammals (Hochachka et al., 1998).

† On initial ascent, an increase in hematocrit is also observed due to a loss of plasma volume. This initial hematocrit increase is not related to an increase in the number of red blood cells, which occurs more slowly over the course of several weeks or months in response to erythropoeitin.

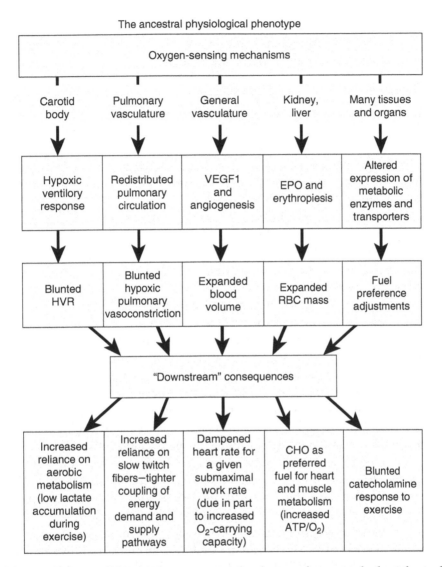

Figure 7.1 Hochachka et al.'s conceptual schema of ancestral physiological phenotype influenced by adaptation to altitude and its close relationship to characteristics of individuals who are well-adapted to endurance performance. Lowlander endurance performers differ primarily by upregulation of mitochondrial function (mitochondrial metabolic enzymes and transporters). (Redrawn from Hochachka, P.W., Gunga, H.C. & Kirsch, K., *Proc. Natl Acad. Sci.*, 95, 1915–1920, 1998. With permission.)

then level off (Burse, Cymerman & Young, 1987). Insulin levels rise and then return to sea-level values after 2 weeks (Young et al., 1987). Blood lactate levels, which initially rise sharply after exercising at 14,000 ft., return toward sea-level baseline after 2 weeks. Plasma glucose levels remain unaffected by altitude or exercise (Young et al., 1987). Taken together, these findings suggest that changes in ammonia accumulation may play a key role in the metabolic acclimatization and improved performance.

It is important to note, however, that acclimatization does not fully counter the effects of hypoxia. Acute performance decrements may have their basis in oxidative stress (Howald & Hoppeler, 2003; Pfeiffer et al., 1999).* However, no acute benefits to health or performance have been observed in relation to the use of antioxidant supplements at altitude (Subudhi et al., 2004). Rather, energy supplementation in the form of carbohydrate reliably improves performance and helps to reduce symptoms of acute mountain sickness (AMS) (Askew, 2004; Fulco et al., 2005).

Physiological and psychological functions and abilities are degraded at altitude and acute illnesses do occur (e.g., AMS, high-altitude pulmonary edema [HAPE], and high-altitude cerebral edema [HACE]). There is much interest in clarifying the pathophysiology of these illnesses to better understand biochemical and genetic markers of susceptibility and to design effective treatments and countermeasures. The picture is far from complete, but recent studies have uncovered several interesting facts. For example, hypoxia associated with high altitude increases the transcription factor hypoxia-inducible factor-1α (HIF-1α). Mairbaurl et al. (2003) found that HIF-1α mRNA increased in the leukocytes of subjects who developed HAPE but not in those who remained well. HIF-1α is known to regulate the genes that control VEGF, which is important to capillary density. Thus, it has been hypothesized that there should occur a measurable increase in capillary density during acclimatization to high altitudes (Lundby et al., 2004). However, this was not found to be the case. After 8 weeks of exposure to altitude (4100 m), messenger RNA of human muscle VEGF did not increase. Maloney, Wang, Duncan, Voelkel, and Ruoss (2000) also found that VEGF levels did not increase with exposure to altitude (4300 m). Thus, the relevance of VEGF to acclimatization remains unknown. Maloney et al. reported a relationship between VEGF level and the incidence of AMS. Specifically, individuals who had the lowest levels of VEGF at sea level were also the least likely to develop AMS at altitude. Moreover, a subgroup of individuals who demonstrated a decrease in VEGF level at altitude also did not develop AMS. The authors concluded that "sustained plasma VEGF at altitude may reflect a phenotype more susceptible to AMS."

Other biochemical and enzymatic factors may predict susceptibility to altitude-related illness. Hanaoka et al. (1998) performed a retrospective study of the frequencies of human leukocyte antigen (HLA) alleles in individuals

---

* It appears that high-altitude inhabitants such as Sherpas have a greater antioxidant capacity.

who developed HAPE. These individuals were more likely to be positive for the antigens HLA-DR6 and HLA-DQ4 compared with their non-HAPE counterparts. Mairbaurl et al. (2003) considered the hypothesis that HAPE susceptibility is related to a diminished expression of transporters involved in alveolar fluid clearance. Mairbaurl et al. observed significant decreases in several factors that control fluid clearance (mRNA of Na-K-ATPase, cystic fibrosis transmembrane regulator [CFTR], and β-actin) among individuals who developed HAPE during a 2-day exposure to 4559 m altitude. However, the authors were unable to take measures that might have definitively established these factors as relevant to the pathophysiology of HAPE.

The renin–angiotensin system is certainly involved in the pathophysiology of pulmonary hypertension and in the development of HAPE. Hotta et al. (2004) measured angiotensin-converting enzyme (ACE) and angiotensin II type 1 receptors in climbers who did and did not develop HAPE. Consistent with earlier findings (Dehnert et al., 2002), climbers who suffered from HAPE did not differ significantly from their healthy counterparts in terms of the polymorphism of the ACE gene. However, investigators observed significant differences in single nucleotide polymorphisms of the angiotensin II type 1 receptor gene (Hotta et al., 2004).

Populations that have lived at high altitudes for many generations demonstrate genetic adaptations. These adaptations have been observed and studied for decades among Andean Quechua Indians. Parallel but different adaptations have been observed in Himalayan Sherpas (Howald & Hoppeler, 2003). There is still much yet to discover about the genomic basis of adaptation to altitude. Moore, Armaza, Villena, and Vargas (2000) identified several differences in Tibetans, including better neonatal oxygenation, greater ventilation and hypoxic ventilatory response, lower hemoglobin concentrations, and reduced susceptibility to chronic altitude sickness. Beall (2000) speculates that such differences reflect a "microevolutionary" process whereby geographically separate populations responded differently when they ascended on altitude for permanent residence. The primary finding of importance here is that highland natives adapt to altitude by decreasing oxidative capacity, rather than by increasing oxidative capacity to manage reduced oxygen availability. As a result, highland natives have an exceptional ability to perform at high altitudes. Sherpas may also be protected by intrinsic antioxidant mechanisms (Howald & Hoppeler, 2003).

With or without the benefit of acclimatization or adaptation, the human body is simply unable to tolerate hypoxia at altitudes higher than 8000 m. Lasting neurological damage has been reported in highly motivated mountaineers who have pushed to the limits of human tolerance (Silber, 2000; West, 1989).

High Work Intensity and Energy Balance

Optimal physical performance involves a unique interplay of physiology, motivation, and environmental constraints. Factors that are important to physical endurance performance include aerobic capacity (e.g., cardiac output, hemoglobin P50, muscle mitochondrial density, vascularity), muscle fiber type (e.g., proportion of Type 1 muscle fibers), biomechanics, substrate availability, and energy metabolism (e.g., fat metabolic efficiency), hydration and thermoregulation, training, and genetics. Nevertheless, psychological motivation may be the most important variable to predict success. First and foremost, motivation is essential for committed physical training, which is in turn essential to the making of an elite competitor. Only through motivation and commitment is it possible to endure the sort of long-term, intense training that is necessary to produce measurable physiological advantage. For example, effective training leads to an increase in type I muscle fibers. By such intense training, Tour de France cycling champion, Lance Armstrong, was able to achieve an 18% improvement in his steady-state power/kg body weight over a period of 7 years (Coyle, 2005; Mena et al., 1991).

Human beings can function in a wide variety of environmental conditions that vary by temperature, humidity, and altitude, but optimal performance is possible only within a fairly narrow range of these environmental factors without sustained training, exposure, and protective clothing and equipment. Hot-dry (desert) and hot-wet (tropic) environments severely restrict work output. Upon first arrival or experimental exposure to such environments, most individuals are severely limited in their ability to accomplish a physical task without risking heat injury (heat exhaustion or heat stroke). Pandolf and Young (1992) demonstrated that with first exposure to a desert environment (120°F, 20% relative humidity), human subjects could not complete a 100 min walk on a treadmill at a moderate pace (3.5 mph) without experiencing an increase in core body temperature beyond safe limits. For reasons discussed earlier in this chapter, altitude also dramatically affects physical performance. Reduced atmospheric pressure affects the body's ability to obtain oxygen from the atmosphere. Physical performance requires an increasing percentage of maximum oxygen uptake as maximum oxygen consumption decreases with increasing altitude (by some measurements as much as 8% for every 1000 m of elevation; Fulco & Cymerman, 2002). This severely limits physical performance ability. For example, Fulco, Rock, and Cymerman (1998) reported that even after 10 days of exposure and training at altitude, human performance in 30 min competitive events such as swimming and running was 5–15% slower at 2000–4000 m, respectively, than at sea level elevation. Hydration status is also a key determinant of sustained physical performance, especially during exercise in high temperatures, with high sweat losses and peripheral vasodilation (Cheuvront, Carter, Castellani & Sawka, 2005).

Habitual physical activity appears to provide benefits to health, including resistance to disease (Dishman et al., 2006); however, connections between excessive training and increased disease susceptibility remain tentative. Although there are anecdotally based claims that excessive training ("overtraining") may lead to an increased frequency of upper respiratory infections, studies designed to test this hypothesis have failed to confirm the claim (Nieman, 2000). Rather, studies of prolonged continuous exertion suggest that preparatory training, adequate energy intake, and rest help to prevent any significant loss of function and protect against decrement in performance (Frykman et al., 2003; Hoyt & Friedl, 2006). In the 3 week-long Tour de France cycling race and in ambitious polar expeditions, peak performances have been achieved over prolonged periods of high-intensity exertion. Reports of significant physical breakdown are usually found related to inadequate energy intake (e.g., Hoyt & Friedl, 2006; Stroud, Jackson & Waterlow, 1996).

Even within well-reasoned models of the effects of prolonged exertion and inadequate energy intake, dramatic variation between the individuals' points to the importance of individual differences in physiological and psychological resilience. For example, two soldiers with the lowest initial body fat composition (~6% body fat) in a group of volunteers who were undergoing the U.S. Army's 8-week Army Ranger course provided extreme contrasts in their responses to the stressors. As part of their training in this course, the soldiers' food intake is deliberately restricted. These two very lean soldiers demonstrated dramatically different metabolic and behavioral responses. One of the soldiers lost the largest amount of lean mass and 23% of his body weight, while the other actually gained a small amount of lean mass (Friedl et al., 1994). The adaptive responses and genetics behind such differences were not readily explainable in this experiment but can include any of a full range of factors, including behavioral responses that improve the economy of motion and energy requirements, as well as the pattern of cytokine responses affecting catabolism, inflammatory, and infectious challenges, all of which were present in varying degrees in the men in this training model.

Thermal Strain

Physiological adaptation to cold is less dramatic than that observed in response to heat. This may be due to human tropical evolutionary heritage or the fact that behavioral responses (e.g., clothing) obviate the need for physiological adaptation.* Nonetheless, several changes can be observed to affect tolerance and performance in cold climates. When tested, fishermen who as part of their work routinely immerse their hands in cold water for several hours a day show a higher finger temperature in response to 10 min hand immersion in cold water (2.5°C) ("Hunting reaction"; LeBlanc, Hildes & Heiroux, 1960). In addition, mean arterial blood pressure is reduced (systemic vascular response). It has also been shown that cold-induced vasodilation (dilation of peripheral blood vessels to warm an area that has been subjected to prolonged cold and possible injury) occurs more rapidly in individuals who routinely work in cold environments (Nelms & Soper, 1962). In whole-body cold immersion experiments, subjects who routinely work in cold environments maintain a higher skin temperature than control subjects (LeBlanc, Pouliot & Rheaume, 1964). Shivering promotes whole-body warmth, but a shivering body also loses heat to the environment more rapidly. In an apparent effort to conserve body heat, individuals who routinely work in the cold begin shivering at lower temperatures (Hong, Lee, Kim, Hong & Rennie, 1969).

Survival in the cold depends on sustained core body temperature, which can be achieved by increases in metabolic rate. This is also important to manual dexterity and to the prevention of peripheral cold injuries that can result from vasoconstriction (Stocks, Taylor, Tipton & Greenleaf, 2004). Although prolonged exposure to extreme cold is often fatal, there are cases in which human beings have survived with full recovery from gradual core body cooling to less than 15°C (Stocks et al., 2004). This raises the question of what unique individual attributes and differences might promote physical or psychological resilience to extreme cold. Scientists at the Defense Institute of Physiology and Allied Sciences (DIPAS) in New Delhi, India, have explored traditional medicines and wisdom as possible means to extend soldier resilience in extreme environments. Selvamurthy and his colleagues studied the effects of yogic meditation and physical training on thermoregulation in normal Indian soldiers (Selvamurthy, Ray, Hegde & Sharma, 1988). In controlled experiments, they discovered evidence for an increase in core temperature that could not be explained by changes in heat loss or shivering. Experiments at this military laboratory are continuing, as they investigate benefits of meditation techniques to enhance soldier physiological resilience (Harinath et al., 2004). Such observations lend credence to anecdotes of resilience in extreme conditions. For example, a Tibetan pilgrim is reported to have slept in light clothing and without shoes or gloves on a cold mountainside

---

* Human beings usually wear protective/insulative clothing when they work and exercise in cold environments. Even in very cold settings, heat load is possible when clothing prevents the dissipation of heat generated by physical activity. Because clothing helps to retain generated metabolic heat, it is usually sufficient to maintain core body temperature without physiological changes.

above 15,000 ft. for 4 days. When later tested in the laboratory, this man demonstrated an ability to maintain an elevated metabolic rate that maintained hand and foot temperatures (Pugh, 1963). This ability to survive by "thinking warm thoughts" is supported by studies involving Tibetan monks (Benson, Malhotra, Goldman, Jacobs & Hopkins, 1990). Techniques of biofeedback have been used to treat Raynaud's syndrome due to previous cold injury. This was a special focus of studies conducted by the U.S. Army Research Institute of Environmental Medicine (USARIEM), involving Argentinian soldiers who suffered cold injury in the Falklands (Ahle, Buroni, Sharp & Hamlet, 1990; Jobe et al., 1985).

Specific neurotransmitters such as neuropeptide Y (NPY) also appear to play a role in peripheral vasodilation. Benson et al. (1990) examined Buddhist meditation techniques and observed metabolic rate increases and decreases greater than 60% accompanied by marked changes in brain electrical activity (EEG). The specific neurochemical pathways involved in such phenomena have not yet been fully characterized, but endocannabinoids appear to play a role (Stefano et al., 2003). Cognitive and psychomotor deficits that occur in some individuals under very high-stress conditions are clearly related to brain NE reductions. These effects can be reversed by providing the rate-limiting precursor substrate, tyrosine, as a dietary supplement (Rauch & Lieberman, 1990; Shurtleff, Thomas, Schrot, Kowalski & Harford, 1994).

Although cold strain modeling indicates that an insulative layer of body fat may be helpful to maintain core body temperature (Xu, Tikuisis, Gonzalez & Giesbrecht, 2005), it does not appear to be the case that obesity (excessive insulative body fat) improves resistance to cold. On the contrary, physically trained individuals generally demonstrate better cardiovascular response to cold, and fit individuals with less body fat compensate with greater shivering thermogenesis (Glickman-Weiss, Goss, Robertson, Metz & Cassinelli, 1991). In a thorough and interesting review of theory and experimental findings reported by competing laboratories over the course of almost 40 years, Armstrong and Pandolf (1986) conclude, "...most authors agree that physical training in a cool environment, or a high level of cardiorespiratory physical fitness, improves physiological responses during exercise at high ambient temperatures and speed the process of heat acclimation" (Armstrong & Pandolf, 1986, p. 223). Bittel, Nonotte-Varly, Livecchi-Gonnot, Sovourey, and Hanniquet (1988) have shown that during exposure to cold, aerobically fit individuals can maintain warmer skin temperatures than their less fit counterparts. Young et al. (1995) observed that subjects exposed to cold after an 8-week endurance training program produced a stronger cutaneous vasoconstrictor response to cold. While undergoing acclimatization to any climate, it is important to maintain adequate hydration because even slight dehydration can degrade physical performance and affect thermoregulatory response. However, very recent studies performed by scientists at USARIEM indicate that dehydration effects on endurance are less of a concern in the cold than in the heat (Cheuvront et al., 2005; Pandolf & Young, 2000; Sawka, 1986).

It is generally well understood that human beings are better able to adapt physiologically to tropical heat than to frigid cold. Numerous studies over the past 50 years have documented the physiological changes that occur when first exposed to hot-wet and hot-dry environments. These same studies have further revealed how well the human body is able to sustain performance in these environments without succumbing to heat injury (cf. Sawka, Wenger & Pandolf, 1996). Individual responses to heat are varied and complex, but in general, after repeated bouts of exercise in hot environments over the course of 7–10 days, most individuals acclimatize in fairly predictable ways. Specifically, they show smaller increases in heart rate, more moderate and less rapid increases in core temperature, improved peripheral (skin) blood flow, and onset of sweating (less salty) at a lower core temperature. These changes have a real and dramatic impact on physical performance capabilities. Pandolf and Young (1992) found that most individuals who were unable to complete even a moderate amount of exercise upon first exposure to a desert environment could do so safely by their seventh consecutive day of exposure. Mountain, Maughan, and Sawka (1996) identified the many aspects of how exercise performance is improved: metabolic rate is lowered, cardiovascular strain is reduced (lower heart rate, increased stroke volume, and better maintenance of blood pressure), and fluid balance is improved (less electrolyte loss, increased total body water and plasma volume). As for hypoxia and cold, the warning signs of heat strain can be voluntarily neglected by highly motivated individuals, often with disastrous consequences. Some well-known athletes (e.g., Alberto Salazar) exemplify motivation to achieve performance beyond safe thermoregulatory limits.

Sleep and Fatigue

Although the purpose of sleep is still not fully understood, it represents a fundamental process that has been preserved across most animal species. Current hypotheses concerning the need for sleep suggest that it may be necessary to essential memory consolidation, restoration of brain energy metabolism, and repair of oxidative stress in neurons. Deprivation of rapid-eye movement (REM, or dream) sleep eventually causes death in a hyper-metabolic state (Montagna, 2005). Whatever processes are involved, marked differences have been observed in human susceptibility for sleep deprivation and related performance degradation (see Figure 7.2).

Inadequate sleep can limit mental performance without affecting physical performance. Severe sleep deprivation leads to progressive

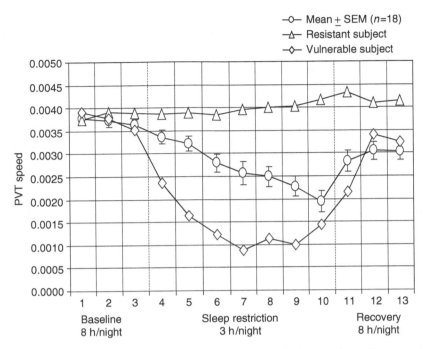

Figure 7.2 Psychomotor vigilance task (PVT) performance (speed) in a group of normal subjects over 1 week of sleep restriction (center line) and two individuals representing opposite outlier responses in performance degradation. The genomic and physiological basis of these differences is currently being explored by researchers at the Walter Reed Army Institute of Research (WRAIR) (Bethesda, MD). With permission, based on data provided by Tom Balkin.

decrements in cognitive function as well as mood (Killgore, Balkin & Wesensten, 2006). Stimulant drugs may induce other behavior changes and provide selective temporary restoration of some functions. In general, though, most effects of sleep deprivation are magnified by ongoing wakefulness. For example, negative effects of sleep deprivation on judgment are not reversed by stimulants such as high-dose caffeine, amphetamine, or modafinil (Wesensten, Killgore & Balkin, 2005). Higher cortical functions such as moral judgment are especially sensitive to sleep deprivation. Amphetamine selectively increases risk-taking behavior without restoring judgment, as demonstrated in one study by the willingness of sleep-deprived soldiers to continue to march on injured feet (Cuthbertson & Know, 1947; Tyler, 1947). Thus, artificially sustained wakefulness is risky.

Convincing data have begun to emerge from animal studies, especially those involving fruit flies (*Drosophila melanogaster*) and mice, supporting the notion that genes may influence sleep patterns and responses to perturbations in normal sleep–wake cycles. At times, these effects can be specific to single mutations. For example, Shaw, Cirelli, Greenspan, and Tononi (2000) found that compared to "wild-type" normal controls, fruit flies with a homozygous mutation for the enzyme arylalkyamine N-acetyl transferase responded atypically to a sleep deprivation paradigm. When deprived of sleep for 12 h and then allowed unlimited recovery sleep, the mutant flies demonstrated significantly greater rebound sleep than controls and the size of this effect was dependent upon the severity of the mutation. Franken, Chollet, and Tafti (2001) studied several strains of inbred mice and observed that differences in recovery sleep (amount of delta power in non-REM sleep) differed among the strains, leading the researchers to conclude that genetic factors influence the rate at which the need for sleep accumulates over time.

Normal sleep patterns may also depend in part upon biochemical pathways that involve cellular messengers such as immediate-early genes. Shiromani et al. (2000) studied two of these genes (c-fos and fos B) in mice and explored the effects of their deletion on sleep. Depending on which gene was deleted, there occurred changes in REM sleep with no change in wakefulness or slow-wave sleep (fos B), or a selective reduction in slow-wave sleep with increased wakefulness (c-fos). The researchers concluded that the induction of these genes in normal mice is important to coding for events critical to sleep regulation and wakefulness.

As noted above, the enzyme arylalkyamine N-acetyl transferase is associated with responses to sleep deprivation. The greater the period of sleep deprivation, the greater is the expression of this enzyme. Similarly, Cirelli, and Tononi (2000) found that induction of another enzyme (arylsulfotransferase [AST]) in rats was proportional to the amount of sleep deprivation. Both arylalkyamine N-acetyl transferase and AST are involved in the metabolic destruction of neurotransmitters such as NE, dopamine, and possibly serotonin. Since the genes that control production of the enzymes are also induced in response to prolonged wakefulness, Cirelli (2002) suggests that their function may be to counter or interrupt the continuous activity of brain catecholaminergic systems during prolonged wakefulness. That is, arylalkyamine N-acetyl transferase and AST levels may be one of the controlling mechanisms of homeostatic processes that regulate sleep and wakefulness. A more thorough understanding of these mechanisms may lead to a refined assessment of individual susceptibility to the effects of sleep deprivation. Such knowledge would enable individuals to be aware of their limitations, understand the implications, and develop effective countermeasures or strategies to avoid difficulties. In addition, pharmacological countermeasures could be tailored to specific enzyme pathways instead of "flogging the system" with the sort of multidimensional stimulants that are currently available.

Psychological Stress

Psychological resilience to stress contributes substantially to the ability (or inability) to withstand environmental stress, and thus presents one of the most accessible avenues for modification of response to environmental demands. For example, in some conditions, resilience can be improved by training human subjects to achieve optimal physiological responses to chronic or acute psychological stress (Crews & Landers, 1987). Acute psychological stress has been studied extensively in sport parachutists and in military trainees who perform dangerous jumping or sliding maneuvers. Experienced parachutists show an initial prejump surge of autonomically mediated heart rate followed by a decline to normal levels when they finally jump. On the contrary, novice jumpers experience a continuous rise in heart rate right up to the moment of the jump (Fenz & Epstein, 1967; Ursin, Levine & Baade, 1978; Wittels, Rosenmayr, Bischof, Hartter & Haber, 1994). These different responses appeared to reflect individual differences in perception of the stressful event, even with increasing experience, and were also associated with jump performance (Fenz & Jones, 1972). The important point of these studies is that training by experience seems to modify the autonomic responses of individuals who will become successful parachutists, and that this modified control of autonomic responses is important for expert performance. Personal spiritual beliefs, self-confidence, and other coping skills contribute to the perception and understanding of psychological stress, and these changes are internalized through brain physiology. Only recently have we begun to unravel some of the mechanisms involved in these effects, such as the role of endocannabinoids, their relationship to nitric oxide and vascular relaxation, and their release by relaxation strategies (produced by repeated mental or physical actions during avoidance of distracting thought) (Stefano et al., 2003).

Chronic stress affects the hypothalamic-pituitary-adrenal (HPA) axis and sustained adrenergic activation produces some maladaptive consequences such as increased susceptibility to infectious disease, impaired short-term memory, and loss of muscle mass and strength (Sapolsky, 1996, 2005). These effects obviously impair health and performance. However, both the response to chronic stress and its outcome can be mediated by psychological resilience, as discussed in other chapters within this volume.

Psychological performance has been studied in relation to environmental stressors such as dehydration, heat, cold, altitude, and workload. One of the more reliable observed effects of environmental stress on cognition is a resulting reduction in short-term memory. Neurobiological mechanisms for this effect appear to be mediated in the hippocampus, possibly through the release of stress hormones. Imaging studies of the hippocampus in individuals suffering from major depression and posttraumatic stress disorder (PTSD) suggest that the size of the hippocampus itself may be reduced (Bremner et al., 2000). Recent work with magnetic resonance imaging indicates that biochemical changes (e.g., reduction in *N*-acetylaspartate) may occur even without anatomical changes (Schuff et al., 2001).

Physiological Limits to Risky Behavior

Were it not for neural mechanisms that limit behavior through fatigue, pain, and other afferent processes, human beings would frequently behave in ways that exceed their physiologically tolerable limits. These processes are adaptive to the extent that they limit voluntary risky behavior under ordinary circumstances. However, their related effects are not necessarily adaptive in extreme environments where fatigue, loss of motivation, disorientation, confusion, and impaired judgment may make it difficult or impossible to survive. Thus, effective psychological resilience to stress in extreme environments should ideally involve knowledge and awareness of one's own limits, and an ability to push to the limits. This is the rationale for some types of brutally intensive military training programs that restrict food and sleep under harsh environmental conditions, such as the Army's Ranger course. By such training, personnel become more aware of how much physical and psychological stress they can tolerate. Nonetheless, highly motivated individuals can exceed their own limits by pushing themselves beyond rational indicators of extreme stress, injury, illness, or performance decrement. This is illustrated by the many documented cases of heat and musculoskeletal overuse injuries that occur among athletes, soldiers, and public safety personnel during training, in real operational environments, and in emergency situations where soldiers and public servants sometimes feel compelled to "do or die" for mission success or survival.

Brain physiological mechanisms support key behavioral limiters of maximal and excessive physical and mental engagement. Central limiters include fatigue, loss of motivation, pain, discomfort, and conditioned avoidance. Physiological effectors include hypoxia, excessive or inadequate glucose levels, fluid compartment shifts, changes in acid–base balance, and stress-induced neurotransmitter release or imbalance. Performance at high altitude is affected by hypoxemia, but hyperventilation and consequent respiratory alkalosis may have central neural effects as well. Dehydration and heat strain affect cardiovascular mechanisms, leading eventually to a reduction in oxygen and glucose delivery to the brain (Cade et al., 1992). During prolonged work effort, glucose delivery to the brain may be the key fatiguing limiter of behavior (Frier, 2001) and sets a lower ceiling by limiting voluntary energy expenditure (Spurr & Reina, 1988). When adequate energy is provided in a readily accessible form (e.g., glucose), very high levels of human sustained effort can be achieved up to what appears to be a limit that is consistent across mammalian species of approximately five times the resting metabolic rate (Hoyt & Friedl, 2006). Higher levels of energy expenditure are limited by a combination of biomechanical, thermoregulatory, and substrate availability factors. However, motivated individuals usually are not stopped by these factors. It appears that there exists some additional sort of central neural mechanism that provides the normal limits. For example, while sleep deprivation causes selective hypometabolic changes in regions of the brain associated with specific types of cognition and emotion, it is also true that one of the most reliable indicators of a sleep-deprived brain is a dramatically shortened sleep latency period (Balkin et al., 2004), which serves to protect against continued wakefulness and resultant impairments in cognitive function. Researchers in this area have suggested that a central protective mechanism may be related to tissue proton accumulation, to an increase in brain levels of 5-hydroxytryptamine, or to some other type of central neural perceptual or biochemical feedback (Abbiss & Laursen, 2005; Newsholme, Blomstrand & Ekblom, 1992; Noakes, 1997).

Cold and hypoxia have been used individually and in combination as stressors to accelerate brain NE secretion rates, and to impair cognition and mood. Rat brain microdialysis studies have demonstrated hypothermia-induced elevated NE concentrations in the hippocampus (Rauch & Lieberman, 1990; Yeghiayan, Luo, Shukitt-Hale & Lieberman, 2001), and tyrosine dietary supplementation has been shown to reverse mood and cognitive decrements in human subjects in cold conditions (Shurtleff et al., 1994) and in cold and hypoxic conditions (Banderet & Lieberman, 1989). Taken together, these studies suggest that the tyrosine substrate is the rate limiter in conditions of extremely high physiological demand. If so, this would provide another modifiable mechanism by which one can prevent or mitigate environmental stress-related impairment. Dienstbier (1991) has suggested that resilience (or "toughness") is closely related to resistance to catecholamine depletion in the brain, and that "catecholamine capacity" can be improved by aerobic training, cold exposure, and psychological challenge.

Neural mechanisms that support resilience to stress may be grouped into at least three areas: reward and motivation, fear responsiveness, and adaptive social behavior. A wide variety of neurochemicals and hormones align with these key mechanisms (Charney, 2004), and deficiencies in each area highlight the behavioral limiting actions of associated neural systems. Thus, classically documented generalized stress-related increases in corticotropin-releasing hormone (CRH), adrenocorticotropic hormone (ACTH), and cortisol during activation of the HPA axis exert interactive effects with other neurobehavioral hormones that play a key role in limiting the motivation of individuals who are under stress. For example, HPA axis activation has been linked to the suppression of testosterone in men, with consequent reductions in vigor and motivation (Friedl, 2005; Zitzmann, Faber & Nieschlag, 2006). This stress-related effect on testosterone secretion has been used by some to justify the use of anabolic steroid "hormone replacement" treatment during stressful athletic training. The behavioral effects (i.e., aggressiveness) may be even more important as a competitive advantage than are more commonly cited physical effects such as increased muscle mass and neuromuscular strength (Friedl, 2005; Pope, Kouri & Hudson, 2000). In older men, testosterone supplementation is advocated as a strategy to maintain vitality and counter depression (Pope, Cohane, Kanayama, Siegel & Hudson, 2003). It is possible that effects of testosterone on male aggressiveness and motivation are mediated through cortical and subcortical dopaminergic systems involved in reward and fear extinction (Hannan, Friedl & Plymate, 1990; Hannan, Friedl, Zold, Kettler & Plymate, 1991). Habitual exercise has also been hypothesized to play an important role in activating these or similar mechanisms (Gilbert, 1995). Exercise and stimulants (e.g., cocaine, amphetamines, caffeine) may also exert their effects by related mechanisms, particularly the DARPP-32 (dopamine- and cAMP-regulated phosphoprotein of 32 kD) signaling pathways (Bastia & Schwarzschild, 2003) (Figure 7.3).*

Dopaminergic systems appear to be central to coping ability and higher order cognitive functioning under stress (Previc, 2005). Additional characterization of mechanisms, which are common for the effects of many drugs, types of behavior, external stimuli, and stressors, will likely help to elucidate key factors of resilience and its possible behavioral outcomes (e.g., motivation, risk taking, motor activity). Additional research in this area is needed to achieve potentially broad scientific and applied benefit. A clear understanding of psychological resilience to stress, and of its physiological basis, would certainly be counted among the most useful and important discoveries of contemporary scientific inquiry in the field of human performance.

Psychosocial Modifiers of Environmental Stress and Health

Although not yet fully mapped or understood, there certainly exists an important relationship between perceived stress and health outcome. Indicators of cumulative stress load have been used to demonstrate dramatic effects on health, especially as associated with immune function, cardiovascular disease, and death. For example, in a carefully controlled study involving deliberate exposure to the common cold virus, Cohen, Tyrrell, and Smith (1991) demonstrated that with increasing levels of life stress, there occurs a linear

---

* Caffeine acts through adenosine 2A receptors to produce physical and mental performance enhancing effects (Kalda, Yu, Oztas & Chen, 2006).

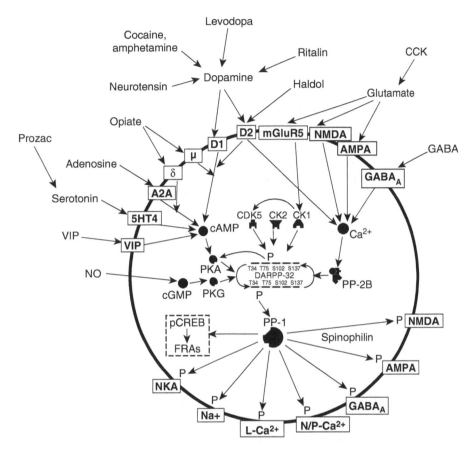

Figure 7.3 The central role of DARPP32 and protein phosphorylation status in mediating the actions of a wide range of stimulants, including exercise, on dopaminergic cells in the brain. Illustration based on Nobel Prize acceptance speech by Paul Greengard (2000), diagram provided with permission from Allan Feinberg.

increase in illness and morbidity. In the military, exposure to significant psychological stress and trauma has also been associated with both short-term somatic complaints and long-term adverse health outcome (McCarroll, Ursano, Fullerton, Liu & Lundy, 2002). A physiological scale developed by Seeman, McEwen, Rowe, and Singer (2001) employs measurable indicators that are generally believed to represent chronic stress (e.g., waist circumference, blood pressure, glycosylated hemoglobin, overnight stress hormone excretion rates). This scale correlates with longer term health outcome measures, including cognitive and physical functions (Seeman et al., 2001). Very long-term health outcomes such as neurodegenerative diseases are more difficult to pinpoint as possibly related to effects of chronic stress but are nonetheless plausibly associated with long-term effects of oxidative stress.

Stress-induced changes in immune function have been well-described in animal models (Glaser & Kiecolt-Glaser, 2005; Kapcala, Chautard & Eskay, 1995) and in human subjects (Cohen et al., 1991). However, some forms of stress may not have any near-term effect on immune function. For example, there appears to be no effect of prolonged aerobic exercise on immune function and susceptibility to disease (Nieman, 2000). Perceptions, attitudes, and attention to stress may play an important role. The near-term effects of environmental stress on immune function are apparently sensitive to psychological stress (Friedl, 2003). When introduced gradually or imperceptibly, some stressors (e.g., heat, hunger) fail to activate any stress-related HPA responses (Mason, 1975). This suggests that perception and neuropsychological processing play a fundamental role in responding to stress, and that accommodation to gradual or continuous stress (allostasis; McEwen, 1998, 2005) can occur without negative health consequences.

Perceived threat is an important determinant in physical responsiveness to stress, particularly when confronted with novel situations or events. Initial experiences with public speaking evoke measurable stress-related responses (e.g., increases in salivary cortisol), but this response is greatly reduced by repeated exposure (Kirschbaum et al., 1995). Personality variables may also play a role. For some individuals, repeated exposure had no effect on stress response as measured by salivary cortisol. Kirschbaum et al. (1995) were able to identify this subgroup of "high responders" as persons with low self-esteem. Apparently, the task of public speaking remained highly stressful for these individuals, even after repeated exposure. Thus, it may be important to consider key personality traits as possible variables of influence on responsiveness to specific stressors.

Psychoneuroimmunology is an emerging interdisciplinary field of study that accesses contributions from psychology, neurology, endocrinology, and immunology to explore relationships between stress, psychological ("mental") outlook, and illness. Findings from studies in this area have a wide impact upon our understanding of the complexities of the brain and behavior, the immune system, and physical health. Most research to date has focused on the question of how physical and psychological stressors affect immune system functions, and how these effects in turn affect physical health. Two leading psychoneuroimmunologists have developed a sophisticated model to represent the interplay between the human central nervous system (CNS) and immune and endocrine systems (see review by Glaser & Kiecolt-Glaser, 2005). Critical to this model is the notion of bidirectional influence. For example, stress-related hormones directly or indirectly (via modulation of cytokines) affect the functioning of T and B cells, neutrophils, macrophages, and other cellular entities (Padgett & Glaser, 2003). In return, cytokines can affect the CNS by actions on the hypothalamic production of stress-related hormones (Figure 7.4).

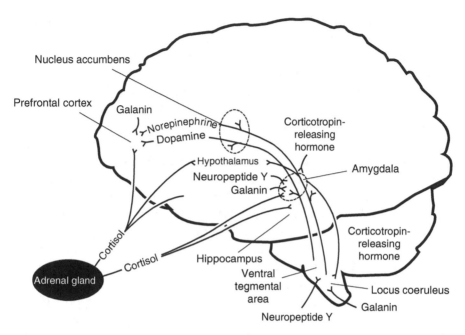

Figure 7.4 Brain connections mediating external stressors and some of the central neuroendocrine pathways currently understood to be involved in adverse stress outcomes. (Adapted from Charney, D.S., *Am. J. Psychiat.*, 161, 195–216, 2004. With permission.)

Stress-related effects on immune function and susceptibility to illness is influenced in part by the intensity of stress. Cohen et al. (1991) combined three inventories to measure psychological stress based on recent life experiences (e.g., divorce, new home) in a sample of 394 men and women. Participants were also assessed based on the degree to which they perceived such life experiences as uncontrollable or unpredictable, and the degree to which they experienced negative emotions (e.g., distressed, sad, upset). The study volunteers were then administered nasal drops, which contained respiratory viruses. Cohen et al. found that higher scores on the composite stress index were related in dose-dependent fashion to more respiratory infections and clinical colds.

Reed, Kemeny, Taylor, and Visscher (1999) studied a group of HIV-positive men to assess their expectations concerning disease progression. Specifically, participants were assessed for their perceptions about infection and disease progression, and the degree to which they felt control over progression of the disease. Additionally, it was noted whether each man had recently experienced the death of a close friend or partner. Results showed an interaction between the recent death of a close friend or partner and high negative scores of disease expectancies. Follow-up study demonstrated that over the course of 2.5 and 3.5 years, previously asymptomatic individuals with high negative expectancies were more likely to develop symptoms. Among these individuals, the disease itself progressed more rapidly.

Social support can exert positive and health-promoting effects on the immune system. Conversely, social isolation is a major risk factor for morbidity and mortality (House, Landis & Umberson, 1988). Kiecolt-Glaser, Garner et al. (1984) found that the number of natural killer cells (a type of lymphocyte) in the immune system and the efficiency with which these cells destroyed diseased cells (such as tumor cells) were reduced in response to stress (studying for and taking medical school exams). Furthermore, and most importantly here, these effects were most dramatic in students who reported greater loneliness. Similar results were found in an in-patient psychiatric setting (Kiecolt-Glaser, Ricker et al., 1984). On the contrary, individuals who have strong social networks (families, friends, social and religious affiliates, coworkers) are generally better able to resist infection (Uchino, Cacioppo & Kiecolt-Glaser, 1996). Immune response to a hepatitis vaccine inoculation during a time of high stress (a three-day series of medical school exams) was stronger among students who reported greater social support (Glaser et al., 1992). Two recent studies by Cohen and colleagues have also demonstrated this effect very convincingly. Individuals who have diverse social networks and individuals who report the least amount of loneliness are least susceptible to infection by viruses that cause colds, and also show the highest antibody responses to flu vaccinations (Cohen, Doyle, Skoner, Rabin & Gwaltney, 1997; Pressman et al., 2005). These findings have direct relevance to resilience in extreme environments. For example, those who participate in expeditions and scientific endeavors in the Antarctic must contend not only with extreme weather, but also with physical isolation in cramped living conditions. Individuals who live and work in such conditions often have reduced cell-mediated immune responses (Mehta, Pierson, Cooley, Dubow & Lugg, 2000; Muller, Lugg & Quinn, 1995; Williams, Climie, Muller & Lugg, 1986).

Resilience Modifiers: Exercise and Other Interventions

Aerobic fitness is intimately tied to optimal physical and cognitive performance. Numerous studies have reported a direct relationship between aerobic fitness and maintenance of cognitive abilities during the aging process. Clarkson-Smith and Hartley (1989, 1990) found that physically active adults performed better than their low-fit counterparts on tests of reaction time, memory, and reasoning. In older adults, these differences are magnified as cognitive tasks become increasingly complex (Shay & Roth, 1992). Moreover, cognitive performance can be improved by improving aerobic fitness. Hawkins, Kramer, and Capaldi (1992) tested older adults (63–82 years) and found that participation in a 10-week exercise program led to significant improvements in auditory and visual reaction time. Hawkins et al. also observed a significant interaction between exercise and task difficulty, such that a more difficult dual-stimulus reaction time task was relatively more sensitive to the exercise effect than either of the single-modality tasks. However, this study did not quantify fitness level and made no attempt to manipulate the intensity of exercise.

Other studies provide additional evidence that physical fitness can serve to attenuate age- and stress-related decline in cognitive abilities (Brown, 1991; Bunce, Barrowclough & Morris, 1996; Roth & Holmes, 1985). Improved cognition may be related to capillary density and general cardiovascular function, which supports the supply of oxygenated blood to the brain (Cotman & Berchtold, 2002), positive effects on the efficiency of neural biochemical and metabolic processes (Gibson & Peterson, 1982; Van Praag, Kempermann & Gage, 1999; Van Praag, Shubert, Zhao & Gage, 2005), maintenance of sensory systems (Era, Parssinen, Pykala, Jokela & Souminen, 1994), and perhaps most critically, maintenance of brain tissue densities (Colcombe et al., 2003). Regular physical training stimulates growth factors (e.g., IGF1, GDNF) that are important to neuro-protection and neurogenesis. It may be through this neuro-protective effect that exercise and physical training protects the brain from damage due to neurotoxin exposure, including intraventricular injection of 6-hydroxydopamine and free radical damage from MPP+ (used in animal models of Parkinson's Disease) (Cohen, Tillerson, Smith, Schallert & Zigmond, 2003; Faherty, Raviie-Shepherd, Herasimtschuk & Smeyne, 2005; Smith & Zigmond, 2003).

Other benefits of exercise are mediated through cytokine responses, such as increases in IL-6, which inhibit proinflammatory cytokines (Petersen & Pedersen, 2005). Through other largely unknown mechanisms, exercise is known to improve mood and sense of well-being (Dishman et al., 2006). Habitual exercisers who stop exercising may suffer mood disturbance (Mondin et al., 1996; Morgan, Costill, Flynn, Raglin & O'Connor, 1988) and in some cases may even develop symptoms of chronic multisymptom illnesses (Glass et al., 2004). One of the most important lessons derived from the medical treatment of chronic multisymptom illness is that physical and mental activity can help to prevent the development of chronic stress-related symptoms and difficulties that might otherwise develop after exposure to traumatic stress (McLean, Clauw, Abelson & Liberzon, 2005). In fact, this factor alone may distinguish those who are least susceptible (most resilient) to chronic symptoms of stress-related trauma (McLean & Clauw, 2004).

Recently, the U.S. Army funded a series of studies to explore cognitive and dietary interventions to overcome effects of lifetime stress on progressive oxidative damage that occurs with aging. The results demonstrated positive effects on learning and memory in dogs that were fed a diet rich in a variety of antioxidants (Milgram et al., 2005). Conceivably, exercise may also stimulate endogenous antioxidant pathways and thus promote resilience to the effects of chronic stress. Repeated damage and oxidative stress leads to long-term loss of muscle function, but proper exercise training provides specific protective benefits that may be mediated through heat shock protein stimulation of the skeletal muscle antioxidant, glutathione (Koh, 2002). Recent studies have also demonstrated the importance of exercise-induced stimulation of brain-derived neurotrophic factor (BDNF) in the hippocampus and elsewhere, and this effect appears to be mediated by astrocytes (Adlard & Cotman, 2004; Zaheer et. al., 2006).

Attempts to extend performance limits through metabolic manipulation are often frustrated by mechanisms that protect individuals from metabolically running amok with every meal. For example, there is a theoretical basis to consider that l-carnitine ingestion increases fatty acid oxidation, which could serve to tilt metabolism towards fat metabolism. Theoretically, this could be used as a strategy to protect lean mass in a semistarvation environment or to increase the availability of energy during high-intensity exercise. However, except for rare individuals with a carnitine deficiency, this strategy simply does not work. Protective mechanisms include limited gut absorption, inhibitory metabolic feedback loops, and mitochondrial energy flux limitations. Effective nutritional supplements are substrates such as basic fuels that are involved in rate-limiting processes. For example, carbohydrates improve physical resilience in extreme environments by extending endurance exercise time (CMNR, 2006), reducing the incidence of AMS in hypobaric hypoxia (Fulco et al., 2005), and improving performance in cold environments (Haman, Legault & Weber, 2004).

Creatine is another energy substrate that can affect specialized types of performance related to short burst strength. However, creatine has failed to provide the benefits originally theorized for brain function (e.g., in hypoxia) and chronic oxidative damage. Likewise, protective mechanisms prevent beneficial effects of direct neurotransmitter administration on the activity of relevant neural pathways. However, it is possible to achieve an effect by providing a substrate for rate-limited resynthesis of neurotransmitters, at least in the case of tyrosine. This may be helpful in high-stress environments, where there occurs substantial depletion of the catecholamines that are synthesized from tyrosine. Cold, wet rats subjected to hypoxia achieve stress levels high enough to reduce the epinephrine content of their adrenals by nearly half (Kiang-Ulrich, 1977). Tyrosine ingestion in stressed rats increases brain resynthesis of NE (Rauch & Lieberman, 1990). Because high levels of stress are required to demonstrate such effects, it is a difficult scientific and ethical challenge to demonstrate the efficacy of such interventions in human subjects.

Kosslyn et al. (2002) present convincing evidence for the importance of individual differences in stress response, activation of the autonomic nervous system, and modulation of the immune response. The individual differences considered by these authors included cortisol responses, heart rate reactivity, and natural killer cell cytotoxic activity. Kosslyn et al. report the results of numerous studies detailing how stress and immune responses differ among individuals and how these processes are related to both short-term (i.e., acute illnesses) and long-term (e.g., diseases such as cancer) health. They propose that as the study of individual differences becomes more refined and is coupled with advances in genomics, a clearer understanding of psychological and biological variations will emerge. This will support a more complete understanding of the interaction between psychology and biology, and will ultimately support an increasingly useful understanding of functions and processes that are essential to stress resilience.

Conclusions and Recommendations for Future Research

Human physiological limits in extreme environments are largely known and understood. Less well understood are exceptional adaptations that make some individuals and populations uniquely capable to perform effectively in extreme environments, and the underlying mechanisms by which behavioral limitations are activated to prevent physiological damage. In some cases, behavioral limits can be exceeded to the detriment of the human body (e.g., heat stroke following extreme physical performance in warm environments) but in other situations, the limiting physiological responses may be maladaptive (e.g., impaired decision making in hypothermia). In a description of the fine line we tread between biological mechanisms that sustain health or produce disease, the Nobel laureate, Aaron Ciechanover, has observed that "man wants to walk in the rain but doesn't want to get wet" (A. Ciechanover, speech in Herzilya, Israel, 24 October 2006). In unique situations where extraordinary performance is required, those who can temporarily push the physiological limits and still survive are considered resilient. Moderators, which can be used to expand human behavioral limits within the range of physiological capacity, are important to our understanding of modifiable resilience. Exercise and fitness appear to be important in this regard. Physical fitness increases resilience in extreme environments, promoting improved performance as well as lasting neuro-protective effects, and this is currently a key research initiative for military medical research. Adaptations noted in specific highland populations indicate a strong genetic influence upon resilience to the effects of altitude. Current technologies such as proteomics and comprehensive approaches using systems biology techniques (Hood, Heath, Phelps & Lin, 2004) will help to explain the underlying mechanisms that provide advantages in various specific extreme environmental conditions. Other potential moderators such as meditation and conditioning may be beneficial as strategies to moderate metabolism, preserve extremity function, and improve psychological coping. Some of these strategies will be aided through training with new technologies that create virtual environments, allowing individuals to safely test their limits and make recoverable mistakes.

Summary

Extreme environments challenge individuals through physiological mechanisms that increase physical and psychological fatigue, adversely affect mood and neurocognitive status, and increase susceptibility to injury and disease. These limiters help prevent more serious injury or death in conditions that may exceed an individual's ability to further compensate in extreme conditions. Resilient individuals are able to push these limits and more fully realize their performance potential in extreme conditions. This thesis is centered on discoveries so that people can learn to "think warm thoughts" and perform better in cold environments; leaders can inspire groups to adopt a positive mental state that enhances their survival in harsh environments; and an attitude of invincibility enables athletes to eke out the winning difference in elite physical performance. This expression of human genetic resilience has been shaped by adaptations favoring endurance performance and is significantly moderated by exercise, mental processes, and psychosocial factors. Examples of resilience extremes provide insights into physiological mechanisms for the variations in human performance, survival, and success. Recent advances in brain physiology can benefit this research frontier, connecting behavior and perception to neurophysiological outcomes in extreme environments.

References

Abbiss, C.R. & Laursen, P.B. (2005). Models to explain fatigue during prolonged endurance cycling. *Sports Medicine, 35*, 865–898.

Adlard, P.A. & Cotman, C.W. (2004). Voluntary exercise protects against stress-induced decreases in brain-derived neurotrophic factor protein expression. *Neuroscience, 124*, 985–992.

Ahle, N.W., Buroni, J.R., Sharp, M.W. & Hamlet, M.P. (1990). Infrared thermographic measurement of circulatory compromise in trenchfoot-injured Argentine soldiers. *Aviation, Space and Environmental Medicine, 61*, 247–250.

Armstrong, L.E., Hubbard, R.W., Jones, B.H. & Daniels, J.T. (1986). Preparing Alberto Salazar for the heat of the 1984 Olympic Marathon. *Physician and Sports Medicine, 14*, 73–81.

Armstrong, L.E. & Pandolf, K.B. (1986). Physical training, cardiorespiratory physical fitness and exercise-heat tolerance. In: K.B. Pandolf, M.N. Sawka & R.R. Gonzalez (Eds.), *Human Performance Physiology and Environmental Medicine at Terrestrial Extremes* (pp. 199–226). Carmel, IN: Cooper Publishing Group.

Askew, E.W. (2004). Food for high-altitude expeditions: Pugh got it right in 1954. *Wilderness and Environmental Medicine, 15*, 121–124.

Balkin, T.J., Bliese, P.D., Belenky, G., Sing, H., Thorne, D.R., Thomas, M., et al. (2004). Comparative utility of instruments for monitoring sleepiness-related performance decrements in the operational environment. *Journal of Sleep Research, 13*, 219–227.

Banderet, L.E. & Lieberman, H.R. (1989). Treatment with tyrosine, a neurotransmitter precursor, reduces environmental stress in humans. *Brain Research Bulletin, 22*, 759–762.

Bastia, E. & Schwarzschild, M.A. (2003). DARPP chocolate: a caffeinated morsel of striatal signaling. *Science Signal Transduction Knowledge Environment, 165*, pe2 [doi: 10.1126/stke.2003.165.pe2]

Beall, C.M. (2000). Tibetan and Andean patterns of adaptation to high-altitude hypoxia. *Human Biology, 72*, 201–228.

Benson, H., Malhotra, M.S., Goldman, R.F., Jacobs, G.D. & Hopkins, P.J. (1990). Three case reports of the metabolic and electroencephalographic changes during advanced Buddhist meditation techniques. *Behavior and Medicine, 16*, 90–95.

Bittel, J.H.M., Nonotte-Varly, C., Livecchi-Gonnot, G.H., Sovourey, G.L.M.J. & Hanniquet, A.M. (1988). Physical fitness and thermoregulatory reactions in a cold environment in men. *Journal of Applied Physiology, 65*, 1984–1989.

Bremner, J.D., Narayan, M., Anderson, E.R., Staib, L.H., Miller, H.L. & Charney, D.S. (2000). Hippocampal volume reduction in major depression. *American Journal of Psychiatry, 157*, 115–118.

Brown, J.D. (1991). Staying fit and staying well: physical fitness as a moderator of life stress. *Journal of Personality and Social Psychology, 60*, 555–561.

Brozek, J., Wells, S. & Keys, A. (1946). Medical aspects of semistarvation in Leningrad (Seige 1941–1942). *American Review of Soviet Medicine, 4*, 70–86.

Bunce, D.J., Barrowclough, A. & Morris, I. (1996). The moderating influence of physical fitness on age gradients in vigilance and serial choice responding tasks. *Psychology and Aging, 11*, 671–682.

Burse, R.L., Cymerman, A. & Young, A. (1987). Respiratory functions and muscle function during isometric handgrip exercise at high altitude. *Aviation, Space and Environmental Medicine, 58*, 39–46.

Cade, R., Packer, D., Zauner, C., Kaufmann, D., Peterson, J., Mars, D., et al. (1992). Marathon running: physiological and chemical changes accompanying late-rate functional deterioration. *European Journal of Applied Physiology, 65*, 485–491.

Cannon, W.B. (1914). The emergency function of the adrenal medulla in pain and the major emotions. *American Journal of Physiology, 33*, 356–372.

Charney, D.S. (2004). Psychophysiological mechanisms of resilience and vulnerability: implications for successful adaptation to extreme stress. *American Journal of Psychiatry, 161*, 195–216.

Cheuvront, S.N., Carter, R., 3rd, Castellani, J.W. & Sawka, M.N. (2005). Hypohydration impairs endurance exercise performance in temperate but not cold air. *Journal of Applied Physiology, 99*, 1972–1976.

Cirelli, C. (2002). How sleep deprivation affects gene expression in the brain: a review of recent findings. *Journal of Applied Physiology, 92*, 394–400.

Cirelli, C. & Tononi, G. (2000). Gene expression in the brain across the sleep-waking cycle. *Brain Research, 885*, 303–321.

Clarkson-Smith, L. & Hartley, A.A. (1989). Relationships between physical exercise and cognitive abilities in older adults. *Psychology and Aging, 4*, 183–189.

Clarkson-Smith, L. & Hartley, A.A. (1990). Structural equation models of relationships between exercise and cognitive abilities. *Psychology and Aging, 5*, 437–446.

Cohen, A.D., Tillerson, J.L., Smith, A.D., Schallert, T. & Zigmond, M.J. (2003). Neuroprotective effects of prior limb use in 6-hydroxydopamine-treated rats: possible role of GDNF. *Journal of Neurochemistry, 85*, 299–305.

Cohen, S., Doyle, W.J., Skoner, D.P., Rabin, B.S. & Gwaltney, J.M. (1997). Social ties and susceptibility to the common cold. *Journal of the American Medical Association, 277*, 1940–1944.

Cohen, S., Tyrrell, D.A.J. & Smith, A.P. (1991). Psychological stress and susceptibility to the common cold. *New England Journal of Medicine, 325*, 606–612.

Colcombe, S.J., Erickson, K.I., Raz, N., Webb, A.G., Cohen, N.J., McAuley, E. & Kramer, A.F. (2003). Aerobic fitness reduces brain tissue loss in aging humans. *Journal of Gerontology: Medical Sciences, 58A*, 176–180.

Committee on Military Nutrition Research (CMNR) (2006). *Nutrient Composition of Rations for Short-term, High-intensity Combat Operations* (pp. 446). Washington, D.C.: The National Academies Press.

Cotman, C.W. & Berchtold, N.C. (2002). Exercise: a behavioral intervention to enhance brain health and plasticity. *Trends in Neuroscience, 25*, 295–301.

Coutu, D.L. (2002) How resilience works. *Harvard Business Review, 80*, 46–50, 52, 55.

Coyle, E.F. (2005). Improved muscular efficiency displayed as Tour de France champion matures. *Journal of Applied Physiology, 98*, 2191–2196.

Crews, D.J. & Landers, D.M. (1987). A meta-analytic review of aerobic fitness and reactivity to psychosocial stressors. *Medicine and Science in Sports and Exercise, 19*, S114–S120.

Cuthbertson, D.P. & Know, J.A.C. (1947). The effects of analeptics on the fatigued subject. *Journal of Physiology, 106*, 42–58.

Dehnert, C., Weymann, J., Montgomery, H.E., Woods, D., Maggiorini, M., Scherrer, U., et al. (2002). No association between high-altitude tolerance and the ACE I/D gene polymorphism. *Medicine and Science in Sports and Exercise, 34*, 1928–1933.

Dienstbier, R.A. (1991). Behavioral correlates of sympathoadrenal reactivity: the toughness model. *Medicine and Science in Sports and Exercise, 23*, 846–852.

Dishman, R.K., Berthoud, H.R., Booth, F.W., Cotman, C.W., Edgerton, V.R., Fleshner, M.R., et al. (2006). Neurobiology of exercise. *Obesity, 14*, 345–356.

Era, P., Parssinen, O., Pykala, P., Jokela, J. & Souminen, H. (1994). Sensitivity of the central visual field in 70- to 81-year old male atheletes and in a population sample. *Aging Clinical and Experimental Research, 6*, 335–342.

Faherty, C.J., Raviie-Shepherd, K., Herasimtschuk, A. & Smeyne, R.J. (2005). Environmental enrichment in adulthood eliminates neuronal death in experimental parkinsonism. *Brain Research and Molecular Brain Research, 134*, 170–179.

Fenz, W.D. & Epstein, S. (1967). Gradients of physiological arousal in parachutists as a function of an approaching jump. *Psychosomatic Medicine, 29*, 33–51.

Fenz, W.D. & Jones, G.B. (1972). Individual differences in physiological arousal and performance in sport parachutists. *Psychosomatic Medicine, 34,* 1–8.

Franken, P., Chollet, D. & Tafti, M. (2001). The homeostatic regulation of sleep need is under genetic control. *Journal of Neuroscience, 21,* 2610–2621.

Friedl, K.E. (2005). Effects of testosterone and related androgens on athletic performance in men. In: W. Kraemer & A. Rogol (Eds.), *The Endocrine System in Sports and Exercise. Olympic Encyclopedia of Sports Medicine* (Vol. 11, pp. 525–543). International Olympic Committee: Blackwell Publishing.

Friedl, K.E. (2003). Military nutritional immunology. In: D.A. Hughes, L.G. Darlington & A. Bendich (Eds.), *Diet and Human Immune Function* (pp. 381–396). Totowa, NJ: Humana Press, Inc.

Friedl, K.E., Moore, R.J., Martinez-Lopez, L.E., Vogel, J.A., Askew, E.W., Marchitelli, L.J., et al. (1994). Lower limits of body fat in healthy active men. *Journal of Applied Physiology, 77,* 933–940.

Frier, B.M. (2001). Hypoglycemic and cognitive function in diabetes. *International Journal of Clinical Practice, 123,* 30–37.

Frykman, P.N., Harman, E.A., Opstad, P.K., Hoyt, R.W., DeLany, J.P. & Friedl, K.E. (2003). Effects of a 3-month endurance event on physical performance and body composition: the G2 *trans*-Greenland expedition. *Wilderness and Environmental Medicine, 14,* 240–248.

Fulco, C.S. & Cymerman, A. (2002). Physical performance at varying terrestrial altitudes. In: K.B. Pandolf & R.E. Burr (Eds.), *Military Aspects of Harsh Environments* (Vol. 2, pp. 693–728). Washington, D.C.: Office of the Surgeon General at Textbook of Military Medicine Publications.

Fulco, C.S., Kambis, K.W., Friedlander, A.L., Rock, P.B., Muza, S.R. & Cymerman, A. (2005). Carbohydrate supplementation improves time-trial cycle performance during energy deficit at 4,300 m altitude. *Journal of Applied Physiology, 99,* 867–876.

Fulco, C.S., Rock, P.B. & Cymerman, A. (1998) Maximal and submaximal exercise performance at altitude. *Aviation, Space, and Environmental Medicine, 69,* 793–801.

Gibson, G.E. & Peterson, C. (1982). Biochemical and behavioral parallels in aging and hypoxia. In: E. Giacobini, G. Filogamo, G. Giacobini & A. Vernadakis (Eds.), *Cellular and Molecular Mechanisms in Aging in the Nervous System* (pp. 107–122). New York: Raven Press.

Gilbert, C. (1995). Optimal physical performance in athletes: key roles of dopamine in a specific neurotransmitter/hormonal mechanism. *Mechanisms of Aging and Development, 84,* 83–102.

Glaser, R. & Kiecolt-Glaser, J.K. (2005). Stress-induced immune dysfunction: implications for health. *Nature Reviews Immunology, 5,* 243–251.

Glaser, R., Kiecolt-Glaser, J.K., Bonneau, R.H., Malarkey, W., Kennedy, S. & Hughes, J. (1992). Stress-induced modulation of the immune response to recombinant hepatitis B vaccine. *Psychosomatic Medicine, 54,* 22–29.

Glass, J.M., Lyden, A.K., Petzke, F., Stein, P., Whalen, G., Ambrose, K., et al. (2004). The effect of brief exercise cessation on pain, fatigue, and mood symptom development in healthy, fit individuals. *Journal of Psychosomatic Research, 57,* 391–398.

Glickman-Weiss, E.L., Goss, F.L., Robertson, R.J., Metz, K.F. & Cassinelli, D.A. (1991). Physiological and thermal responses of males with varying body compositions during immersion in moderately cold water. *Aviation, Space and Environmental Medicine, 62,* 1063–1067.

Haman, F., Legault, S.R. & Weber, J.M. (2004). Fuel selection during intense shivering in humans: EMG pattern reflects carbohydrate oxidation. *Journal of Physiology, 556(Pt 1),* 305–313.

Hanaoka, M., Kubo, K., Yamazaki, Y., Miyahara, T., Matsuzawa, Y., Kobayashi, T., et al. (1998). Association of high-altitude pulmonary edema with the major histocompatibility complex. *Circulation, 97,* 1124–1128.

Hannan, Jr., C.J., Friedl, K.E. & Plymate, S.R. (1990). Effect of Testosterone on Apomorphine Induced Movements in the Rat. Workshop Conference on Androgen Therapy: Biologic and Clinical Consequences, 17–20 January 1990, Marco Island, FL.

Hannan, Jr., C.J., Friedl, K.E., Zold, A., Kettler, T.M. & Plymate, S.R. (1991). Psychological and serum homovanillic acid changes in men administered androgenic steroids. *Psychoneuroendocrinology, 16,* 335–343.

Harinath, K., Malhotra, A.S., Pal, K., Prasad, R., Kumar, R., Kain, T.C., et al. (2004). Effects of hatha yoga and omkar meditation on cardiorespiratory performance, psychological profile, and melatonin secretion. *Journal of Alternative and Complementary Medicine, 10,* 261–268.

Hawkins, H.L., Kramer, A.F. & Capaldi, D. (1992). Aging, exercise, and attention. *Psychology and Aging, 7,* 643–653.

Hehir, P. (1922). Effects of chronic starvation during the siege of Kut. *British Medical Journal, 1,* 865–869.

Hochachka, P.W., Gunga, H.C. & Kirsch, K. (1998). Our ancestral physiological phenotype: an adaptation for hypoxia tolerance and for endurance performance? *Proceedings of the National Academy of Sciences, 95,* 1915–1920.

Hong, S.K., Lee, C.K., Kim, J.K., Hong, S.H. & Rennie, D.W. (1969). Peripheral blood flow and heat flux of Korean women divers. *Federation Proceedings, 28,* 1143–1148.

Hood, L., Heath, J.R., Phelps, M.E. & Lin, B. (2004). Systems biology and new technologies enable predictive and preventative medicine. *Science, 306,* 640–643.

Hotta, J., Hanaoka, M., Droma, Y., Katsuyama, Y., Ota, M. & Kobayashi, T. (2004). Polymorphisms of rennin-angiotensin system genes with high-altitude pulmonary edema in Japanese subjects. *Chest, 126,* 825–830.

House, J.S., Landis, K.R. & Umberson, D. (1988). Social relationships and health. *Science, 241,* 540–545.

Howald, H. & Hoppeler, H. (2003). Performing at extreme altitude: muscle cellular and subcellular adaptations. *European Journal of Applied Physiology, 90,* 360–364.

Hoyt, R.W. & Friedl, K.E. (2006). Field studies of exercise and food deprivation. *Current Opinion in Clinical Nutrition and Metabolic Care, 9,* 685–690.

Huntford, R. (2000). *The Last Place on Earth: Scott and Amundsen's Race to the South Pole.* London: Abacus.

Jobe, J.B., Beetham, Jr., W.P., Roberts, D.E., Silver, G.R., Larsen, R.F., Hamlet, M.P. & Sampson, J.B. (1985). Induced vasodilation as a home treatment for Raynaud's disease. *Journal of Rhematology, 12,* 953–956.

Kalda, A., Yu, L., Oztas, E. & Chen, J.F. (2006). Novel neuroprotection by caffeine and adenosine A(2A) receptor antagonists in animal models of Parkinson's disease. *Journal of Neurological Science*, [Epub http://dx.doi.org/10.1016/j.jns.2006.05.003].

Kapcala, L.P., Chautard, T. & Eskay, R.L. (1995). The protective role of the hypothalamic-pituitary-adrenal axis against lethality produced by immune, infectious, and inflammatory stress. *Annals of the New York Academy of Sciences*, 771, 419–437.

Kiang-Ulrich, M.K.S. (1977). The Adrenal and Cold Acclimation. Doctoral Dissertation. University of California, Santa Barbara, California.

Kiecolt-Glaser, J.K., Garner, W., Speicher, C., Penn, G.M., Holliday, J. & Glaser, R. (1984). Psychosocial modifiers of immunocompetence in medical students. *Psychosomatic Medicine*, 46, 7–14.

Kiecolt-Glaser, J.K., Ricker, D., George, J., Messick, G., Speicher, C.E., Garner, W. & Glaser, R. (1984). Urinary cortisol levels, cellular immunocompetency, and loneliness in psychiatric inpatients. *Psychosomatic Medicine*, 46, 15–23.

Killgore, W.D., Balkin, T.J. & Wesensten, N.J. (2006). Impaired decision making following 49 h of sleep deprivation. *Journal of Sleep Research*, 15, 7–13.

King, L.A., King, D.W., Fairbank, J.A., Keane, T.M. & Adams, G.A. (1998). Resilience-recovery factors in post-traumatic stress disorder among female and male Vietnam veterans: hardiness, postwar social support, and additional stressful life events. *Journal of Personality and Social Psychology*, 74, 420–434.

Kirschbaum, C., Prussner, J.C., Stone, A.A., Federenko, I., Gaab, J., Lintz, D., et al. (1995). Persistent high cortisol responses to repeated psychological stress in a subpopulation of healthy men. *Psychosomatic Medicine*, 57, 468–474.

Kobasa, S.C. (1979). Stressful life events, personality, and health: an inquiry into hardiness. *Journal of Personality and Social Psychology*, 37, 1–11.

Koh, T. (2002). Do small heat shock proteins protect skeletal muscle from injury? *Exercise and Sport Sciences Reviews*, 30, 117–121.

Kosslyn, S.M., Cacioppo, J.T., Davidson, R.J., Hugdahl, K., Lovallo, W.R., Spiegel, D. & Rose, R. (2002). Bridging psychology and biology: the analysis of individuals in groups. *American Psychologist*, 57, 341–351.

LeBlanc, J., Hildes, J.A. & Heiroux, O. (1960). Tolerance of Gaspe' fishermen to cold water. *Journal of Applied Physiology*, 15, 1031–1034.

LeBlanc, J., Pouliot, M. & Rheaume, S. (1964). Thermal balance and biogenic amine excretion in Gaspe' fishermen exposed to cold. *Journal of Applied Physiology*, 19, 9–12.

Lundby, C., Pilegaard, H., Andersen, J.L., van Hall, G., Sander, M. & Calbet, J.A.L. (2004). Acclimatization to 4100m does not change capillary density or mRNA expression of potential angiogenesis regulatory factors in human skeletal muscle. *Journal of Experimental Biology*, 207, 3865–3871.

Maddi, S.R. (1999). The personality construct of hardiness I: effects on experiencing, coping, and strain. *Consulting Psychology Journal*, 51, 83–94.

Mairbaurl, H., Schwobel, F., Hoschele, S., Maggiorini, M., Gibbs, S., Swenson, E.R. & Bartsch, P. (2003). Altered ion transporter expression in bronchial epithelium in mountaineers with high-altitude pulmonary edema. *Journal of Applied Physiology*, 95, 1843–1850.

Maloney, J., Wang, D., Duncan, T., Voelkel, N. & Ruoss, S. (2000). Plasma vascular endothelial growth factor in acute mountain sickness. *Chest, 118,* 47–52.

Maron, M.B. & Horvath, S.M. (1978). The marathon: a history and review of the literature. *Medicine and Science in Sports and Exercise, 10,* 137–150.

Mason, J.W. (1975). A historical view of the stress field. *Journal of Human Stress, 1,* 6–12.

McCarroll, J.E., Ursano, R.J., Fullerton, C.S., Liu, X. & Lundy, A. (2002). Somatic symptoms in Gulf War mortuary workers. *Psychosomatic Medicine, 64,* 29–33.

McEwen, B.S. (1998). Stress, adaptation, and disease. Allostasis and allostatic load. *Annals of the New York Academy of Sciences, 840,* 33–44.

McEwen, B.S. (2005). Stressed or stressed out: what is the difference? *Journal of Psychiatry and Neurosciences, 30,* 315–318.

McLean, S.A. & Clauw, D.J. (2004). Predicting chronic symptoms after an acute "stressor"—lessons learned from 3 medical conditions. *Medical Hypotheses, 63,* 653–658.

McLean, S.A., Clauw, D.J., Abelson, J.L. & Liberzon, I. (2005). The development of persistent pain and psychological morbidity after motor vehicle collision: integrating the potential role of stress response systems into a biopsychosocial model. *Psychosomatic Medicine, 67,* 783–790.

Mehta, S.K., Pierson, D.L., Cooley, H., Dubow, R. & Lugg, D. (2000). Epstein-Barr virus reactivation associated with diminished cell-mediated immunity in Antarctic expeditioners. *Journal of Medical Virology, 61,* 235–240.

Mena, P., Maynar, M., Gutierrez, J.M., Maynar, J., Timon, J. & Campillo, J.E. (1991). Erythrocyte free radical scavenger enzymes in bicycle professional racers—adaptation to training. *International Journal of Sports Medicine, 12,* 563–566.

Messner, R. (1979). Everest. Novara: Instituto Geograifco De Agostini.

Milgram, N.W., Head, E., Zicker, S.C., Ikeda-Douglas, C.J., Murphey, H., Muggenburg, B., et al. (2005). Learning ability in aged beagle dogs is preserved by behavioral enrichment and dietary fortification: a two-year longitudinal study. *Neurobiology of Aging, 26,* 77–90.

Mondin, G.W., Morgan, W.P., Piering, P.N., Stegner, A.J., Stotesbery, C.L., Trine, M.R. & Wu, M.Y. (1996). Psychological consequences of exercise deprivation in habitual exercisers. *Medicine and Science in Sports and Exercise, 28,* 1199–1203.

Montagna, P. (2005). Fatal familial insomnia: a model disease in sleep physiopathology. *Sleep Medicine Review, 9,* 339–353.

Moore, L.G., Armaza, F., Villena, M. & Vargas, E. (2000). Comparative aspects of high-altitude adaptation in human populations. *Advances in Experimental Medicine and Biology, 475,* 45–62.

Morgan, W.P. & Costill, D.L. (1972). Psychological characteristics of the marathon runner. *Journal of Sports Medicine and Physical Fitness, 12,* 42–46.

Morgan, W.P. & Costill, D.L. (1996). Selected psychological characteristics and health behaviors of aging marathon runners: a longitudinal study. *International Journal of Sports Medicine, 17,* 305–312.

Morgan, W.P., Costill, D.L., Flynn, M.G., Raglin, J.S. & O'Connor, P.J. (1988). Mood disturbance following increased training in swimmers. *Medicine and Science in Sports and Exercise, 20,* 408–414.

Morrell, M. & Capparelli, S. (2001). *Shackleton's Way: Leadership Lessons from the Great Antarctic Explorer.* New York: Penguin Putnam Inc.

Mountain, S.J., Maughan, R.J. & Sawka, M.N. (1996). Heat acclimatization strategies for the 1996 summer Olympics. *Athletic Therapy Today, 1*, 42–46.

Muller, H.K., Lugg, D.J. & Quinn, D. (1995). Cell mediated immunity in Antarctic wintering personnel: 1984–1992. *Immunology and Cell Biology, 73*, 316–320.

Nelms, J.D. & Soper, D.J.G. (1962). Cold vasodilation and cold acclimatization in the hands of British fish filleters. *Journal of Applied Physiology, 12*, 444–448.

Newsholme, E.A., Blomstrand, E. & Ekblom, B. (1992). Physical and mental fatigue: metabolic mechanisms and importance of plasma amino acids. *British Medical Bulletin, 48*, 477–495.

Nieman, D.C. (2000). Is infection risk linked to exercise workload? *Medicine and Science in Sports and Exercise, 32*, S406–S411.

Noakes, T.D. (1997). Challenging beliefs: ex Africa simper aliquid novi. *Medicine and Science in Sports and Exercise, 29*, 571–590.

Padgett, D.A. & Glaser, R. (2003). How stress influences the immune response. *Trends in Immunology, 24*, 444–448.

Page, W.F. & Tanner, C.M. (2000). Parkinson's disease and motor-neuron disease in former prisoners-of-war. *Lancet, 355*, 843.

Pandolf, K.B. & Young, A.J. (2000). Assessment of environmental extremes and competitive strategies. In: R.J. Shephard & P.O. Astrand (Eds.), *Endurance in Sport* (pp. 287–300). Oxford: Blackwell.

Pandolf, K.B. & Young, A.J. (1992). Environmental extremes and performance. In: R.J. Shephard & P.O. Astrand (Eds.), *Endurance in Sport* (pp. 270–282). Oxford: Blackwell.

Perkins, D.N.T., Holtman, M.P. & Kessler, P.R. (2000). *Leading at the Edge: Leadership Lessons from the Extraordinary Saga of Shackleton's Antarctic Expedition.* New York: American Management Association (AMACOM).

Petersen, A.M. & Pedersen, B.K. (2005). The anti-inflammatory effect of exercise. *Journal of Applied Physiology, 98*, 1154–1162.

Pfeiffer, J.M., Askew, E.W., Roberts, E.E., Wood, S.M., Benson, J.E., Johnson, S.C. & Freedman, M.S. (1999). Effect of antioxidant supplementation on urine and blood markers of oxidative stress during extended moderate-altitude training. *Wilderness and Environmental Medicine, 10*, 66–74.

Pope, Jr., H.G., Cohane, G.H., Kanayama, G., Siegel, A.J. & Hudson, J.I. (2003). Testosterone gel supplementation for men with refractory depression: a randomized, placebo-controlled trial. *American Journal of Psychiatry, 160*, 105–111.

Pope, Jr., H.G., Kouri, E.M. & Hudson, J.I. (2000). Effects of supraphysiologic doses of testosterone on mood and aggression in normal men. *Archives of General Psychiatry, 57*, 133–140.

Pressman, S.D., Cohen, S., Miller, G.E., Barkin, A., Rabin, B.S. & Treanor, J.J. (2005). Loneliness, social network size, and immune response to influenza vaccination in college freshmen. *Health Psychology, 24*, 297–306.

Previc, F.H. (2005). An integrated neurochemical perspective on human performance measurement. In: J.W. Ness, V. Tepe & D. Ritzer (Eds.), *The Science and Simulation of Human Performance* (pp. 327–390). Amsterdam: Elsevier.

Pugh, L.G. (1963). Tolerance to extreme cold at altitude in a Nepalese pilgrim. *Journal of Applied Physiology, 18*, 1234–1238.

Rauch, T.M. & Lieberman, H.R. (1990). Tyrosine pretreatment reverses hypothermia-induced behavioral depression. *Brain Research Bulletin, 24*, 147–150.

Reed, G.M., Kemeny, M.E., Taylor, S.E. & Visscher, B.R. (1999). Negative HIV-specific expectancies and AIDS-related bereavement as predictors of symptom onset in asymptomatic HIV-positive gay men. *Health Psychology, 18*, 354–363.

Roth, D.L. & Holmes, D.S. (1985). Influence of physical fitness in determining the impact of stressful life events on physical and psychologic health. *Psychosomatic Medicine, 47*, 164–173.

Sapolsky, R.M. (2005). The influence of social hierarchy on primate health. *Science, 308*, 648–652.

Sapolsky, R.M. (1996). Why stress is bad for your brain. *Science, 273*, 749–750.

Sawka, M.N. (1986). Body fluid responses and hypohydration during exercise-heat stress. In: K.B. Pandolf, M.N. Sawka & R.R. Gonzalez (Eds.), *Human Performance Physiology and Environmental Medicine at Terrestrial Extremes* (pp. 227–266). Carmel, IN: Cooper Publishing Group.

Sawka, M.N., Wenger, C.B. & Pandolf, K.B. (1996). Thermoregulatory responses to acute exercise-heat stress and heat acclimation. In: M.J. Fregley & C.M. Blatteis (Eds.), *Handbook of Physiology, Section 4: Environmental Physiology* (pp. 157–185). New York: Oxford University Press.

Schuff, N., Neylan, T.C., Lenoci, M.A., Du, A.T., Weiss, D.S., Marmar, C.R. & Weiner, M.W. (2001). Decreased hippocampal N-acetylaspartate in the absence of atrophy in posttraumatic stress disorder. *Biological Psychiatry, 50*, 952–959.

Seeman, T.E., McEwen, B.S., Rowe, J.W. & Singer, B.H. (2001). Allostatic load as a marker of cumulative biological risk: MacArthur studies of successful aging. *Proceedings of the National Academy of Sciences USA, 98*, 4470–4475.

Selvamurthy, W., Ray, U.S., Hegde, K.S. & Sharma, R.P. (1988). Physiological responses to cold (10°C) in men after six months practice of yoga exercises. *International Journal of Biometeorology, 32*, 188–193.

Selye, H. (1950). Stress and the general adaptation syndrome. *British Medical Journal, 1*, 1383–1392.

Shaw, P.J., Cirelli, C., Greenspan, R.J. & Tononi, G. (2000). Correlates of sleep and waking in Drosophila melanogaster. *Science, 287*, 1834–1837.

Shay, K.A. & Roth, D.L. (1992). Association between aerobic fitness and visuospatial performance in healthy older adults. *Psychology and Aging, 7*, 15–24.

Shiromani, P.J., Basheer, R., Thakkar, J., Wagner, D., Greco, M.A. & Charnes, M.E. (2000). Sleep and wakefulness in *c-fos* and *fos B* gene knockout mice. *Molecular Brain Research, 80*, 75–87.

Shurtleff, D., Thomas, J.R., Schrot, J., Kowalski, K. & Harford, R. (1994). Tyrosine reverses a cold-induced working memory deficit in humans. *Pharmacology Biochemistry and Behavior, 47*, 935–941.

Silber, E. (2000). Upper limb motor function at 5000 metres: determinants of performance and residual sequaelae. *Journal of Neurology, Neurosurgery, and Psychiatry, 69*, 233–236.

Smith, A.D. & Zigmond, M.J. (2003). Can the brain be protected through exercise? Lessons from an animal model of parkinsonism. *Experimental Neurology, 184*, 31–39.

Spurr, G.B. & Reina, J.C. (1988). Influence of dietary intervention on artificially increased activity in marginally undernourished Columbian boys. *European Journal of Clinical Nutrition, 42*, 835–846.

Stefano, G.B., Esch, T., Cadet, P., Zhu, W., Mantione, K. & Benson, H. (2003). Endocannabinoids as autoregulatory signaling molecules: coupling to nitric oxide and a possible association with the relaxation response. *Medical Science Monitor, 9*, RA83–RA95.

Stocks, J.M., Taylor, N.A., Tipton, M.J. & Greenleaf, J.E. (2004). Human physiological responses to cold exposure. *Aviation Space and Environmental Medicine, 75*, 444–457.

Stroud, M.A., Jackson, A.A. & Waterlow, J.C. (1996). Protein turnover rates of two human subjects during an unassisted crossing of Antarctica. *British Journal of Nutrition, 76*, 165–174.

Subudhi, A.W., Jacobs, K.A., Hagobian, T.A., Fattor, J.A., Fulco, C.S., Muza, S.R., et al. (2004). Antioxidant supplementation does not attenuate oxidative stress at high altitude. *Aviation, Space and Environmental Medicine, 75*, 881–888.

Tyler, D.B. (1947). The effect of amphetamine sulfate and some barbiturates on the fatigue produced by prolonged wakefulness. *American Journal of Physiology, 150*, 253–262.

Uchino, B.N., Cacioppo, J.T. & Kiecolt-Glaser, J.K. (1996). The relationship between social support and physiological processes: a review with emphasis on underlying mechanisms. *Psychological Bulletin, 119*, 488–531.

Ursin, H., Levine, S. & Baade, E. (Eds.) (1978). *Psychobiology of Stress: A Study of Coping Men*. New York: Academic Press.

Van Praag, H., Kempermann, G. & Gage, F.H. (1999). Running increases cell proliferation and neurogenesis in the adult mouse dentate gyrus. *Nature and Neuroscience, 2*, 266–270.

Van Praag, H., Shubert, T., Zhao, C. & Gage, F.H. (2005). Exercise enhances learning and hippocampal neurogenesis in aged mice. *The Journal of Neuroscience, 25*, 8680–8685.

Wesensten, N.J., Killgore, W.D. & Balkin, T.J. (2005). Performance and alertness effects of caffeine, dextroamphetamine, and modafinil during sleep deprivation. *Journal of Sleep Deprivation, 14*, 255–266.

West, J.B. (1989). Physiological responses to severe hypoxia in man. *Canadian Journal of Physiology and Pharmacology, 67*, 173–178.

Williams, D.L., Climie, A., Muller, H.K. & Lugg, D.J. (1986). Cell-mediated immunity in healthy adults in Antarctic and the sub-Antarctic. *Journal of Clinical Laboratory Immunology, 20*, 43–49.

Wittels, P., Rosenmayr, G., Bischof, B., Hartter, E. & Haber, P. (1994). Aerobic fitness and sympatho-adrenal response to short-term psycho-emotional stress under field conditions. *European Journal of Applied Physiology, 68*, 418–424.

Xu, X., Tikuisis, P., Gonzalez, R. & Giesbrecht, G. (2005). Thermoregulatory model of prediction of long-term cold exposure. *Computers in Biology and Medicine, 35*, 287–298.

Yeghiayan, S.K., Luo, S., Shukitt-Hale, B. & Lieberman, H.R. (2001). Tyrosine improves behavioral and neurochemical deficits caused by cold exposure. *Physiology and Behavior, 72*, 311–316.

Young, A.J., Sawka, M.N., Levine, L., Burgoon, P.W., Latzka, W.A., Gonzalez, R.R. & Pandolf, K.B. (1995). Metabolic and thermal adaptations from endurance training in hot or cold water. *Journal of Applied Physiology, 78*, 793–801.

Young, P.M., Rock, P.B., Fulco, C.S., Trad, L.A., Forte, V.A. & Cymerman, A. (1987). Altitude acclimatization attenuates plasma ammonia accumulation during submaximal exercise. *Journal of Applied Physiology, 63*, 758–764.

Zaheer, A., Haas, J.T., Reyes, C., Mathur, S.N., Yang, B. & Lim, R. (2006). GMF-knockout mice are unable to induce brain-derived neurotrophic factor after exercise. *Neurochemical Research, 31*, 579–584.

Zitzmann, M., Faber, S. & Nieschlag, E. (2006). Association of specific symptoms and metabolic risks with serum testosterone in older men. *Journal of Clinical Endocrinology and Metabolism,* Epub doi:10.1210/jc.2006–0401.

Posttraumatic Stress Disorder: Genetic and Environmental Risk Factors

8

DEWLEEN G. BAKER

University of California San Diego
Veterans Affairs Center for Stress and Mental Health

VICTORIA B. RISBROUGH

University of California San Diego

NICHOLAS J. SCHORK

The Scripps Research Institute

Contents

Introduction

Civilian exposure to accidents, physical and sexual assaults, human-made and natural disasters, and other life-threatening and traumatic events is common. In societies where rates of exposure have been measured, the lifetime prevalence of experiencing such events is reported to be between 17% and 80% (Alonso et al., 2004; Creamer, Burgess & McFarlane, 2001; Frans, Rimmo, Aberg & Fredrikson, 2005; Kessler, Sonnega, Bromet, Hughes & Nelson, 1995; Norris et al., 2003; Perkonigg, Kessler, Storz & Wittchen, 2000). Individuals working in professions such as firefighting, law enforcement, or the military are potentially confronted with random, ubiquitous life-threatening events as a part of their jobs. Exposure to traumatic or life-threatening events is associated with a subsequent increase in psychiatric illness, including posttraumatic stress disorder (PTSD) (Green, Lindy, Grace & Leonard, 1992; Kang, Dalager, Mahan & Ishii, 2005; Kang, Natelson, Mahan, Lee & Murphy, 2003). Longitudinal data from the Vietnam Veteran Twin Registry demonstrate that this link persists over time (Roy-Byrne et al., 2004). Indeed a causal link between the experience of a traumatic event and the diagnosis of PTSD is codified as part of the diagnostic definition (designated Category A1 criterion) in Diagnostic and Statistical Manual of Mental Disorders-IV (DSM-IV; American Psychiatric Association, 1994).

There appears to be a dose–response relationship between the duration and intensity of specific types of trauma exposure and the resulting risk for PTSD, with some types of events being more "pathogenic" than others (Green, Grace, Lindy, Gleser & Leonard, 1990; King et al., 2000; Stein, Jang, Taylor, Vernon & Livesley, 2002; Wolfe et al., 2000). But, psychiatric outcomes (including PTSD) that follow exposure to life-threatening events show considerable variability across the population, suggesting that individual differences play an important role in determining resilience versus vulnerability to stress. For the purpose of this chapter, we view resilience primarily as a descriptor of outcome. That is, resilient individuals are defined here as those who experience only transient PTSD symptoms or none at all. In contrast, those at risk are less able to function in daily life as a result of chronic, persistent PTSD symptoms (Breslau & Davis, 1992; Davidson, Hughes, Blazer & George, 1991; North et al., 1999; Roy-Byrne et al., 2004).

The purpose of this chapter is to consider the genetic and environmental bases of PTSD. We begin with an historical review of genetic research relevant to risk and resilience with respect to PTSD. The existing research literature suggests that vulnerability to PTSD is influenced in part by a heritable or genetic component. Our historical review includes consideration of gene association studies of specific genetic variations hypothesized to be correlated with PTSD and PTSD-related outcomes. We address studies that make use of microarray-based gene expression technologies, and discuss the possible problems and issues that plague these studies. We will also consider and address new strategies for the identification and characterization of genetic factors that contribute to risk versus resilience for negative mental health outcome from exposure to life-threatening events. Our purpose is to expose the reader to the current state-of-the-art in the field, and to put in perspective potentially novel approaches to uncovering the genetic basis of resilience to PTSD.

PTSD is the only psychiatric disorder, that is, by definition, causally linked to a specific type of life experience. Thus, it is arguable that the study of PTSD and its genetic determinants offers a potentially informative paradigm for investigations of true interactions between an individual's genetic makeup and his or her exposure to environmental influences. This opportunity raises a number of issues, challenges, and potential strategies for exploring the interaction of environmental and genetic contributions to risk and resilience to PTSD. We will outline a strategic approach to state-of-the-art research of disorders that result from complex gene–environmental interactions such as hypertension, diabetes, asthma, PTSD, and other psychiatric syndromes. It should be emphasized that as we consider the potential influence of gene × environment interactions on PTSD, we refer specifically to DSM-IV PTSD category A-1 life-threat events and risk for developing PTSD. In this context, we will highlight challenges and limitations inherent in successfully completing genetic research in PTSD.

As an essential part of this chapter, we consider how new scientific approaches (e.g., translational models) might be used to better understand the specific contribution of genetics to risk versus resilience. This discussion includes model systems for endophenotypes. We consider in detail how fear-potentiated startle (FPS) or "anxiety"-potentiated startle might prove useful as a translational model for exploring genes that may mediate responses to environmental stressors.

Finally, we provide a roadmap for genetics researchers by considering pharmacologic studies that leverage information about biochemical pathways, and novel genomic research techniques that take advantage of very recently developed resources such as data emerging from the International HapMap Project (IHP) and microarray-based single nucleotide polymorphism (SNP) technologies. As a guide to those contemplating research in this area, we discuss several pathways and genes involved in neurological signaling, biosynthesis, and release. This discussion further highlights the fact that PTSD, and resilience to PTSD, are complex, multifactorial conditions with many environmental and genetic determinants.

Historical Overview

Genetic Epidemiology

Genetic epidemiologic methods have been used in studies of twins to quantify the genetic contribution to the risk of developing PTSD. Two twin studies stand out as relevant in this regard. Making use of the Vietnam Veteran Twin Registry, True et al. (1993) estimated that the genetic contribution to PTSD is approximately 30%, after accounting for the genetic influence on specific personality traits (e.g., extroversion and propensity to high-risk behavior) that mediate the risk of being exposed to life-threatening situations in the first place. Whereas the Vietnam twin registry study is the largest study, and therefore provides the strongest evidence for a genetic contribution to PTSD risk, a subsequent twin study of civilians exposed to trauma produced heritability estimates similar to those found in the large veteran study (~20% heritability) (Stein et al., 2002). Thus, it seems that despite differences in the populations studied and the environmental exposures assessed, there are consistent and identifiable genetic or heritable contributors to PTSD susceptibility.

Additional studies suggest that the genetic contribution to PTSD is complex, and that inherited genetic factors may play a role in the likelihood of exposure to trauma itself. Although Roy-Byrne et al. (2004) compared monozygotic versus dizygotic twins and found no evidence that the genetic influence on vulnerability to PTSD is related to genetic influence on exposure to trauma, other studies clearly indicate that genetic factors may play a role in the likelihood of exposure to trauma. For example, Stein et al. (2002) compared traumatic event exposure levels of monozygotic and dizygotic twins, and found that monozygotic twins shared a greater likelihood of exposure to assaultive trauma, and an especially strong correlation between assaultive trauma and the development of PTSD symptoms. These authors argued that shared genetic factors, which influence the likelihood of exposure to trauma, may also increase vulnerability to PTSD after individuals have been exposed (Stein et al., 2002). Koenen et al. (2003b) examined PTSD risk factors among Vietnam veteran twins and concluded that the likelihood of exposure to traumatic events is not random, but rather that it is influenced by both individual and familial risk factors, some of which increase vulnerability to exposure and other which increase PTSD risk in individuals who have been exposed (Koenen et al., 2003b).

Specific psychiatric and lifestyle variables have been identified as risk factors for PTSD among military personnel. For example, there is some evidence that service members, previously diagnosed with juvenile conduct disorder (CD) and those who have a history of substance abuse or dependence, are at increased risk for the development of PTSD (Koenen, Fu et al., 2005; Koenen, Hitsman et al., 2005). Koenen et al. observed that CD symptoms increased the risk for both trauma exposure and PTSD in a dose-dependent fashion—that is, the greater the number of CD symptoms, the greater the increased risk—and that this relationship was partially mediated by environmental influence such as substance abuse and dependence. However, the researchers found no evidence for pleiotopy,* that is, that a single gene or gene variation exerted an influence upon multiple traits simultaneously in a manner that would influence the underlying risk for both CD and PTSD (Koenen, Fu et al., 2005).

A subsequent study of over 6000 veterans from the same registry provided evidence that after accounting for shared risk factors, there was a robust association between nicotine dependence (ND) and PTSD. Environmental effects explained 38% of the covariation between ND and PTSD, but the authors of this study concluded that the bulk (63%) of the PTSD–ND association was explained by pleiotropic gene effects (Koenen, Hitsman et al., 2005). Despite limitations imposed by the retrospective nature of the study, the authors made an attempt to examine the direction of the association using temporal ordering of the disorders. Although the results were not definitive, they concluded that preexisting ND increased the risk of developing PTSD (Koenen, Hitsman et al., 2005). These results need to be replicated, especially because the appearance of a link between substance abuse/dependence and risk for trauma exposure and the development of PTSD is inconsistent with conclusions derived from civilian studies (Chilcoat & Breslau, 1998). Further investigation is needed to explain these differences, which may in some part reflect limitations inherent to experimental designs and statistical methodologies (Kendler, 2005). It is important to note that many inferences derived from the genetic study of a single sample or database can be unique to the specific population or group being studied because a given population may possess a unique gene pool and set of experiences. Thus, although the findings reported by Koenen et al. are of great interest, it remains possible that conclusions drawn from studies of the Vietnam Veteran Twin Registry database may not fully generalize to other (e.g., civilian and mixed gender) populations (Kendler, 2005).

---

* "Pleiotropy" describes the phenomenon whereby a single gene or genetic variation influences multiple phenotypes or traits.

Gene Association Studies

Gene association studies seek to identify specific inherited genetic variations (known as DNA sequence "polymorphisms") that correlate or are
overrepresented in individuals who possess certain phenotypes or "traits."
A small number of these studies have been performed to address genetic
risk for PTSD, and only a few of their results have thus far been replicated.
Non-replication of study results is not uncommon for association studies in
general (Hirschhorn & Daly, 2005). Factors that complicate study replication
are numerous, including the fact that medical and psychiatric diseases are
complex and multifactorial, influenced in their expression and severity by a
number of genetic and nongenetic factors. Therefore, it is difficult to isolate
the relevance of any single factor whose influence might be obscured or confounded by the effects of multiple (and potentially unknown) other factors
(Lander & Schork, 1994; Lohmueller, Pearce, Pike, Lander & Hirschhorn,
2003). Scientific and methodological issues may also limit the validity or generalizability of some studies (Ioannidis, Trikalinos, Ntzani & Contopoulos-
Ioannidis, 2003; Kendler, 2005; Newton-Cheh & Hirschhorn, 2005).

Despite these limitations, researchers have pursued studies to identify
evidence of genetic influences on PTSD and related diseases and syndromes.
In fact, there is large body of work suggesting that PTSD vulnerability may be
influenced indirectly or secondarily by a specific functional polymorphism
located in the 5' region (5 HTTLPR) of the human serotonin transporter gene
(SLC6A4). This polymorphism has already been linked to depressive and
anxiety disorders (Caspi et al., 2003; Eley et al., 2004; Gillespie, Whitfield,
Williams, Heath & Martin, 2005; Grabe et al., 2005; Kaufman et al., 2004;
Kendler, 2005), anxiety traits (Hariri et al., 2005), and differential acquisition of conditioned fear and increased amygdala excitability in humans
(Garpenstrand, Annas, Ekblom, Oreland & Fredrikson, 2001; Lesch et al.,
1996). In a first published case-controlled study, Lee et al. (2005) report
evidence that the serotonin transporter gene (SLC6A4) polymorphism
moderates vulnerability to PTSD in individuals who have been exposed to
life-threatening events (Lee et al., 2005). In a less specific set of genetic studies, Koenen et al. (2003a) found that monozygotic co-twins born to PTSD
probands experienced significantly more symptoms of mood disorder than
the monozygotic co-twins of combat controls or dizygotic co-twins of veterans
diagnosed with PTSD. This finding suggests that genetic factors mediate a
shared familial vulnerability to the comorbidity that is frequently observed
between PTSD and major depression (Koenen et al., 2003a).

There are additional lines of evidence to suggest the possible involvement of
specific genetic factors in mediating vulnerability to the development of PTSD
and related symptoms. For example, preclinical data indicate that uncontrollable
stress is associated with serotonin and dopamine efflux in the medial prefrontal

cortex of the brain (Bland et al., 2003). Such effects have been associated with changes in anxiety (Hashimoto, Inoue & Koyama, 1999) and coping (Berridge, Mitton, Clark & Roth, 1999; Horger & Roth, 1996). Thus, it is reasonable to consider that genes involved in brain dopaminergic activity might also play a role in PTSD, although at present there is only modest clinical evidence to support a direct association between dopamine neurotransmission and PTSD (Geracioti, Jr. et al., 1999; Spivak et al., 1999; Strawn et al., 2002). Three studies have considered the possible involvement of dopamine-2 (D2) receptor polymorphisms and PTSD risk, with mixed results (Comings, Muhleman & Gysin, 1996; Gelernter et al., 1999; Young et al., 2002). However, these studies were limited in several respects, including small sample size, failure to assess trauma exposure in control subjects, and failure to exclude substance-abusing probands. Segman et al. (2002) reported a statistically significant relationship between the SLCA3 9-repeat allele and PTSD in a large, well-characterized, population-stratified sample ($N = 206$). However, the authors of this study did not find evidence that the genetic variation was associated with comorbid depression in the PTSD subjects.

Based upon reports of an association between glucocorticoid (GC) receptor sensitivity and PTSD (Yehuda, Boisoneau, Lowy & Giller, 1995), Bachmann et al. (2005) recently investigated GC receptor polymorphisms (N363S and *Bcll*) in a small cohort of Australian Vietnam veterans with PTSD. This study revealed no evidence for association between variations in either the N363S gene or the *Bcll* gene and PTSD diagnosis. Nor was there evidence for an association between variations in N363S or *Bcll* and a specific measure of GC receptor sensitivity known as the "low-dose dexamethasone suppression test" (Bachmann et al., 2005).

Gene Expression Profiling

Gene expression studies attempt to identify genes that are differentially expressed in disparate individuals, for example, in those with or without a particular disease, and which might therefore serve as putative molecular markers for the disease in question. In the case of PTSD, Segman et al. (2005) have attempted to identify a peripheral blood mononuclear cell (PBMC) gene expression profile that might predict individual risk for developing PTSD after exposure to life-threatening events. The investigators used oligonucleotide microarrays, which have been designed to interrogate the expression levels of thousands of genes simultaneously, and PBMCs that were obtained immediately after exposure and again 4 months later. For the gene expression data collected both immediately after exposure and 4 months later, the expression levels of specific genes could be used to distinguish between individuals who met DSM-IV diagnostic criteria for PTSD and individuals who did not. Specifically, Segman et al. (2005) found a general reduction in

PBMC gene expression for transcription activators among PTSD-vulnerable individuals, and also found that the genes, which differentiated PTSD subjects from non-PTSD subjects included stress-related response genes. Moreover, these same expression patterns correlated with the severity of each of three PTSD symptom clusters that were assessed at 4 months postexposure (Segman et al., 2005).

Although findings such as those reported by Segman et al. (2005) are of great interest and potentially informative, it is important to note that there remain unresolved issues and questions surrounding the use of gene expression microarrays and blood cells to identify genes that influence complex traits such as PTSD risk or resilience. For example, to the extent that a specific disorder or disease has its source in lesions that affect the brain, the tissue specificity of gene expression raises the question of whether gene variations derived from a peripheral blood source are biologically relevant.

Issues and Approaches to the Study of PTSD

Several authors have addressed challenges inherent to the design of studies that are intended to identify and characterize the combined effects of genes and environmental factors on phenotypic expression (Eaves & Erkanli, 2003; Grigorenko, 2005; Kelada, Eaton, Wang, Rothman & Khoury, 2003; Kramer et al., 2005; Rutter, 2005). Moffitt, Caspi, and Rutter (2005) offer an especially useful discussion of the feasibility of such studies with respect to neuropsychiatric phenotypes. Moffitt et al. (2005) discuss seven specific strategic "steps" that should be taken in the conduct of such research. In this section, we apply this same series of strategic recommendations as an approach to address the challenges and limitations associated with the scientific effort to identify genetic factors that contribute to PTSD.

Step 1: Consult quantitative behavioral-genetic models. This first step calls upon prospective researchers to first consider existing evidence that a behavioral trait may have any genetic basis at all (Moffitt et al., 2005). In the case of PTSD, twin studies provide initial evidence that risk and resilience to PTSD are heritable tendencies. Additional evidence can be found in retrospective studies of probands from families whose members suffer from PTSD or other mental illnesses such as depression, anxiety disorders, and even psychosis (Breslau, Davis, Andreski & Peterson, 1991; Breslau, Davis, Peterson & Schultz, 1997; Bromet, Sonnega & Kessler, 1998; Cottler, Nishith & Compton, III, 2001; Reich, Lyons & Cai, 1996; Sack, Clarke & Seeley, 1995; Skre, Onstad, Torgersen, Lygren & Kringlen, 1993). However, no such effect has been found for individuals from families with alcohol or illicit substance abuse (Breslau et al., 1997; Cottler et al., 2001).

Step 2: Identify the candidate environmental pathogen. In the case of PTSD, the proximal "pathogen" is defined as traumatic stress. There is robust evidence suggesting that such traumatic stress is, in fact, causally related to PTSD. Thus, when PTSD symptoms occur, they are reliably linked to trauma. Animal models provide additional evidence that behavioral changes subsequent to severe stress are related to specific protein synthesis and neurotransmitter changes that occur in the same brain circuits and neurotransmitters, which are known to play a role in PTSD (Adamec, Blundell & Burton, 2005, 2006; Inda, gado-Garcia & Carrion, 2005; Rattiner, Davis & Ressler, 2004; Weaver et. al., 2005). Charney and his colleagues provide a comprehensive review of relevant stress neuropeptides and neurocircuitry (Bonne, Grillon, Vythilingam, Neumeister & Charney, 2004; Charney, 2004).

Step 3: Optimize environmental risk measurement. Reliable measurement of environmental risk requires attention to a number of factors. These include the potential cumulative nature of environmental influences, age-specific effects of environmental pathogens, and the scientific dangers of using retrospective recall data (Moffitt et al., 2005). To date, instruments and methods that have been developed to assess trauma exposure rely upon subjective recall of the trauma (Keane et al., 1989). Ideally, assessment should employ some additional, objective evaluation to verify the occurrence of the event, to understand its potential impact in the context of cumulative effect, and to generate an informed estimate of its intensity or severity. In principle, it should be possible to develop such an assessment in the context of military combat. Data from World War II show that the number of acute psychiatric (combat stress) casualties could be predicted by the intensity of fighting (numbers of physical casualties), mediated by the nature of the fight and the quality of the troops involved (Jones & Wessely, 2001). Although the precise relationship between combat-related stress and PTSD is not yet fully understood, it may be possible to develop an objective measure of environmental "pathogenesis" based on evidence that negative outcome and severity of symptoms are generally related to the intensity of the precipitating traumatic event(s) (Green et al., 1990; King et al., 2000; Stein et al., 2002; Wolfe et al., 2000). To be fully informative, such a measure should also take into account the potentially cumulative nature of combat experience and exposure. With these goals in mind, objective assessment can be achieved by careful documentation of structured interviews with well-informed cohorts (e.g., fellow soldiers, squad leaders). This approach could be used to support retrospective and prospective studies to elucidate the environmental pathogenesis of PTSD and to identify specific conditions, behavior, or characteristics that render individuals more or less resilient to the disorder.

Step 4: Identify candidate susceptibility genes. Certainly, it would be ideal if a researcher were able to identify candidate genes that reliably moderate phenotypic outcomes and could be shown to regulate one or more neuro-biological pathways of known relevance to those outcomes. However, Moffitt et al. (2005) acknowledge that these criteria are difficult to meet because, despite recent advances in the neurobiological study of stress and resilience (Charney, 2004; Moffitt et al., 2005; Nemeroff et al., 2005), relatively little is currently known about the effects of various environmental factors on brain physiology. Moreover, experimental designs must take into account human development and the possibility that gene–environment interactions and their effects may change over the human lifespan (Fazel, Wheeler & Danesh, 2005; Kohn, Levav, Garcia, Machuca & Tamashiro, 2005; Maercker, Michael, Fehm, Becker & Margraf, 2004; Perkonigg et al., 2000). Preclinical and clinical data suggest that during certain periods of early development, gene–environment interactions have uniquely profound and lasting effects, possibly through epigenetic and gene expression adaptations (Gardner, Thrivikraman, Lightman, Plotsky & Lowry, 2005; Kramer et al., 2005; Ladd, Huot, Thrivikraman, Nemeroff & Plotsky, 2004; Plotsky et al., 2005; Sanchez et al., 2005; Weaver et al., 2005). Such periods of unique effect do not persist into adulthood, but rather allow long-term alterations in the underlying neurobiology that will later define the individual adult phenotype (Kramer et al., 2005; Rutter, 2005). These alterations may have potentially profound effects on responsiveness to stress in adulthood because they affect neurocircuits that control physiological responses to stress (e.g., corticotropin-releasing factor [CRF]). For example, exposure to stress in childhood can produce long-term changes in hypothalamic pituitary adrenal (HPA) axis reactivity, cortisol diurnal rhythm, and serotonergic neurons in areas of the brain that project to central autonomic and emotional motor control systems (Gardner et al., 2005; Plotsky et al., 2005; Sanchez et al., 2005). In turn, these changes in the brain produce changes in behavior. Animals exposed to environmental stress during early development demonstrate a more fearful phenotype as their adults do. This effect is evident in an increased startle response* concurrent with CRF and HPA changes, and in an altered pattern of social interaction concurrent with changes in the serotonergic system (Gardner et al., 2005; Plotsky et al., 2005; Sanchez et al., 2005). Mirescu, Peters, and Gould (2004) have reported similar findings to suggest that neurogenesis in adulthood is altered when individual mice are stressed at younger ages. In human clinical research, history of childhood trauma is a well-documented risk factor for PTSD onset subsequent to adult exposure to trauma (Yehuda, Halligan & Grossman, 2001). Thus, PTSD studies of specific genotype influences in adult subjects should account for childhood trauma and, if possible,

---

* The startle response is putatively a defensive behavior evolved to protect the body from impact during attack (Graham, 1975; Yeomans et al., 2002).

other factors (e.g., intelligence, neurological soft signs, personality, coping style, physiologic responsiveness) that might be due to direct genetic effects or to phenotypic changes stemming from exposure to stress in early life (Grigorenko, 2005; Kramer et al., 2005; McNally, 2003).

Given the difficulties inherent to identifying specific candidate genes for a PTSD phenotype, an alternative strategy is to address subclinical but measurable "endophenotypes" that can be associated with PTSD based upon data derived from preclinical models and other biological abnormalities associated with PTSD. For example, FPS provides a measure of fear-based learning (acquisition learning) that can be modeled in animals and is thought to occur reliably in response to life-threatening events. Researchers have recently made significant progress toward understanding the neurocircuitry and neurochemical basis of fear-based learning (Bonne et al., 2004; Charney, 2004).

Step 5: Test for an interaction. In order to test a putative interaction between a gene and environment, the researcher, among other things, must include a cohort that is sufficient to represent genetic variation in the population-at-large and a cohort or sample of individuals who vary in their responses to the environmental pathogen(s) of interest (Collins, Lau & De La Vega, 2004; Moffitt et al., 2005). In the context of PTSD research, longitudinal cohort studies are desirable because they provide an opportunity to observe subjects before and after trauma exposure and onset of PTSD symptoms. Unfortunately, while such studies are theoretically possible in cohorts of individuals exposed to high-risk environments (e.g., war or law enforcement), they can be difficult to execute for a number of reasons, including cost. A longitudinal study of PTSD would have to assume that the base rate of potentially traumatic stress would be sufficiently severe and frequent to produce high enough rates of PTSD in cohort subjects to allow use of standard statistical measures. These conditions cannot be met in the average civilian environment, because even though the prevalence of PTSD is higher than for many other mental disorders, it is not possible to predict *a priori* who will be exposed to trauma, and consequently be potentially susceptible to PTSD. Thus, it would be necessary to longitudinally follow large numbers of subjects for an unpredictable length of time. Consequently, researchers typically favor more efficient and affordable designs such as those that add trauma exposure information to more conventional gene-association studies (Moffitt et al., 2005; Yang & Khoury, 1997).

Step 6: Evaluate whether effects of the gene–environment interaction extend beyond initially hypothesized relationships. The researcher should take an additional exploratory step to determine if the gene–environment interaction of interest has effects that extend to other genes or environmental pathogens, which activate the same neural or physiologic systems to produce similar outcomes.

Step 7: Replicate and meta-analyze. Finally, it is important to replicate positive results to rule out false positive or spurious findings. Unfortunately, as noted, genetic association studies are inherently difficult to replicate (Hirschhorn, Lohmueller, Byrne & Hirschhorn, 2002). However, resources such as the "The Genetic Association Study Database" (http://geneticassociationdb.nih.gov/) provide information that may help researchers to identify and understand the results of other genetic association studies whose findings that can be reconciled with new or unique observations.

Model Systems and the Genetic Basis of PTSD

The Startle Response

Model systems are routinely used to identify candidate biological pathways, neuroanatomical circuits, and genes that may influence specific phenotypes in human beings. For example, the startle response is a highly conserved, cross-species phenomenon that is well-suited to translational studies of pathology across animal and human subjects. The startle response manifests as a series of involuntary reflexes elicited by a sudden, intense auditory stimulus or sudden tactile stimulus to the throat or face. The startle response is modulated by cortical and limbic brain regions, many of which are abnormally activated or exhibit altered volumes in individuals who suffer from anxiety disorders (Davis, 1998; Funayama, Grillon, Davis & Phelps, 2001; Gilbertson et al., 2002; Hull, 2002; Kumari et al., 2003; Lorberbaum et al., 2004; Neumeister et al., 2004; Schneider et al., 1999; Swerdlow, Geyer & Braff, 2001; Weike et al., 2005). The magnitude of the startle response can be increased by the presentation of fear-inducing stimuli or by administration of anxiogenic compounds (Brown, Kalish & Farber, 1951; Davis, Walker & Lee, 1997; Swerdlow, Geyer, Vale & Koob, 1986), and can be decreased by the use of threat-reducing stimuli (Lang, Bradley & Cuthbert, 1990), anxiolytic and sedative drugs (Abduljawad, Langley, Bradshaw & Szabadi, 2001), or sensory input in the case of prepulse inhibition (PPI) (Braff, Geyer & Swerdlow, 2001; Geyer, Krebs-Thomson, Braff & Swerdlow, 2001; Graham, 1975; Swerdlow et al., 2001). Abnormal startle responses have been observed in subjects with anxiety disorders (Butler et al., 1990; Ludewig et al., 2005; Ludewig S., Ludewig K., Geyer, Hell & Vollenweider, 2002; Morgan, Grillon, Southwick, Davis & Charney, 1995, 1996; Orr, Lasko, Shalev & Pitman, 1995). Children of patients with anxiety and depressive disorders also exhibit exaggerated startle, indicating that startle responsiveness could be a marker of vulnerability to the development of clinical anxiety (Grillon, Dierker & Merikangas, 1998) or depression (Grillon et al., 2005). Thus, startle behavior may be useful as a model basis for the study of both state- and trait-related anxiety.

The Startle Response as a Tool for Translational Research

The measurement of rodent startle response plasticity has face validity, predictive validity, and construct validity for the study of startle plasticity in human subjects (Davis, Walker & Myers, 2003; Funayama et al., 2001; Grillon, 2002; Swerdlow, Braff, Taaid & Geyer, 1994). Unlike other anxiety measures that depend on responsiveness to novel stimuli or environments, startle behavior is relatively stable across repeated sessions and is thus ideal for longitudinal and prospective studies of change in response to stress or trauma. This stability is also observed in healthy human subjects, including clinically stable psychiatric patients (e.g., Shalev et al., 2000). The startle response may be helpful as an index of posttrauma behavioral recovery, and may also be particularly useful as a means to develop animal models of PTSD and resilience (Cohen & Zohar, 2004; Rothbaum & Davis, 2003).

Startle response paradigms offer multiple advantages over other preclinical models of anxiety. For example, measures of startle plasticity are less likely to be confounded by differences in locomotor activity (Davis, 1993; Davis, Cassella, Wrean & Kehne, 1986). Startle behavior paradigms are generally easier to use and to reproduce because they involve simple, well-controlled stimuli. The neuroanatomical and neurochemical substrates that mediate and modulate startle plasticity are already relatively well-defined. These advantages support the development of more precise experimental hypotheses and more robust interpretation of experimental results (Braff et al., 2001; Davis, Falls, Campeau & Kim, 1993; Geyer et al., 2001; Heldt, Sundin, Willott & Falls, 2000; Mansbach & Geyer, 1988; Risbrough, Hauger, Pelleymounter & Geyer, 2003; Risbrough, Hauger, Roberts, Vale & Geyer, 2004; Swerdlow et al., 2001; Walker, Ressler, Lu & Davis, 2002).

A series of elegant FPS studies conducted by the Davis laboratory (see Walker et al., 2002) found that extinction training is enhanced by the administration of D-cycloserine (a glutamate partial agonist). A subsequent clinical study found that D-cycloserine also significantly enhanced the efficacy of extinction therapy in phobic patients (Ressler et al., 2004). Thus, the FPS-extinction model has demonstrated predictive utility as a means to identify successful pharmaceutical intervention to modulate extinction processes in human subjects. Additional support for the usefulness of this model can be found in a recent meta-analysis, which indicates that enhanced fear learning may be a characteristic of clinical anxiety (Lissek et al., 2005). PTSD patients may also have deficits in the ability to extinguish learned fear (Orr et al., 2000).

Startle Endophenotypes Specific
to the Genetic Basis of Human PTSD

In human subjects, baseline startle and inhibition of startle via PPI appear to be heritable traits. PPI of the startle response occurs when a low-intensity stimulus or "prepulse" preceding an intense startling stimulus results in an inhibited startle response (Graham, 1975). This behavior is a simple operational measure of startle inhibition and sensorimotor gating. PPI is deficient in individuals with some neuropsychiatric disorders such as schizophrenia, Tourette's disease, Huntington's disorder, panic disorder, and PTSD (Braff et al., 2001; Ludewig et al., 2002, 2005). Researchers who perform twin studies report concordance as high as 50% and 70% for PPI and baseline startle (Anokhin, Heath, Myers, Ralano & Wood, 2003; Kumari, Das, Zachariah, Ettinger & Sharma, 2005). A recent study of mice found that PPI was the only one of several genetically linked types of behavior that was relatively insensitive to the epigenetic influence of maternal environment (Francis, Szegda, Campbell, Martin & Insel, 2003). PPI is currently under investigation as a potential marker for vulnerability to the development of schizophrenia (Cadenhead & Braff, 2002). PPI has also been shown to be reduced in PTSD patients, although the effect size is smaller than that shown for other neuropsychiatric disorders (Grillon, Morgan, Davis & Southwick, 1998; Grillon, Morgan, Southwick, Davis & Charney, 1996; Ornitz & Pynoos, 1989).

It is important to note that genetic studies of startle response alone do not specifically address PTSD-related phenotypes such as anxiety and fear (see Grillon & Baas, 2002, 2003; DSMIV). In animal studies, baseline abnormalities of the startle response (increased startle, reduced PPI, reduced habituation) are often observed outside the context of stress or anxiety (Geyer, McIlwain & Paylor, 2002). In human studies, changes in startle plasticity are also not specific to anxiety disorders, but rather are observed in many other neuropsychiatric disorders as well (see review by Braff et al., 2001). Thus, baseline startle or PPI phenotypes alone are not specific probes for the discovery of gene candidates involved in anxiety or PTSD (Joober, Zarate, Rouleau, Skamene & Boksa, 2002; Liu et al., 2003; Palmer et al., 2003; Swerdlow, Talledo & Braff, 2005). However, the startle response can be used in conjunction with the study of anxiety-related endophenotypes such as increased amygdala activation (Nutt & Malizia, 2004; Protopopescu et al., 2005; Rauch et al., 2000), reductions in hippocampal volume (Gilbertson et al., 2002; Gurvits et al., 1996), and excessive central CRF release (Baker et al., 1999; Bremner et al., 1997; Sautter et al., 2003). This approach is more likely to reveal genes or systems of independent or combined relevance to PTSD. It is important to note, however, that each behavioral measure of anxiety (e.g., in animals: startle responding, avoidance behavior, freezing) may probe only one specific aspect of a complex construct. Hence, each "anxiety-like" phenotype may survey a different genetic system (Crabbe, Metten, Cameron & Wahlsten, 2005).

Another important consideration is that baseline startle differences may vary between studies due to differences in the type or extent of uncontrolled experimental stressors (Grillon, 2002) or other nonspecific effects

(Swerdlow et al., 2005). More consistent and interpretable results are likely when startle changes are elicited by an experimental stimulus (e.g., prepulse or stressor), which permits baseline normalization (percentage change) and baseline matching (Baas, Nugent, Lissek, Pine & Grillon, 2004; Cornwell, Johnson, Berardi & Grillon, 2006; de Jongh, Groenink, van der Gugten & Olivier, 2003; Swerdlow et al., 2005; Walker & Davis, 2002b).

The startle response can also be used to measure fear learning or stress recovery, which have been found to be altered in individuals with PTSD and other anxiety disorders (Lissek et al., 2005; Orr et al., 2000; Rothbaum & Davis, 2003). In this way, the startle response may be used as a more specific means to identify genes or systems that mediate PTSD. For example, enhanced fear conditioning and reduced fear extinction can be measured by acquisition and extinction of FPS (Jovanovic et al., 2005; Orr et al., 2000; Walker & Davis, 2002a), stress-induced sensitization of startle (Grillon & Morgan, 1999; Yilmazer-Hanke, Faber-Zuschratter, Linke & Schwegler, 2002; Yilmazer-Hanke, Roskoden, Zilles & Schwegler, 2003; Yilmazer-Hanke, Wigger, Linke, Landgraf & Schwegler, 2004), or delayed behavioral recovery from stress (Adamec, 1997; Shalev et al., 2000). Divergent endophenotypes of highly heritable traits (e.g., FPS; Falls, Carlson, Turner & Willott, 1997; McCaughran, Bell & Hitzemann, 2000; Risbrough, Brodkin & Geyer, 2003; Risbrough & Geyer, 2005) may provide a basis for the modeling of genetic mechanisms. Cohen and Zohar (2004) observed that only a small percentage of rats demonstrate exaggerated and prolonged stress responses after "trauma" (in this case, predator odor). Selective breeding of trauma-responsive and trauma-nonresponsive rats could support the development of an animal model of genetic vulnerability to PTSD.

Animal Models of Fear Learning

Animal models of fear responding (e.g., conditioned fear) have revealed a wealth of new candidate genes and systems that may be important for acquiring, maintaining, and inhibiting conditioned fear responses. For example, researchers at the Eric Kandel Research Laboratory have recently discovered two genes, gastrin-related peptide (GRP) and oncoprotein 18/stathmin, that modulate performance in learned fear (amygdala dependent) tasks without affecting spatial working memory (hippocampus dependent) (Shumyatsky et al., 2002, 2005). The stathmin gene appears to be required for normal fear learning, while the GRP appears to inhibit anxiety and learned fear responsiveness. The apparent specificity of these genes for fear-related memory functions (versus cognition in general) is very exciting, because it suggests that these genes might also be specifically involved with anxiety disorders such as PTSD, or with putative alterations in fear learning and extinction. The impact of functional mutations to these genes on anxiety in human subjects is unknown, although genes that regulate GRP signaling have been implicated in autism (Ishikawa-Brush et al., 1997).

Because the GRP and stathmin genes are potential candidates for PTSD-related phenotypes (e.g., vulnerability to alteration of fear memory encoding or expression), researchers are now trying to determine whether stress neuropeptides in either gene are relevant to amygdala function in normal human subjects and in anxiety disorder patient populations. Targeting these genes or their peptides for therapy may be difficult, however, as both have fairly ubiquitous functions. For example, stathmin gene expression plays an important role in cell mitosis and has been associated with oncogenesis and malignant tumor growth in peripheral cells (e.g., Mistry, Bank & Atweh, 2005). Thus, manipulation of stathmin expression could produce unwanted, perhaps even deleterious side effects.

Another pathway of interest for fear memory formation and expression is the extracellular signal-regulated kinase (ERK) pathway. ERK is an intracellular second messenger system that appears to be required for amygdala-dependent fear acquisition and extinction (Apergis-Schoute, Debiec, Doyere, LeDoux & Schafe, 2005; Lin, Chakravarti & Cutler, 2004; Lu, Walker & Davis, 2001; Schafe et al., 2000). ERK signaling pathways produce transcription factors to modulate gene expression. ERK signaling has been shown to play a role in neuronal plasticity, is activated by acute stress (Meller et al., 2003; Shen, Tsimberg, Salvadore & Meller, 2004), and might also play a role in the mediation of responses to acute stress. Stress-induced enhancement of fear learning appears to occur via activation of ERK signaling (perhaps via CRF release; Sananbenesi, Fischer, Schrick, Spiess & Radulovic, 2003). Thus, the molecules that regulate ERK signaling present an exciting new avenue for the study of anxiety and fear.

As animal models improve our understanding of the cellular mechanisms that underlie learned fear and anxiety responses, they will also help to reveal additional gene candidates for the study of heritable vulnerability versus resilience to stress. In the next section, we address the need for translational research to further explore CRF using cross-species behavioral indices of fear responding.

Combining Behavioral and Biological Markers of PTSD Pathology

Several studies have documented exaggerated startle response in human subjects with PTSD. Specifically, these individuals may demonstrate increased baseline startle, increased startle in the presence of threatening or unpleasant stimuli (e.g., stimuli that predict shock, trauma-specific stimuli), reduced threshold for startle responding, and reduced PPI (Butler et al., 1990; Grillon et al., 1998, 1996; Morgan, Grillon, Southwick, Davis &

Charney, 1996; Ornitz & Pynoos, 1989; Orr et al., 1995). These differences are similar to those reported in animal subjects (mice) after administration of CRF (Conti, Murry, Ruiz & Printz, 2002; Risbrough et al., 2004; Risbrough, Hauger et al., 2003; Swerdlow et al., 1986). Studies are currently underway to determine if both phenotypes—altered startle response and CRF effects—are evident in human subjects with PTSD. If so, this could provide the basis for a unique genetic profile of PTSD. Human subjects with other disorders (e.g., panic disorder, depression) have been shown to demonstrate one effect or the other, but not both (Fossey et al., 1996; Ludewig et al., 2005; Nemeroff et al., 1984; Perry, Minassian & Feifel, 2004).

Because CRF studies with human subjects are technically difficult and time consuming, animal models are helpful to refine hypotheses and identify candidate genes. For example, inbred mouse strains can be screened for central CRF expression levels combined with specific startle phenotypes (Hovatta et al., 2005). Rats bred for differing levels of innate fearful behavior have been shown to differ both in terms of CRF peptide levels (in the amygdala) and FPS, suggesting that these two markers are linked (Yilmazer-Hanke et al., 2002). Studies of mice also suggest a causal link between CRF expression and startle behavior such that the startle phenotype may depend upon the quantity of CRF gene expression or overexpression in particular cell populations (Dirks et al., 2002; also Risbrough, Deussing, Holsboer & Geyer, unpublished observations). A combined PTSD phenotype study to screen for startle response as well as CRF expression (quantified expression levels over specific brain regions) would significantly advance our understanding of PTSD as a disorder, and would help to clarify putative CRF mechanisms for the startle response.

Pharmacologic Manipulation of CRF Systems and Startle Response

Another valuable avenue of research is found in the effort to identify genes that contribute to CRF sensitivity. Because the magnitude of CRF effects on startle varies substantially among different rodent strains (Conti, 2005; Conti, Costello, Martin, White, Abreu, 1994), it is likely that many genetic factors contribute to CRF responsiveness. CRF action involves two known G-protein receptor subtypes, CRF-R1 and CRF-R2 (Dautzenberg & Hauger, 2002; Perrin & Vale, 1999). Changes in the expression or peptide levels of these receptors are also linked to startle traits in rodents. For example, CRF-R1 receptor expression may contribute to the enhancement of the startle reflex after isolation-induced stress (Nair, Gutman, Davis & Young, 2005). The absence of such effects in CRF-R1 null mutations mice (or mice treated with CRF1 antagonists) indicates that CRF-R1 receptors mediate CRF effects on startle (Risbrough et al., 2004; Risbrough, Hauger et al., 2003). CRF-R2 mutant mice exhibit slightly prolonged recovery from CRF effects on startle and exaggerated effects of CRF on PPI (Risbrough, Hauger, Coste, Stenzel, Geyer, 2005); this supports the hypothesis that CRF-R2 receptors inhibit CRF-R1 effects on startle behavior.

It has been suggested that CRF-R2 receptor functions may be important for stress recovery or "stress coping" and "resilience" (Coste, Heard, Phillips & Stenzel-Poore, 2006; Coste, Murray & Stenzel-Poore, 2001; Reul & Holsboer, 2002; Valdez, Sabino & Koob, 2004). CRF receptor genes have been identified as good candidates for future genetic association studies of anxiety phenotypes and startle phenotypes. To date, few association studies have reported finding CRF system gene abnormalities in patients with anxiety disorders. However, one interesting observation is that polymorphism in the CRF gene is associated with behavioral inhibition, which is a risk factor for the development of clinical anxiety (Smoller et al., 2003, 2005). This area of research is new, but promising. Next, we consider novel approaches to the identification of putative genetic links between biological systems and PTSD.

Genomic Approaches to the Study of PTSD and Resilience

Contemporary large-scale DNA sequencing and polymorphism discovery initiatives such as the Human Genome Project (HGP; www.genome.gov), the ENCODE project (www.genome.gov), and the IHP (www.genome.gov and www.hapmap.org) provide researchers with access to a wealth of information and resources useful for the identification of genes that are involved in traits and diseases of all sorts. These resources can also be useful to the study of PTSD and resilience, provided that researchers recognize specific caveats, cautions, and guidelines.

Genome-Wide Human Association Studies

In the absence of prior knowledge concerning specific genes or polymorphic DNA markers, one can "search" the genome for functionally relevant variations. Although family-based genome-wide linkage analyses have long been used to support human gene discovery initiatives, the idea of sequentially testing individual polymorphic sites directly for their possible association with a particular trait was only recently proposed as a viable alternative to studies based on prior knowledge of specific genes or polymorphic markers.*

---

* Lander and Schork (1994) provide a useful description of human gene discovery strategies. See Risch and Merikangas (1996) for a discussion of the feasibility and merits of linkage-based versus association-based genome-wide approaches to gene discovery.

Although there are many difficulties associated with this broad approach, some difficulties are gradually being overcome such that whole-genome association studies may soon hold promise for the genetic study of PTSD.

If the purpose of a genome-wide study is to query all the essential components of the human genome (~3 billion nucleotides in length), then the researcher must have access to a large number of polymorphic sites in order to avoid inadvertent neglect of potentially important genomic locations. The IHP was initiated to address this need among others (Altshuler et al., 2005; www.hapmap.org). The project's recent data release and resources provide comprehensive information about human DNA polymorphism. In addition to providing information about the locations and frequencies of specific DNA sequence variations in four different populations (West African, Northern European, Chinese, and Japanese), the IHP also provides detailed information about polymorphic site "coverage" (correlation of variations, or "linkage disequilibrium" between variations). This information helps to ensure that all (or most) genomic regions can be interrogated as part of a whole-genome association study.

Whole-genome association studies are currently very expensive. For example, a researcher may need to test ~400,000 polymorphic sites in order to adequately "cover" all the polymorphic variation that exists in the genome (Altshuler et al., 2005). Using traditional genotyping assays (~$1.00 per assay), the total cost of such a study could reach as high as $80,000,000. Fortunately, new technologies and strategies can be used to reduce these costs. DNA microarrays can now be fabricated on chips to provide multiplex genotyping assays that currently cost $800–1200 per chip (see, e.g., http://www.affymetrix.com/index.affx and http://www.illumina.com/). Despite the reduced costs of large-scale genotyping via chip technology, the cost of genome-wide research is still very high (e.g., $1000 per chip × 2000 experimental subjects = $2,000,000). It is hoped that cost will be further reduced as chip technology continues to improve.

An alternative strategy for genome-wide association research is more affordable, but also problematic. DNA can be "pooled" across individuals within groups of interest (e.g., trait-positive versus trait-negative subjects). Using genotyping technology such as a chip, allele frequencies can then be estimated at each locus (Craig et al., 2005) and the resulting estimates can be compared to identify variations related to the phenotype of interest. This strategy dramatically reduces the cost of genotyping. However, pooled DNA allele frequency estimates may be unreliable, and disequilibrium patterns cannot be leveraged as they can for individual genotype studies (Salem, Wessel & Schork, 2005).

Statistical methodology is another challenge in genome-wide research. It is no small feat to yield compelling and meaningful results by the analysis of hundreds of thousands of individual DNA sequence variations. In order to avoid false positive or spurious findings, the researcher must somehow correct for the large number of statistical tests that are necessary to identify associations in a large dataset (Taylor & Tibshirani, 2006). The researcher must also carefully consider the manner in which effects of individual variations are to be modeled for the phenotype of interest. For example, each individual locus and its variations can be tested for their association with the phenotype of interest, but this strategy ignores linkage disequilibrium relationships that might exist between variations at adjacent loci. Alternatively, the researcher might consider testing haplotypes composed of variations at multiple loci. However, this strategy raises questions concerning the biological meaningfulness of the haplotypes tested.* There are also questions about how best to model gene $\times$ gene interactions, gene $\times$ environment interactions, and variant $\times$ variant interactions within a gene. With ~400,000 loci and perhaps 15–20 environmental risk factors for consideration, there are a potentially enormous number of resulting possible interactions that might be tested. Fortunately, there has been recent progress toward the development of rational and compelling approaches to the analysis of genome-wide association data (see de Bakker et al., 2005; Lin et al., 2004; Schork et al., 2001).

Genome-wide association studies require large sample sizes to provide appropriate statistical power and to account for the potential heterogeneity of factors that may contribute to phenotype expression. For example, if it is believed that a particular phenotype may be influenced by demographic or behavioral variables of relevance, these variables must be represented and controlled for by including a sufficiently large number of individuals in each of multiple groups of experimental subjects. This method can be very difficult to achieve if the phenotype in question is rare or hard to diagnose, or if the researcher is interested in an endophenotype that is particularly expensive and difficult to gather (e.g., functional imaging-derived phenotypes). The genetic analysis of large human samples also poses the issue of genetic background heterogeneity, that is, the fact that individual subjects may have unique genetic predispositions to disease or phenotypes associated with ancestry (Campbell et al., 2005; Freedman et al., 2004; Marchini, Cardon, Phillips & Donnelly, 2004). When the entire subject sample is analyzed, genetic background heterogeneity may obscure the contribution of another gene or genetic variation to the phenotype (see Berger et al., 2006). Fortunately, this problem can be overcome by the use of sophisticated statistical methods (Pritchard, Stephens, Rosenberg & Donnelly, 2000; Pritchard & Rosenberg, 1999; Schork et al., 2001).

---

* In the process of defining a haplotype and testing it for association with a particular phenotype, one typically assumes that there exist additional, unobserved variations for each haplotype that influence the phenotype. This assumption may be incorrect.

Table 8.1   Single Nucleotide Polymorphism Characteristics of Candidate Genes for PTSD

Label	Gene Name	Chrom	Size (bases)	Total SNPs	Trans Fac	Splice	ns cSNPs	Intron
CRH	Corticotropin releasing hormone	8q13	2,214	7	1	5	1	0
CRHR1	Corticotropin releasing hormone receptor 1	17q12	51,524	115	1	1	0	63
CRHR2	Corticotropin releasing hormone receptor 2	7p14	47,519	131	0	6	5	46
TH	Tyrosine hydroxylase	11p15	7,875	99	1	1	0	52
HTT	Serotonin transporter	17q11	37,799	38	0	3	1	11

Key: Label: gene label; chrom: chromosomal position; size: size of the gene in bases; total SNPs: total number of SNPs in public domain databases associated with the gene; trans fac: SNPs known to be within a transcription factor binding site; splice: SNPs in genic positions likely to effect splicing; ns cSNPs: nonsynonymous amino acid substitutions; intron: SNPs in intronic positions.

Bioinformatically Informed Candidate Gene Studies

Rather than contend with the costs and challenges inherent to genome-wide association studies, researchers may opt to conduct investigations that target specific candidate genes or genetic variations. Increasingly sophisticated genetic databases and information resources can help researchers to overcome difficulties associated with the identification of candidate genes. For example, there now exists a very large body of publicly accessible information about gene expression patterns (see http://ntddb.abcc.ncifcrf.gov/cgi-bin/nltissue.pl), the interaction of genes and proteins at the molecular level (see http://www.hpid.org/), and the effects of gene silencing and gene knockouts* in model organisms (Austin et al., 2004). Other databases contain very detailed information about actual gene variations and their likely functional or physiological significance. This information can also be obtained from computational (or *in silico*) studies such as those that address the three-dimensional structure of an encoded protein, gene transcription factors, or protein interactions with other proteins or molecules.

Table 8.1 represents detailed information about five genes of specific relevance to PTSD. This information was obtained by accessing the GeneCards database (www6.unito.it/cards/index.shtml) and the PupaSNP Web site (http://www.pupasnp.org).

---

* A gene knockout is a genetically engineered organism. One or more genes in its chromosomes have been rendered inoperative.

These publicly available databases gave us direct access to information about genetic variations that reside in different parts of each gene and also identify some properties of those variations that suggest physiological importance. This information, which we summarize in Table 8.1, allows the researcher to consider how many variations are located in transcription factor ("trans fac") binding sites and thus are likely to affect gene expression; how many variations are located in exon–intron boundaries and other relevant positions that might influence gene splicing ("splice") and thus protein formation; and how many variations are located in coding regions that create amino acid substitutions ("ns cSNPs") and thus are likely to influence protein structure.

Pharmacological Studies and the Exploitation of Genetic Network Information

In the effort to identify genes that mediate a complex phenotype such as PTSD, researchers can leverage existing pharmacologic knowledge about biochemical pathways of known or putative relevance. This approach may also provide additional insight into factors that influence response to specific treatments. In fact, the field of pharmacogenetics itself is based on the notion that it is possible to identify inherited DNA variations, which influence individual responses to particular drugs or treatments (see also PharmGKB at www.pharmgkb.org; Weber, 1997).

Table 8.2 presents a list of studies relevant to the administration of tyrosine, which has been shown to influence both animal and human responses to stress, as well as cognitive and physiologic functional abilities in the face of various types of stressors (Deijen, 2005).

Tyrosine is known to play a critical role in the biosynthesis and ultimate release of catecholamines (Lieberman, 2003) and can be administered to combat negative effects of stress (Banderet & Lieberman, 1989; Brady, Brown & Thrumond, 1980; Dollins, Krock, Storm, Wurtman & Leiberman, 1995; Lieberman, et al., 1984; Lieberman, Georgelis, Maher & Yeghiayan, 2005; Magill et al., 2003; Schurleff, Thomas, Ahlers & Schrot, 1993; Shukitt-Hale, Stillman & Leiberman, 1996; Shurleff, Thomas, Schrot, Kowalski & Harford, 1994; Waters et al., 2003; Yeghiayan, Luo, Shukitt-Hale & Leiberman, 2001). The gene encoding tyrosine hydroxylase (TH) is involved in tyrosine production. Therefore, variation in the TH gene might influence the ability of the cell to generate and utilize tyrosine, which in turn might also affect catecholamine production. Recently, Zhang et al. (2004) identified a number of naturally occurring variations in the TH gene, some of which were shown to influence blood pressure and catecholaminergic response to stress. It is of great interest then to determine whether TH gene

Table 8.2   Studies Examining the Influence of Oral Administration of Tyrosine on Stress

Reference	Species	Phenotypes/Stressors	Results
Magill et al. (2003)	Human	Cognitive; motor/sleep deprivation	Improved performance
Waters et al. (2003)	Human	Cognitive; motor/sleep deprivation	No difference
Dollins et al. (1995)	Human	Auditory potential/lower body pressure	Improved potential
Deijen et al. (1999)	Human	Combat training effects on cognitive tasks	Improved performance
Shurtleff et al. (1994)	Human	Cold stress effects on working memory	Improved performance
Deijen and Orlebeke (1994)	Human	90 dB noise while performing tasks	Improved performance
Banderet and Lieberman (1989)	Human	Mood; performance/ hypothermia; hypoxia	Improved performance
Lieberman et al. (1984)	Human	General mood/no stressor	No difference
Lieberman et al. (2005)	Rats (Fisher 344)	Water maze; swim test/ hyperthermia	Improved performance
Yeghiayan et al. (2001)	Rats	Swim test/hypothermia	Improved performance
Shukitt-Hale et al. (1996)	Rats (Fisher 344)	Swim test; memory/hypoxia	Improved performance
Shurtleff et al. (1993)	Rats	Matching tests/hypothermia	Improved performance
Ahlers et al. (1992)	Rats	Earned reinforcement/ CRF administration	Improved performance
Rauch and Lieberman (1990)	Rats	Behavioral/hypothermia	Improved performance
Reinstein et al. (1984)	Rats	Behavioral/acute stress	Improved performance
Brady et al. (1980)	Mice	Cold-swim test	Improved performance

variations may also affect responsiveness to tyrosine and vulnerability to stress-related disorders such as PTSD.

There is ample preclinical evidence that a variety of physical and emotional stressors activate cell bodies in the hindbrain locus coeruleus (LC), where TH is readily detectable in cell bodies (Aston-Jones & Cohen, 2005; Aston-Jones, Rajkowski & Cohen, 1999; Pickel, Joh & Reis, 1975; Berridge & Waterhouse, 2003). There is also now preclinical evidence that chronic stress increases the coexpression of TH in the rat prefrontal cortex, providing a means by which neuronal terminals switch from a state of low activity to one of increased TH activity in response to behavioral demand (Miner et al., 2006). Moreover, this increased TH expression demonstrates considerable variability among subjects, suggesting the possibility that there is a genetic variation.

Neuroendocrine, pharmacologic, and brain imaging studies provide compelling evidence for a persistent increase in noradrenergic activity in human subjects with PTSD. This increase is generally not observable under baseline or resting conditions, but is readily observable in response to a variety of stressors (see review by Southwick et al., 1999). Measurement of norepinephrine (NE) concentrations in cerebrospinal fluid under resting (basal) conditions does provide direct evidence of persistent central hyperarousal in PTSD. Like those who suffer from melancholic depression, individuals with PTSD demonstrate increased concentrations of cerebrospinal fluid NE (Geracioti, Jr. et al., 2001; Wong et al., 2000). Moreover, NE concentrations in subjects with PTSD correlate strongly with PTSD symptom levels (Geracioti et al., 2001).

Certainly, there are many other pharmacologic compounds and relevant genes that can and should be investigated with respect to PTSD and by reference to findings in the fields of pharmacology and neuroscience. Candidate compounds and genes of particular interest are those that influence the serotonergic, dopaminergic, noradrenergic, and CRF systems.

Conclusions and Recommendations

PTSD and resilience to PTSD are complex, multifactorial phenotypes whose genetic and environmental influences are likely to be difficult to identify with any single research paradigm. Thus, for example, association studies, especially those pursued on a genome-wide scale, will need replication in order to provide compelling results. In addition, in order for any gene that might be found to be associated with PTSD risk or resilience to play a convincing role in the etiology of PTSD-related phenotypes, its biological role in mediating PTSD must be characterized. Characterization of the "functional" role that genes play with respect to human physiology is not trivial and requires the use of state-of-the-field molecular and subclinical phenotyping technologies. In addition, model species studies—which are often used to interrogate the functional effects of genes via knockout, transgenic, and gene expression manipulations—are not likely to reveal all relevant and important details about the evolutionarily unique neural circuitry and genetic networks of relevance in human subjects. Thus, the most logical and compelling option is to apply an integrated approach by which the results of different studies and methodologies can be used to inform and confirm the results of one another.

Acknowledgments

D.G.B. is funded in part by VA grants: MERIT ("Cerebrospinal Fluid and Plasma Interleukin-6 Concentrations: Relationship to Combat Exposure, PTSD and Health Status"), Postdeployment MERIT ("Serotonin and Dopamine Transporter Genetics: A Factor in PTSD Risk?"), and Cooperative Study ("VA Cooperative Study Grant # 519, Integrated Smoking Cessation Treatment for Veterans with PTSD"). N.J.S. is funded in part by NIMH grant R01 HLMH065571-02 ("The Consortium on the Genetics of Schizophrenia"). VBR is funded in part by NIMH grant R21 MH076850-01.

References

Abduljawad, K.A.J., Langley, R.W., Bradshaw, C.M. & Szabadi, E. (2001). Effects of clonidine and diazepam on prepulse inhibition of the acoustic startle response and the N1/P2 auditory evoked potential in man. *J. Psychopharmacol., 15,* 237–242.

Adamec, R. (1997). Transmitter systems involved in neural plasticity underlying increased anxiety and defense—implications for understanding anxiety following traumatic stress. *Neurosci. Biobehav. Rev., 21,* 755–765.

Adamec, R.E., Blundell, J. & Burton, P. (2005). Neural circuit changes mediating lasting brain and behavioral response to predator stress. *Neurosci. Biobehav. Rev., 29,* 1225–1241.

Adamec, R.E., Blundell, J. & Burton, P. (2006). Relationship of the predatory attack experience to neural plasticity, pCREB expression and neuroendocrine response. *Neurosci. Biobehav. Rev., 30,* 356–375.

Ahlers, S.T., Salander, M.K., Shurtleff, D. & Thomas, J.R. (1992). Tyrosine pretreatment alleviates suppression of schedule-controlled responding produced by corticotropin releasing factor (CRF) in rats. *Brain Res. Bull., 29,* 567–571.

Alonso, J., Angermeyer, M.C., Bernert, S., Bruffaerts, R., Brugha, T.S., Bryson, H., et al. (2004). Prevalence of mental disorders in Europe: results from the European Study of the Epidemiology of Mental Disorders (ESEMeD) project. *Acta Psychiatr. Scand. Suppl.,* 21–27.

Altshuler, D., Brooks, L.D., Chakravarti, A., Collins, F.S., Daly, M.J. & Donnelly, P. (2005). International HapMap Consortium: a haplotype map of the human genome. *Nature, 437,* 1299–1320.

Anokhin, A.P., Heath, A.C., Myers, E., Ralano, A. & Wood, S. (2003). Genetic influences on prepulse inhibition of startle reflex in humans. *Neurosci. Lett., 353,* 45.

Apergis-Schoute, A.M., Debiec, J., Doyere, V., LeDoux, J.E. & Schafe, G.E. (2005). Auditory fear conditioning and long-term potentiation in the lateral amygdala require ERK/MAP kinase signaling in the auditory thalamus: a role for presynaptic plasticity in the fear system. *J. Neurosci., 25,* 5730–5739.

Aston-Jones, G. & Cohen, J.D. (2005). Adaptive gain and the role of the locus coeruleus-norepinephrine system in optimal performance. *J. Comp. Neurol., 493,* 99–110.

Aston-Jones, G., Rajkowski, J. & Cohen, J. (1999). Role of locus coeruleus in atten-
    tion and behavioral flexibility. *Biol. Psychiatr., 46*, 1309–1320.
Austin, C.P., Battey, J.F., Bradley, A., Bucan, M., Capecchi, M., Collins, F.S., et al.
    (2004). The knockout mouse project. *Nat. Genet., 36*, 921–924.
Baas, J.M., Nugent, M., Lissek, S., Pine, D.S. & Grillon, C. (2004). Fear conditioning
    in virtual reality contexts: a new tool for the study of anxiety. *Biol. Psychiatr.,
    55*, 1056–1060.
Bachmann, A.W., Sedgley, T.L., Jackson, R.V., Gibson, J.N., Young, R.M. & Torpy,
    D.J. (2005). Glucocorticoid receptor polymorphisms and post-traumatic stress
    disorder. *Psychoneuroendocrinology, 30*, 297–306.
Baker, D.G., West, S.A., Nicholson, W.E., Ekhator, N.N., Kasckow, J.W., Hill, K.K.,
    et al. (1999). Serial CSF corticotropin-releasing hormone levels and adreno-
    cortical activity in combat veterans with posttraumatic stress disorder. *Am. J.
    Psychiatr., 156*, 585–588.
Banderet, L.E. & Lieberman, H.R. (1989). Treatment with tyrosine, a neurotrans-
    mitter precursor, reduces environmental stress in humans. *Brain Res. Bull.,
    22*, 759–762.
Berger, M., Stassen, H.H., Kohler, K., Krane, V., Monks, D., Wanner, C., et al.
    (2006). Hidden population substructures in an apparently homogeneous
    population bias association studies. *Eur. J. Hum. Genet., 14*, 236–244.
Berridge, C.W., Mitton, E., Clark, W. & Roth, R.H. (1999). Engagement in a non-
    escape (displacement) behavior elicits a selective and lateralized suppression of
    frontal cortical dopaminergic utilization in stress. *Synapse, 32*, 187–197.
Berridge, C.W. & Waterhouse, B.D. (2003). The locus coeruleus-noradrenergic
    system: modulation of behavioral state and state-dependent cognitive pro-
    cesses. *Brain Res. Rev., 42*, 33–84.
Bland, S.T., Hargrave, D., Pepin, J.L., Amat, J., Watkins, L.R. & Maier, S.F. (2003).
    Stressor controllability modulates stress-induced dopamine and serotonin
    efflux and morphine-induced serotonin efflux in the medial prefrontal cortex.
    Neuropsychopharmacology, 28, 1589–1596.
Bonne, O., Grillon, C., Vythilingam, M., Neumeister, A. & Charney, D.S. (2004).
    Adaptive and maladaptive psychobiological responses to severe psychologi-
    cal stress: implications for the discovery of novel pharmacotherapy. *Neurosci.
    Biobehav. Rev., 28*, 65–94.
Brady, K., Brown, J.W. & Thurmond, J.B. (1980). Behavioral and neurochemical
    effects of dietary tyrosine in young and aged mice following cold-swim stress.
    Pharmacol. Biochem. Behav., 12, 667–674.
Braff, D.L., Geyer, M.A. & Swerdlow, N.R. (2001). Human studies of prepulse inhibi-
    tion of startle: normal subjects, patient groups, and pharmacological studies.
    Psychopharmacology (Berl), 156, 234–258.
Bremner, J.D., Licinio, J., Darnell, A., Krystal, J.H., Owens, M.J., Southwick, S.M.,
    et al. (1997). Elevated CSF corticotropin-releasing factor concentrations in
    posttraumatic stress disorder. *Am. J. Psychiatr., 154*, 624–629.
Breslau, N. & Davis, G.C. (1992). Posttraumatic stress disorder in an urban popula-
    tion of young adults: risk factors for chronicity. *Am. J. Psychiatr., 149*, 671–675.
Breslau, N., Davis, G.C., Andreski, P. & Peterson, E. (1991). Traumatic events and
    posttraumatic stress disorder in an urban population of young adults. *Arch.
    Gen. Psychiatr., 48*, 216–222.

Breslau, N., Davis, G.C., Peterson, E.L. & Schultz, L. (1997). Psychiatric sequelae of posttraumatic stress disorder in women. *Arch. Gen. Psychiatr., 54*, 81–87.

Bromet, E., Sonnega, A. & Kessler, R.C. (1998). Risk factors for DSM-III-R posttraumatic stress disorder: findings from the National Comorbidity Survey. *Am. J. Epidemiol., 147*, 353–361.

Brown, J.S., Kalish, H.I. & Farber, I.E. (1951). Conditioned fear as revealed by magnitude of startle response to an auditory stimulus. *J. Exp. Psychol., 41*, 317–328.

Butler, R.W., Braff, D.L., Rausch, J.L., Jenkins, M.A., Sprock, J. & Geyer, M.A. (1990). Physiological evidence of exaggerated startle response in a subgroup of Vietnam veterans with combat-related PTSD. *Am. J. Psychiatr., 147*, 1308–1312.

Cadenhead, K.S. & Braff, D.L. (2002). Endophenotyping schizotypy: a prelude to genetic studies within the schizophrenia spectrum. *Schizophr. Res., 54*, 47–57.

Campbell, C.D., Ogburn, E.L., Lunetta, K.L., Lyon, H.N., Freedman, M.L., Groop, L.C., et al. (2005). Demonstrating stratification in a European American population. *Nat. Genet., 37*, 868–872.

Caspi, A., Sugden, K., Moffitt, T.E., Taylor, A., Craig, I.W., Harrington, H., et al. (2003). Influence of life stress on depression: moderation by a polymorphism in the 5-HTT gene. *Science, 301*, 386–389.

Charney, D.S. (2004). Psychobiological mechanisms of resilience and vulnerability: implications for successful adaptation to extreme stress. *Am. J. Psychiatr., 161*, 195–216.

Chilcoat, H.D. & Breslau, N. (1998). Investigations of causal pathways between PTSD and drug use disorders. *Addict. Behav., 23*, 827–840.

Cohen, H. & Zohar, J. (2004). An animal model of posttraumatic stress disorder: the use of cut-off behavioral criteria. *Ann. New York Acad. Sci., 1032*, 167–178.

Collins, A., Lau, W. & De La Vega, F.M. (2004). Mapping genes for common diseases: the case for genetic (LD) maps. *Hum. Hered., 58*, 2–9.

Comings, D.E., Muhleman, D. & Gysin, R. (1996). Dopamine D2 receptor (DRD2) gene and susceptibility to posttraumatic stress disorder: a study and replication. *Biol. Psychiatr., 40*, 368–372.

Conti, L.H. (2005). Characterization of the effects of corticotropin-releasing factor on prepulse inhibition of the acoustic startle response in Brown Norway and Wistar-Kyoto rats. *Eur. J. Pharmacol., 507*, 125–134.

Conti, L.H., Costello, D.G., Martin, L.A., White, M.F. & Abreu, M.E. (1994). Mouse strain differences in the behavioral effects of corticotropin-releasing factor (CRF) and the CRF antagonist alpha-helical CRF9-41. *Pharmacol. Biochem. Behav., 48*, 497–503.

Conti, L.H., Murry, J.D., Ruiz, M.A. & Printz, M.P. (2002). Effects of corticotropin-releasing factor on prepulse inhibition of the acoustic startle response in two rat strains. *Psychopharmacology (Berl), 161*, 296–303.

Cornwell, B.R., Johnson, L., Berardi, L. & Grillon, C. (2006). Anticipation of public speaking in virtual reality reveals a relationship between trait social anxiety and startle reactivity. *Biol. Psychiatr., 59*, 664–666.

Coste, S.C., Heard, A.D., Phillips, T.J. & Stenzel-Poore, M.P. (2006). Corticotropin-releasing factor receptor type 2-deficient mice display impaired coping behaviors during stress. *Gene. Brain Behav., 5*, 131–138.

Coste, S.C., Murray, S.E. & Stenzel-Poore, M.P. (2001). Animal models of CRH excess and CRH receptor deficiency display altered adaptations to stress. *Peptides, 22,* 733–741.

Cottler, L.B., Nishith, P. & Compton, W.M. 3rd (2001). Gender differences in risk factors for trauma exposure and post-traumatic stress disorder among inner-city drug abusers in and out of treatment. *Compr. Psychiatr., 42,* 111–117.

Crabbe, J.C., Metten, P., Cameron, A.J. & Wahlsten, D. (2005). An analysis of the genetics of alcohol intoxication in inbred mice. *Neurosci. Biobehav. Rev., 28,* 785.

Craig, D.W., Huentelman, M.J., Hu-Lince, D., Zismann, V.L., Kruer, M.C., Lee, A.M., et al. (2005). Identification of disease causing loci using an array-based genotyping approach on pooled DNA. *Genomics, 6,* 138.

Creamer, M., Burgess, P. & McFarlane, A.C. (2001). Post-traumatic stress disorder: findings from the Australian National Survey of Mental Health and Well-being. *Psychol. Med., 31,* 1237–1247.

Dautzenberg, F.M. & Hauger, R.L. (2002). The CRF peptide family and their receptors: yet more partners discovered. *Trends Pharmacol. Sci., 23,* 71–77.

Davidson, J.R., Hughes, D., Blazer, D.G. & George, L.K. (1991). Post-traumatic stress disorder in the community: an epidemiological study. *Psychol. Med., 21,* 713–721.

Davis, M. (1998). Are different parts of the extended amygdala involved in fear versus anxiety? *Biol. Psychiatr., 44,* 1239–1247.

Davis, M. (1993). Pharmacological analysis of fear-potentiated startle. *Braz. J. Med. Biol. Res., 26,* 235–260.

Davis, M., Cassella, J.V., Wrean, W.H. & Kehne, J.H. (1986). Serotonin receptor subtype agonists: differential effects on sensorimotor reactivity measured with acoustic startle. *Psychopharmacol. Bull., 22,* 837–843.

Davis, M., Falls, W.A., Campeau, S. & Kim, M. (1993). Fear-potentiated startle: a neural and pharmacological analysis. *Behav. Brain Res., 58,* 175–198.

Davis, M., Walker, D.L. & Lee, Y. (1997). Roles of the amygdala and bed nucleus of the stria terminalis in fear and anxiety measured with the acoustic startle reflex. Possible relevance to PTSD. *Ann. New York Acad. Sci., 821,* 305–331.

Davis, M., Walker, D.L. & Myers, K.M. (2003). Role of the amygdala in fear extinction measured with potentiated startle. *Ann. New York Acad. Sci., 985,* 218–232.

de Bakker, P.I., Yelensky, R., Pe'er, I., Gabriel, S.B., Daly, M.J. & Altshuler, D. (2005). Efficiency and power in genetic association studies. *Nat. Genet., 37,* 1217–1223.

Deijen, J.B. (2005). Tyrosine. In: Lieberman, H.R., Kanarek, R.B. & Prasad,C. (Eds.), *Nutritional Neuroscience.* Boca Raton, FL: CRC Press, pp. 363–382.

Deijen, J.B. & Orlebeke, J.F. (1994). Effect of tyrosine on cognitive function and blood pressure under stress. *Brain Res. Bull., 33,* 319–323.

Deijen, J.B., Wientjes, C.J., Vullinghs, H.F., Cloin, P.A. & Langefeld, J.J. (1999). Tyrosine improves cognitive performance and reduces blood pressure in cadets after one week of a combat training course. *Brain Res. Bull., 48,* 203–209.

de Jongh, R., Groenink, L., van der Gugten, J. & Olivier, B. (2003). Light-enhanced and fear-potentiated startle: temporal characteristics and effects of alpha-helical corticotropin-releasing hormone. *Biol. Psychiatr., 54,* 1041–1048.

Diagnostic and Statistical Manual of Mental Disorders IV. (1994). Washington, DC: American Psychiatric Association Press.

Dirks, A., Groenink, L., Schipholt, M.I., van der Gugten, J., Hijzen, T.H., Geyer, M.A. & Olivier, B. (2002). Reduced startle reactivity and plasticity in transgenic mice overexpressing corticotropin-releasing hormone. *Biol. Psychiatr., 51*, 583–590.

Dollins, A.B., Krock, L.P., Storm, W.F., Wurtman, R.J. & Lieberman, H.R. (1995). L-tyrosine ameliorates some effects of lower body negative pressure stress. *Physiol. Behav., 57*, 223–230.

Eaves, L.J. & Erkanli, A. (2003). Markov chain Monte Carlo approaches to analysis of genetic and environmental components of human developmental change and G x E interaction. *Behav. Genet., 33*, 279–299.

Eley, T.C., Sugden, K., Corsico, A., Gregory, A.M., Sham, P., McGuffin, P., et al. (2004). Gene-environment interaction analysis of serotonin system markers with adolescent depression. *Mol. Psychiatr., 9*, 908–915.

Falls, W.A., Carlson, S., Turner, J.G. & Willott, J.F. (1997). Fear-potentiated startle in two strains of inbred mice. *Behav. Neurosci., 111*, 855–861.

Fazel, M., Wheeler, J. & Danesh, J. (2005). Prevalence of serious mental disorder in 7000 refugees resettled in western countries: a systematic review. *Lancet, 365*, 1309–1314.

Fossey, M.D., Lydiard, R.B., Ballenger, J.C., Laraia, M.T., Bissette, G. & Nemeroff, C.B. (1996). Cerebrospinal fluid corticotropin-releasing factor concentrations in patients with anxiety disorders and normal comparison subjects. *Biol. Psychiatr., 39*, 703–707.

Francis, D.D., Szegda, K., Campbell, G., Martin, W.D. & Insel, T.R. (2003). Epigenetic sources of behavioral differences in mice. *Nat. Neurosci., 6*, 445–446.

Frans, O., Rimmo, P.A., Aberg, L. & Fredrikson, M. (2005). Trauma exposure and post-traumatic stress disorder in the general population. *Acta Psychiatr. Scand., 111*, 291–299.

Freedman, M.L., Reich, D., Penney, K.L., McDonald, G.J., Mignault, A.A., Patterson, N., et al. (2004). Assessing the impact of population stratification on genetic association studies. *Nat. Genet., 36*, 388–393.

Funayama, E.S., Grillon, C., Davis, M. & Phelps, E.A. (2001). A double dissociation in the affective modulation of startle in humans: effects of unilateral temporal lobectomy. *J. Cognit. Neurosci., 13*, 721–729.

Gardner, K.L., Thrivikraman, K.V., Lightman, S.L., Plotsky, P.M. & Lowry, C.A. (2005). Early life experience alters behavior during social defeat: focus on serotonergic systems. *Neuroscience, 136*, 181–191.

Garpenstrand, H., Annas, P., Ekblom, J., Oreland, L. & Fredrikson, M. (2001). Human fear conditioning is related to dopaminergic and serotonergic biological markers. *Behav. Neurosci., 115*, 358–364.

Gelernter, J., Southwick, S., Goodson, S., Morgan, A., Nagy, L. & Charney, D.S. (1999). No association between D2 dopamine receptor (DRD2) "A" system alleles, or DRD2 haplotypes, and posttraumatic stress disorder. *Biol. Psychiatr., 45*, 620–625.

Geracioti, T.D. Jr., Baker, D.G., Ekhator, N.N., West, S.A., Hill, K.K., Bruce, A.B., et al. (2001). CSF norepinephrine concentrations in posttraumatic stress disorder. *Am. J. Psychiatr., 158*, 1227–1230.

Geracioti, T.D. Jr., West, S.A., Baker, D.G., Hill, K.K., Ekhator, N.N., Wortman, M.D., et al. (1999). Low CSF concentration of a dopamine metabolite in tobacco smokers. *Am. J. Psychiatr., 156*, 130–132.

Geyer, M.A., Krebs-Thomson, K., Braff, D.L. & Swerdlow, N.R. (2001). Pharmacological studies of prepulse inhibition models of sensorimotor gating deficits in schizophrenia: a decade in review. *Psychopharmacology (Berl), 156,* 117–154.

Geyer, M.A., McIlwain, K.L. & Paylor, R. (2002). Mouse genetic models for prepulse inhibition: an early review. *Mol. Psychiatr., 7,* 1039–1053.

Gilbertson, M.W., Shenton, M.E., Ciszewski, A., Kasai, K., Lasko, N.B., Orr, S.P. & Pitman, R.K. (2002). Smaller hippocampal volume predicts pathologic vulnerability to psychological trauma. *Nat. Neurosci., 5,* 1242–1247.

Gillespie, N.A., Whitfield, J.B., Williams, B., Heath, A.C. & Martin, N.G. (2005). The relationship between stressful life events, the serotonin transporter (5-HTTLPR) genotype and major depression. *Psychol. Med., 35,* 101–111.

Grabe, H.J., Lange, M., Wolff, B., Volzke, H., Lucht, M., Freyberger, H.J., et al. (2005). Mental and physical distress is modulated by a polymorphism in the 5-HT transporter gene interacting with social stressors and chronic disease burden. *Mol. Psychiatr., 10,* 220–224.

Graham, F.K. (1975). Presidential address, 1974. The more or less startling effects of weak prestimulation. *Psychophysiology, 12,* 238–248.

Green, B.L., Grace, M.C., Lindy, J.D., Gleser, G.C. & Leonard, A. (1990). Risk factors for PTSD and other diagnoses in a general sample of Vietnam veterans. *Am. J. Psychiatr., 147,* 729–733.

Green, B.L., Lindy, J.D., Grace, M.C. & Leonard, A.C. (1992). Chronic posttraumatic stress disorder and diagnostic comorbidity in a disaster sample. *J. Nerv. Ment. Dis., 180,* 760–766.

Grigorenko, E.L. (2005). The inherent complexities of gene-environment interactions. *J. Gerontol. B Psychol. Sci. Soc. Sci., 60 Spec No 1,* 53–64.

Grillon, C. (2002). Associative learning deficits increase symptoms of anxiety in humans, *Biol. Psychiatr., 51,* 851–858.

Grillon, C. & Baas, J. (2003). A review of the modulation of the startle reflex by affective states and its application in psychiatry. *Clin. Neurophysiol., 114,* 1557–1579.

Grillon, C. & Baas, J.M. (2002). Comments on the use of the startle reflex in psychopharmacological challenges: impact of baseline startle on measurement of fear-potentiated startle. *Psychopharmacology (Berl), 164,* 236–238.

Grillon, C., Dierker, L. & Merikangas, K.R. (1998). Fear-potentiated startle in adolescent offspring of parents with anxiety disorders. *Biol. Psychiatr., 44,* 990–997.

Grillon, C. & Morgan, C.A. 3rd (1999). Fear-potentiated startle conditioning to explicit and contextual cues in Gulf War veterans with posttraumatic stress disorder. *J. Abnorm. Psychol., 108,* 134–142.

Grillon, C., Morgan, C.A. 3rd., Davis, M. & Southwick, S.M. (1998). Effects of experimental context and explicit threat cues on acoustic startle in Vietnam veterans with posttraumatic stress disorder. *Biol. Psychiatr., 44,* 1027–1036.

Grillon, C., Morgan, C.A., Southwick, S.M., Davis, M. & Charney, D.S. (1996). Baseline startle amplitude and prepulse inhibition in Vietnam veterans with posttraumatic stress disorder. *Psychiatr. Res., 64,* 169–178.

Grillon, C., Warner, V., Hille, J., Merikangas, K.R., Bruder, G.E., Tenke, C.E., et al. (2005). Families at high and low risk for depression: a three-generation startle study. *Biol. Psychiatr., 57,* 953.

Gurvits, T.V., Shenton, M.E., Hokama, H., Ohta, H., Lasko, N.B., Gilbertson, M.W., et al. (1996). Magnetic resonance imaging study of hippocampal volume in chronic, combat-related posttraumatic stress disorder. *Biol. Psychiatr., 40,* 1091–1099.

Hariri, A.R., Drabant, E.M., Munoz, K.E., Kolachana, B.S., Mattay, V.S., Egan, M.F., et al. (2005). A susceptibility gene for affective disorders and the response of the human amygdala. *Arch. Gen. Psychiatr., 62,* 146–152.

Hashimoto, S., Inoue, T. & Koyama, T. (1999). Effects of conditioned fear stress on serotonin neurotransmission and freezing behavior in rats. *Eur. J. Pharmacol., 378,* 23–30.

Heldt, S., Sundin, V., Willott, J.F. & Falls, W.A. (2000). Posttraining lesions of the amygdala interfere with fear-potentiated startle to both visual and auditory conditioned stimuli in C57BL/6J mice. *Behav. Neurosci., 114,* 749–759.

Hirschhorn, J.N. & Daly, M.J. (2005). Genome-wide association studies for common diseases and complex traits. *Nat. Rev. Genet., 6,* 95–108.

Hirschhorn, J.N., Lohmueller, K., Byrne, E. & Hirschhorn, K. (2002). A comprehensive review of genetic association studies. *Genet. Med., 4,* 45–61.

Horger, B.A. & Roth, R.H. (1996). The role of mesoprefrontal dopamine neurons in stress. *Crit. Rev. Neurobiol., 10,* 395–418.

Hovatta, I., Tennant, R.S., Helton, R., Marr, R.A., Singer, O., Redwine, J.M., et al. (2005). Glyoxalase 1 and glutathione reductase 1 regulate anxiety in mice. *Nature, 438,* 662–666.

Hull, A.M. (2002). Neuroimaging findings in post-traumatic stress disorder. Systematic review. *Br. J. Psychiatr., 181,* 102–110.

Inda, M.C., gado-Garcia, J.M. & Carrion, A.M. (2005). Acquisition, consolidation, reconsolidation, and extinction of eyelid conditioning responses require *de novo* protein synthesis. *J. Neurosci., 25,* 2070–2080.

Ioannidis, J.P., Trikalinos, T.A., Ntzani, E.E. & Contopoulos-Ioannidis, D.G. (2003). Genetic associations in large versus small studies: an empirical assessment. *Lancet, 361,* 567–571.

Ishikawa-Brush, Y., Powell, J.F., Bolton, P., Miller, A.P., Francis, F., Willard, H.F., et al. (1997). Autism and multiple exostoses associated with an X; 8 translocation occurring within the GRPR gene and 3' to the SDC2 gene. *Hum. Mol. Genet., 6,* 1241–1250.

Jones, E. & Wessely, S. (2001). Psychiatric battle casualties: an intra- and interwar comparison. *Br. J. Psychiatr., 178,* 242–247.

Joober, R., Zarate, J.M., Rouleau, G.A., Skamene, E. & Boksa, P. (2002). Provisional mapping of quantitative trait loci modulating the acoustic startle response and prepulse inhibition of acoustic startle. *Neuropsychopharmacology, 27,* 765–781.

Jovanovic, T., Keyes, M., Fiallos, A., Myers, K.M., Davis, M. & Duncan, E.J. (2005). Fear potentiation and fear inhibition in a human fear-potentiated startle paradigm. *Biol. Psychiatr., 57,* 1559.

Kang, H., Dalager, N., Mahan, C. & Ishii, E. (2005). The role of sexual assault on the risk of PTSD among Gulf War veterans. *Ann. Epidemiol., 15,* 191–195.

Kang, H.K., Natelson, B.H., Mahan, C.M., Lee, K.Y. & Murphy, F.M. (2003). Posttraumatic stress disorder and chronic fatigue syndrome-like illness among Gulf War veterans: a population-based survey of 30,000 veterans. *Am. J. Epidemiol., 157,* 141–148.

Kaufman, J., Yang, B.Z., Douglas-Palumberi, H., Houshyar, S., Lipschitz, D., Krystal, J.H., et al. (2004). Social supports and serotonin transporter gene moderate depression in maltreated children. *Proc. Natl Acad. Sci. U.S.A., 101*, 17316–17321.

Keane, T.M., Fairbank, J.A., Caddell, J.M., Zimering, R.T., Taylor, K.I. & Mora, C.A. (1989). Brief reports: clinical evaluation of a measure to assess combat exposure. *J. Consult. Clin. Psychol., 1*, 53–55.

Kelada, S.N., Eaton, D.L., Wang, S.S., Rothman, N.R. & Khoury, M.J. (2003). The role of genetic polymorphisms in environmental health. *Environ. Health Perspect., 111*, 1055–1064.

Kendler, K.S. (2005). "A gene for...": the nature of gene action in psychiatric disorders. *Am. J. Psychiatr., 162*, 1243–1252.

Kessler, R.C., Sonnega, A., Bromet, E., Hughes, M. & Nelson, C.B. (1995). Posttraumatic stress disorder in the National Comorbidity Survey. *Arch. Gen. Psychiatr., 52*, 1048–1060.

King, D.W., King, L.A., Erickson, D.J., Huang, M.T., Sharkansky, E.J. & Wolfe, J. (2000). Posttraumatic stress disorder and retrospectively reported stressor exposure: a longitudinal prediction model. *J. Abnorm. Psychol., 109*, 624–633.

Koenen, K.C., Fu, Q.J., Lyons, M.J., Toomey, R., Goldberg, J., Eisen, S.A., et al. (2005). Juvenile conduct disorder as a risk factor for trauma exposure and posttraumatic stress disorder. *J. Trauma. Stress, 18*, 23–32.

Koenen, K.C., Hitsman, B., Lyons, M.J., Niaura, R., McCaffery, J., Goldberg, J., et al. (2005). A twin registry study of the relationship between posttraumatic stress disorder and nicotine dependence in men. *Arch. Gen. Psychiatr., 62*, 1258–1265.

Koenen, K.C., Lyons, M.J., Goldberg, J., Simpson, J., Williams, W.M., Toomey, R., et al. (2003a). A high risk twin study of combat-related PTSD comorbidity. *Twin Res., 6*, 218–226.

Koenen, K.C., Lyons, M.J., Goldberg, J., Simpson, J., Williams, W.M., Toomey, R., et al. (2003b). Co-twin control study of relationships among combat exposure, combat-related PTSD, and other mental disorders. *J. Trauma. Stress, 16*, 433–438.

Kohn, R., Levav, I., Garcia, I.D., Machuca, M.E. & Tamashiro, R. (2005). Prevalence, risk factors and aging vulnerability for psychopathology following a natural disaster in a developing country. *Int. J. Geriatr. Psychiatr., 20*, 835–841.

Kramer, J.H., Rosen, H.J., Du, A.T., Schuff, N., Hollnagel, C., Weiner, M.W., et al. (2005). Dissociations in hippocampal and frontal contributions to episodic memory performance. *Neuropsychology, 19*, 799–805.

Kumari, V., Das, M., Zachariah, E., Ettinger, U. & Sharma, T. (2005). Reduced prepulse inhibition in unaffected siblings of schizophrenia patients. *Psychophysiology, 42*, 588–594.

Kumari, V., Gray, J.A., Geyer, M.A., Ffytche, D., Soni, W., Mitterschiffthaler, M.T., et al. (2003). Neural correlates of tactile prepulse inhibition: a functional MRI study in normal and schizophrenic subjects. *Psychiatr. Res. Neuroimaging, 122*, 99–113.

Ladd, C.O., Huot, R.L., Thrivikraman, K.V., Nemeroff, C.B. & Plotsky, P.M. (2004). Long-term adaptations in glucocorticoid receptor and mineralocorticoid receptor mRNA and negative feedback on the hypothalamo-pituitary-adrenal axis following neonatal maternal separation. *Biol. Psychiatr., 55*, 367–375.

Lander, E.S. & Schork, N.J. (1994). Genetic dissection of complex traits. *Science, 265,* 2037–2048.

Lang, P.J., Bradley, M.M. & Cuthbert, B.N. (1990). Emotion, attention, and the startle reflex. *Psychol. Rev., 97,* 377–395.

Lee, H.J., Lee, M.S., Kang, R.H., Kim, H., Kim, S.D., Kee, B.S., et al. (2005). Influence of the serotonin transporter promoter gene polymorphism on susceptibility to posttraumatic stress disorder. *Depress. Anxiety, 21,* 135–139.

Lesch, K.P., Bengel, D., Heils, A., Sabol, S.Z., Greenberg, B.D., Petri, S., et al. (1996). Association of anxiety-related traits with a polymorphism in the serotonin transporter gene regulatory region. *Science, 274,* 1527–1531.

Lieberman, H.R. (2003). Nutrition, brain function and cognitive performance. *Appetite, 40,* 245–254.

Lieberman, H.R., Corkin, S., Spring, B.J., Garfield, G.S., Growdon, J.H. & Wurtman, R.J. (1984). The effects of tryptophan and tyrosine on human mood and performance. *Psychopharmacol. Bull., 20,* 595–598.

Lieberman, H.R., Georgelis, J.H., Maher, T.J. & Yeghiayan, S.K. (2005). Tyrosine prevents effects of hyperthermia on behavior and increases norepinephrine. *Physiol. Behav., 84,* 33–38.

Lin, S., Chakravarti, A. & Cutler, D.J. (2004). Exhaustive allelic transmission disequilibrium tests as a new approach to genome-wide association studies. *Nat. Genet., 36,* 1181–1188.

Lissek, S., Powers, A.S., McClure, E.B., Phelps, E.A., Woldehawariat, G., Grillon, C. & Pine, D.S. (2005). Classical fear conditioning in the anxiety disorders: a meta-analysis. *Behav. Res. Ther., 43,* 1391–1424.

Liu, D., Singh, R.P., Khan, A.H., Bhavsar, K., Lusis, A.J., Davis, R.C. & Smith, D.J. (2003). Identifying loci for behavioral traits using genome-tagged mice. *J. Neurosci. Res., 74,* 562–569.

Lohmueller, K.E., Pearce, C.L., Pike, M., Lander, E.S. & Hirschhorn, J.N. (2003). Meta-analysis of genetic association studies supports a contribution of common variants to susceptibility to common disease. *Nat. Genet., 33,* 177–182.

Lorberbaum, J.P., Kose, S., Johnson, M.R., Arana, G.W., Sullivan, L.K., Hamner, M.B., et al. (2004). Neural correlates of speech anticipatory anxiety in generalized social phobia. *Neuroreport, 15,* 2701–2705.

Ludewig, S., Geyer, M.A., Ramseier, M., Vollenweider, F.X., Rechsteiner, E. & Cattapan-Ludewig, K. (2005). Information-processing deficits and cognitive dysfunction in panic disorder. *J. Psychiatr. Neurosci., 30,* 37–43.

Ludewig, S., Ludewig, K., Geyer, M.A., Hell, D. & Vollenweider, F.X. (2002). Prepulse inhibition deficits in patients with panic disorder. *Depress. Anxiety, 15,* 55–60.

Lu, K.T., Walker, D.L. & Davis, M. (2001). Mitogen-activated protein kinase cascade in the basolateral nucleus of amygdala is involved in extinction of fear-potentiated startle. *J. Neurosci., 21,* RC162.

Maercker, A., Michael, T., Fehm, L., Becker, E.S. & Margraf, J. (2004). Age of traumatisation as a predictor of post-traumatic stress disorder or major depression in young women. *Br. J. Psychiatr., 184,* 482–487.

Magill, R.A., Waters, W.F., Bray, G.A., Volaufova, J., Smith, S.R., Lieberman, H.R., et al. (2003). Effects of tyrosine, phentermine, caffeine D-amphetamine, and placebo on cognitive and motor performance deficits during sleep deprivation. *Nutr. Neurosci., 6,* 237–246.

Mansbach, R.S. & Geyer, M.A. (1988). Blockade of potentiated startle responding in rats by 5-hydroxytryptamine1A receptor ligands. *Eur. J. Pharmacol., 156,* 375–383.

Marchini, J., Cardon, L.R., Phillips, M.S. & Donnelly, P. (2004). The effects of human population structure on large genetic association studies. *Nat. Genet., 36,* 512–517.

McCaughran, J.A. Jr., Bell, J. 3rd & Hitzemann, R.J. (2000). Fear-potentiated startle response in mice: genetic analysis of the C57BL/6J and DBA/2J intercross. *Pharmacol. Biochem. Behav., 65,* 301–312.

McNally, R.J. (2003). Psychological mechanisms in acute response to trauma. *Biol. Psychiatr., 53,* 779–788.

Meller, E., Shen, C., Nikolao, T.A., Jensen, C., Tsimberg, Y., Chen, J. & Gruen, R.J. (2003). Region-specific effects of acute and repeated restraint stress on the phosphorylation of mitogen-activated protein kinases. *Brain Res., 979,* 57–64.

Miner, L.H., Jedema, H.P., Moore, F.W., Blakely, R.D., Grace, A.A. & Sesack, S.R. (2006). Chronic stress increases the plasmalemmal distribution of the norepinephrine transporter and the coexpression of tyrosine hydroxylase in norepinephrine axons in the prefrontal cortex. *J. Neurosci., 26,* 1571–1578.

Mirescu, C., Peters, J.D. & Gould, E. (2004). Early life experience alters response of adult neurogenesis to stress. *Nat. Neurosci., 7,* 841–846.

Mistry, S.J., Bank, A. & Atweh, G.F. (2005). Targeting stathmin in prostate cancer. *Mol. Canc. Therapeut., 4,* 1821–1829.

Moffitt, T.E., Caspi, A. & Rutter, M. (2005). Strategy for investigating interactions between measured genes and measured environments. *Arch. Gen. Psychiatr., 62,* 473–481.

Morgan, C.A. 3rd., Grillon, C., Southwick, S.M., Davis, M. & Charney, D.S. (1996). Exaggerated acoustic startle reflex in Gulf War veterans with posttraumatic stress disorder. *Am. J. Psychiatr., 153,* 64–68.

Morgan, C.A. 3rd., Grillon, C., Southwick, S.M., Davis, M. & Charney, D.S. (1995). Fear-potentiated startle in posttraumatic stress disorder. *Biol. Psychiatr., 38,* 378–385.

Nair, H.P., Gutman, A.R., Davis, M. & Young, L.J. (2005). Central oxytocin, vasopressin, and corticotropin-releasing factor receptor densities in the basal forebrain predict isolation potentiated startle in rats. *J. Neurosci., 25,* 11479–11488.

Nemeroff, C.B., Bremner, J.D., Foa, E.B., Mayberg, H.S., North, C.S. & Stein, M.B. (2006). Posttraumatic stress disorder: a state-of-the-science review. *J. Psychiatr. Res., 40,* 1–21.

Nemeroff, C.B., Widerlov, E., Bissette, G., Walleus, H., Karlsson, I., Eklund, K., et al. (1984). Elevated concentrations of CSF corticotropin-releasing factor-like immunoreactivity in depressed patients. *Science, 226,* 1342–1344.

Neumeister, A., Bain, E., Nugent, A.C., Carson, R.E., Bonne, O., Luckenbaugh, D.A., et al. (2004). Reduced serotonin type 1A receptor binding in panic disorder. *J. Neurosci., 24,* 589–591.

Newton-Cheh, C. & Hirschhorn, J.N. (2005). Genetic association studies of complex traits: design and analysis issues. *Mutat. Res., 573,* 54–69.

Norris, F.H., Murphy, A.D., Baker, C.K., Perilla, J.L., Rodriguez, F.G. & Rodriguez, J.J. (2003). Epidemiology of trauma and posttraumatic stress disorder in Mexico. *J. Abnorm. Psychol., 112,* 646–656.

North, C.S., Nixon, S.J., Shariat, S., Mallonee, S., McMillen, J.C., Spitznagel, E.L., et al. (1999). Psychiatric disorders among survivors of the Oklahoma city bombing. *J. Am. Med. Assoc., 282*, 755–762.

Nutt, D.J. & Malizia, A.L. (2004). Structural and functional brain changes in post-traumatic stress disorder. *J. Clin. Psychiatr., 65 Suppl. 1*, 11–7.

Ornitz, E.M. & Pynoos, R.S. (1989). Startle modulation in children with posttraumatic stress disorder. *Am. J. Psychiatr., 146*, 866–870.

Orr, S.P., Lasko, N.B., Shalev, A.Y. & Pitman, R.K. (1995). Physiologic responses to loud tones in Vietnam veterans with posttraumatic stress disorder. *J. Abnorm. Psychol., 104*, 75–82.

Orr, S.P., Metzger, L.J., Lasko, N.B., Macklin, M.L., Peri, T. & Pitman, R.K. (2000). De novo conditioning in trauma-exposed individuals with and without post-traumatic stress disorder. *J. Abnorm. Psychol., 109*, 290–298.

Palmer, A., Breen, L., Flodman, P., Conti, L., Spence, A. & Printz, M. (2003). Identification of quantitative trait loci for prepulse inhibition in rats. *Psychopharmacology., 165*, 270.

Perkonigg, A., Kessler, R.C., Storz, S. & Wittchen, H.U. (2000). Traumatic events and post-traumatic stress disorder in the community: prevalence, risk factors and comorbidity. *Acta Psychiatr. Scand., 101*, 46–59.

Perrin, M. & Vale, W. (1999). The role of corticotropin-releasing factor receptors in stress and anxiety. In: Bale, T.L., Lee, K.F., Vale, W.W. (Eds.), *Integrative and Comparative Biology.* New York: Oxford University Press, pp. 505–526.

Perry, W., Minassian, A. & Feifel, D. (2004). Prepulse inhibition in patients with non-psychotic major depressive disorder. *J. Affect. Disord., 81*, 179–184.

Pickel, V.M., Joh, T.H. & Reis, D.J. (1975). Ultrastructural localization of tyrosine hydroxylase in noradrenergic neurons of brain. *Proc. Natl Acad. Sci. U.S.A., 72*, 659–663.

Plotsky, P.M., Thrivikraman, K.V., Nemeroff, C.B., Caldji, C., Sharma, S. & Meaney, M.J. (2005). Long-term consequences of neonatal rearing on central corticotropin-releasing factor systems in adult male rat offspring. *Neuropsychopharmacology, 30*, 2192–2204.

Pritchard, J.K. & Rosenberg, N.A. (1999). Use of unlinked genetic markers to detect population stratification in association studies. *Am. J. Hum. Genet., 65*, 220–228.

Pritchard, J.K., Stephens, M., Rosenberg, N.A. & Donnelly, P. (2000). Association mapping in structured populations. *Am J Hum Genet., 67*, 170–181.

Protopopescu, X., Pan, H., Tuescher, O., Cloitre, M., Goldstein, M., Engelien, W., et al. (2005). Differential time courses and specificity of amygdala activity in posttraumatic stress disorder subjects and normal control subjects. *Biol. Psychiatr., 57*, 464–473.

Rattiner, L.M., Davis, M. & Ressler, K.J. (2004). Differential regulation of brain-derived neurotrophic factor transcripts during the consolidation of fear learning. *Learn. Mem., 11*, 727–731.

Rauch, S.L., Whalen, P.J., Shin, L.M., McInerney, S.C., Macklin, M.L., Lasko, N.B., et al. (2000). Exaggerated amygdala response to masked facial stimuli in posttraumatic stress disorder: a functional MRI study. *Biol. Psychiatr., 47*, 769–776.

Rauch, T.M. & Lieberman, H.R. (1990). Tyrosine pretreatment reverses hypothermia-induced behavioral depression. *Brain Res. Bull., 24*, 147–150.

Reich, J., Lyons, M. & Cai, B. (1996). Familial vulnerability factors to post-traumatic stress disorder in male military veterans. *Acta Psychiatr. Scand., 93*, 105–112.

Reinstein, D.K., Lehnert, H., Scott, N.A. & Wurtman, R.J. (1984). Tyrosine prevents behavioral and neurochemical correlates of an acute stress in rats. *Life Sci., 34*, 2225–2231.

Ressler, K.J., Rothbaum, B.O., Tannenbaum, L., Anderson, P., Graap, K., Zimand, E., et al. (2004). Cognitive enhancers as adjuncts to psychotherapy: use of D-cyclo-serine in phobic individuals to facilitate extinction of fear. *Arch. Gen. Psychiatr., 61*, 1136–1144.

Reul, J.M. & Holsboer, F. (2002). Corticotropin-releasing factor receptors 1 and 2 in anxiety and depression. *Curr. Opin. Pharmacol., 2*, 23–33.

Risbrough, V.B., Brodkin, J.D. & Geyer, M.A. (2003). GABA-A and 5-HT1A receptor agonizts block expression of fear-potentiated startle in mice. *Neuropsychopharmacology, 28*, 654–663.

Risbrough, V.B. & Geyer, M.A. (2005). Anxiogenic treatments do not increase fear-potentiated startle in mice. *Biol. Psychiatr., 57*, 33–43.

Risbrough, V.B., Hauger, R.L., Pelleymounter, M.A. & Geyer, M.A. (2003). Role of corticotropin releasing factor (CRF) receptors 1 and 2 in CRF-potentiated acoustic startle in mice. *Psychopharmacology (Berl), 170*, 178–187.

Risbrough, V.B., Hauger, R.L., Roberts, A.L., Vale, W.W. & Geyer, M.A. (2004). Corticotropin-releasing factor receptors CRF1 and CRF2 exert both additive and opposing influences on defensive startle behavior. *J. Neurosci., 24*, 6545–6552.

Risbrough, V., Hauger, R., Coste, S.C., Stenzel, P. & Geyer, M.A. (2005). Role of CRF2 receptors in maintenance and recovery from CRF-R1 receptor-induced alterations in defensive startle. ACNP 44th Annual Meeting, Vol 30S1. Waikoloa, Hawaii: American College of Neuropsychopharmacology, p. S234.

Risch, N. & Merikangas, K. (1996). The future of genetic studies of complex human diseases. *Science, 273*, 1516–1517.

Rothbaum, B.O. & Davis, M. (2003). Applying learning principles to the treatment of post-trauma reactions. *Ann. New York Acad. Sci., 1008*, 112–121.

Roy-Byrne, P., Arguelles, L., Vitek, M.E., Goldberg, J., Keane, T.M., True, W.R., et al. (2004). Persistence and change of PTSD symptomatology—a longitudinal co-twin control analysis of the Vietnam Era Twin Registry. *Soc. Psychiatr. Psychiatr. Epidemiol., 39*, 681–685.

Rutter, M. (2005). Environmentally mediated risks for psychopathology: research strategies and findings. *J. Am. Acad. Child Adolesc. Psychiatr., 44*, 3–18.

Sack, W.H., Clarke, G.N. & Seeley, J. (1995). Posttraumatic stress disorder across two generations of Cambodian refugees. *J. Am. Acad. Child Adolesc. Psychiatr., 34*, 1160–1166.

Salem, R.M., Wessel, J. & Schork, N.J. (2005). A comprehensive literature review of haplotyping software and methods for use with unrelated individuals. *Hum. Genom., 2*, 39–66.

Sananbenesi, F., Fischer, A., Schrick, C., Spiess, J. & Radulovic, J. (2003). Mitogen-activated protein kinase signaling in the hippocampus and its modulation by corticotropin-releasing factor receptor 2: a possible link between stress and fear memory. *J. Neurosci., 23*, 11436–11443.

Sanchez, M.M., Noble, P.M., Lyon, C.K., Plotsky, P.M., Davis, M., Nemeroff, C.B., et al. (2005). Alterations in diurnal cortisol rhythm and acoustic startle response in nonhuman primates with adverse rearing. *Biol. Psychiatr., 57*, 373–381.

Sautter, F.J., Bissette, G., Wiley, J., Manguno-Mire, G., Schoenbachler, B., Myers, L., et al. (2003). Corticotropin-releasing factor in posttraumatic stress disorder (PTSD) with secondary psychotic symptoms, nonpsychotic PTSD, and healthy control subjects. *Biol. Psychiatr., 54*, 1382–1388.

Schafe, G.E., Atkins, C.M., Swank, M.W., Bauer, E.P., Sweatt, J.D. & LeDoux, J.E. (2000). Activation of ERK/MAP kinase in the amygdala is required for memory consolidation of pavlovian fear conditioning. *J. Neurosci., 20*, 8177–8187.

Schneider, F., Weiss, U., Kessler, C., Muller-Gartner, H.W., Posse, S., Salloum, J.B., et al. (1999). Subcortical correlates of differential classical conditioning of aversive emotional reactions in social phobia. *Biol. Psychiatr., 45*, 863–871.

Schork, N.J., Fallin, D., Thiel, B., Xu, X., Broeckel, U., Jacob, H.J. & Cohen, D. (2001). The future of genetic case-control studies. *Adv. Genet., 42*, 191–212.

Segman, R.H., Cooper-Kazaz, R., Macciardi, F., Goltser, T., Halfon, Y., Dobroborski, T., et al. (2002). Association between the dopamine transporter gene and post-traumatic stress disorder. *Mol. Psychiatr., 7*, 903–907.

Segman, R.H., Shefi, N., Goltser-Dubner, T., Friedman, N., Kaminski, N. & Shalev, A.Y. (2005). Peripheral blood mononuclear cell gene expression profiles identify emergent post-traumatic stress disorder among trauma survivors. *Mol. Psychiatr., 10*, 500–513, 425.

Shalev, A.Y., Peri, T., Brandes, D., Freedman, S., Orr, S.P. & Pitman, R.K. (2000). Auditory startle response in trauma survivors with posttraumatic stress disorder: a prospective study. *Am. J. Psychiatr., 157*, 255–261.

Shen, C.P., Tsimberg, Y., Salvadore, C. & Meller, E. (2004). Activation of Erk and JNK MAPK pathways by acute swim stress in rat brain regions. *BMC Neurosci., 5*, 36.

Shukitt-Hale, B., Stillman, M.J. & Lieberman, H.R. (1996). Tyrosine administration prevents hypoxia-induced decrements in learning and memory. *Physiol. Behav., 59*, 867–871.

Shumyatsky, G.P., Malleret, G., Shin, R.M., Takizawa, S., Tully, K., Tsvetkov, E., et al. (2005). Stathmin, a gene enriched in the amygdala, controls both learned and innate fear. *Cell, 123*, 697–709.

Shumyatsky, G.P., Tsvetkov, E., Malleret, G., Vronskaya, S., Hatton, M., Hampton, L., et al. (2002). Identification of a signaling network in lateral nucleus of amygdala important for inhibiting memory specifically related to learned fear. *Cell, 111*, 905–918.

Shurtleff, D., Thomas, J.R., Ahlers, S.T. & Schrot, J. (1993). Tyrosine ameliorates a cold-induced delayed matching-to-sample performance decrement in rats. *Psychopharmacology (Berl), 112*, 228–232.

Shurtleff, D., Thomas, J.R., Schrot, J., Kowalski, K. & Harford, R. (1994). Tyrosine reverses a cold-induced working memory deficit in humans. *Pharmacol. Biochem. Behav., 47*, 935–941.

Skre, I., Onstad, S., Torgersen, S., Lygren, S. & Kringlen, E. (1993). A twin study of DSM-III-R anxiety disorders. *Acta Psychiatr. Scand., 88,* 85–92.

Smoller, J.W., Rosenbaum, J.F., Biederman, J., Kennedy, J., Dai, D., Racette, S., et al. (2003). Association of a genetic marker at the corticotropin-releasing hormone locus with behavioral inhibition. *Biol. Psychiatr., 54,* 1376–1381.

Smoller, J.W., Yamaki, L.H., Fagerness, J.A., Biederman, J., Racette, S., Laird, N.M., et al. (2005). The corticotropin-releasing hormone gene and behavioral inhibition in children at risk for panic disorder. *Biol. Psychiatr., 57,* 1485–1492.

Southwick, S.M., Bremner, J.D., Rasmusson, A., Morgan, C.A. 3rd., Arnsten, A. & Charney, D.S. (1999). Role of norepinephrine in the pathophysiology and treatment of posttraumatic stress disorder. *Biol. Psychiatr., 46,* 1192–1204.

Spivak, B., Vered, Y., Graff, E., Blum, I., Mester, R. & Weizman, A. (1999). Low platelet-poor plasma concentrations of serotonin in patients with combat-related posttraumatic stress disorder. *Biol. Psychiatr., 45,* 840–845.

Stein, M.B., Jang, K.L., Taylor, S., Vernon, P.A. & Livesley, W.J. (2002). Genetic and environmental influences on trauma exposure and posttraumatic stress disorder symptoms: a twin study. *Am. J. Psychiatr., 159,* 1675–1681.

Strawn, J.R., Ekhator, N.N., Anthenelli, R.M., Baker, D.G., Maxwell, R.A., Hill, K.K., et al. (2002). Intra- and inter-individual relationships between central and peripheral serotonergic activity in humans: a serial cerebrospinal fluid sampling study. *Life Sci., 71,* 1219–1225.

Swerdlow, N.R., Braff, D.L., Taaid, N. & Geyer, M.A. (1994). Assessing the validity of an animal model of deficient sensorimotor gating in schizophrenic patients. *Arch. Gen. Psychiatr., 51,* 139–154.

Swerdlow, N.R., Geyer, M.A. & Braff, D.L. (2001). Neural circuit regulation of pre-pulse inhibition of startle in the rat: current knowledge and future challenges. *Psychopharmacology (Berl), 156,* 194–215.

Swerdlow, N.R., Geyer, M.A., Vale, W.W. & Koob, G.F. (1986). Corticotropin-releasing factor potentiates acoustic startle in rats: blockade by chlordiazepoxide. *Psychopharmacology (Berl), 88,* 147–152.

Swerdlow, N.R., Talledo, J.A. & Braff, D.L. (2005). Startle modulation in Caucasian-Americans and Asian-Americans: a prelude to genetic/endophenotypic studies across the 'Pacific Rim'. *Psychiatr. Genet., 15,* 61–65.

Taylor, J. & Tibshirani, R. (2006). A tail strength measure for assessing the overall univariate significance in a dataset. *Biostatistics, 7,* 167–181.

True, W.R., Rice, J., Eisen, S.A., Heath, A.C., Goldberg, J., Lyons, M.J., et al. (1993). A twin study of genetic and environmental contributions to liability for post-traumatic stress symptoms. *Arch. Gen. Psychiatr., 50,* 257–264.

Valdez, G.R., Sabino, V. & Koob, G.F. (2004). Increased anxiety-like behavior and ethanol self-administration in dependent rats: reversal via corticotropin-releasing factor-2 receptor activation. *Alcohol. Clin. Exp. Res., 28,* 865–872.

Walker, D.L. & Davis, M. (2002a). The role of amygdala glutamate receptors in fear learning, fear-potentiated startle, and extinction. *Pharmacol. Biochem. Behav., 71,* 379–392.

Walker, D.L. & Davis, M. (2002b). Quantifying fear potentiated startle using absolute versus proportional increase scoring methods: implications for the neuro-circuitry of fear and anxiety. *Psychopharmacology (Berl), 164,* 318–328.

Walker, D.L., Ressler, K.J., Lu, K.T. & Davis, M. (2002). Facilitation of conditioned fear extinction by systemic administration or intra-amygdala infusions of D-cycloserineas assessed with fear-potentiated startle in rats. *J. Neurosci.*, 22, 2343–2351.

Waters, W.F., Magill, R.A., Bray, G.A., Volaufova, J., Smith, S.R., Lieberman, H.R., et al. (2003). A comparison of tyrosine against placebo, phentermine, caffeine, and D-amphetamine during sleep deprivation. *Nutr. Neurosci.*, 6, 221–235.

Weaver, C.G., Cervoni, N., Champagne, F.A., D'Allesio, A.C., Sharma, S., Seckl, J.R., et al. (2005). Epigentic programming by maternal behavior. *Nat. Neurosci.*, 7, 847–854.

Weber, W.W. (1997). *Pharmacogenomics*. New York: Oxford University Press.

Weike, A.I., Hamm, A.O., Schupp, H.T., Runge, U., Schroeder, H.W.S. & Kessler, C. (2005). Fear conditioning following unilateral temporal lobectomy: dissociation of conditioned startle potentiation and autonomic learning. *J. Neurosci.*, 25, 11117–11124.

Wolfe, J., Chrestman, K.R., Ouimette, P.C., Kaloupek, D., Harley, R.M. & Bucsela, M. (2000). Trauma-related psychophysiological reactivity in women exposed to war-zone stress. *J. Clin. Psychol.*, 56, 1371–1379.

Wong, M.L., Kling, M.A., Munson, P.J., Listwak, S., Licinio, J., Prolo, P., et al. (2000). Pronounced and sustained central hypernoradrenergic function in major depression with melancholic features: relation to hypercortisolism and corticotropin-releasing hormone. *Proc. Natl Acad. Sci. U.S.A.*, 97, 325–330.

Yang, Q. & Khoury, M.H. (1997). Evolving methods in genetic epidemiology, III: gene-environmental interaction in epidemiological research. *Epidemiol. Rev.*, 19, 33–43.

Yeghiayan, S.K., Luo, S., Shukitt-Hale, B. & Lieberman, H.R. (2001). Tyrosine improves behavioral and neurochemical deficits caused by cold exposure. *Physiol. Behav.*, 72, 311–316.

Yehuda, R., Boisoneau, D., Lowy, M.T. & Giller, E.L. Jr. (1995). Dose-response changes in plasma cortisol and lymphocyte glucocorticoid receptors following dexamethasone administration in combat veterans with and without posttraumatic stress disorder. *Arch. Gen. Psychiatr.*, 52, 583–593.

Yehuda, R., Halligan, S.L. & Grossman, R. (2001). Childhood trauma and risk for PTSD: relationship to intergenerational effects of trauma, parental PTSD and cortisol secretion. *Dev. Psychopathol.*, 13, 733–753.

Yeomans, J.S., Li, L., Scott, B.W. & Frankland, P.W. (2002). Tactile, acoustic and vestibular systems sum to elicit the startle reflex. *Neurosci. Biobehav. Rev.*, 26, 1–11.

Yilmazer-Hanke, D.M., Faber-Zuschratter, H., Linke, R. & Schwegler, H. (2002). Contribution of amygdala neurons containing peptides and calcium-binding proteins to fear-potentiated startle and exploration-related anxiety in inbred Roman high- and low-avoidance rats. *Eur. J. Neurosci.*, 15, 1206–1218.

Yilmazer-Hanke, D.M., Roskoden, T., Zilles, K. & Schwegler, H. (2003). Anxiety-related behavior and densities of glutamate, GABAA, acetylcholine and serotonin receptors in the amygdala of seven inbred mouse strains. *Behav. Brain Res.*, 145, 145–159.

Yilmazer-Hanke, D.M., Wigger, A., Linke, R., Landgraf, R. & Schwegler, H. (2004). Two wistar rat lines selectively bred for anxiety-related behavior show opposite reactions in elevated plus maze and fear-sensitized acoustic startle tests. *Behav. Genet., 34*, 309–318.

Young, R.M., Lawford, B.R., Noble, E.P., Kann, B., Wilkie, A., Ritchie, T., et al. (2002). Harmful drinking in military veterans with post-traumatic stress disorder: association with the D2 dopamine receptor A1 allele. *Alcohol Alcohol., 37*, 451–456.

Zhang, L., Rao, F., Wessel, J., Kennedy, B.P., Rana, B.K., Taupenot, L., et al. (2004). Functional allelic heterogeneity and pleiotropy of a repeat polymorphism in tyrosine hydroxylase: prediction of catecholamines and response to stress in twins. *Physiol. Genom., 19*, 277–291.

Section III

Psychosocial Aspects
of Resilience

Resilience and Personality

9

4

MAREN WESTPHAL AND GEORGE A. BONANNO
Teachers College, Columbia University

PAUL T. BARTONE
*Center for Technology and National Security Policy,
National Defense University*

Contents

Bad things happen. During the course of our lives, most of us will be confronted with at least one potentially traumatic event (PTE) (e.g., physical or sexual assault or a life-threatening accident). Virtually everyone must contend at some point with the death of close friends and relatives. In the aftermath of such events, many people feel anxious and confused. Some may find it difficult to concentrate or to stop thinking about the event. They might experience loss of appetite or difficulty in sleeping. Reactions of this sort are usually temporary, lasting for just a few hours or days. However, for a small but important minority of individuals, trauma can have strong and enduring effects that interfere with normal function for a long period of time, perhaps even for many years after the event. These individuals usually meet the diagnostic criteria for posttraumatic stress disorder (PTSD) (American Psychiatric Association, 2000).

The trauma literature is dominated by studies of PTSD, its course, and its treatment. Although the percentage of those who develop PTSD varies by duration, severity, and type of traumatic exposure, in general, PTSD occurs in 5–10% of individuals who are exposed to PTEs (Ozer, Best, Lipsey & Weiss, 2003). Among those exposed to extreme (e.g., life-threatening) events, the proportion of those who develop PTSD tends to be higher (Bonanno, Galea & Bucciarelli, 2006). For example, a recent study of U.S. soldiers exposed to war-zone stress in Iraq reported estimated PTSD rates of up to 18% (Hoge, Castro, McGurk, Cotting & Koffman, 2004). Because PTSD can impair social and occupational functioning, these percentages suggest a substantial health cost.

By contrast, little attention has been paid to the fact that most people exposed to PTEs do not develop PTSD and that the majority often demonstrate resilience, which is to say they maintain a healthy, symptom-free functioning. Until recently, little was known about the prevalence and the characteristics of resilience among adults or about the factors that might foster or suppress resilience. Over the past few years, there has been a welcome surge of research and theory on the subject of resilience. Nonetheless, misconceptions and misunderstandings persist.

The purpose of this chapter is to review and clarify recent conceptual distinctions that have emerged in the study of resilience, with particular emphasis on personality factors of relevance to resilient outcomes in adults. We begin with a brief review of concepts and distinctions concerning resilience in children versus adults. We then offer arguments in support of the notion that adult resilience to trauma is both common and empirically distinct from the outcome trajectory that is normally associated with recovery from trauma (Bonanno, 2004). Finally, we review two distinct dispositional coping styles—flexible adaptation and pragmatic coping—that have been associated with resilient outcomes in adults.

Resilience in Children versus Adults

Resilience to extreme adversity is not a new construct. Much of the original theorizing in this area emerged during the 1970s from within the fields of developmental psychology and psychiatry. Garmezy (1971, 1974) and other pioneering researchers observed and documented that contrary to expectations, many children growing up in caustic socioeconomic circumstances followed healthy developmental trajectories (Garmezy, 1971, 1974; Murphy & Moriarity, 1976; Rutter, 1979; Werner & Smith, 1992). Prompted by the finding that this unexpected resilience among at-risk children was in fact quite a common rather than rare phenomenon, Masten (2001) described resilience as an "ordinary magic."

During that same period of time, there were also sporadic reports of widespread resilience among adults who had been exposed to isolated PTEs (e.g., Rachman, 1978). However, only recently adult resilience to trauma has become a focus of research and the differences between adults and children have become evident (Bonanno, 2004, 2005a, 2005b). Some differences appear to hinge on the temporal and contextual characteristics of stress and adaptation at different points in the human life span. Defining healthy adaptation in children presents an enormously complex task (Luthar & Cicchetti, 2000; Masten, 2001). For example, at-risk children may evidence competence in one domain while failing to meet long-term developmental challenges in other domains (Luthar, Doernberger & Zigler, 1993). The situation is arguably more straightforward for researchers who study resilience in developmentally mature adults (Bonanno, 2004, 2005a). Most, but certainly not all, PTEs can be classified as isolated stressor events (e.g., an automobile accident) that occur in a broader context of otherwise normative, low-stress circumstances. Although specific accompanying stressors such as enduring health problems or financial difficulties may exacerbate or prolong the effects of PTEs, variability in these concomitant stressors usually can be measured with a reasonable degree of reliability (Bonanno, Moskowitz, Papa & Folkman, 2005). Finally, because developmental factors tend to be less pronounced in adults, their responses to PTEs can be assessed as deviation from and return to a baseline level of functioning (Carver, 1998).

The present chapter focuses on resilience in adults. We discuss this research from a person-centered perspective based on Bonanno's (2004) definition of resilience as "the ability of adults in otherwise normal circumstances who are exposed to an isolated and potentially highly disruptive event such as the death of a close relation or a violent or life-threatening situation to maintain relatively stable, healthy levels of psychological and physical functioning … as well as the capacity for generative experiences and positive emotions" (pp. 20–21). This definition contrasts resilient outcomes with the more traditional concept of recovery, a pathway characterized by observable elevations in psychological symptoms that endure for at least several months before gradually returning to baseline, pretrauma levels. A key point is that although resilient individuals may experience some short-term dysregulation and variability in their emotional and physical well-being (Bisconti, Bergman & Boker, 2004; Carver, 1998), their reactions to a marker PTE tend to be relatively brief and usually do not impede their functioning to a significant degree. Thus, one would expect resilient individuals among a trauma-exposed population to report few or no psychological symptoms, to continue fulfilling their personal and social responsibilities, and to be able to embrace new tasks and experiences.

It is worth noting that this type of resilient response is probably not limited to acute and isolated stressor events (PTEs). Some individuals may demonstrate a similar level of resilience to more chronic or enduring stressors (e.g., diagnosis of a catastrophic illness). Some studies do address resilience to acute as well as chronic stress. However, it is not clear whether personality factors that promote resilience to acute stressors are as adaptive or as helpful in the context of chronic stress. Given the current scarcity of studies that offer clear definitions of resilient outcomes in adults and the difficulty inherent in defining resilience and resilient outcomes, we prefer, for now, to focus on acute stressor events because they offer more precise and operationally definable outcome trajectories.

Resilience versus Recovery

Within the trauma literature, there have been few attempts to distinguish subgroups within the broad category of trauma-exposed individuals who do not develop PTSD. When resilience to trauma has been addressed in the trauma literature, it is often conceived in terms of factors that "favor a path to recovery" (McFarlane & Yehuda, 1996, p. 156). Trauma theorists typically use the terms "resilience" and "recovery" interchangeably, sometimes pooling the two outcomes into a single category (King, King, Foy, Keane & Fairbank, 1999). Moreover, without an adequate database from which to consider a full range or incidence of reactions to trauma, it has been widely assumed that a positive outcome, that is, few or no symptoms of PTSD is rare and occurs only in individuals who possess exceptional physical or emotional strength.

Most early studies of adults exposed to PTEs were anecdotal and relied upon retrospective data, small sample sizes, and variable levels of trauma exposure. For example, published accounts of British civilians exposed to repeated aerial bombardment during World War II have been cited as evidence for widespread resilience (Janis, 1951; Rachman, 1978). However, these accounts were typically based on retrospective and relatively unsystematic assessments. Recent trauma studies have provided more systematic, although indirect evidence, for resilience in adults exposed to trauma. For example, Bryant, Moulds, and Guthrie (2000) studied hospitalized survivors of motor vehicle accidents and observed that the vast majority did not develop PTSD and demonstrated very few PTSD symptoms within the first week after hospitalization. Although these findings suggest that many accident survivors suffer few or no symptoms of posttraumatic stress, this study, as most similar studies in this area, was not specifically designed to address the issue of resilience. Therefore, more precise estimates of resilience were not possible.

In one of the few prospective studies of adult resilience, Saigh (1988) measured adjustment among Lebanese university students before and after they had been exposed to intense and prolonged aerial bombardment. Although most students showed signs of acute distress immediately after the bombing, almost all had returned to baseline levels of function within 1 month after the bombing. Unfortunately, the very small sample size used in this study ($n = 12$) severely limits the generalizability of its findings.

Over the past decade, several prospective and longitudinal studies have been published, which have made it possible to begin mapping the characteristics of adults who demonstrate resilience in the aftermath of PTEs. Much of our current knowledge base stems from studies of bereavement after the death of a spouse, child, or life partner (Bonanno, Keltner, Holen & Horowitz, 1995; Bonanno et al., 2005; Bonanno, Wortman et al., 2002; Bonanno, Wortman & Nesse, 2004; Bonanno, Znoj, Siddique & Horowitz, 1999; Boerner, Wortman & Bonanno, 2005). However, more recent studies also document the prevalence of resilience following potentially more traumatic events such as the September 11th terrorist attack in New York City (Bonanno et al., 2006; Bonanno, Rennicke & Dekel, 2005). This research has produced findings that not only support many of the ideas originally proposed by developmental researchers, but that also add some important new insights about the characteristics and the correlates of resilience.

In particular, more recent research has demonstrated that resilience to trauma and recovery from trauma can be mapped as discrete and empirically separable outcome trajectories (Bonanno, 2004, 2005b). These distinct trajectories were evidenced, for example, in the aftermath of spousal bereavement (e.g., Bonanno, Wortman et al., 2002) and among individuals who had experienced high levels of exposure to terrorist attack (Bonanno et al., 2005). In these studies, recovery from trauma was operationally defined as initially moderate to severe levels of psychological sequelae and significant disruptions in daily functioning that abate gradually over the course of many months before returning to baseline, pretrauma levels. By contrast, resilience was defined as either the absence of symptoms or the presence of a few mild, transient symptoms (e.g., several weeks of variability in negative affect, difficulty in concentrating, or sleeplessness) in conjunction with a relatively stable level of healthy adjustment over time.

Resilience Is Common

The traditional assumption that resilience is a rare phenomenon implies that only individuals who have exceptional mental or emotional health can be resilient to extreme adversity. However, recent empirical research indicates that resilience actually constitutes the most frequently observed outcome. For example, in a recent bereavement study, resilience to loss was operationally defined in terms of normative levels of symptoms (e.g., distressing dreams, muscle tension, headaches, decreased attention span, anxiety) observed among individuals in a matched group of nonbereaved individuals (Bonanno et al., 2005). Using this approach, it was shown that more than half the members of a sample of middle-aged, conjugally bereaved individuals had symptom levels within the normal range of symptoms for the married comparison group measured at 4 and 18 months postbereavement. In other words, resilient, bereaved individuals were no more symptomatic than their married counterparts. In a second study that used this same normative comparison approach, more than half the members of a sample of bereaved HIV+ caregivers were found to have symptom levels within the normal range of symptoms for a comparable group of non-bereaved, noncaregiving HIV+ men (Bonanno et al., 2005).

Resilience was also observed in a large probability sample ($N = 2752$) of New York Metropolitan area residents during the first 6 months after the September 11th terrorist attack in 2001 (Bonanno et al., 2006). Using random digit phone dialing, investigators were able to recruit a representative sample that closely mirrored the most recent census data for the New York area (Galea et al., 2003; Galea, Ahern et al., 2002; Galea, Resnick et al., 2002). Because assessments of PTSD symptoms were found to be highly reliable in this sample when obtained at 1, 4, and 6 months (Resnick, Galea, Kilpatrick & Vlahov, 2004), it was possible to employ a relatively conservative definition of resilience as either zero or one PTSD symptom at any point during the first 6 months after the attack. Mild trauma/recovery was defined as two or more PTSD symptoms in the absence of the PTSD diagnosis. Based on these definitions, nearly two-thirds (65%) of the sample was found to be resilient. When the sample was narrowed to include only those people who had either witnessed the attack in person or were directly affected by it (e.g., were injured or lost a friend or loved one), the proportion of the sample that demonstrated resilience was still more than 50%. In some categories of exposure (e.g., witnessing another person's death), the percentage of individuals who showed resilience dropped to slightly lower levels, but never fell below one-third of the sample even among those who experienced the most extreme levels of exposure that generated the highest levels of PTSD among their nonresilient cohorts.

Another study of high-trauma-exposed survivors who were either in or near the World Trade Center (WTC) during the September 11th attack employed a more conservative approach, requiring low symptom levels on multiple outcome measures. However, even within this more stringent context, more than one-third (35%) of survivors met the criteria for a resilient outcome (Bonanno et al., 2005). Moreover, in each of the New York studies, recovery was less frequent than resilience.

Flexible Adaptation and Pragmatic Coping

In the following sections, we describe different personality dimensions that appear to serve a protective function in the face of PTEs. Bonanno (2005) recently proposed that these person-centered factors could be cataloged into two broad categories, flexible adaptation and pragmatic coping (Bonanno, 2005).

Flexible adaptation to adverse circumstances can operate through a variety of cognitive, emotional, and interpersonal processes, but its common denominator is the capacity to shape and modify one's behavior to meet the demands of a given stressor. Flexible adaptation can be observed very early in development and appears to result from the dynamic interaction of biologically based individual differences (e.g., extroversion, emotional reactivity, and affect-intensity) and social interactions, particularly those involving attachment figures. We distinguish here between two different types of flexible adaptations that we refer to as appraisal-based flexibility and expressive flexibility. Appraisal-based flexibility refers to the ability to reduce the negative impact of potentially stressful events by appraising them in a way that promotes active engagement and enables individuals to protect and potentially enhance their sense of self-efficacy and self-esteem. Expressive flexibility refers to the ability to foster intrapersonal and interpersonal adjustment in response to potentially stressful events by regulating the expression or suppression of emotion in accordance with situational demands.

Pragmatic coping is a distinct but related construct that represents a "whatever it takes" response to PTEs that may also be referred to as "coping ugly" (Bonanno, 2006). Pragmatic coping involves single-minded goal-directed coping strategies that evoke many of the meanings pragmatic has in both colloquial language and academic usage, for example, business-like, efficient, hard-boiled, hardheaded, logical, matter-of-fact, philistine, practical, realistic, sober, and utilitarian. Unlike flexible adaptation, pragmatic coping probably does not manifest until adolescence or adulthood and involves protective factors that reflect learning, cultural influences, and gender differences as well as stable personality dispositions associated with approach and avoidance behaviors, respectively. Although some of their protective components are similar (e.g., positive emotions, self-esteem), flexible adaptation and pragmatic coping are likely to be differentially effective in response to chronic versus acute stressors. We will argue that flexible adaptation represents generally salutary personality traits and types of behavior that contribute to resilience in response to both acute stressful events and chronically corrosive environments. In contrast, pragmatic coping may promote resilience to extremely aversive events but can carry enduring social costs and other liabilities as well as have potentially maladaptive consequences when exhibited in less acute circumstances. Thus, whereas flexible adaptation is a generally healthy disposition, pragmatic coping represents something more of a "mixed blessing" (Paulhus, 1998).

Appraisal-Based Flexibility

When considering resilience, it is crucial to recognize that as horrific as many catastrophic events may be, the events themselves are not inherently traumatic. Rather, trauma represents a subjective response to PTEs that is shaped by one's view, perception, or interpretation of the event. Depending on the context, certain personal attributes serve as protective internal resources in adversity, while others increase vulnerability to psychopathology. Personality traits and coping styles are a part of a larger set of personal attributes that include intelligence, genetic predispositions, abilities and disabilities, motivation, and values. In this section, we examine personality traits that contribute to resilience by influencing the ways in which individuals appraise potentially stressful circumstances.

Optimism

The tendency to hold positive expectancies about the future is described as *dispositional optimism* (Scheier, Carver & Bridges, 1994). Optimistic individuals characteristically attribute negative events to temporary, specific, and external causes. Thus, their appraisals of stressful events tend to be relatively benign. In contrast, pessimistic people tend to believe that difficulties in life are permanent and will have a negative impact on all areas of life (Seligman, 1992). The optimistic explanatory style is associated with greater motivation and achievement, lower levels of depressive symptoms, and better physical well-being (for reviews, see Buchanan & Seligman, 1995; Peterson & Steen, 2002). Moreover, individuals who have positive expectancies are more likely to employ effective coping strategies and typically report fewer physical symptoms than their pessimistic counterparts (for reviews, see Scheier & Carver, 1992, 1993).

Although optimism has not yet been studied specifically with respect to resilience, studies of dispositional optimism and positive explanatory style suggest that the tendency toward optimistic appraisal serves as a protective resource for coping with stress. However, it may also be the case that optimistic people are relatively more vulnerable to stress when it accumulates or intensifies to a degree that defies their positive expectations. Prospective studies have found that the benefits of positive expectancies may depend on the perceived controllability of the acute or the chronic stressor (e.g., Fournier, de Ridder & Bensing, 2002). Additionally, at least in women, optimistic expectations may change over time in response to role changes that are perceived as being outside the individual's control (Atienza, Stephens & Townsend, 2004). There is also evidence that individuals with an internal locus of control, who tend to assume responsibility for the outcomes of their own actions (Rotter, 1966), may feel particularly threatened by uncontrollable events (Tomaka & Blascovich, 1994; Tomaka et al., 1999).

Another possible disadvantage of a generalized expectation of positive outcomes is that it may lead the optimist to underestimate the seriousness of a potentially threatening situation and thus to invest too little effort in coping with it. This is particularly problematic in circumstances that require careful attention and consideration of positive as well as negative information to protect oneself or other people. Research examining the effects of emotions on cognitive appraisal has demonstrated that people who experience negative affect tend to apply more stringent standards when they are asked to evaluate potentially problematic events (Ellsworth & Scherer, 2003; Schwarz & Skurnik, 2003). Thus, when faced with threatening situations, it may be more adaptive to maintain flexible and balanced expectations than to be biased toward indiscriminately positive appraisals. The ability to flexibly appraise highly threatening or stressful situations has been referred to as "hardiness" in personality and health psychology research (Gentry & Kobasa, 1984; Kobasa, 1979; Kobasa, Maddi & Courington, 1981; Kobasa, Maddi & Kahn, 1982; Kobasa, Maddi, Puccetti & Zola, 1985; Kobasa & Puccetti, 1983; Suls & Rittenhouse, 1990; Westman, 1990).

Hardiness

The construct known as hardiness was first conceived by Kobasa (1979) to describe a constellation of personality characteristics apparent in individuals who exhibit surprisingly low levels of illness in response to highly stressful life events. Specifically, Kobasa found that stress-resistant or "hardy" individuals generally (1) believe that they can control or influence events, (2) demonstrate commitment to activities, relationships, and self by adhering to distinctive values, goals and priorities in life, and (3) seek meaning in their lives and thus view adverse life events and other changes as challenges rather than as threats (Kobasa, 1979).

Although hardy and optimistic individuals share a belief in their ability to master stressful situations, hardy individuals are able to recognize the possible benefits of a challenging situation as well as the reality of potential danger and loss. We propose that this unique ability—to maintain a differentiated view of positive as well as negative information—is indicative of a more flexible appraisal style that enables hardy individuals to manage difficult circumstances and life events in a highly adaptive way.

The tendency to find positive meaning in life is considered by some researchers as the defining characteristic of hardiness and as a key contributor to the stress resistance that is observed in hardy individuals (Kobasa, 1979; Maddi, 1987; Maddi & Kobosa, 1984). Kobasa et al. (1981, 1982) proposed that hardy individuals perceive potentially stressful events as less threatening than nonhardy individuals do. Several studies have supported this hypothesis by finding that despite experiencing no more or fewer negative life events than nonhardy individuals, hardy individuals tend to evaluate negative events as less stressful and are more confident that they will cope successfully (Allred & Smith, 1989; Rhodewalt & Zone, 1989; Westman, 1990; Wiebe, 1991). Kobasa et al. (1982) found that hardy individuals reported finding more meaning in their work activities and were less vulnerable to the negative effects of stress than people scoring low on this personality dimension (Bartone, Ursano, Wright & Ingraham, 1989; Kobasa et al., 1982). A survey conducted by Rhodewalt and Zone (1989) also found that hardy women were less likely than their low-hardy female counterparts to view their life experiences as undesirable and as requiring greater adjustment. Research findings from numerous studies suggest that hardiness is positively associated with both physical and mental health (Kobasa, 1979; Kobasa et al., 1981, 1982, 1985; Kobasa & Puccetti, 1983; Maddi, 1998; Maddi & Khoshaba, 1994). Hardiness has been found to be inversely correlated with measures of anxiety and depression (Allred & Smith, 1989; Drory & Florian, 1991; Funk & Houston, 1987; Nowack, 1989, 1990; Rhodewalt & Zone, 1989) and positively correlated with well-being and adjustment (for reviews, see Blaney & Ganellen, 1990; Hull, Van Treuren & Virnelli, 1987; Orr & Westman, 1990).

The buffering effect of hardiness against adverse effects of stress on psychological well-being appears to be robust across diverse occupational groups that involve different levels of work-related stress (Bartone, 1989, 1996; Contrada, 1989; de Vries & van Heck, 2000; Kobasa et al., 1982; Roth, Wiebe, Fillingim & Shay, 1989; Wiebe, 1991). For example, Kobasa et al. (1985) studied the health of 85 business executives who experienced a high number of stressful life events and found that out of three variables known to be associated with stress resistance (personality hardiness, exercise, and social support), personality hardiness was the most important predictor of concurrent and prospective health. Optimism and health-related hardiness have also been found to predict a significant proportion of variability in the health and well-being of older women, above and beyond factors such as socioeconomic status, social support, physical illness, and access to services (Smith, Young & Lee, 2004). In a study of older people (65–80 years), Sharpley and Yardley (1999) found that hardiness was a strong predictor of scores along a mood scale (continuum from depression to happiness), with high-hardy individuals tending to score higher on the happiness end of the continuum.

Although hardiness has often been viewed as a moderator of stress-related illness, research findings are inconsistent on this point. Some studies— particularly those that measure hardiness as a composite construct—have failed to support the hypothesis that hardiness buffers against stress-related illness (Blaney & Ganellen, 1990; Funk, 1992). For example, a study of the impact of hardiness, exercise participation, self-perceived fitness level, and stress resistance found no moderator effect for hardiness, although further analyses indicated that hardiness may have had an indirect effect on health by influencing either the occurrence or the subjective interpretation of stressful life events. Clark and Hartman (1996) also found that while hardiness predicted psychological distress, it did not predict physical health. A more recent study by Klag and Bradley (2004) found that the statistical relationship between hardiness and illness was reduced when controlled for the effect of negative affectivity.

Research concerning the presumed moderating effect of hardiness has been limited by reliance upon cross-sectional, main-effect experimental designs. Very few prospective investigations have been performed to consider the interactions among variables associated with stress resistance. However, some important exceptions do provide compelling evidence that hardiness exerts a protective effect. In particular, Bartone and his colleagues have studied the relation between hardiness and resilience of military personnel who are engaged in peacekeeping and other military missions. In these populations, Bartone and Adler (1999) found that hardiness is associated with less depression and fewer other psychiatric symptoms. Bartone (1999) also explored the potential stress-moderating role of personality hardiness as predictive of psychiatric symptoms in a sample of U.S. Army reserve personnel who served in the Persian Gulf War. This study revealed a significant interaction among hardiness, combat-related stress, and stressful life events. Importantly, the relationship between hardiness and various indicators of health was strongest for individuals who had been exposed to high-stress and multiple-stress conditions (Bartone, 1999). Overall, these findings lend support to the hypothesis that hardiness may increase resistance to even the most extreme forms of stress.

Biological Correlates of Appraisal Flexibility

Experts in the research field of psychoneuroendocrinology* have used the concept of "allostatic load" to explain observed relations between hardiness and stress (McEwen, 1998; McEwen & Seeman, 2003). Allostatic load refers to the cumulative impact of stress ("wear and tear") on an individual's ability to maintain physiological homeostasis as indicated by various indices of health such as sleep and metabolic functioning. For example, several studies

---

* Psychoneuroendocrinology is a subspecialty of health psychology, concerned with interactions between the brain, hormonal systems, and other body processes.

have found that stress-related malfunctions such as insomnia and obesity are mediated, at least in part, through imbalanced levels of stress hormones such as cortisol (Brown, Varghese & McEwen, 2004; Epel, Lapidus, McEwen & Brownell, 2000; Epel et al., 2000; McEwen & Wingfield, 2003).

In a recent paper on the psychobiology of PTSD, Olff, Langeland, and Gersons (2005b) proposed that appraising potentially stressful events as an opportunity for gain (challenge) mediates the strength of the neuroendocrine stress response. Several studies have also shown that the perceived controllability of an event may not only buffer against negative biological stress responses, but may also contribute to physical thriving via neuroendocrine processes (Brosschot et al., 1998; Epel, McEwen & Ickovics, 1998; Ursin & Olff, 1993). There is evidence, for example, that challenge appraisals are associated with an adaptive neuroendocrine response pattern involving a short-term increase in catecholamine, strong anabolic counter-regulatory responses, and cortisol adaptation or habituation to subsequent stressors (Epel et al., 1998). Challenge appraisals may also contribute to increased cardiac activity and rapid cortisol responses with faster recovery (Epel et al., 1998; Frankenhaeuser, 1983; Vaernes, Ursin, Darragh & Lambe, 1982). Ursin and Olff (1993) have argued that because challenge appraisals are "nonalarming," they put less demand on one's perceived coping needs. Moreover, challenge appraisals of highly stressful events appear to facilitate a shift from negative emotions to positive arousal, which in turn might support resistance to the development of PTSD symptoms (Olff, Langeland & Gersons, 2005a, 2005b).

Reduced arousal and positive affect.   Several experimental studies suggest that when faced with stressful or challenging tasks, hardy individuals experience less negative physiological arousal and more positive affect than their nonhardy counterparts. For example, Contrada (1989) found that high-hardy individuals evidenced lower diastolic blood pressure and reported feeling the least amount of anger during a challenging cognitive (mirror-tracing) task. Similar results were reported by Wiebe (1991) who compared responses of high-hardy and low-hardy students to a stress evaluation task. Specifically, Wiebe found that high-hardy individuals appraised the experimental stressor as less threatening. Moreover, hardy male (but not female) subjects demonstrated lower levels of physiological arousal (slower heart rate response). Finally, supporting the proposed relation between hardiness and positive affect, individuals who scored high on hardiness responded with more positive and less negative affect and also evidenced higher levels of tolerance to frustration (Wiebe, 1991).

Subsequent studies have produced similar results, showing that individuals who appraise stressful events as challenging (versus threatening) tend to evidence better cardiovascular functioning, including reduced duration of cardiovascular reactivity (Tomaka, Blascovich, Kelsey & Leitten, 1993; Tomaka, Blascovich, Kibler & Ernst, 1997). In a recent experimental study, Tugade and Fredrickson (2004) observed that positive cognitive appraisal and positive emotion enabled people who scored high on the personality variable ego resilience to recover more quickly from negative emotional arousal induced by an experimental stressor. Ego resilience is a unique personality construct that will be discussed in detail later in this chapter.

Facilitation of Coping

Several studies have provided evidence that flexible appraisal may facilitate adaptive coping behavior. For example, hardy individuals tend to employ more problem-focused coping strategies and are less likely to use maladaptive, emotion-focused coping strategies such as behavioral withdrawal (Blaney & Ganellen, 1990; Kobasa & Puccetti, 1983; Westman, 1990; Williams, Wiebe & Smith, 1992). Maddi, Wadhwa, and Haier (1996) compared hardiness and optimism as mediators of everyday stress among college students and found that hardiness was associated with more decisive coping strategies (e.g., planning, positive reinterpretation, and seeking of instrumental help) and less regressive coping efforts (e.g., behavioral disengagement, denial, and alcohol or drug use; see also Maddi & Kobasa, 1984).

Particularly relevant to the current chapter are findings from a prospective study conducted by Florian, Mikulincer, and Taubman (1995). Florian et al. examined the relationship between hardiness, mental health (psychological distress and psychological well-being), cognitive appraisal, and coping style in a sample of 276 young and healthy Israeli men during a 4-month period of intensive basic combat training that forms part of their compulsory 2-year service in the Israeli Defense Forces (IDF). Self-report data on participants' hardiness and mental health (as measured by the Mental Health Inventory (MHI); Veit & Ware, 1983) were obtained at the beginning and end of the training period. Results showed that two components of hardiness—commitment and control—predicted improved mental health (reduced psychological distress and increased psychological well-being) compared with baseline measures. Path analysis revealed further that commitment exerted a positive effect on mental health. Individuals who scored high on commitment appraised combat training as less threatening, were less reliant on emotion-focused coping strategies (e.g., their coping efforts focused on understanding and controlling negative emotions), and were more likely to view themselves as capable of coping with threat. Control contributed to mental health by diminishing threat appraisals, by increasing positive secondary appraisals, and by increasing the use of problem-solving and support-seeking strategies (Florian et al., 1995).

A recent prospective study has provided intriguing data on the relationships between hardiness, habitual coping style, emotional distress, and quality of life in a prolonged stressful situation. Eid, Johnsen, Saus, and Risberg (2005) measured self-reported emotional stress symptoms and quality of life in a sample of 18 male Norwegian sailors who were confined to a disabled submarine for 1 week as part of a simulated emergency exercise. Sailors who scored high on a questionnaire measure of personality hardiness (a Norwegian translation of the short form of the Dispositional Resiliency Scale) reported lower levels of emotional distress (as measured by a questionnaire measure of posttraumatic symptoms) and improved quality of life (as measured by a General Health Questionnaire). Most interestingly, although all crew members experienced a reduction in emotional distress over the course of the week-long exercise, only hardy individuals also reported an improvement in the quality of life.

In summary, there is a growing body of evidence to support the argument that flexible appraisal styles (hardiness, optimism) may promote resilience to stress. However, relatively few studies have specified the emotion self-regulatory processes that might underlie the observed relationship between stress resilience and appraisal style. In the following section, we focus on the role of flexible regulation of emotional expression (expressive flexibility) in resilience.

Emotional Flexibility

Emotion self-regulatory processes are implicated in most aspects of the stress response, in particular physical arousal and psychological distress. The inability to downregulate negative emotions such as anger and fear are likely to play a key role in the development of stress-related syndromes such as PTSD (Briere, 1997; Chemtob, Novaco, Hamada & Gross, 1997; Herman, 1992; Kubany & Watson, 2002; Pelcovitz et al., 1997; Resick, 2001; van der Kolk et al., 1996; van der Kolk, Roth & Pelcovitz, 1993). One way in which emotion self-regulatory ability may affect vulnerability to PTSD is by influencing the impact emotional states can have on different stages of information processing such as the encoding, storage, and retrieval of memories associated with highly stressful events (Foa & Kozak, 1986; Horowitz, 1986; Litz, 1993; McNally, Kaspi, Riemann & Zeitlin, 1991). Although emotion regulation is mentioned frequently in the PTSD literature, few assessment measures have been developed to operationally define this construct (Price, Monson, Callahan & Rodriguez, 2006).

Emotion self-regulation has been defined as referring to "the processes by which we influence which emotions we have, when we have them and how we experience and express them" (Gross, 1998b, p. 275). This model of emotion regulation distinguishes between antecedent emotion self-regulation strategies that influence the occurrence of an emotional episode (e.g., angry outburst) and response-focused regulatory processes that operate after the onset of an emotional response (e.g., regulating feelings or expressions of disappointment after receiving bad news). Antecedent strategies include active selection or avoidance of situations that may trigger negative emotions, actions taken to change a situation in order to modify its (potential) emotional impact, selective focus on emotional aspects of a situation, and cognitive reappraisal of the meaning of a situation that may provoke an unwanted or negative emotional response. Response-focused self-regulation strategies include enhancing or suppressing the experience or the expression of an emotional response (Gross, 1998a, b, 1999).

Applying this theoretical framework to hardiness, the appraisal style of hardy individuals would fall under the category of antecedent regulation. Note, however, that our conceptualization of hardy appraisal style is not limited to the type of intentional and conscious antecedent and response-focused regulatory strategies that are emphasized in Gross' model of emotional self-regulation. Rather, we view the adaptive cognitive style of hardy individuals as a manifestation of dispositional appraisal-based flexibility that involves both conscious goal-directed and automatic or habitual emotion-regulatory processes. Similarly, in our following discussion of expressive flexibility, we consider both conscious and automatic or habitual uses of expression and suppression of emotion in response to stress and discuss their potential benefits and drawbacks. We will argue that the ability to flexibly shift between these two regulatory strategies is most conducive to a resilient trajectory. We also highlight the crucial role played by positive emotions in this process.

The ability to express and perceive emotions plays a crucial role in child development and continues to serve a myriad of communicative and regulatory functions throughout the human life span. The experience and expression of emotion provide structure to interpersonal encounters (Averill, 1980), help to maintain social order (Keltner, 1995; Rozin, Lowery, Imada & Haidt, 1999), and support awareness of the needs, desires, and behavioral intentions of oneself and others.

By the same token, the suppression of emotion has been linked to various adaptive costs. Defined as the conscious inhibition of emotion while emotionally aroused (Gross & Levenson, 1993), emotion suppression has been linked to poorer self-reported and objective memory (Richards & Gross, 2000), increased sympathetic activation (Gross, 1998a; Gross & Levenson, 1993, 1997), intrusive and ruminative thought (Pennebaker, 1993, 1995; Pennebaker & Beall, 1986; Pennebaker & Seagal, 1999; Pennebaker & Susman, 1988), and reduced rapport and less willingness to affiliate in dyadic partnership (Butler et al., 2003). As a trait-based regulation style, suppression has also been associated with increased vulnerability to stress-related diseases as well as adverse outcome in cancer and cardiovascular disease (Cooper & Faragher, 1992, 1993; Ornish, Brown, Scherwitz, Billings & Armstrong, 1990; Pennebaker, Kiecolt-Glaser & Glaser, 1988; Sapolsky, 1998, 1999; Stein & Spiegel, 2000).

By focusing primarily on the expressive regulation of negative emotion, the clinical literature has contributed to a polarized portrayal of emotion expression as healthy and of emotion suppression as unhealthy (e.g., Consedine, Magai & Bonanno, 2002; Salovey, 2001). The construct of expressive flexibility encapsulates the idea that the expression and the suppression of emotion each have both costs and benefits. For example, although verbal disclosure of emotionally charged information is necessary at times to elicit practical and emotional support, it may also incur significant social and psychological costs depending on what is expressed, to whom, and how (Kelly & McKillop, 1996; Kennedy-Moore & Watson, 2001). The listener may misinterpret the speaker's intent or minimize or dismiss the importance of the information being shared, leaving the communicator to feel rejected and humiliated (e.g., Lehman, Ellard & Wortman, 1986; Major et al., 1990; Silver, Boon & Stones, 1983; Silver & Wortman, 1980; Silver, Wortman & Crofton, 1990). In close relationships, the expression of emotional distress can instigate or intensify negative escalation cycles, particularly if the listener perceives that he or she is being blamed (e.g., Gottman & Levenson, 1986; Julien, Markman, Leveille, Chartrand & Begin, 1994). The duration and intensity of negative emotional expression tends to increase when negative emotion is expressed as anger (Ebbesen, Duncan & Konecni, 1975).

The psychological and social implications of negative emotion expression may differ depending upon personal and cultural standards (e.g., Kitayama & Markus, 1996; Mesquita & Frijda, 1992; Porter & Samovar, 1998; Surgenor & Joseph, 2000). For example, in Japan or China, it is considered socially desirable to inhibit the expression of negative emotion (Markus & Kitayama, 1991; Mesquita, 2001). Thus, while some individuals may feel quite comfortable about the expression of negative emotion, others may view it as a shameful lapse in self-control (Kennedy-Moore & Watson, 1999).

There is evidence to suggest that the ability to modify negative emotional expression may support recovery of normal functioning in adverse circumstances. Bonanno and Keltner (1997) studied reactions to bereavement in a normal population and found that facial expressions of negative emotion, and anger in particular, predicted a more protracted course of grief even when initial levels of grief and self-reported emotional experience were statistically controlled. By contrast, the expression of positive emotion while relating distressing information about the loss of one's spouse predicted reduced levels of grief at subsequent assessments. Recently, researchers have drawn attention to the adaptive value of positive emotional expression as a strategy to cope with stress. According to Fredrickson's' "broaden and build" theory (Fredrickson, 2001; Fredrickson & Levenson, 1998; Fredrickson, Tugade, Waugh & Larkin, 2003; Tugade & Fredrickson, 2004), positive emotional expressions (e.g., laughter) broaden cognitive resources, thus facilitating perception of a wider range of possibilities. Laughter and smiling may also help to build resources such as stable interpersonal bonds, which in turn may facilitate reciprocal and cooperative behavior in times of need (Isen, 1987; Oatley & Jenkins, 1996; Owren & Bachorowski, 2001).

Although emotions are often expressed spontaneously, people sometimes express emotion in a deliberate or strategic manner as a means to attract interest or goodwill (Bonanno, 2001; Gross, 1998b). Bonanno and colleagues have proposed that the psychologically adaptive benefits of emotional expression or suppression depend upon the extent to which self-regulatory processes can be employed in a flexible and goal-directed manner to meet situational demands (Bonanno, Papa, Lalande, Westphal & Coifman, 2004). Bonanno et al. (2004) tested this hypothesis in a study of New York City college students during the aftermath of the September 11th terrorist attacks in 2001 and found that flexibility (versus ability or frequency) of emotional expression and suppression predicted better adaptation across a 2-year period. However, it remains to be seen whether flexibility of emotional expression also predicts better adjustment in populations that are directly exposed to high levels of stress such as combat.

A Dynamic Model of Affect

Flexibility is also evidenced in the subjective experience of emotion. Emotion theorists have noted that affective experience can vary greatly between individuals, in different situations, and over time (Green, Salovey & Truax, 1999; Rafaeli, Rogers & Revelle, 2007; Russell & Feldman-Barrett, 1999). In an effort to address this issue, Zautra and colleagues proposed an integrative model, the dynamic model of affect (DMA; Davis, Zautra & Smith, 2004; Pruchno & Meeks, 2004; Reich, Zautra & Davis, 2003; Zautra, 2003; Zautra, Berkhof & Nicolsen, 2002). These authors argue that during periods of stress, as cognitive resources become increasingly narrow and focused, affective space becomes more limited. Under ordinary circumstances, most people demonstrate a capacity for complex affect, including simultaneous and contiguous awareness of positive and negative affects. Normally, positive and negative affective states are only loosely correlated and tend to function independently. DMA predicts that stress will tend to limit the conscious experience of affect such that individuals under stress might only be aware of negative or positive emotions. Under stress, affective experiences should become more highly correlated and polarized (for more detailed explication, see Zautra, 2003; Reich et al., 2003).

Bisconti, Bergeman, and Boker (2004) recently reported findings that are consistent with these predictions. These investigators attempted to test the idea that "a stressful life event, such as the death of a spouse, perturbs the emotional well-being state of the individual away from equilibrium, contributing to emotional shifts that vacillate between negative and positive affect" (p. 164). Bisconti et al. obtained daily measures of emotional well-being and depression from a sample of widows during the first through the fourth month of bereavement following the death of their spouses. Within the framework of DMA, the authors predicted that the widows' daily well-being ratings would conform to a linear oscillator model that resembles a "pendulum with friction" (p. 159). Because the death of a loved one typically evokes acute reactions, oscillations would tend to be more frequent and extreme soon after a loss and then gradually lessen in intensity and frequency over time. Bisconti et al.'s results confirmed these predictions.

In another recent study, Coifman, Bonanno, and Rafaeli (2007) examined reports of positive and negative affects at multiple points during a single interview in which recently bereaved individuals discussed various aspects of their loss. These authors included a measure of the resilient outcome trajectory. Again consistent with the DMA, bereaved individuals who followed the resilient trajectory also demonstrated weaker (or less polarized) correlations between positive and negative affects. This finding held even when the current level of overall distress was statistically controlled. Together, these studies suggest that resilient individuals may possess a capacity for more complex and flexible affective experiences and further that this capacity helps them to deal more adaptively with the potentially dysregulating impact of highly aversive events.

Salutary functions of positive emotions.   Positive emotion appears to be a core element of emotional flexibility. Until recently, little attention had been paid to the possible usefulness of positive emotions in the context of coping with PTEs. In fact, researchers and theorists have commonly dismissed the occurrence of positive emotions during or following stressful events, as suggestive of unhealthy denial (e.g., Bowlby, 1980). A more recent and growing body of empirical evidence indicates that positive emotions can help reduce personal distress following aversive events by reducing or "undoing" negative emotion and arousal (Fredrickson & Levenson, 1998; Keltner & Bonanno, 1997; Tugade & Fredrickson, 2004) and by fostering social connectedness and integration (Bonanno & Keltner, 1997). Recently, Papa and Bonanno (in press) have observed that these effects can occur simultaneously and independently.

Several other recent studies have demonstrated the salutary effects of positive emotion in the specific context of PTEs. Genuine laughs and smiles known as Duchenne expressions* can be reliably coded from muscle contractions of the orbicularis oculi muscles around the eye. By contrast, non-Duchenne expressions—laughs or smiles that are not accompanied by a contraction of the orbicularis oculi muscles—are typically not associated with the genuine experience of positive emotion (e.g., Ekman & Friesen, 1982; Bonanno & Keltner, 2004). Rather, non-Duchenne expressions are usually polite social markers, attempts to mask true feelings or to communicate appeasement (Bonanno, Keltner et al., 2002; Bugental, 1986; Ekman & Friesen, 1982; Ekman, Friesen & O'Sullivan, 1988; Hecht & LaFrance, 1988; Keltner, 1995; Prkachin & Silverman, 2002). Bonanno and colleagues have observed that Duchenne expressions of genuine positive emotions are evidenced by the majority of bereaved individuals in the early months after their loss (Bonanno, Wortman et al., 2002; Keltner & Bonanno, 1997) and further that these early expressions of genuine positive emotions are predictive of better psychological and social adjustments over subsequent years of bereavement. Consistent with the hypothesized social integration function of positive emotions, Duchenne expressions also tend to evoke more favorable responses in observers (Keltner & Bonanno, 1997).

The expression of positive emotion may also exert a salutary effect in the context of traumatic events more broadly defined. For example, Duchenne expressions among young adult survivors of childhood sexual abuse have been found to predict better adjustment and better social relationships (Bonanno, Colak et al., 2005). It is important to note, however, that although positive emotional expression in the context of a socially stigmatized event such as childhood sexual abuse may predict better adjustment, it may also carry certain costs such as decreased social competence. Recently, Fredrickson et al. (2003) found that the relation between personal resilience and adjustment after the September 11th terrorist attacks was mediated by the experience of positive emotions (e.g., gratitude, interest, love). Several studies have also linked the salutary coping effects of positive emotions to personality variables such as self-enhancement (Bonanno et al., 2005), emotional dissociation or repressive coping (Bonanno & Keltner, 1997), and ego resilience (Fredrickson et al., 2003).

Ego resilience. Several decades ago, Block and his colleagues found that children who had high levels of ego control[†] were more likely to respond in

---

* This term was coined in honor of nineteenth century physiologist Duchenne de Bologne, who first identified the marker for the expression (Duchenne de Bologne, 1962). Duchenne expressions have been consistently and unambiguously associated with genuine positive emotion (Duchenne de Bologne, 1962; Ekman & Friesen, 1982; Frank, Ekman & Friesen, 1993; Keltner & Bonanno, 1997).
† Ego control refers to the ability to inhibit aggressive impulses and to postpone gratification of immediate desires in order to pursue long-term goals and intentions.

a constructive way to frustrating situations (Block & Martin, 1955; Funder & Block, 1989). Block (1982) also observed that adults who are high in ego control are well-organized, goal-oriented, and tend to inhibit their emotions. For adults, ego control is also associated with avoidant behavior and difficulty tolerating ambiguity. By contrast, individuals who have low levels of ego control tend to be more spontaneous and express their feelings openly and directly to other people (Block, 2002; Letzring, Block & Funder, 2005). This tendency to experience and express a wide range of emotions comes at the cost of higher distractibility and low impulse control, which may in turn increase the vulnerability of low-ego control individuals to maladaptive behavior such as drug use and smoking (Barefoot, Smith, Dahlstrom & Williams, 1989; Block, Block & Keyes, 1988).

Perhaps most interesting, Block and Block (1980) observed that positive outcomes were most often achieved by individuals who have a moderate (versus extreme) level of ego control. Thus, the concept of ego resilience was proposed to identify individuals who are neither over-controlled nor under-controlled and who are thought to possess an elastic (flexible) emotion self-regulatory system that facilitates matching expressive and regulatory behaviors to situational demands irrespective of personal disposition (Block, 1950; Block, 2002; Block, 1951; Block & Block, 1980).

Ego resilience has been associated with several variables and measures of interest with respect to coping with stress. Block and Kremen (1996) found that ego resilience predicts positive interpersonal and emotional function, and a study conducted by Spangler (1997) provided additional support for the hypothesized relation between ego resilience and flexible coping. Specifically, Spangler observed that ego-resilient subjects had lower levels of physiological reactivity during a stressful examination and evidenced a more rapid return to baseline after the exam. More recently, Tugade and Fredrickson (2004) found that resilient individuals not only were less reactive to a stressful task but also returned more quickly to baseline levels of emotional arousal. In a subsequent prospective study, Fredrickson et al. (2003) showed that ego resilience was associated with better coping in everyday life and better overall adjustment (among Midwestern college students) immediately following the September 11th terrorist attack. Specifically, Fredrickson et al. found that individuals who scored high on Block's measure of ego resilience were less likely to develop depressive symptoms and reported higher levels of life satisfaction, optimism, and tranquility after 9/11. Fredrickson et al.'s statistical analyses also showed that positive emotions fully mediated the relation between ego resilience and positive adjustment. Similarly, findings from longitudinal studies using nonstudent samples indicate that ego resiliency may support coping with various challenges confronted across the human life span (e.g., aging; Klohnen, Vandewater & Young, 1996) as well as with more traumatic events such as physical abuse (Flores, Rogosch & Cicchetti, 2005).

Pragmatic Coping

So far, we have focused on protective personality variables and have linked their protective effects to flexibility in appraising events and regulating emotion. Here, we turn to a very different kind of protective personality factor that, under normal conditions, does not necessarily involve positive interpersonal interactions. On the contrary, the characteristics and behavior that typify pragmatic coping may be viewed as socially undesirable or even ugly (Bonanno, 2006).

Trait Self-Enhancement

Most people occasionally view themselves and the world around them through self-serving biases and other forms of positive illusion. There is a considerable body of empirical evidence to indicate that self-serving bias is a necessary feature of psychological adjustment and healthy coping, particularly in the context of extreme adversity (Taylor & Brown, 1988). For example, people may exaggerate their abilities and downplay their limitations. In an effort to enhance self-image or reputation, people might accept credit for positive events or results in which they played little or no causal role or eschew responsibility for negative events or results for which they were directly responsible. The tendency to engage in self-enhancing bias is known as trait self-enhancement. Trait self-enhancement can be measured by the administration of a self-report questionnaire that contains many items suggestive of exaggerated and self-serving attributions (e.g., "I don't care what other people think of me," "I am a completely rational person," and "I always know why I like things"; Paulhus, 1984, 1991). Another method of measurement is to compare self-ratings against peer-ratings; self-enhancers typically rate themselves more favorably than they are rated by their peers (Bonanno, Field, Kovacevic & Kaltman, 2002; John & Robins, 1994; Paulhus, 1998).

There is considerable disagreement about whether trait self-enhancement should be seen as generally adaptive or as generally maladaptive. Self-enhancers have been described as self-centered, self-aggrandizing, dominant, and manipulative (e.g., Emmons, 1987; Paulhus, 1998; Paulhus & Williams, 2002). Some researchers argue that self-enhancers possess an illusory view of their own adjustment (e.g., Shedler, Mayman & Manis, 1993) and that self-enhancement serves to mask social ineptitudes (Colvin, Block & Funder, 1995) and personal difficulties (e.g., Robins & Beer, 2001). Although self-enhancers often make a favorable first impression (Paulhus, 1998), with repeated contact, people quickly come to view self-enhancers in negative terms (John & Robins, 1994; Paulhus, 1998). Moreover, the self-enhancer may respond to bereavement (Bonanno et al., 2002) or disaster (Bonanno et al., 2005) in ways that clash with culture-based expectations of appropriate or expectable behavior. In a study conducted by Bonanno et al. (2002) bereaved individuals were rated by untrained observers who viewed participants on videotape. The observers rated self-enhancers in this sample less favorably than other participants in that study. The authors speculated that this may have been due to self-enhancers' failure to exhibit the expected levels of distress, as was evident in follow-up analyses of facial expressions of emotion. However, it is important to note that the negative impressions self-enhancers evoked in their observers (and presumably in other people as well) had no apparent effect on their ability to maintain relatively low levels of psychological symptoms during bereavement.

While self-enhancing behavior often backfires in the long run, it may nonetheless facilitate coping in the near term (for reviews, see Taylor & Brown, 1994, 1999; Taylor & Armor, 1996). When confronted by adversity, self-enhancement strategies may boost personal confidence and courage by positive reframing (Taylor, Wood & Lichtman, 1984) and downward social comparison (Helgeson & Taylor, 1993; Taylor, Kemeny, Reed & Aspinwall, 1991). Self-enhancement has been linked to healthy adjustment as measured by self-report and peer ratings of mental health (Taylor, Lerner, Sherman, Sage & McDowell, 2003a), and to physiological indices of healthy coping such as lower baseline cortisol levels, lower cardiovascular responses to stress, and faster cardiovascular recovery in response to an experimental stressor (Taylor, Lerner, Sherman, Sage & McDowell, 2003b).

Several studies also provide compelling evidence that trait self-enhancers cope well with extreme adversity. Bonanno et al. (2002) examined trait self-enhancement among individuals dealing with real-world stressors such as the premature death of a spouse or civilian exposure to urban combat during wartime. In the bereavement study, high scores on the trait self-enhancement questionnaire were inversely associated with symptoms of grief and PTSD over the first 25 months of bereavement. A particularly relevant finding from this study was that self-enhancement interacted with the severity of the loss. Specifically, self-enhancement was more strongly inversely correlated with PTSD symptoms for bereaved participants who had lost their spouse to a violent death, which as several studies have now shown, generally results in more severe and enduring trauma reactions (e.g., Kaltman & Bonanno, 2003; Zisook, Chenstova-Dutton & Shuchter, 1998). In other words, self-enhancement appeared to be particularly adaptive in extremely aversive events. In the wartime study, self-enhancement was measured by self-peer discrepancies among a sample of citizens of Sarajevo who had endured several years of the stress and deprivation associated with urban combat in Bosnia. Self-enhancers in this group also demonstrated better adjustment than their nonself-enhancing peers.

A recent study by Bonanno et al. (2005) has particular relevance to the question of psychological resilience to stress. Participants in this study were high-exposure survivors of the September 11th terrorist attack in New York City. These were people who were either inside or very near the WTC on the day of the attack. Most had witnessed death or injury to others and were themselves in serious physical danger during the attack. Participants were assigned to the resilient trajectory if they had few or no PTSD symptoms and scored within the normal (nondepressed) range. Assignment to the resilient trajectory and other outcome trajectories (e.g., "recovery" from trauma) was validated against similar assignments made independently in anonymous ratings by study participants' close friends and relatives. To explore the assumption that resilience involves the "capacity for generative experiences and positive emotions" (Bonanno, 2004, p. 21), affective experiences were measured during an interview in which participants discussed their experiences on the day of the attack. Finally, participants' friends and relatives were asked to rate the participant on various aspects of adjustment such as mental and physical health, goal accomplishment, and coping ability.

The results of this study indicated that self-enhancers were more likely to follow a resilient outcome trajectory, whether defined by self-reported symptom levels or based on ratings by their close friends/relatives. Self-enhancers also demonstrated more positive affect when they described their experiences during the attack. They were rated by their friends and relatives as having consistently higher levels of mental and physical health, goal accomplishment, and coping ability. However, consistent with the potential social liabilities of trait self-enhancement, self-enhancers' friends/relatives also rated them as decreasing in social adjustment over time and, among those with the highest levels of exposure, as less honest. This pattern of findings supports the view that self-enhancers are able to maintain generally high levels of function in most areas of life except their social relations. Perhaps most interesting was the finding that self-enhancers perceived their social relationships in relatively more positive terms than did other participants, and this factor fully mediated their reduced PTSD symptomology. In other words, it seems that self-enhancers can be blissfully unaware of the critical reactions they may evoke in others, and this self-serving bias plays a crucial role in their ability to maintain healthy function in other areas.

Dispositional processes such as self-enhancement may be generally effective because they function at a habitual or relatively automatic level. While other individuals often find it difficult to self-promote in stressful situations that tend to increase cognitive load (e.g., job interviews; see Muraven, Tice & Baumeister, 1998), self-enhancers may need to invest less cognitive effort because they can rely on habitual patterns of positive self-presentation.

Repressive Coping and Emotional Dissociation

Repressive coping is another dispositional self-regulatory process that may function in a relatively automated fashion (Bonanno, Davis, Singer & Schwartz, 1991; Bonanno & Singer, 1990; Weinberger & Davidson, 1994; Weinberger,

Schwartz & Davidson, 1979). Individuals who score high on trait-repressive coping habitually avoid negative emotional stimuli (e.g., by screening out or not paying attention to negative feedback from other people) and as a result tend to experience low levels of negative emotions (Weinberger et al., 1979). Although there is a considerable body of literature on repressive coping, there remains disagreement over how to operationalize and measure this construct. Many studies in this area have utilized a questionnaire approach originally developed by Weinberger et al. (1979). In this methodological framework, repressive copers are characterized as individuals who self-report low-trait anxiety but score high on measures of defensiveness (e.g., Marlowe–Crowne Social Desirability Scale; Crowne & Marlowe, 1964). Unfortunately, there are numerous problems with this approach. For example, the determination of high versus low scores is typically achieved by artificially dichotomizing two continuous variables (continuous anxiety and defensiveness) that are moderately correlated. This leads to a biased distribution of scores across resulting quadrants (Maxwell & Delaney, 1993) and may thus over-represent repressive coping.

To avoid this problem, researchers have more recently begun to measure repressive coping in terms of more reliable behavioral manifestations related to emotional dissociation (Bonanno et al., 1995). Emotional dissociation is characterized by a transient shift of attentional focus away from a particular and usually negative emotional response toward other, relatively more benign content (Bonanno, 2001). This attentional shift can help to attenuate emotional distress that would normally accompany physiological arousal triggered by stressful events.

One of the most widely used measures of emotional dissociation is affective-autonomic response dissociation, which is observed when subjective emotional distress is disproportionately low compared to an observed increase in autonomic response (Newton & Contrada, 1992). Individuals identified by questionnaire as repressive copers consistently demonstrate high affective-autonomic discrepancy scores (Bonanno et al., 1995; Bonanno, Keltner et al., 2002; Newton & Contrada, 1992; Weinberger et al., 1979). Moreover, the relationship between repressive coping and emotional dissociation is reliable over time (Bonanno et al., 1995). Repressive copers demonstrate an apparently automatic propensity to selectively attend away from threatening information (e.g., Bonanno et al., 1991; Fox, 1993; Mogg et al., 2000) toward positive content and stimuli (Boden & Baumeister, 1997; Tomarken & Davidson, 1994).

Traditionally, repressive coping has been viewed as maladaptive denial. Indeed, shifting awareness away from distressing emotion may incur deleterious physical and emotional costs over the long term (Shedler, Mayman & Manis, 1993). However, emotional dissociation may also reduce demand on limited cognitive resources and thus leave more resources available to others, relatively more effortful processes associated with appraisal and self-control. Support for the view that emotional avoidance may serve an adaptive purpose can be found in studies that link affective-autonomic dissociation to better overall adjustment among sexually abused adolescent girls (Bonanno, Keltner et al., 2002) and middle-aged adults coping with the recent death of a spouse (Bonanno et al., 1995, 1999; Coifman, Bonanno, Ray & Gross, 2007). Emotional dissociation may enable individuals under stress to minimize the disruptive impact of intense negative emotions. Affective-autonomic dissociation has also been linked to the generation of positive states such as laughter (Bonanno & Keltner, 1997; Bonanno, Noll, Putnam, O'Neill & Trickett, 2003). Keltner and Bonanno (1997) found that bereaved individuals who exhibit genuine laughter while talking about their loss were significantly more likely to evidence autonomic-affective dissociation than those who did not laugh.

Laughter often occurs in negative contexts that seem incongruous with the experience of positive emotion. By creating a mental distance from negative stimuli, dissociation may help to preserve or restore the cognitive flexibility that is needed to recognize novel aspects of a situation that afford humorous interpretations. As an individual begins to laugh, regulatory processes are set into motion with relaxing effects that may affect other people through processes of emotional contagion and thus generate additional opportunities for experiencing positive emotions. The expression of positive emotion might also offset physiological arousal and benefit well-being by eliciting positive responses from other people in the individual's social environment, which in turn enables the individual to maintain old or form new social support networks (Keltner & Bonanno, 1997). Thus, the ability to experience positive affect in an otherwise aversive situation may offer a number of benefits that outweigh potential social costs associated with regulatory strategies that tend to reduce awareness of threatening information.

Conclusion

In this chapter, we reviewed a number of different pathways to resilience. These pathways vary in automaticity and permeability (resistance to change) as well in the extent to which they inform the quality of social relations. Individual differences shape responses to potentially stressful events by affecting the ability to modulate emotional experience and expressions, by predisposing individuals to focus on particular types of information and draw positive versus negative conclusions, and by influencing the extent to which individuals can elicit and benefit from social support. Some, if not all, of the adaptive psychological and social benefits are mediated by positive emotions.

Based on the research reviewed in this chapter, we argue that appraisal-based flexibility promotes resilience because it fosters feelings of mastery, competence, commitment, and other aspects of positive self-perceptions that maintain or restore self-esteem after potentially threatening experiences. Expressive flexibility, that is, the ability to express and suppress emotions in accordance with situational demands, contributes to resilience by facilitating goal-directed interpersonal behaviors. The ability to express positive emotions is particularly important because of its potential to produce mutually satisfying interactions with other people. Such interactions tend to confirm positive self-perceptions and thereby help to maintain or increase self-esteem. In high-stress situations that present a threat to survival, pragmatic coping strategies such as self-enhancement help people to maintain a stable and positive sense of self.

The arguments and the ideas discussed in this chapter are intended to encourage and foster the development of a more encompassing and pre-cise taxonomy of individual differences that are relevant to resilience. Cer-tainly, there still is much to learn about how personality traits and associated behaviors contribute to or detract from resilience to stress and how they might interact with other variables and vary under different conditions or at different periods of human development. One recent study of resilience in response to disaster highlights the potential importance of demographic variables, material and social resources, and prior as well as current life stress (Bonanno et al., 2006). We hope that future research will clarify the interrela-tions between these and other factors. A better understanding of the psycho-logical mechanisms, biological processes, and social factors that contribute to resilient outcome trajectories is an essential prerequisite for developing effective real-life applications (e.g., in human resources) and informing interventions for individuals who have been or may currently be exposed to chronic or acute stress.

References

Allred, K.D. & Smith, T.W. (1989). The hardy personality: cognitive and physiological responses to evaluative threat. *Journal of Personality and Social Psychology, 56,* 257–266.

American Psychiatric Association (2000). *Diagnostic and Statistical Manual of Mental Disorders (DSM-IV-TR)* (4th ed.). Washington, D.C.: American Psy-chiatric Association.

Atienza, A.A., Stephens, M.A.P. & Townsend, A.L. (2004). Role stressors as predic-tors of changes in women's optimistic expectations. *Personality and Individual Differences, 37,* 471–484.

Averill, J.R. (1980). A constructivist view of emotion. In: R. Plutchik & H. Kellerman (Eds.), *Emotion: Theory, Research, and Experience* (pp. 305–339). Orlando, FL: Academic Press.

Barefoot, J.C., Smith, R.H., Dahlstrom, W.G. & Williams, R.B. (1989). Personality predictors of smoking behavior in a sample of physicians. *Psychology & Health, 3*, 37–43.

Bartone, P.T. (1999). Hardiness protects against war-related stress in army reserve forces. *Consulting Psychology Journal: Practice and Research, 51*, 72–82.

Bartone, P.T. (1989). Predictors of stress related illness in city bus drivers. *Journal of Occupational Medicine, 31*, 657–663.

Bartone, P.T. & Adler, A.B. (1999). Cohesion over time in a peacekeeping medical task force. *Military Psychology, 11*, 85–107.

Bartone, P.T., Ursano, R.J., Wright, K.M. & Ingraham, L.H. (1989). The impact of a military air disaster on the health of assistance workers: a prospective study. *Journal of Nervous and Mental Disease, 177*, 317–328.

Bisconti, T.L., Bergman, C.S. & Boker, S.M. (2004). Emotional well-being in recently bereaved widows: a dynamic systems approach. *The Journals of Gerontology: Series B: Psychological Sciences and Social Sciences, 59B*, 158–168.

Blaney, P.H. & Ganellen, R.J. (1990). Hardiness and social support. In: B. Sarason, G. Sarason & G. Pierce (Eds.), *Social Support: An Interactional View*. New York: Wiley.

Block, J. (1950). An experimental investigation of the construct of ego-control. Unpublished doctoral dissertation, Stanford University.

Block, J. (1982). Assimilation, accommodation, and the dynamics of personality development. *Child Development, 53*, 281–295.

Block, J. (2002). *Personality as an Affect-Processing System*. Mahwah, NJ: Lawrence Erlbaum.

Block, J., Block, J.H. & Keyes, S. (1988). Longitudinally foretelling drug usage in adolescence: early childhood personality and environmental precursors. *Child Development, 59*, 336–355.

Block, J. & Kremen, A.M. (1996). IQ and ego-resiliency: conceptual and empirical connections and separateness. *Journal of Personality and Social Psychology, 70*, 349.

Block, J.H. (1951). An experimental study of a topological representation of ego-structure. Unpublished doctoral dissertation, Stanford University.

Block, J.H. & Block, J. (1980). The role of ego-control and ego-resiliency in the origination of behavior. In: W.A. Collings (Ed.), *The Minnesota Symposia on Child Psychology, 13* (pp. 39–101). Hillsdale, NJ: Erlbaum.

Block, J.H. & Martin, B. (1955). Predicting the behavior of children under frustration. *Journal of Abnormal and Social Psychology, 51*, 281–285.

Boden, J.M. & Baumeister, R.F. (1997). Repressive coping: distraction using pleasant thoughts and memories. *Journal of Personality and Social Psychology, 73*, 45–62.

Boerner, K., Wortman, C.B. & Bonanno, G.A. (2005). Resilient or at risk? A 4-year study of older adults who initially showed high or low distress following conjugal loss. *Journals of Gerontology: Series B: Psychological Sciences and Social Sciences, 60B*, 67–73.

Bonanno, G.A. (2001). Emotion self-regulation. In: T.J. Mayne & G.A. Bonanno (Eds.), *Emotions: Current Issues and Future Directions* (pp. 251–285). New York: Guilford Press.

Bonanno, G.A. (2004). Loss, trauma, and human resilience: have we under-estimated the human capacity to thrive after extremely aversive events? *American Psychologist, 59*, 20–28.

Bonanno, G.A. (2005a). Clarifying and extending the construct of adult resilience. *American Psychologist, 60*, 265–267.

Bonanno, G.A. (2005b). Resilience in the face of potential trauma. *Current Directions in Psychological Science, 14*, 135–138.

Bonanno, G.A. (2006). Grief, trauma, and resilience. In: E.K. Rynearson (Ed.), *Violent Death: Resilience and Intervention Beyond the Crisis* (pp. 31–46). New York: Routledge.

Bonanno, G.A., Colak, D.M., Keltner, D., Shiota, L., Papa, A., Noll, J.G., Putnam, F.W. & Trickett, P.K. (in press). Context matters: The benefits and costs of expressing positive emotion among survivors of childhood sexual abuse. *Emotion*.

Bonanno, G.A., Davis, P.J., Singer, J.L. & Schwartz, G.E. (1991). The repressor personality and avoidant information processing: a dichotic listening study. *Journal of Research in Personality, 25*, 386–401.

Bonanno, G.A., Field, N.P., Kovacevic, A. & Kaltman, S. (2002). Self-enhancement as a buffer against extreme adversity: civil war in Bosnia and traumatic loss in the United States. *Personality and Social Psychology Bulletin, 2*, 194–196.

Bonanno, G.A., Galea, S. & Bucciarelli, A. (2006). Psychological resilience after disaster. *Psychological Science, 17*, 181–183.

Bonanno, G.A. & Keltner, D. (1997). Facial expressions of emotion and the course of conjugal bereavement. *Journal of Abnormal Psychology, 106*, 126–137.

Bonanno, G.A. & Keltner, D. (2004). The coherence of emotion systems: comparing "on-line" measures of appraisal and facial expressions, and self-report. *Cognition & Emotion, 18*, 431–444.

Bonanno, G.A., Keltner, D., Holen, A. & Horowitz, M.J. (1995). When avoiding unpleasant emotions might not be such a bad thing: verbal-autonomic response dissociation and midlife conjugal bereavement. *Journal of Personality and Social Psychology, 69(5)*, 975–989.

Bonanno, G.A., Keltner, D., Noll, J.G., Putnam, F.W., Trickett, P.K., LeJeune, J. et al. (2002). When the face reveals what words do not: facial expressions of emotion, smiling, and the willingness to disclose childhood sexual abuse. *Journal of Personality and Social Psychology, 83*, 94–110.

Bonanno, G.A., Moskowitz, J.T., Papa, A. & Folkman, S. (2005). Resilience to loss in bereaved spouses, bereaved parents, and bereaved gay men. *Journal of Personality and Social Psychology, 88*, 827–843.

Bonanno, G.A., Noll, J.G., Putnam, F.W., O'Neill, M. & Trickett, P.K. (2003). Predicting the willingness to disclose childhood sexual abuse from measures of repressive coping and dissociative tendencies. *Child Maltreatment: Journal of the American Professional Society on the Abuse of Children, 8*, 302–318.

Bonanno, G.A., Papa, A., Lalande, K., Westphal, M. & Coifman, K. (2004). The importance of being flexible: the ability to both enhance and suppress emotional expression predicts long-term adjustment. *Psychological Science, 15*, 482–487.

Bonanno, G.A., Rennicke, C. & Dekel, S. (2005). Self-enhancement among high-exposure survivors of the September 11th terrorist attack: resilience or social maladjustment? *Journal of Personality and Social Psychology, 88*, 984–998.

Bonanno, G.A. & Singer, J.L. (1990). Repressive personality style: theoretical and methodological implications for health and pathology. In: J.L. Singer (Ed.), *Repression and Dissociation* (pp. 435–470). Chicago, IL: University of Chicago Press.

Bonanno, G.A., Wortman, C.B., Lehman, D.R., Tweed, R.G., Haring, M., Sonnega, J. et al. (2002). Resilience to loss and chronic grief: a prospective study from preloss to 18-months postloss. *Journal of Personality and Social Psychology, 83*, 1150–1164.

Bonanno, G.A., Wortman, C.B. & Nesse, R.M. (2004). Prospective patterns of resilience and maladjustment during widowhood. *Psychology and Aging, 19*, 260–271.

Bonanno, G.A., Znoj, H., Siddique, H.I. & Horowitz, M.J. (1999). Verbal-autonomic dissociation and adaptation to midlife conjugal loss: a follow-up at 25 months. *Cognitive Therapy and Research, 23*, 605–624.

Bowlby, J. (1980). *Sadness and Depression (Vol. 3)*. New York: Basic Books.

Briere, J.N. (1997). Treating adults severely abused as children: the self-trauma model. In: D.H. Wolfe, R.J. McMahon & R.D. Peters (Eds.), *Child Abuse: New Directions in Prevention and Treatment Across the Lifespan* (pp. 177–204). Thousand Oaks, CA: Sage Publications.

Brosschot, J.F., Godaert, G.L.R., Benschop, R.J., Olff, M., Ballieux, R.E. & Heijnen, C.J. (1998). Experimental stress and immunological reactivity: a closer look at perceived uncontrollability. *Psychosomatic Medicine, 60*, 359–361.

Brown, E.S., Varghese, F.P. & McEwen, B.S. (2004). Association of depression with medical illness: does cortisol play a role? *Biological Psychiatry, 55*, 1–9.

Bryant, R.A., Moulds, M.L. & Guthrie, R.M. (2000). Acute stress disorder scale: a self-report measure of acute stress disorder. *Psychological Assessment, 12*, 61–68.

Buchanan, G.M. & Seligman, M.E.P. (1995). *Explanatory Style*. Hillsdale, NJ: Erlbaum.

Bugental, D.B. (1986). Unmasking the "polite smile": situational and personal determinants of managed affect in adult–child interaction. *Personality and Social Psychology Bulletin, 12*, 7–16.

Butler, E.A., Egloff, B., Wilhelm, F.H., Smith, N.C., Erickson, E.A. & Gross, J.J. (2003). The social consequences of expressive suppression. *Emotion, 3*, 48–67.

Carver, C.S. (1998). Resilience and thriving: issues, models, and linkages. *Journal of Social Issues, 54*, 245–266.

Chemtob, C.M., Novaco, R.W., Hamada, R.S. & Gross, D.M. (1997). Cognitive-behavioral treatment for severe anger in posttraumatic stress disorder. *Journal of Consulting and Clinical Psychology, 65*, 184–189.

Clark, L. & Hartman, M. (1996). Effects of hardiness and appraisal on the well-being of caregivers to elderly relatives. *Research on Aging, 18*, 379–401.

Coifman, K.G., Bonanno, G.A. & Rafaeli, E. (2007). Affective dynamics, bereavement, and resilience to loss. *Journal of Happiness Studies, 8*, 371–392.

Coifman, K.G., Bonanno, G.A., Ray, R. & Gross, J.J. (2007). Does repressive coping promote resilience? affective-autonomic response discrepancy during bereavement. *Journal of Personality and Social Psychology, 92*, 745–758.

Colvin, C.R., Block, J. & Funder, D.C. (1995). Overly positive self-evaluations and personality: negative implications for mental health. *Journal of Personality and Social Psychology, 68*, 1152–1162.

Consedine, N.S., Magai, C. & Bonanno, G.A. (2002). Moderators of the emotion inhibition—health relationship: a review and research agenda. *Review of General Psychology, 6*, 204–228.

Contrada, R.J. (1989). Type A behavior, personality hardiness, and cardiovascular responses to stress. *Journal of Personality and Social Psychology, 57,* 895–903.

Cooper, C.L. & Faragher, E.B. (1992). Coping strategies and breast disorders/cancer. *Psychological Medicine, 22,* 447–455.

Cooper, C.L. & Faragher, E.B. (1993). Psychosocial stress and breast cancer: the interrelationships between stress events, coping strategies and personality. *Psychological Medicine, 23,* 653–662.

Crowne, D.P. & Marlowe, D. (1964). *The Approval Motive.* New York: Wiley.

Davis, M.C., Zautra, A.J. & Smith, B.W. (2004). Chronic pain, stress, and the dynamics of affective differentiation. *Journal of Personality, 72,* 1133–1159.

de Vries, J. & van Heck, G.L. (2000). Personality and emotional exhaustion: a review of the literature. *Gedrag and Gezondheid: Tijdschrift voor Psychologie and Gezondheid, 28,* 90–105.

Drory, Y. & Florian, V. (1991). Long-term psychosocial adjustment to coronary artery disease. *Archives of Physical Medicine and Rehabilitation, 72,* 326–331.

Duchenne de Bologne, G.B. (1962). *The Mechanism of Human Facial Expression.* New York: Cambridge University Press.

Ebbesen, E.B., Duncan, B. & Konecni, V.J. (1975). Effects of content of verbal aggression on future verbal aggression. A field study. *Journal of Experimental Social Psychology, 11,* 192–204.

Eid, J., Johnsen, B.H., Saus, E.-R. & Risberg, J. (2005). Stress and coping in a week-long disabled submarine exercise. *Aviation, Space, and Environmental Medicine, 75,* 616–621.

Ekman, P. & Friesen, W.V. (1982). Felt, false, and miserable smiles. *Journal of Nonverbal Behavior, 6,* 238–258.

Ekman, P., Friesen, W.V. & O'Sullivan, M. (1988). Smiles when lying. *Journal of Personality and Social Psychology, 54,* 414–420.

Ellsworth, P.C. & Scherer, K.R. (2003). Appraisal processes in emotion. In: J.R. Davidson, K.R. Scherer & H.H. Goldsmith (Eds.), *Handbook of Affective Sciences* (pp. 572–595). New York: Oxford University Press.

Emmons, R.A. (1987). Narcissism: theory and measurement. *Journal of Personality and Social Psychology, 52,* 11–17.

Epel, E., Lapidus, R., McEwen, B. & Brownell, K. (2000). Stress may add bite to appetite in women: a laboratory study of stress-induced cortisol and eating behavior. *Psychoneuroendocrinology, 26,* 37–49.

Epel, E., McEwen, B., Seeman, T., Matthews, K., Castellazzo, G., Brownell, K. et al. (2000). Can stress shape your body? Consistently greater stress-induced cortisol secretion among women with abdominal fat. *Psychosomatic Medicine, 62,* 623–632.

Epel, E.S., McEwen, B.S. & Ickovics, J.R. (1998). Embodying psychological thriving: physical thriving in response to threat. *Journal of Social Issues, 54,* 301–322.

Flores, E., Rogosch, F.A. & Cicchetti, D. (2005). Predictors of resilience in maltreated and nonmaltreated latino children. *Developmental Psychology, 41,* 338–351.

Florian, V., Mikulincer, M. & Taubman, O. (1995). Does hardiness contribute to mental health during a stressful real-life situation? The roles of appraisal and coping. *Journal of Personality and Social Psychology, 68,* 687–695.

Foa, E.B. & Kozak, M.J. (1986). Emotional processing of fear: exposure to corrective information. *Psychological Bulletin, 99,* 20–35.

Fournier, M., de Ridder, D. & Bensing, J. (2002). How optimism contributes to the adaptation of chronic illness. A prospective study into the enduring effects of optimism on adaptation moderated by the controllability of chronic illness. *Personality and Individual Differences, 33,* 1163–1183.

Fox, E. (1993). Allocation of visual attention and anxiety. *Cognition & Emotion, 7,* 207–215.

Frankenhaeuser, M. (1983). The sympathetic-adrenal and pituitary-adrenal response to challenge: comparison between the sexes. In: T.M. Dembroski, T.H. Schmidt & G. Bluemchen (Eds.), *Biobehavioral Bases of Coronary Heart Diseases* (pp. 91–105). Basel: Karger.

Frank, M.G., Ekman, P. & Friesen, W.V. (1993). Behavioral markers and recognizability of the smile of enjoyment. *Journal of Personality and Social Psychology, 64,* 83–93.

Fredrickson, B.L. (2001). The role of positive emotions in positive psychology: the broaden-and-build theory of positive emotions. *American Psychologist, 56,* 218–226.

Fredrickson, B.L. & Levenson, R.W. (1998). Positive emotions speed recovery from the cardiovascular sequelae of negative emotions. *Cognition & Emotion, 12,* 191–220.

Fredrickson, B.L., Tugade, M.M., Waugh, C.E. & Larkin, G.R. (2003). What good are positive emotions in crises? A prospective study of resilience and emotions following the terrorist attacks on the United States on September 11th, 2001. *Journal of Personality and Social Psychology, 84,* 365–376.

Funder, D.C. & Block, J. (1989). The role of ego-control, ego-resiliency, and IQ in delay of gratification in adolescence. *Journal of Personality and Social Psychology, 57,* 1041–1050.

Funk, S.C. (1992). Hardiness: a review of theory and research. *Health Psychology, 11,* 335–345.

Funk, S.C. & Houston, B.K. (1987). A critical analysis of the hardiness scale's validity and utility. *Journal of Personality and Social Psychology, 53,* 572–578.

Galea, S., Ahern, J., Resnick, H., Kilpatrick, D., Bucuvalas, M., Gold, J. et al. (2002). Psychological sequelae of the September 11 terrorist attacks in New York city [see comment]. *New England Journal of Medicine, 346,* 982–987.

Galea, S., Resnick, H., Ahern, J., Gold, J., Bucuvalas, M., Kilpatrick, D. et al. (2002). Posttraumatic stress disorder in Manhattan, New York city, after the September 11th terrorist attacks. *Journal of Urban Health, 79,* 340–353.

Galea, S., Vlahov, D., Resnick, H., Ahern, J., Susser, E., Gold, J. et al. (2003). Trends of probable post-traumatic stress disorder in New York city after the September 11 terrorist attacks. *American Journal of Epidemiology, 158,* 514–524.

Garmezy, N. (1974). Children at risk: the search for the antecedents of schizophrenia: II. Ongoing research programs, issues, and intervention. *Schizophrenia Bulletin, 9,* 55–125.

Garmezy, N. (1971). Vulnerability research and the issue of primary prevention. *American Journal of Orthopsychiatry, 41,* 101–116.

Gentry, W.D. & Kobasa, S.C. (1984). Social and psychological resources mediating stress–illness relationships in humans. In: W.D. Gentry (Ed.), *Handbook of Behavioral Medicine* (pp. 87–116). New York: Guilford Press.

Gottman, J.M. & Levenson, R.W. (1986). Assessing the role of emotion in marriage. *Behavioral Assessment, 8*, 31–48.

Green, D.P., Salovey, P. & Truax, K.M. (1999). Static, dynamic, and causative bipolarity of affect. *Journal of Personality and Social Psychology, 76*, 856–867.

Gross, J.J. (1998a). Antecedent and response-focused emotion self-regulation: divergent consequences for experience, expression, and physiology. *Journal of Personality and Social Psychology, 74*, 224–237.

Gross, J.J. (1999). Emotion self-regulation: past, present, future. *Cognition & Emotion, 13*, 551–573.

Gross, J.J. (1998b). The emerging field of emotion self-regulation: an integrative review. *Review of General Psychology, 2*, 271–299.

Gross, J.J. & Levenson, R.W. (1993). Emotional suppression: physiology self-report and expressive behavior. *Journal of Social and Personality Psychology, 64*, 970–86.

Gross, J.J. & Levenson, R.W. (1997). Hiding feelings: the acute effects of inhibiting negative and positive emotion. *Journal of Abnormal Psychology, 106*, 95.

Hecht, M.A. & LaFrance, M. (1988). License or obligation to smile: the effect of power and gender on amount and type of smiling. *Personality and Social Psychology Bulletin, 24*, 1326–1336.

Helgeson, V.S. & Taylor, S.E. (1993). Social comparisons and adjustment among cardiac patients. *Journal of Applied Social Psychology, 23*, 1171–1185.

Herman, J.L. (1992). *Trauma and Recovery.* New York: Basic Books.

Hoge, C.W., Castro, C.A., McGurk, D., Cotting, D.I. & Koffman, R.L. (2004). Combat duty in Iraq and Afghanistan, mental health problems, and barriers to care. *New England Journal of Medicine, 351*, 13–22.

Horowitz, M.J. (1986). *Stress Response Syndromes* (2nd ed.). Northvale, NJ: Jason Aronson.

Hull, J.G., Van Treuren, R.R. & Virnelli, S. (1987). Hardiness and health: a critique and alternative approach. *Journal of Personality and Social Psychology, 53*, 518–530.

Isen, A.M. (1987). Positive affect, cognitive processes, and social behavior. *Advances in Experimental Social Psychology, 20*, 203–253.

Janis, I.L. (1951). *Air War and Emotional Stress: Psychological Studies of Bombing and Civilian Defense.* New York: McGraw-Hill.

John, O.P. & Robins, R.W. (1994). Accuracy and bias in self-perception: individual differences in self-enhancement and the role of narcissism. *Journal of Personality and Social Psychology, 66*, 206–219.

Julien, D., Markman, H.J., Leveille, S., Chartrand, E. & Begin, J. (1994). Networks' support and interference with regard to marriage: disclosures of marital problems to confidants. *Journal of Family Psychology, 8*, 16–31.

Kaltman, S. & Bonanno, G.A. (2003). Trauma and bereavement: examining the impact of sudden and violent deaths. *Journal of Anxiety Disorders, 17*, 131–147.

Kelly, A.E. & McKillop, K.J. (1996). Consequences of revealing personal secrets. *Psychological Bulletin, 120*, 450–465.

Keltner, D. (1995). Signs of appeasement: evidence for the distinct displays of embarrassment, amusement, and shame. *Journal of Personality and Social Psychology, 68*, 441–454.

Keltner, D. & Bonanno, G.A. (1997). A study of laughter and dissociation: distinct correlates of laughter and smiling during bereavement. *Journal of Personality and Social Psychology, 73*, 687–702.

Kennedy-Moore, E. & Watson, J.C. (1999). *Expressing Emotion: Myths, Realities, and Therapeutic Strategies*. New York: Guilford Press.

Kennedy-Moore, E. & Watson, J.C. (2001). How and when does emotional expression help? *Review of General Psychology, 5*, 187–212.

King, D.W., King, L.A., Foy, D.W., Keane, T.M. & Fairbank, J.A. (1999). Posttraumatic stress disorder in a national sample of female and male Vietnam veterans: risk factors, war-zone stressors, and resilience-recovery variables. *Journal of Abnormal Psychology, 108*, 164–170.

Kitayama, S. & Markus, H.R. (1996). *Emotion and Culture*. Washington, D.C.: American Psychological Association.

Klag, S. & Bradley, G. (2004). The role of hardiness in stress and illness: an exploration of the effect of negative affectivity and gender. *British Journal of Health Psychology, 9*, 137–161.

Klohnen, E.C., Vandewater, E.A. & Young, A. (1996). Negotiating the middle years: ego-resiliency and successful midlife adjustment in women. *Psychology and Aging, 11*, 431–442.

Kobasa, S.C. (1979). Stressful life events, personality, and health: an inquiry into hardiness. *Journal of Personality and Social Psychology, 37*, 1–11.

Kobasa, S.C., Maddi, S.R. & Courington, S. (1981). Personality and constitution as mediators in the stress-illness relationship. *Journal of Health and Social Behavior, 22*, 368–378.

Kobasa, S.C., Maddi, S.R. & Kahn, S. (1982). Hardiness and health: a prospective study. *Journal of Personality and Social Psychology, 42*, 168–177.

Kobasa, S.C., Maddi, S.R., Puccetti, M.C. & Zola, M.A. (1985). Effectiveness of hardiness, exercise and social support as resources against illness. *Journal of Psychosomatic Research, 29*, 525–533.

Kobasa, S.C. & Puccetti, M.C. (1983). Personality and social resources in stress resistance. *Journal of Personality and Social Psychology, 45*, 839–850.

Kubany, E.S. & Watson, S.B. (2002). Cognitive trauma therapy for formerly battered women with PTSD: conceptual bases and treatment outlines. *Cognitive and Behavioral Practice, 9*, 111–127.

Lehman, D.R., Ellard, J.H. & Wortman, C.B. (1986). Social support for the bereaved: recipients' and providers' perspectives on what is helpful. *Journal of Consulting and Clinical Psychology, 54*, 438–446.

Letzring, T.D., Block, J. & Funder, D.C. (2005). Ego-control and ego-resiliency: generalization of self-report scales based on personality descriptions from acquaintances, clinicians, and the self. *Journal of Research in Personality, 39*, 395–422.

Litz, B.T. (1993). Emotional numbing in combat-related post-traumatic stress disorder: a critical review and reformulation. *Clinical Psychology Review, 12*, 417–432.

Luthar, S.S. & Cicchetti, D. (2000). The construct of resilience: implications for interventions and social policies. *Development and Psychopathology, 12*, 857–885.

Luthar, S.S., Doernberger, C.H. & Zigler, E. (1993). Resilience is not a unidimensional construct: insights from a prospective study of inner-city adolescents. *Development and Psychopathology, 5,* 703–717.

Maddi, S.R. (1987). Hardiness training at Illinois bell telephone. In: J.P. Opatz (Ed.), *Health Promotion Evaluation.* Stevens Point, WI: National Wellness Institute.

Maddi, S.R. (1998). Hardiness in health and effectiveness. In: H.S. Friedman (Ed.), *Encyclopedia of Mental Health* (pp. 323–335). San Diego, CA: Academic Press.

Maddi, S.R. & Khoshaba, D.M. (1994). Hardiness and mental health. *Journal of Personality Assessment, 63,* 265–274.

Maddi, S.R. & Kobosa, S.C. (1984). *The Hardy Executive: Health Under Stress.* Homewood, IL: Dow Jones-Irwin.

Maddi, S.R., Wadhwa, P. & Haier, R.J. (1996). Relationship of hardiness to alcohol and drug use in adolescents. *American Journal of Drug and Alcohol Abuse, 22,* 247–257.

Major, F., Cozzarelli, C., Sciacchitano, A.M., Cooper, M.L., Testa, M. & Mueller, P.M. (1990). Perceived social support, self-efficacy, and adjustment to abortion. *Journal of Personality and Social Psychology, 77,* 735–745.

Markus, H.R. & Kitayama, S. (1991). Culture and self: implications for cognition, emotion, and motivation. *Psychological Review, 98,* 224–253.

Masten, A.S. (2001). Ordinary magic: resilience processes in development. *American Psychologist, 56,* 227–238.

Maxwell, S.E. & Delaney, H.D. (1993). Bivariate median splits and spurious statistical significance. *Psychological Bulletin, 113,* 181–190.

McEwen, B.S. (1998). Protective and damaging effects of stress mediators. *New England Journal of Medicine, 338,* 171–179.

McEwen, B.S. & Seeman, T. (2003). Stress and affect: applicability of the concepts of allostasis and allostatic load. In: R.J. Davidson, K.R. Scherer & H.H. Goldsmith (Eds.), *Handbook of Affective Sciences* (pp. 1117–1137). New York: Oxford University Press.

McEwen, B.S. & Wingfield, J.C. (2003). The concept of allostasis in biology and biomedicine. *Hormones and Behavior, 43,* 2–15.

McFarlane, A.C. & Yehuda, R.A. (1996). Resilience, vulnerability, and the course of posttraumatic reactions. In: B.A. van der Kolk, A.C. McFarlane & L. Weisaeth (Eds.), *Traumatic Stress: The Effects of Overwhelming Experience on Mind, Body, and Society* (pp. 155–181). New York: Guilford Press.

McNally, R.J., Kaspi, S.P., Riemann, B.C. & Zeitlin, S.B. (1991). Selective processing of threat cues in posttraumatic stress disorder. *Journal of Abnormal Psychology, 99,* 398–402.

Mesquita, B. (2001). Emotions in collectivist and individualist contexts. *Journal of Personality and Social Psychology, 80,* 68–74.

Mesquita, B. & Frijda, N.H. (1992). Cultural variations in emotions: a review. *Psychological Bulletin, 412,* 179–204.

Mogg, K., Bradley, B.P., Dixon, C., Fisher, S., Twelftree, H. & McWilliams, A. (2000). Trait anxiety, defensiveness and selective processing of threat: an investigation using two measures of attentional bias. *Personality and Individual Differences, 28,* 1063–1077.

Muraven, M., Tice, D.M. & Baumeister, R.F. (1998). Self-control as a limited resource: regulatory depletion patterns. *Journal of Personality and Social Psychology, 74*, 774–789.

Murphy, L.B. & Moriarity, D. (1976). *Vulnerability, Coping, and Growth*. New Haven, CT: Yale University Press.

Newton, T.L. & Contrada, R.J. (1992). Repressive coping and verbal-autonomic response dissociation: the influence of social context. *Journal of Personality and Social Psychology, 62*, 159–167.

Nowack, K.M. (1989). Coping style, cognitive hardiness, and health status. *Journal of Behavioral Medicine, 12*, 145–158.

Nowack, K.M. (1990). Initial development of an inventory to assess stress and health risk. *American Journal of Health Promotion, 4*, 173–180.

Oatley, K. & Jenkins, J.M. (1996). *Understanding Emotions*. Cambridge, MA: Blackwell.

Olff, M., Langeland, W. & Gersons, B.P.R. (2005a). Effects of appraisal and coping on the neuroendocrine response to extreme stress. *Neuroscience & Biobehavioral Reviews, 29*, 457–467.

Olff, M., Langeland, W. & Gersons, B.P.R. (2005b). The psychobiology of PTSD: coping with trauma. *Psychoneuroendocrinology, 30*, 974–982.

Ornish, D., Brown, S.E., Scherwitz, L.W., Billings, J.H. & Armstrong, W.T. (1990). Can lifestyle changes reverse coronary heart disease? *Lancet, 336*, 129–133.

Orr, E. & Westman, M. (1990). Does hardiness moderate stress, and how? A review. *Springer Series on Behavior Therapy and Behavioral Medicine, 24*, 64–94.

Owren, M.J. & Bachorowski, J.A. (2001). The evolution of emotional expression: a "selfishgene" account of smiling and laughter in early hominids and humans. In: T.J. Mayne & G.A. Bonanno (Eds.), *Emotions: Current Issues and Future Directions* (pp. 152–191). New York: Guildford Press.

Ozer, E.J., Best, S.R., Lipsey, T.L. & Weiss, D.S. (2003). Predictors of posttraumatic stress disorder and symptoms in adults: a meta-analysis. *Psychological Bulletin, 129*, 52–73.

Papa, A. & Bonanno, G.A. (in press). Smiling in the face of adversity: interpersonal and intrapersonal functions of smiling. *Emotion*.

Paulhus, D.L. (1998). Interpersonal and intrapsychic adaptiveness of trait self-enhancement: a mixed blessing? *Journal of Personality and Social Psychology, 74*, 1197–1208.

Paulhus, D.L. (1991). Measurement and control of response bias. In: J.P. Robinson, P.R. Shaver & L.S. Wrightsman (Eds.), *Measures of Personality and Social Psychological Attitudes* (pp. 17–59). New York: Academic Press.

Paulhus, D.L. (1984). Two-component models of socially desirable responding. *Journal of Personality and Social Psychology, 46*, 598–609.

Paulhus, D.L. & Williams, K.M. (2002). The dark triad of personality: narcissism, Machiavellianism, and psychopathy. *Journal of Research in Personality, 36*, 556–563.

Pelcovitz, D., van der Kolk, B.A., Roth, S., Mandel, F., Kaplan, S. & Resick, P. (1997). Development of a criteria set and a structured interview for disorders of extreme stress (SIDES). *Journal of Traumatic Stress, 10*, 3–16.

Pennebaker, J.W. (1995). *Emotion, Disclosure, and Health*. Washington, D.C.: American Psychological Association.

Pennebaker, J.W. (1993). Putting stress into words: health, linguistic, and therapeutic implications. *Behaviour Research and Therapy, 31*, 539–548.

Pennebaker, J.W. & Beall, S.K. (1986). Confronting a traumatic event: toward an understanding of inhibition and disease. *Journal of Abnormal Psychology, 95*, 274–281.

Pennebaker, J.W., Kiecolt-Glaser, J.K. & Glaser, R. (1988). Confronting traumatic experience and immunocompetence: a reply to Neale, Cox, Valdimarsdottir, and Stone. *Journal of Consulting and Clinical Psychology, 56*, 638–639.

Pennebaker, J.W. & Seagal, J.D. (1999). Forming a story: the health benefits of narrative. *Journal of Clinical Psychology, 55*, 1243–1254.

Pennebaker, J.W. & Susman, J.R. (1988). Disclosure of traumas and psychosomatic processes. *Social Science and Medicine, 26*, 327–332.

Peterson, C. & Steen, T.A. (2002). Optimistic explanatory style. In: C.R. Snyder & S.J. Lopez (Eds.), *Handbook of Positive Psychology* (pp. 244–256). New York: Oxford University Press.

Porter, R.E. & Samovar, L.A. (1998). Cultural influences on emotional expression: implications for intercultural communication. In: P.A. Andersen & L.K. Guerrero (Eds.), *Handbook of Communication and Emotion: Research, Theory, Applications, and Contexts* (pp. 451–472). San Diego, CA: Academic Press.

Price, J.L., Monson, C.M., Callahan, K. & Rodriguez, B.F. (2006). The role of emotional functioning in military-related PTSD and its treatment. *Journal of Anxiety Disorders, 20*, 661–674.

Prkachin, K.M. & Silverman, B.E. (2002). Hostility and facial expression in young men and women: is social regulation more important than negative affect? *Health Psychology, 21*, 33–39.

Pruchno, R.A. & Meeks, S. (2004). Health-related stress, affect, and depressive symptoms experienced by caregiving mothers of adults with a developmental disability. *Psychology and Aging, 19*, 394–401.

Rachman, S.J. (1978). *Fear and Courage*. New York: Freeman.

Rafaeli, E., Rogers, G.M. & Revelle, W. (2007). Affective synchrony: individual differences in mixed emotions. *Personality and Social Psychology Bulletin, 33*, 915–932.

Reich, J.W., Zautra, A.J. & Davis, M. (2003). Dimensions of affect relationships: models and their integrative implications. *Review of General Psychology, 7*, 66–83.

Resick, P.A. (2001). Cognitive therapy for posttraumatic stress disorder. *Journal of Cognitive Psychotherapy: An International Quarterly, 15*, 321–329.

Resnick, H., Galea, S., Kilpatrick, D. & Vlahov, D. (2004). Research on trauma and PTSD in the aftermath of 9/11. *PTSD Research Quarterly, 15*, 1–8.

Rhodewalt, F. & Zone, J.B. (1989). Appraisal of life change, depression, and illness in hardy and nonhardy women. *Journal of Personality and Social Psychology, 56*, 81–88.

Richards, J.M. & Gross, J.J. (2000). Emotion regulation and memory: the cognitive costs of keeping one's cool. *Journal of Personality and Social Psychology, 79*, 410–424.

Robins, R.W. & Beer, J.S. (2001). Positive illusions about the self: short-term benefits and long-term costs. *Journal of Personality and Social Psychology, 80*, 340–352.

Roth, D.L., Wiebe, D.J., Fillingim, R.B. & Shay, K.A. (1989). Life events, fitness, hardiness, and health: a simultaneous analysis of proposed stress-resistance effects. *Journal of Personality and Social Psychology, 57*, 136–142.

Rotter, J.B. (1966). Generalized expectancies for internal versus external control of reinforcement. *Psychological Monographs, 80*, 1–28.

Rozin, P., Lowery, L., Imada, S. & Haidt, J. (1999). The CAD triad hypothesis: a mapping between three moral emotions (contempt, anger, disgust) and three moral codes (community, autonomy, divinity). *Journal of Personality and Social Psychology, 76*, 574–586.

Russell, J.A. & Feldman-Barrett, L.F. (1999). Core affect, prototypical emotional episodes, and other things called emotion: dissecting the elephant. *Journal of Personality and Social Psychology, 69*, 805–819.

Rutter, M. (1979). Maternal deprivation, 1972–1978: new findings, new concepts, new approaches. *Child Development, 50*, 283–305.

Saigh, P.A. (1988). Anxiety, depression, and assertion across alternating intervals of stress. *Journal of Abnormal Psychology, 97*, 338–341.

Salovey, P. (2001). Applied emotional intelligence: regulating emotions to become healthy, wealthy, and wise. In: J. Ciarrochi, J.P. Forgas & J.D. Meyer (Eds.), *Emotional Intelligence in Everyday Life: A Scientific Inquiry* (pp. 168–184). Philadelphia, PA: Psychology Press/Taylor & Francis.

Sapolsky, R.M. (1999). The physiology and pathophysiology of unhappiness. In: K. Kahneman, E. Diener & N. Schwarz (Eds.), *Well-being: The Foundations of Hedonic Psychology* (pp. 453–469). New York: Russell Sage Foundation.

Sapolsky, R.M. (1998). *Why Zebras Don't Get Ulcers. An Updated Guide to Stress, Stress-related Diseases, and Coping.* New York: Freeman & Company.

Scheier, M.F. & Carver, C.S. (1992). Effects of optimism on psychological and physical well-being: theoretical overview and empirical update. *Cognitive Therapy and Research, 16*, 201–228.

Scheier, M.F. & Carver, C.S. (1993). On the power of positive thinking. *Current Directions in Psychological Science, 2*, 26–30.

Scheier, M.F., Carver, C.S. & Bridges, M.W. (1994). Distinguishing optimism from neuroticism (and trait anxiety, self-mastery, and self-esteem): a reevaluation of the life orientation test. *Journal of Personality and Social Psychology, 67*, 1063–1078.

Schwarz, N. & Skurnik, I. (2003). Feeling and thinking: implications for problem solving. In: J.R. Davidson & R.J. Sternberg (Eds.), *The Nature of Problem Solving* (pp. 263–292). Cambridge, UK: Cambridge University Press.

Seligman, M.E.P. (1992). Power and powerlessness: comments on "cognates of personal control." *Applied and Preventive Psychology: Current Scientific Perspectives, 1*, 119–120.

Sharpley, C.F. & Yardley, P. (1999). The relationship between cognitive hardiness, explanatory style and depression-happiness in post-retirement men and women. *Australian Psychologist, 34*, 198–203.

Shedler, J., Mayman, M. & Manis, M. (1993). The illusion of mental health. *American Psychologist, 48*, 1117–1131.

Silver, R.L., Boon, C. & Stones, M.H. (1983). Searching for meaning in misfortune: making sense of incest. *Journal of Social Issues, 39*, 81–102.

Silver, R.L. & Wortman, C.B. (1980). Coping with undesirable life events. In: J. Garber & M.E.P. Seligman (Eds.), *Human Helplessness: Theory and Applications* (pp. 279–340). New York: Academic Press.

Silver, R.L., Wortman, C.B. & Crofton, C. (1990). The role of coping in support provision: the self-representational dilemma of victims of life crises. In: B.R. Sarason, I.G. Sarason & G.R. Pierce (Eds.), *Social Support: An Interactional View* (pp. 397–426). New York: Wiley.

Smith, N., Young, A. & Lee, C. (2004). Optimism, health-related hardiness and well-being among older Australian women. *Journal of Health Psychology*, 9, 741–752.

Spangler, G. (1997). Psychological and physiological responses during an exam and their relation to personality characteristics. *Psychoneuroendocrinology*, 22, 423–441.

Stein, S. & Spiegel, D. (2000). Psychoneuroimmune and endocrine effects on cancer progression. In: K. Goodkin & A.P. Visser (Eds.), *Psychoneuroimmunology: Stress, Mental Disorders, and Health. Progress in Psychiatry*, 59 (pp. 105–151). Washington, D.C.: American Psychiatric Publishing, Inc.

Suls, J. & Rittenhouse, J.D. (1990). Models of linkages between personality and disease. *Wiley Series on Health Psychology/Behavioral Medicine*, 38–64.

Surgenor, T. & Joseph, S. (2000). Attitudes to emotional expression and personality in predicting post-traumatic stress disorder. *Review of Personality and Social Psychology*, 5, 170–191.

Taylor, S.E. & Armor, D.A. (1996). Positive illusions and coping with adversity. *Journal of Personality*, 64, 873–898.

Taylor, S.E. & Brown, J.D. (1988). Illusion and well being: a social-psychological perspective on mental health. *Psychological Bulletin*, 103, 193–213.

Taylor, S.E. & Brown, J.D. (1999). Illusion and well-being: a social psychological perspective on mental health. In: R.F. Baumeister (Ed.), *The Self in Social Psychology*. Philadelphia, PA: Psychology Press.

Taylor, S.E. & Brown, J.D. (1994). Positive illusions and well-being revisited: separating fact from fiction. *Psychological Bulletin*, 116, 21–27.

Taylor, S.E., Kemeny, M.E., Reed, G.M. & Aspinwall, L.G. (1991). Assault on the self: positive illusions and adjustment to threatening events. In: G.A. Goethals & J.A. Strauss (Eds.), *The Self: An Interdisciplinary Perspective* (pp. 239–254). New York: Springer-Verlag.

Taylor, S.E., Lerner, J.S., Sherman, D.K., Sage, R.M. & McDowell, N.K. (2003a). Portrait of the self-enhancer: well adjusted and well liked or maladjusted and friendless? *Journal of Personality and Social Psychology*, 84, 165–176.

Taylor, S.E., Lerner, J.S., Sherman, D.K., Sage, R.M. & McDowell, N.K. (2003b). Are self-enhancing cognitions associated with healthy or unhealthy biological profiles? *Journal of Personality and Social Psychology*, 85, 605–615.

Taylor, S., Wood, J. & Lichtman, R. (1984). Attributions, beliefs about control, and adjustment to breast cancer. *Journal of Personality and Social Psychology*, 46, 489–502.

Tera, D., Letzring, T.D., Block, J. & Funder, D.C. (2005). Ego-control and ego-resiliency: generalization of self-report scales based on personality descriptions from acquaintances, clinicians, and the self. *Journal of Research in Personality*, 39, 395–422.

Tomaka, J. & Blascovich, J. (1994). Effects of justice beliefs on cognitive appraisal of and subjective, physiological, and behavioral responses to potential stress. *Journal of Personality and Social Psychology, 67,* 732–740.

Tomaka, J., Blascovich, J., Kelsey, R.M. & Leitten, C.L. (1993). Subjective, physiological, and behavioral effects of threat and challenge appraisal. *Journal of Personality and Social Psychology, 65,* 248–260.

Tomaka, J., Blascovich, J., Kibler, J. & Ernst, J.M. (1997). Cognitive and physiological antecedents of threat and challenge appraisal. *Journal of Personality and Social Psychology, 73,* 63–72.

Tomaka, J., Palacios, R., Schneider, K.T., Colotla, M., Concha, J.B. & Herrald, M.M. (1999). Assertiveness predicts threat and challenge reactions to potential stress among women. *Journal of Personality and Social Psychology, 76,* 1008–1021.

Tomarken, A.J. & Davidson, R.J. (1994). Frontal brain activation in repressors and nonrepressors. *Journal of Abnormal Psychology, 103,* 339–349.

Tugade, M.M. & Fredrickson, B.L. (2004). Resilient individuals use positive emotions to bounce back from negative emotional experiences. *Journal of Personality and Social Psychology, 86,* 320–333.

Ursin, H. & Olff, M. (1993). Psychobiology of coping and defence strategies. *Neuropsychobiology, 28,* 66–71.

Vaernes, R., Ursin, H., Darragh, A. & Lambe, R. (1982). Endocrine response patterns and psychological correlates. *Journal of Psychosomatic Research, 26,* 123–131.

van der Kolk, B.A., Pelcovitz, D., Roth, S., Mandel, F.S., McFarlane, A. & Herman, J.L. (1996). Dissociation, somatization, and affect dysregulation: the complexity of adaptation to trauma. *American Journal of Psychiatry, 153,* 83–93.

van der Kolk, B.A., Roth, S. & Pelcovitz, D. (1993). *Complex PTSD: Results of the PTSD field trials for DSM-IV.* Washington, D.C.: American Psychiatric Association.

Veit, C.T. & Ware, J.E. (1983). The structure of psychological stress and well-being in general populations. *Journal of Consulting and Clinical Psychology, 51,* 730–742.

Weinberger, D.A. & Davidson, M.N. (1994). Styles of inhibiting emotional expression: distinguishing repressive coping from impression management. *Journal of Personality, 62,* 587–613.

Weinberger, D.A., Schwartz, G.E. & Davidson, R.J. (1979). Low-anxious, high-anxious, and repressive coping styles: psychometric patterns and behavioral and physiological responses to stress. *Journal of Abnormal Psychology, 88,* 369–380.

Werner, E.E. & Smith, R.S. (1992). *Overcoming the Odds: High Risk Children from Birth to Adulthood.* Ithaca, NY: Cornell University Press.

Westman, M. (1990). The relationship between stress and performance: the moderating effect of hardiness. *Human Performance, 3,* 141–155.

Wiebe, D.J. (1991). Hardiness and stress moderation: a test of proposed mechanisms. *Journal of Personality and Social Psychology, 60,* 89–99.

Williams, P.G., Wiebe, D.J. & Smith, T.W. (1992). Coping processes as mediators of the relationship between hardiness and health. *Journal of Behavioral Medicine, 15,* 237–255.

Zautra, A.J. (2003). *Emotions, Stress, and Health.* New York: Oxford University Press.

Zautra, A.J., Berkhof, J. & Nicolsen, N.A. (2002). Changes in affect interrelations as a function of stressful events. *Cognition & Emotion, 16,* 309–318.

Zisook, S., Chentsova, Y. & Schucter, S.R. (1998). Post-traumatic stress disorder following bereavement. *Annals of Clinical Psychiatry, 10,* 157–163.

Cognitive Performance and Resilience to Stress* 10

MARK A. STAAL

Air Force Special Operations Command

AMY E. BOLTON

Strategic Analysis Inc.

RITA A. YAROUSH AND LYLE E. BOURNE Jr.

University of Colorado at Boulder

Contents

* The preparation of this chapter was supported in part by Army Research Institute Contracts DASW01-99-K-0002 and DASW01-03-K-0002, Army Research Office Grant W9112NF-05-1-0153, and National Aeronautic and Space Administration Contract NAG2-1561 to the University of Colorado.

Cognitive resilience is a construct that has recently attracted the attention of researchers but is not yet well understood. The research literature in this area addresses a loose association of related concepts such as hardiness, stress vulnerability, coping style, protective factors, and self-efficacy (Bandura, 2001; Florian, Mikulincer & Taubman, 1995; Kobasa, 1979, 1982; Kobasa & Puccetti, 1983; Lazarus & Folkman, 1984; Nowack, 1989; Rhodewalt & Zone, 1989). A constellation of factors have been shown to contribute to cognitive resilience. These factors include cognitive appraisal, locus of control, perception of predictability and control, dispositional optimism, learning, experience/expertise, affectivity, motivation, effort, social support systems, and other individual difference characteristics (Bandura, 2001; Kobasa, 1979; Lazarus, 1966, 1990; Lazarus & Folkman, 1984; Seligman, 1998; Seligman & Csikszentmihalyi, 2000).

In general, cognitive resilience describes the capacity to overcome the negative effects of setbacks and associated stress on cognitive function or performance. As such, cognitive resilience can be understood to manifest as a continuum of functionality or behavioral outcome. On one end of the continuum, cognitive processes are overwhelmed by stress and consequently might be ineffective. On the other end of the continuum, there are few or no negative effects of stress on cognitive performance. Within and between these two extremes, individual differences may interact to enhance or diminish resilience to the effects of stress on various specific cognitive processes under different conditions, settings, and levels of demand. The focus of most of this research has been on the effects of stressful conditions on cognitive performance. Although the evidence is presently quite limited, cognitive resilience can be thought of in another, quite different way. That is, cognition itself can influence or moderate adverse effects of stress on other types of behavior (Gilbertson et al., 2006). We have more to say about results of this sort later in this chapter.

The resilience literature has historically focused on specific contexts in which some individuals succumb to stress while others are better able to withstand or overcome it. For example, some children are able to overcome negative life circumstances (e.g., poverty, poor health, violence, lack of family support) that can be devastating to other children (Cesarone, 1999; Comer, 1984; Garmezy, 1991; Kumpfer, 1999; Luthar, Cicchetti & Becker, 2000;

O'Neal, 1999). These and related studies of resilience have informed our understanding of individual vulnerability to mental health problems such as depression, posttraumatic stress disorder (PTSD), and the onset of schizophrenia (Bonanno, Field, Kovavecic & Kaltman, 2002; King, King, Foy, Keane & Fairbanks, 1999; Robbins, 2005; Robinson & Alloy, 2003). Resilience may also help to explain patterns of cognitive decline associated with normal aging and other degenerative processes (DeFrias, Dixon & Backman, 2003; Mackinnon, Christensen, Hofer, Korten & Jorm, 2003; Seeman, Lusignolo, Berkman & Albert, 2001; Wilson et al., 2002).

There is also an extensive body of research devoted to the study of human performance under stress. Studies in this area reveal and emphasize primarily negative effects of stress on cognition (Bourne & Yaroush, 2003; Driskell, Mullen, Johnson, Hughes & Batchelor, 1992; Driskell & Salas, 1996; Hancock & Desmond, 2001; Staal, 2004; Stokes & Kite, 1994). Unfortunately, beyond addressing training and experience levels, the human performance literature generally fails to address individual differences that may explain or promote resilience to stress.

In the following sections, we provide a brief overview of how stress affects the primary cognitive processes of attention, memory, and judgment/ decision making. Although this initial discussion is general in concept and limited in scope, it provides the basis for consideration of specific moderating factors that promote cognitive resilience. Finally, we address how these factors might be applied for practical purposes in military and other operational environments.

What Is Stress?

There are two traditional models of psychological stress. A stimulus-based model treats stress as a function of external influence (e.g., demanding workload, heat/cold, time constraint). Critics of the stimulus-based model argue that it ignores individual differences, does not adequately evaluate contextual circumstances, and neglects entirely the role of emotion (Stokes & Kite, 1994). By contrast, a response-based model holds that stress is a composite of response patterns (behavioral, cognitive, and affective) that result from exposure to a given stressor.

More recently, a third approach has emerged to conceptualize stress more broadly as an interaction between the individual and his or her environment. Transactional models of stress emphasize the role of the individual in appraising a situation and shaping responses to it. For the purpose of this chapter, we view stress as the interaction between three transactional elements: perceived demand, ability to cope, and perceived importance of coping with the demand (McGrath, 1976).

Stress and Human Performance

Human performance under stress depends on multiple factors related to the individual performer and to specific attributes of the situation in which he or she must perform. As noted earlier, research in cognitive science reveals a continuum of outcome, ranging from no effect on cognitive processes to extreme dysfunction (Bourne & Yaroush, 2003; Driskell & Salas, 1996; Hancock & Desmond, 2001; Staal, 2004). However, effects of stress on human performance in general and on cognition in particular can be very difficult to predict at the individual level. The intensity of a particular stressor or condition might be increased without coincident or measurable effect on the performance of one individual, while the same increase might be associated with dramatic degradation in the performance of another individual. Whether by disposition or experience or both, some individuals are simply better able or equipped than others to handle stress. It may be possible to mitigate vulnerability to stress by experience and training, although there is little research available yet to guide the development of resilience training *per se*.

Quantitatively, it has long been known that stress effects on human performance generally follow an inverted U-shaped function. According to the Yerkes–Dodson law (Yerkes & Dodson, 1908) and a considerable body of evidence consistent with it, increasing amounts of stress (arousal) are associated initially with improved performance. However, at some point, stress level reaches an optimal level, beyond which performance will degrade as stress continues to increase. This performance pattern is well-established, but does not tell the whole story and has limited explanatory value for a number of reasons documented elsewhere (see Hancock, 2002). We suggest that for the purpose of understanding stress effects on cognition, the usefulness of the Yerkes–Dodson framework can be improved by a more detailed consideration of specific effects or stress states (Bourne & Yaroush, 2003) at and between the extremes of the inverted U curve. Figure 10.1 depicts the Yerkes–Dodson inverted U function and its relationship to stress states identified specifically as facilitation, optimization, mobilization, degradation, choking, and panic.

As noted, initial increases in stress are typically associated with improvement in performance. This phenomenon is known as facilitation, and it may be related to positive effects of increased arousal on cognitive function. For example, Chappelow (1988) conducted an analysis of aircrew performance errors and found that performance was improved in a slightly more stressful environment. A certain amount of stress-related arousal may be conducive to specific cognitive functions such as attention and memory.

At some point for any given task and individual, performance under stress will reach its optimal level. Beyond that optimal level, additional stress typically exerts a detrimental effect on performance. However, if a performer is sufficiently motivated, he or she may be able to maintain or

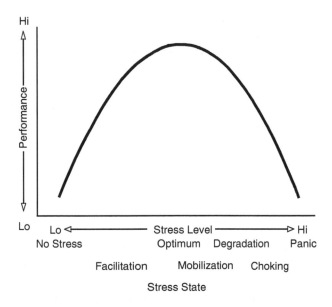

Figure 10.1 The Yerkes–Dodson inverted "U" function and its relationship to identifiable stress states: facilitation, optimization, mobilization, degradation, choking, and panic.

improve performance beyond the optimal level. This phenomenon is attributed to mobilization of mental effort, which is invoked when performance level is recognized as insufficient for success. Indeed, mobilization of mental effort will tend to maintain or improve performance at any level of stress. Effort mobilization plays a prominent role in Kahneman's classical analysis of attention (Kahneman, 1973) and has received empirical support in research conducted by Kahneman and others (e.g., Doerner & Pfeifer, 1993; Hockey, 1997).

At some point, as stress continues to increase, there begins to occur an unavoidable degradation in performance. At this point, the performer will find it increasingly difficult or impossible to perform successfully. Ordinarily, performance will degrade gradually (or gracefully; see Norman & Bobrow, 1975, 1976). However, extreme stress may produce a catastrophic degradation that manifests as choking or panic. These phenomena have been demonstrated experimentally by Lehner, Seyed-Solorforough, O'Connor, Sak, and Mullin (1997), who observed among other things that when human operators were subjected to extreme stress (e.g., extreme time pressure), they abandoned procedures they had been trained to follow and reverted instead to more familiar, intuitive procedures that produced inferior results.

Strictly quantitative formulations, such as the Yerkes–Dodson law, fail to capture the more qualitative character of phenomena such as facilitation, optimization, mobilization, degradation, choking, and panic. By expanding our consideration to include these qualitative phenomena, we can interpret more fully the empirical effects of stress on primary cognitive functions such as attention, memory, and judgment and decision making. These effects are reviewed in the next section as a critical first step toward identifying factors, processes, and relationships that may serve to mitigate the negative effects of stress and thus promote cognitive resilience.

Stress Effects on Cognition

Attention

Because attention is a critical gateway to other cognitive processes, it is among the most widely studied phenomena in cognitive science. Although the full scope of information processing begins with preattentive, preparatory functions such as orientation and pattern recognition (see Duckworth, Bargh, Gracia & Chaiken, 2002; Sokolov, 1975), these early processes are largely unaffected by ambient stress and are immune to effects of resource sharing (see cognitive resources). Effects of stress- and task-related demands are generally not observed until formal attentive and higher order cognitive processes are called into play.

In general, studies of stress and attention converge on findings first reported by Easterbrook (1959) concerning the relationships between motivation, drive, arousal, and cue utilization (range of informational cues attended). Extensive research in this area has shown that individuals under stress tend to reduce their use of peripherally relevant information. These individuals tend instead to centralize or limit their focus of attention to stimuli they perceive to be the most important or the most relevant to a main or primary task. This tunneling hypothesis has been echoed by numerous other investigators (Baron, 1986; Broadbent, 1958, 1971; Bundesen, 1990; Bursill, 1958; Cohen, 1980; Combs & Taylor, 1952; Cowan, 1999; Davis, 1948; Driskell, Salas & Johnston, 1999; Hockey, 1970, 1978; Hockey & Hamilton, 1970; James, 1890; Murata, 2004; Pamperin & Wickens, 1987; Salas, Driskell & Hughes, 1996; Stokes, Wickens & Kite, 1990; Vroom, 1964; Wickens, 1984; Williams, Tonymon & Anderson, 1990; Zhang & Wickens, 1990). Research has also demonstrated that the tunneling of attention may be helpful or harmful to performance, depending on the nature of the task at hand and the circumstances under which it must be performed. For example, when peripheral cues are irrelevant to the primary task, it may be helpful to ignore them. However, if peripheral cues are ignored when they might otherwise bear relevance to an important task, performance on that task may suffer.

Several theories have been proposed to explain why stress affects attention as it does. Chajut and Algom (2003) posited that stress depletes attentional resources and thus reduces the bandwidth of attention such that peripheral information is neglected and attentional selectivity is improved. When we speak of cognitive resources, we refer to a theoretical reservoir of mental capacity that can be drawn from to meet the demands of various cognitive tasks. Although many previous investigators have sought to define this concept precisely, empirical research in the area has remained vague and ill-defined. Wickens (1984) has suggested that the term "resources" can be considered synonymous with a number of other common terms such as capacity, attention, and effort. Kahneman (1973) is frequently cited as the first to propose a limited-capacity resource model although Norman and Bobrow (1975, 1976) are typically credited with coining the term. Kahneman suggested that there exists a limited pool of mental resources that can be divided across tasks. Kinsbourne and Hicks (1978) argued that resources can be construed as competing for actual cerebral space although there is no solid empirical evidence for this claim. Others have related resource management and consumption to the brain's metabolism of glucoproteins and changes in blood flow (Sokolov, 1975), but again supporting evidence is minimal.

A second explanatory framework is the capacity-resource theory (Chajut & Algom, 2003), which suggests that when stress occurs, attention is narrowed to the direction of whatever information is most proximal, accessible, or automatic (e.g., primed cues) without consideration of its task relevance. Working from a capacity-resource model, a number of workload studies have focused on the siphoning of attentional resources by task-irrelevant activities during driving (Hughes & Cole, 1986; Matthews & Desmond, 1995; Matthews, Sparkes & Bygrave, 1996; Metzger & Parasuraman, 2001; Recarte & Nunes, 2000, 2003; Renge, 1980; Suzuki, Nakamura & Ogasawara, 1966). Research in this area indicates that automobile drivers tend to pay a significant amount of attention (perhaps as much as 50%) to activities or objects that are unrelated to driving. Evidence from a series of studies by Strayer and his colleagues (e.g., Strayer & Drews, 2004; Strayer, Drews & Johnston, 2003), using a driving simulator, shows that drivers who are involved in cell phone conversations have slower brake response times and are more likely to miss roadside sign information and traffic signals than drivers who are not so engaged. Indeed, driving performance during cell phone use is sometimes inferior to that accomplished while under the influence of alcohol. Horrey, Wickens, and Consalus (2006) extended these findings to other in-vehicle technologies such as navigational devices or traffic, road, and vehicle status information. Strayer et al. attributed the adverse effects of cell phone use to a shift of attention away from visual input toward auditory information that is necessary to comprehend phone conversations, whereas Horrey et al. emphasized the interfering effects of expanding attentional bandwidth. Both ideas are consistent with an interpretation of stress effects based on capacity-resource theory.

A third theoretical framework proposed to explain stress effects on attention is known as thought suppression (Chajut & Algom, 2003), which holds that tunneling effects are due to competition between consciously controlled attention and an unconscious search for "to-be-suppressed" material. The supposed competitive effect of secondary monitoring is believed to be the result of additional demands placed on attentional resources when an individual becomes sensitized to information he or she should ignore (e.g., "whatever you do, don't look down"). This effect may be amplified under stress and produce hypersensitivity toward task-irrelevant information (Wegner, 1994; Wenzlaff & Wegner, 2000).

The study of attentional decrement under stress has focused heavily on specific attentional processes, especially sustained attention (vigilance). The type of stress associated with vigilance tasks is often related to task demands and to boredom associated with those demands (Frankenhaeuser, Nordheded, Myrsten & Post, 1971; Galinsky, Rosa, Warm & Dember, 1993; Hancock & Warm, 1989; Hovanitz, Chin & Warm, 1989; Mackworth, 1948; Scerbo, 2001). Empirical studies of vigilance usually apply stress in the form of fatigue (e.g., due to prolonged work shifts or sleep deprivation; Baranski et al., 2002), although other stress conditions such as noise, temperature, time pressure, and workload have also been applied (Kjellberg, 1990; Pepler, 1958; Van Galen & van Huygevoort, 2000; Wickens, Stokes, Barnett & Hyman, 1991). Similar cognitive performance decrements have been found for a variety of tasks and measures, including serial response times, logical reasoning, visual comparison, mathematical problem solving, vigilance, and multitasking (Samel et al., 1997; Wilkinson, 1964; Williams, Lubin & Goodnow, 1959). Interestingly, some studies have demonstrated that the direct effects of stress can be modulated by individual differences and by psychological processes that mobilize resources such as motivation and effort. Unfortunately, these studies are few in number and have failed to address stress modulation effects in detail.

Attention researchers have also observed that well-learned tasks are associated with fewer lapses in attention. Well-learned skills are performed more automatically in the sense that they require fewer mental resources and less deliberate or conscious control of attention. Presumably, more cognitive resources are left available to support the performance of other or additional tasks (Beilock, Carr, MacMahon & Starkes, 2002).

The observations reported above will be considered again later in this chapter, with specific emphasis on their potential utility and relevance to cognitive resilience.

Memory

The study of memory involves two important construct distinctions that are essential to defining the character and the role of memory in any given situation. First, researchers draw a distinction between explicit and implicit memories to describe the extent to which task performance is consciously and deliberately controlled (Schacter, 1989). On learning a new task or skill set, an individual usually must think through each step of the task in a deliberate manner and explicitly encode new information into memory (a necessary precondition for automatic task performance; Logan & Klapp, 1991; Zbrodoff & Logan, 1986). As learning proceeds, task performance requires less deliberation, less step-by-step attention, and less conscious information processing. With practice and repetition, task-related responses eventually become more automatic in the sense that they require little or no conscious control (Shiffrin & Schneider, 1977). Task performance improves as task-related responses become more fluid and less effortful. At this point, task-relevant information and knowledge retrieval is said to be implicit (Reber, 1989; Schacter, 1987).

Another important distinction is based on a temporal continuum from the remote past (retrospective long-term memory; Atkinson & Shiffrin, 1968) to the present or near present (short-term memory, immediate or working memory; Atkinson & Shiffrin, 1968; Baddeley, 1986, 1992) and into the future (prospective memory; Brandimonte, Einstein & McDaniel, 1996; Winograd, 1988). Long-term memory constitutes a repository of facts and skills acquired in the past. Short-term memory refers to an assortment of facts and skills that are relevant to the current or recent focus of attention. Prospective memory preserves intentions or reminders of actions that must be executed at some point in the future. Stress and other variables may exert selective effects on these different types of memory.

In general, stress provokes a shift of attention to the here-and-now and thus can introduce potential consequent degradation of performance on tasks that involve either retrospective or prospective memory (see Healy & Bourne, 2005). There is little empirical evidence concerning stress effects on long-term retrospective memory in particular, but recent studies suggest that stress due to distraction may have specific adverse effects on short-term memory (Larsen & Baddeley, 2003; Neath, Farley & Surprenant, 2003). Other studies have demonstrated that tests of prospective memory are particularly sensitive to extraneous or secondary task demands (Einstein, McDaniel, Williford, Pagan & Dismukes, 2003). These results, although limited, are consistent with a memory constriction hypothesis, which holds that the time span from which knowledge can easily be retrieved and used in a given context will tend to shrink with increasing levels of stress (e.g., Berntsen, 2002). The consequent neglect of facts or procedures held in long-term memory and failure to execute required responses at appointed future times might explain many of the performance errors that tend to occur under stress. This reasoning is also consistent with attention tunneling effects commonly observed under stress (see Easterbrook, 1959). Although empirical evidence is currently somewhat limited as to broad time-based stress effects on memory, this type of theoretical framework may prove useful as a guide to future research.

General Stress Effects on Memory

A variety of stressful conditions influence the way in which memory functions. For example, Gomes, Martinho-Pimenta, and Castelo-Branco (1999) showed a significant negative impact of stressful noise on immediate verbal memory. Fowler, Prlic, and Brabant (1994) reported a similar effect of hypoxia on the executive function of working memory. Finally, Parker, Bahrick, Fivush, and Johnson (2006) observed a full-range Yerkes–Dodson function on memory for events during a major hurricane, with moderate stress associated with best recall. Mandler (1979) was one of the first cognitive psychologists to speculate theoretically about the effects of stress on memory, arguing that stress creates cognitive system "noise," which in turn competes with task-related demands on limited cognitive (conscious) resources. According to this view, memory processes that rely upon conscious elaboration of current sensory input and relatively new memory representations (explicit memory) should be especially sensitive to stress. Van Gemmert and Van Galen (1997) share Mandler's view (1979), arguing that stress-related noise in the cognitive system results either in reduced sensitivity to task-related sources of information or in less exacting motor movements.

Mandler's theoretical framework is logically consistent with the memory constriction (tunneling) hypothesis. It is reasonable to suppose that when attention is focused on the here-and-now, the likely result will be greater reliance upon explicit (deliberate, conscious) memory processes, which are in turn relatively more vulnerable to stress effects than are automatic (implicit) memory processes. However, this possibility raises the question of whether short-term memory is more or less resilient to stress and why. It is certainly possible that short-term memory is inherently more vulnerable to degradation by stress and that tunneling of attention and memory serve to mitigate this vulnerability. Additional research is needed to examine this and other possible interpretations of effects of stress on memory.

Van Overschelde and Healy (2001) have demonstrated that stress can be provoked by information overload during a learning task, but that negative effects can be mitigated by elucidating connections between new facts (i.e., new information to be learned under stress) and information that already resides in long-term memory. The general principle illustrated here is that the acquisition and retention of new information and associations is facilitated by linkage to existing knowledge. This strategy is based on a theory of long-term working memory (Ericsson & Kintsch, 1995), which postulates that information held in long-term memory can be temporally activated or primed for easy access by task-related cues from short-term memory. This proposed mechanism has been useful as a means to explain text comprehension and expert-level performance on memory span tasks as well as resilience to information overload.

A different view on the role of working memory can be found in the study of individuals who suffer from math anxiety (Ashcraft, 2002; see also Ashcraft & Kirk, 2001), in which it has been proposed that high math anxiety (susceptibility to stress) leads to reduced working memory capacity. When the working memory capacity of nonanxious subjects is limited by added task demands, they show performance decrements that are similar to those observed in high-math-anxious subjects. Ashcraft concludes that stress generally tends to reduce working memory capacity and that any task which involves explicit learning or memory processes should thus be especially vulnerable to stress.

Matthews (1997) has argued that intrusive thoughts and other worries occupy space in working memory and thereby interfere with the performance of tasks that rely upon working memory. Matthews' research has also shown that worries, daily hassles, and intrusive thoughts tend to occupy more space in working memory among high-anxious than among low-anxious subjects (see also Dutke & Stoebber, 2001). Matthews et al. (2006) demonstrated that measures of emotional intelligence (EI) and the stress coping strategies that EI entails do relate positively to subjective feelings of concern and worry. However, Matthews et al. were unable to show any significant impact of EI on performance under stress in tasks that required little or no working memory. In a review of the literature, Miyake and Shah (1999b) identified emotion, stress, and anxiety as major modulating factors in memory but noted the need for additional research to address how these variables affect particular aspects of memory (especially working memory) such as memory maintenance, executive control, and content.

Context and State Dependency
It is well known that memory is context-dependent (e.g., Johnson, Hashtroudi & Lindsay, 1993) in that memory task performance is typically better when it is tested in a context identical or very similar to the context in which the task was originally learned. Few studies of stress effects on memory have taken into account the potentially confounding influence of context dependency. One of the very few exceptions is a study conducted by Thompson, Williams, L'Esperance, and Cornelius (2001), which directly examined context effects by testing the recall of experienced skydivers who learned word lists while in the air (stressful context) or on the ground (less stressful context) prior to participating in a skydiving event. The skydivers' recall was poor in air-learning

conditions, regardless of the context in which they were later tested for recall. That is, there was no context effect on memory when learning took place under stress. But when lists were learned on land, later recall was better when it was also tested on land, demonstrating a clear effect of context dependency.

The researchers also tested other subjects in less stressful conditions. Instead of participating in a skydiving event, these subjects merely watched a skydiving video. In this case, recall was better when contexts matched, regardless of stress condition. Thompson et al. thus proposed that under extremely emotionally arousing circumstances (e.g., preparing in the air for a sky dive), environmental cues (context) are less likely to be encoded or linked to newly acquired information and thus are unavailable to serve as cues to later retrieval under less emotional circumstances. Expressed simply, the generally strong context and state dependency effects on memory might be overridden under extremely stressful conditions.

The findings reported by Thompson et al. call attention to the need for similar research in operational paradigms. This type of research may improve our understanding of resilient behavior and task performance in occupations and settings that expose individuals to emotional stress during initial training and/or subsequent recall of trained information. One implication is that individuals who experience less extreme emotional responses to stress might also demonstrate more persistent (spared) context dependency effects on memory. If so, context-dependent recall under stress might be useful as a marker of cognitive resilience.

Judgment and Decision Making

Although judgment and decision making can be viewed as processes or as outcomes—or as one (decision making) the result of the other (judgment)—they are more typically combined (JDM) as an end state, which culminates from attention and memory processes. Broadbent (1979) observed that JDM is largely dependent on the perceived probability of possible outcomes. Building on Broadbent's work, Gigerenzer and Selten (2001) suggested that decision makers rely on a number of heuristics ranging from the simple to the complex. They theorized that human beings are equipped with an adaptive toolbox that contains a different types of strategies. Accordingly, when faced with the need to make a decision, we are able to employ the most adaptive heuristic available (Gigerenzer, Hoffrage & Kleinbolting, 1991; Gigerenzer & Selten, 2001).

JDM can be degraded by a wide variety of stressors, including noise (Rotton, Olszewski, Charleton & Soler, 1978), fatigue (Soetens, Hueting & Wauters, 1992), fear (Yamamoto, 1984), interruption (Speier, Valacich & Vessey, 1999), and time pressure (Ben Zur & Breznitz, 1981; Stokes, Kemper

& Marsh, 1992; Wickens, Stokes, Barnett & Hyman, 1991; Zakay & Wooler, 1984). Wickens, Stokes, Barnett, and Hyman (1991) examined the effects of time pressure on decision making in aircraft pilots. Building on the earlier work of Broadbent (1971) and Hockey (1983), these authors identified three main effects of stress on JDM: a reduction in cue sampling, a reduction in the resource-limited capacity of working memory, and, when time was limited, a speed–accuracy trade-off in performance outcome.

In general, when human subjects are under stress, they become less flexible to alternative JDM strategies (Broder, 2000, 2003; Dougherty & Hunter, 2003; Janis, Defares & Grossman, 1983; Janis & Mann, 1977; Keinan, 1987; Streufert & Streufert, 1981; Walton & McKersie, 1965; Wright, 1974). Stressed subjects also tend to persist with a particular problem-solving method or strategy even after it fails to be useful (Cohen, 1952; Staw, Sandelands & Dutton, 1981). These effects seem to be clear enough, but it remains uncertain exactly what aspects or processes of JDM are degraded and why. Janis and Mann (1977) were among the first to observe that stress can lead to hypervigilance, defined as a state of disorganized and haphazard attentional processing. Janis and Mann proposed a decision-conflict theory in which hypervigilance provokes frantic search, rapid attentional shifting, and a reduction in the number and quality of considered alternatives. Hypervigilance thus degrades JDM and, in its extreme, may lead to choking or panic (see below; see also Baradell & Klein, 1993; Janis, Defares & Grossman, 1983; Keinan, 1987).

Although it is generally true that extreme emotional responses to stress interfere with information processing, it is also the case that a manageable negative emotional response might help to sustain JDM under stressful conditions. Sinclair and Mark (1995) explored the effects of mood state on judgment accuracy and found that when individuals experienced a positive mood state, they tended to make less effortful, less detail-oriented, and fewer correct decisions. By contrast, negative and neutral mood states tended to enlist greater effort; decisions made in these conditions were more detailed, more systematic, and more often correct. Therefore, to the extent that a state of stress invokes a manageable level of negative emotion, it may facilitate greater effort and detailed attention, leading in turn to more accurate judgment and improved decision making.

As noted above, good JDM may depend to a large extent on the ability to consider and use alternative heuristics. Support for this idea comes from individual and team performance research. Team studies identify strategy shifting (e.g., from explicit to implicit coordination) as critical to effective team performance (Entin & Serfaty, 1990; Entin, Serfaty & Deckert, 1994; Entin, Serfaty, Entin & Deckert, 1993; Serfaty, Entin & Johnston, 1998). Bowers et al. (2002) have also observed this to be true for team performance under stressful time and mental workload conditions. Orasanu (1990) reported similar findings for aircrew performance. Entin and Serfaty (1990) have suggested that teams tend to draw upon shared mental models of situation and task. Shared mental models may facilitate team members' ability to shift from explicit to implicit strategies, thereby reducing the mental resource costs incurred by explicit strategies. In effect, teams may respond to cognitive stress much as individuals do and thus be more or less resilient to it for similar reasons.

Human operators may also respond and adapt to stress by shedding or simplifying task demands (Rothstein & Markowitz, 1982). For example, Davis (1948) studied the effects of fatigue and continuous flying operations on pilots. He observed that over time, pilots reduced their attention to peripheral instrumentation and limited their visual scanning to focus primarily on instruments directly relevant to the central task of flying. Bursill (1958) replicated these findings on laboratory tasks. More recently, Raby and Wickens (1994) examined aeronautical decision making in an experimental setting and found that when pilots became task-saturated and stressed, they reduced their own workload by dropping tasks in reverse order of criticality. (It is worthwhile to note that judgment and decision-making processes were necessarily involved in making this adjustment.) Sperandio (1971) examined task simplification strategies employed by air traffic controllers and found that they tend to regulate their workload by strategy shifting. When air traffic controllers found themselves under increased traffic load conditions, they tended to reduce the volume of information they provided to each aircrew, eventually reducing it to the minimum amount of information required for safe operations. Sperandio concluded that controllers economized their workload by reducing the amount of redundant or nonessential information they themselves might have to process.

The ability to prune or simplify task demands in a strategic manner is an adaptive skill in most circumstances. This ability enhances cognitive resiliency by task prioritization and organization, the positive effect of which is an improved economy of resource mobilization. There is evidence to suggest that strategic shedding and task prioritization can be learned and improved by training (e.g., Gopher, 1992; Gopher, Weil & Bareket, 1994). Effective training of this type may be invaluable to improve JDM in potentially stressful settings. However, it is also important to recognize that adjustment strategies may themselves draw upon already strained cognitive resources and thus may be difficult or impossible to achieve under conditions that impose a very high level of workload or extreme stress.

Summary

Taken together, documented effects of stress on attention, memory, and JDM suggest that effective cognitive performance depends heavily upon the extent to which cognitive resources can be preserved and managed. Resource management appears to be directly related to the state of stress experienced by the performer. When cognitive resources are strained or depleted by stress or workload, performance (attention, memory, JDM) is degraded. By contrast, when resources are effectively managed, spared, or mobilized, performance is preserved or facilitated. Training and experience can play a critical role to the extent that well-learned tasks can be performed less deliberately, placing fewer demands on cognitive resources.

Research also indicates that strategy shifting and economizing workload (by reduction or task simplification) can be an effective means to mitigate the potentially negative effects of stress on cognitive task performance. These adjustments may help to sustain resource capacity by reducing the need for attention to and processing of redundant or nonessential information. This type of resource management seems to happen logically and effectively at first, but under extremely stressful conditions, the resource management process itself may impose additional limitations on performance.

Cognitive Resilience: Moderators, Factors, and Strategies

Studies of psychological resilience have identified a number of moderating variables, protective factors, and behavioral strategies that appear to promote resilience to stress. Here, we address findings of particular relevance to cognitive resilience.

Cognitive Appraisal

Research has provided consistent support for the notion that cognitive evaluations of threat or perceived control are influenced by the subjective experience of stress and, conversely, that positive evaluations may offer some level of protection from stress. The basis for this idea is not new. Lazarus (1966) was among the first to observe that when human subjects viewed a situation as negative or threatening, they experienced psychological stress as a direct result of their own negative appraisal (Lazarus, 1990; Lazarus & Folkman, 1984).

The works of many other researchers and theorists suggest that anxiety exerts an important influence on cognitive appraisal. In particular, high-trait and high-state anxious individuals demonstrate an attentional bias toward threatening stimuli (Beck, 1976; MacLeod & Mathews, 1988). Bower (1981) proposes a network theory, which holds that emotional states prompt the activation of mood-congruent memory representations and the consequent selective processing of available information. Taken together, these and a number of other related works support the notion that anxious individuals are more likely to attend and negatively appraise emotionally threatening stimuli (Broadbent & Broadbent, 1988; Calvo & Castillo, 2001; Mogg, Bradley & Hallowell, 1994; Williams, Watts, MacLeod & Mathews, 1988).

The work of Wofford and colleagues indicates that low-trait anxious individuals are relatively less vulnerable to negative effects of stress on cognition than are their high-trait anxious counterparts (Wofford, 2001; Wofford & Goodwin, 2002; Wofford, Goodwin & Daly, 1999). Not surprisingly, negative attitude has been linked to reduced resilience and increased risk for depression following exposure to stressful events (Abela & Alessandro, 2002). Thus, it is reasonable to consider that interventions to reduce anxiety and to support positive emotional orientation may also facilitate positive cognitive appraisal, reduce negative effects of stress on cognition, and promote cognitive resilience.

In addition to its role in emotion and attitude, cognitive appraisal may play a key role in the mobilization of cognitive resources. That is, one's appraisal of a particular stressor or situation might exert a direct impact on one's preparation or direct attention to it and allocate mental resources to meet the challenge. There are no empirical data currently available to support this notion, but it is reasonable to expect that situations which are perceived as very important, challenging, or threatening would tend to attract the most attention and inspire the most determined preparation or allocation of cognitive resources. This is an area that invites additional research with particular attention as to whether resource allocation under stress is deliberate (conscious) or involuntary.

Disposition and Coping

Dispositional optimism is a psychological concept that has received increasing scientific attention in recent years. The positive psychological movement has brought advanced constructs such as optimism, explanatory style, and self-efficacy theories to the forefront of behavioral science research (Bandura, 2001; Seligman, 1998; Seligman & Csikszentmihalyi, 2000). These constructs emphasize the importance of dispositional viewpoint and outlook as factors that exert a significant influence on psychological health. There is a growing body of evidence to support the belief that individuals who are predisposed to optimism enjoy a number of benefits to their well-being, including better overall health and less susceptibility to depression (Seligman, 1998). Similar findings have been reported in studies of self-efficacy (the belief that one has the power to positively influence one's own circumstances). For example, perceived self-efficacy has been associated with reduced anxiety and increased perceived control over a variety of stressors (Endler, Speer, Johnson & Flett, 2001).

Although optimism and self-efficacy surely represent the combined effects of emotion and cognition, we need not disentangle these effects to recognize their potential joint benefits. To the extent that optimism and self-efficacy represent or encourage positive cognitive appraisal, these dispositional tendencies may also provide some measurable basis for the promotion and the prediction of cognitive resilience.

Zakowski, Hall, Cousino-Klein, and Baum (2001) found that coping strategies tend to be congruent with situation appraisal. That is, one's approach to coping with a stressful situation will tend to reflect one's appraisal of the situation itself. Positive appraisals are more often associated with positive outcome and negative appraisals with less successful outcome. Positive appraisal appears to mediate subjective outcome (e.g., self-reported measures of feeling better) as well as objective outcome (e.g., scored task performance). When individuals view an event in positive (but realistic) terms, they tend to copeup more effectively, enjoy positive feelings, and experience greater confidence (Janis, 1983; Skinner & Brewer, 2002).

Finally, there is a robust literature examining the extent to which so-called "hardy" individuals respond to stress. Hardiness describes an assortment of dispositional characteristics, including a strong sense of self and self-efficacy, an internal locus of control (Rotter, 1954), and the perspective that life has meaning and purpose (Kobasa, 1979). In general, hardy individuals are better able to perform well under stress (Westman, 1990) and are less likely to suffer stress-related illnesses (Kobasa, 1979; Kobasa & Puccetti, 1983; Pengilly & Dowd, 2000). Research also indicates that hardy individuals are more likely to engage in solution-focused problem-solving strategies, while less hardy individuals tend toward avoidant and emotion-focused coping strategies (Pollock, 1989; Williams, Wiebe & Smith, 1992).

Predictability and Control

An important outcome of cognitive appraisal is the extent to which stressors are perceived as predictable or controllable. Perceived control and predictability are directly related to subjective distress and cognitive performance. When a situation or stressor is perceived as within one's control, it tends to provoke less subjective stress (Lazarus, 1966). For example, it has been shown that the psychological stress associated with the threat of electric shock can be reduced when an individual perceives control over stimulus intensity, timing, frequency, or termination (Bowers, 1968).

Individuals who perceive themselves as being able to exert some form of control over a stressful stimulus report less anticipatory anxiety (Champion, 1950; Houston, 1972) and demonstrate a corresponding decrease in physiological arousal (Geer, Davison & Gatchel, 1970; Szpiler & Epstein, 1976). Control also facilitates prediction. Predictable stimuli—even those that may be threatening—are perceived as less aversive than similar but unpredictable stressors. This effect can be measured by subjective report and by physiological markers (Badia & Culbertson, 1970; Baum & Paulus, 1987; Bell & Greene, 1982; Burger & Arkin, 1980; D'Amato & Gumenik, 1970; Epstein, 1982; Evans & Jacobs, 1982; Monat, Averill & Lazarus, 1972; Weinberg & Levine, 1980).

Experience and Expertise

The highest standards of cognitive performance are often necessitated by demanding and/or high-risk situations where the consequences of failure may be severe or even catastrophic. Individuals who work in such settings know well that training and experience are critical to job performance and may even be essential to survival. For example, it is for good reason that aircraft pilots are judged and qualified on the basis of the number of hours they spend in training and in flight. In the cockpit, good decision-making strategies and outcomes are supported by experience and familiarity (Doane, Woo Sohn & Jodlowski, 2004; Klein & Thordsen, 1991; Shafto & Coley, 2003; Stokes, Kemper & Marsh, 1992; Wiggins & O'Hare, 1995). Similar findings have been reported for automobile drivers (Lansdown, 2001), firefighters (Klein, 1989; Klein & Klinger, 1991; Taynor, Crandall & Wiggins, 1987), air traffic controllers (Hutton, Thordsen & Mogford, 1997), and parachutists (Burke, 1980; Doane, Woo Sohn & Jodlowski, 2004; MacDonald & Lubac, 1982; Stokes, 1995). In general, individuals who have more experience (experts) attend and process task-relevant information more efficiently and with better results than do individuals with lesser experience (novices). When the stakes are high, expertise may literally make the difference between life and death (Kornovich, 1992; Li, Baker, Lamb, Grabowski & Rebok, 2001; Stokes, 1995).

Recent evidence (Gilbertson et al., 2006) shows that experience is aided and abetted by cognitive skill. In this study, soldiers who scored high on tests of cognitive ability were found to be less vulnerable to the development of combat-related PTSD. Thus, beyond the question of how stress affects cognition, it must also be considered that cognitive ability or skill might exert a protective or mitigating effect against the lasting, negative psychological impact of stress.

The Presence of Others

The social psychology literature refers to social facilitation and social impairment to describe positive (facilitation) or negative (impairment) effects of performing in the presence of others. In general, the presence of others tends to exert a facilitative effect on the performance of simple or well-learned tasks while it tends to impair performance on complex, novel, or poorly learned tasks (Allport, Antonis & Reynolds, 1972; Beilock & Carr, 2001; Beilock, Carr, MacMahon & Starkes, 2002; Carver & Scheier, 1981; Katz & Epstein, 1991).

These findings have interesting implications for cognitive resiliency, specifically with respect to training, complex tasks and systems, human–machine interaction, and augmented cognition. For instance, much has been written about using computer-aided technologies to enhance performance through the reduction of task complexity and the introduction of in-the-moment performance feedback (Cooke, 2005; Nicholson, Lackey, Arnold & Scott, 2005).

Training for Extreme Stress States

As noted earlier, under extremely stressful conditions, human performance degradation can be catastrophic. Choking is a term commonly used to describe severe performance degradation that may occur as an extreme response to stress (i.e., "choking under pressure"). This extreme response is characterized by an unintentional and paradoxical transition away from well-learned, highly practiced, essentially automatic action toward more deliberate, time-consuming, and less effective strategies. When an otherwise highly skilled individual reverts to conscious deliberation to meet each requirement of an otherwise familiar task, he or she loses the ability to generate fluid and efficient results. Response time is increased as each aspect of the task is approached with cautious reference to explicit memories that may not have been accessed for quite some time. In lay terms, this phenomenon is sometimes described as "over-thinking" or "paralysis by analysis."

Recent research suggests that it might be possible to inoculate individuals against the adverse influence of extreme stress. Inoculation techniques involve preexposure to stress and training under conditions that incorporate stressful contexts. In one of a very few laboratory studies to address this phenomenon, Beilock and Carr (2001) observed the performance of golfers who had been trained to putt while under audience observation, while performing a distraction task, or in quiet solitude without distraction. When subsequently tested under low-pressure conditions, no performance differences were found among golfers who had been trained under the three different conditions. However, in high-pressure conditions—when a large monetary prize hung in the balance—golfers who had been trained in the presence of an audience significantly out-performed their counterparts in other training conditions and in fact exceeded their own training performance. The authors (see also Beilock, Carr, MacMahon & Starkes, 2002) argued that training in an environment in which one is forced to attend to performance (self-focus) from the outset can immunize the performer against negative effects of pressure on later performance. Expressed simply, training scenarios can be designed to anticipate stress on performance, to avoid choking, and to promote resilience.

More recently, Beilock and colleagues have reported somewhat different findings from a study of cognitive task performance. Beilock, Kulp, Holt, and Carr (2004; see also Beilock & Carr, 2005) examined problem-solving performance on familiar (highly practiced) versus unfamiliar (infrequently practiced) mathematical problems. In this paradigm, pressure adversely affected performance only on unfamiliar mathematical problems. Beilock et al. concluded that skilled individuals are far less likely to choke under pressure when performing cognitive (versus sensory-motor/coordination) tasks and further that when choking does occur during a cognitive task, the effect is likely attributable to a reduction in working or immediate memory capacity rather than to the invocation of explicit memories (see also Ashcraft, 2002).

History, folklore, and sports literature contain numerous examples of choking due to heightened self-consciousness or stress. Relatively recent examples include Greg Norman's collapse in the final round of the Masters' Golf Tournament in 1996 and Jana Novotna's last-set loss to Steffi Graf at Wimbledon in 1993. However, as noted above, the effects of stress are likely to be different for different types of skills and, in particular, for cognitive skills that require involvement of conscious working memory even for highly developed skills and well-learned tasks. What is needed is a taxonomy that can help to clarify if, when, and how various resources and processes are required for particular skills. Such a taxonomy would help to predict when and how stress might adversely affect performance on specific types of tasks, in what circumstances choking might be more or less likely to occur, and when or how it might be possible to reduce the probability of choking (i.e., improve resilience) through training or other interventions.

Panic is qualitatively different from choking and usually results in even more severe performance degradation. Panic is associated with primitive behavior and maladaptive automatic thinking (Katz & Epstein, 1991). Rather than over-thinking the stressful situation, a panicked person essentially stops thinking altogether and is inclined instead to react in the most basic possible way to escape or avoid the situation entirely. Sport coaches sometimes refer to panic as "brain lock." Explicit memories become inaccessible. Short-term memory seems to cease functioning. The panicked individual responds in an unskilled way, reverts to primal instincts, or simply fails to respond at all. At best, the panicked individual will focus on a single aspect of the environment, usually to the neglect of information that might resolve or eliminate the stressful condition. Although the panicked individual's exclusive goal is to survive, his or her performance becomes functionally maladaptive and may in fact make survival less likely (Katz & Epstein, 1991).

Conditions of panic are virtually impossible to recreate in the laboratory. Further, it is not at all clear how preexposure or training to mitigate panic might be accomplished. Most of what we know about stress-induced panic comes from case histories and self-reports by athletes and others who have experienced panic in real-world settings. For example, skydivers typically carry two parachutes and are well-trained to release the secondary chute immediately if the primary chute fails to open. Nonetheless, accidents sometimes do occur when skydivers panic and find themselves unable to perform as trained. Langewiesche (1998) documents other poignant accounts of panic as experienced by aircraft pilots.

Clearly, panic is a state one should try to avoid if one wishes to survive an emergency situation. There is an obvious value in efforts to develop training strategies and scenarios that may improve preparation in ways that minimize the likelihood of panic. To this end, it may be helpful to train individuals to recognize early symptoms of panic and to offer strategies to prevent its full onset. Unfortunately, at the time of this writing, little or no known progress has been made toward the development of effective panic mitigation procedures.

Summary

So far, behavioral researchers have identified several variables that appear consistently to mitigate negative effects of stress on cognition. These include specific individual traits or tendencies (positive appraisal, optimism, expertise) as well as task or situational attributes (predictability and control, the presence of others). It is likely that these are but a few of the many variables that will ultimately be identified as bearing direct or indirect influence upon human cognitive resilience to stress.

Although cognitive task performance under stress seems to depend heavily upon the effective preservation, allocation, or management of cognitive resources, it cannot be assumed that this is the only mechanism by which moderators of cognitive resilience must act. Moreover, there are different strategies (e.g., tunneling, workload reduction, strategy shifting) by which cognitive resource management can be achieved or maintained. Thus, researchers should seek to explain how and when specific moderating variables exert their effects.

The identification of predictive moderators also implies a need to better understand at what point along the theoretical inverted U curve specific moderating variables come into play. There is no reason to assume that all moderators of cognitive resilience exert relevant or measurable effects at all times during a stressful task or experience. For example, it may well be the case that a given trait or state variable is specifically conducive to improved cognitive performance by enhanced mobilization, while another is specifically linked to panic deterrence.

Finally, there is the question of which, if any, moderating variable might be achieved or improved by training or experience. Effective training strategies would be especially valuable to prevent choking or panic in response to extreme stress. There is a pressing need for research in this area to determine how existing and new information about cognitive resilience might be put to practical use in real-world operational environments.

Military Applications and Other Considerations

There are several areas of military activity in which cognitive resilience can play a significant role to enhance performance. These include training, personnel selection/assessment, operational performance, and human operator interface with weapons platforms and related systems. Each of these areas has been addressed quite extensively elsewhere in this volume and in the military scientific literature. Here, we offer a brief review of military needs and activities as they relate specifically to cognition, stress, and resilience. We further consider how resilience might be promoted by anticipating specifically relevant cognitive processes and identifying appropriate potential moderators of stress effects in each case. For example, Table 10.1 summarizes potential areas of application for the various moderators of cognitive resilience discussed above.

Training and Preparation

The U.S. military's primary business is to fight and win our nation's wars. Crudely expressed, warfighters are trained to kill people, break things, and support their brothers in arms and allies who do the same. By the very nature of their work, soldiers, sailors, airmen, and Marines are placed in harm's way and are asked to perform tasks that demand a high degree of stress resiliency that is rarely needed in the course of an ordinary civilian life. Even when warfighters are not directly involved in combat, they must be prepared to endure a variety of extreme physical, psychological, and environmental stressors. For those who experience combat, resilience to stress is critical. The U.S. military selects men and women who, they believe, stand the greatest chance of performing well under the most extremely stressful circumstances conceivable. These individuals are trained, tested, and prepared through the use of rigorous physical, mental, and emotional conditioning. They are placed in challenging situations, and their performance is examined critically under simulated but realistic training conditions.

As behavioral science yields new information about how to train individuals to perform under high-stress work conditions, the U.S. military is eager to incorporate these lessons into its training protocols. There is a fairly robust literature already in place to show that well-learned tasks are most resistant to negative effects of stress. There is also a growing body of research whose purpose is to develop and optimize training conditions for jobs that require

Table 10.1 Possible Applications for Moderators of Cognitive Resilience

Moderators	Training	Selection and Assessment	Operational Support	Benefit(s)
Cognitive appraisal	Develop resource allocation strategies	Select for low-state and trait-anxious individuals	Optimize resources	Anxiety reduction Improved coping
Disposition and coping	Increase self-efficacy Increase perceived control	Select for predisposition to optimism		Anxiety reduction Hardiness
Predictability and control	Cope with uncertainty		Supply predictive information	Stress reduction
Experience and expertise	Increase level of experience and improve skills	Select for criterion level of expertise		Expert performance Improved efficiency Improved survivability
The presence of others	Improve performance under observation		Reduce task complexity	Anxiety reduction Improved performance on new and complex tasks
Extreme stress states	Expose and rehearse to performance under extreme pressure	Select out individuals predisposed to anxiety/ panic attacks	Intervene and maintain operations	Stress management Prevention of panic and choking

resilience to stress. Although training under pressure may be helpful to prevent choking or panic during subsequent performance under pressure, high levels of stress may also tend to degrade knowledge acquisition during training (Keinan, Friedland & Sarig-Naor, 1990). As noted earlier in this chapter, Thompson et al. (2001) found that learning under the stressful conditions of skydiving had a significantly deleterious effect on subsequent cognitive task (recall) performance. Research in this area supports the need for a balanced emphasis on learning (knowledge acquisition and retention) and real-world preparation. At present, the most effective approach is delivered as phased training,* which provides for initial knowledge acquisition under minimal stress conditions. During a subsequent intermediate stage of phased training, trainees are familiarized with relevant criterion stressors and thus begin to develop more realistic expectations about field conditions. Finally, trainees are exposed to realistic stressors and practice their newly learned skills in conditions that successively approximate a true performance environment† (Keinan, Friedland & Sarig-Naor, 1990).

Virtual environments (VEs) are an appealing alternative to live training exercises because they provide a safer and more cost-effective context for learning and practicing operational skills. It would be beneficial to determine how phased training toward cognitive resilience might be achieved in a low-cost VE. VEs offer distinct advantages such as the opportunity to manipulate task performance requirements and environmental demands and thus expose trainees to a broader repertoire of experiences and a full variety of positive and negative effects of stress on attention, memory, and JDM. It is reasonable to expect that multiple practice opportunities in a VE would support the development of an expertise, advance task training and performance from controlled to automatic processing, increase the bandwidth of attentional resources and executive function, reduce demands on memory resources required for task performance (Atkinson & Shiffrin, 1968; Shiffrin & Schneider, 1977), and enable rapid recognition-primed decision making (Klein, 1989). Reduced demands on cognitive resources may, in turn, promote more efficient information processing and cognitive resilience to stress in real-life environments such as combat. These suggested training effects could be empirically tested in VE with more flexibility and at less expense than in traditional live training environments. Attention and fatigue management

---

* Phased training should not be confused with graduated stress training, which exposes trainees to increasing levels of stress over time. Graduated stress training programs have been shown to yield inferior outcomes (Friedland & Keinan, 1992).
† Typically, the final phase of military training involves live fire exercises. Because live fire exercises are costly and can cause environmental and safety problems, exposure is generally limited. Thus, the final phase of basic military training may not fully prepare service members to achieve a high level of cognitive resilience to stress prior to deployment.

techniques should also be considered for their potential impact as training techniques to sustain or improve cognitive performance under stress. Currently, there is little empirical evidence concerning the degree of transfer from VEs to real environments, but we anticipate that pertinent studies and assessments will be conducted and reported in the near future.

Contemporary theories of learning and instruction may provide generally helpful guidance, but are not adequate to identify specific conditions under which cognitive resilience might be promoted through training. To achieve a well-defined, integrated, and useful body of empirical evidence, researchers should consider and examine the effects of specific variables, factors, and conditions that may serve to moderate stress effects on cognition and thus advance our understanding of how best to promote cognitive resilience.

Selection, Assessment, and Measurement

The purpose of military selection and assessment is to identify individuals who are most likely to succeed in specific jobs. This effort is usually based on a series of target attributes that have been established as characteristic of candidates who succeed (select-in criteria) or not (select-out criteria) on the job. Most selection and assessment instruments include demographic, psychographic, and behavioral performance indicators.

There are a number of assessment instruments that claim to measure constructs related to cognitive resiliency (e.g., scales of hardiness, locus of control, optimism, and self-efficacy). Many of these tools have been used for the selection of special mission unit personnel and special duty positions within the military. Selection programs that implement screening procedures of this type typically compare results against previously identified profiles of successful operators. It is presumed that these characteristics are relevant to performance success and are thus desirable to replicate in prospective candidates.

Although psychometric instruments are often helpful to narrow the field of potential job candidates, it is not yet clear whether they effectively identify or predict resilience to stress *per se*. Unfortunately, as yet, there is no direct method to assess cognitive resilience to stress, primarily because resilience itself is not yet sufficiently well-defined. Moreover, it seems that the more we learn about stress, the more we are forced to expand our understanding of resilience to accommodate potential direct and interactive influences of myriad individual differences and psychobiological system variables. This suggests the need for a fairly complex assessment instrument that is adequate to assess a variety of domain characteristics (e.g., emotion, personality, physiology) and moderating variables (e.g., outlook, disposition, training or experience).

The U.S. military and other organizations have devoted substantial efforts and resources to the research and development of high-fidelity training environments (VEs; Durlach & Mavor, 1995; National Research Council, 1999) that can mimic real operational environments for the purpose of training. Recently, sponsors of VE development have suggested that VEs might also be useful to support selection and assessment (Schmorrow, in press). The reasoning here is that if simulated environments are sufficiently realistic to promote learning, they can also be used to represent operational environments for selection based upon performance assessment.

Existing VEs already have the capability to record a wide variety of performance data and to apply assessment techniques. Currently available VE performance measures include body motion/gestures, eye movements, interaction with others (synthetic or real) in the environment, actions, arousal (via physiological measurement), and neurophysiological measures. These and other indices could be applied to construct a multivariate assessment of cognitive resilience based on task performance in combination with other variable measures. For example, specific neurophysiological signals associated with attention, memory, or JDM as recorded from individuals who perform well on cognitive tasks in stressful environments might provide an additional basis for job candidate assessment.

Certainly, more research is needed to define resilience operationally, to identify critical factors and markers of resilience, and to guide the design of scenarios to provide an informative context for the assessment of cognitive resilience. With respect to resilience assessment, it would likely be most efficient to begin with careful consideration of currently available and well-documented psychological and physiological measures. As noted previously, future research should also address known and putative moderators of stress effects on cognition as possible contributors to resilience.

Human–Computer Interfaces and Operational Performance Support

The U.S. military uses state-of-the-art technology to support increased automation of the battlefield (FFW, 2004). For the purpose of this chapter, we define operational performance support as any human performance intervention whose purpose is to improve operational task performance. Human factors engineering is an essential part of designing military operational systems and interfaces such that they will not exert a negative impact on performance. Human factors research and engineering can also be used to develop automated performance support systems. Computational decision-making models, cybernetic support systems, and augmented cognition are just a few of the information management systems that are under recent or current development as tools to reduce demands on operators' mental resources (attention and memory) and to facilitate more accurate and efficient information processing and JDM (Girolamo, 2005; Ververs, Whitlow, Dorneich, Mathon & Sampson, 2005). Augmented cognition is an emerging field that seeks to extend operators' abilities and ultimately their performance using computational technologies. These technologies are explicitly designed to address bottlenecks, limitations, and biases in cognition and to improve decision-making capabilities (D.D. Schmorrow, personal communication, July 25, 2005). For example, the demonstrated benefits of individual performance improvement through augmented cognition technologies (Schmorrow, 2005; Schmorrow, Kruse, Reeves & Bolton, submitted) have the potential to generalize to distributed team decision making. Through the use of computer-aided situational updating, the goal would be to reduce the time and the cognitive effort required of the team to make decisions about emerging problems or threats. It is thus likely that augmented cognition may be an effective means to reduce task load- and workload-related stress (Schmorrow, 2005; Schmorrow, Kruse, Reeves & Bolton, 2007), and to encourage more positive cognitive appraisal. The net effect of these benefits might improve cognitive resilience in operational environments.

To the extent that automated systems could help to reduce negative effects of stress on cognition, they offer a promising new basis for cognitive resilience research and development. Tools and techniques that augment the capabilities of individual soldiers, team leaders, and commanders provide the greatest opportunity to improve their performance in the battle space. For example, augmenting technologies could be used to assess individual physiological stress state and adjust information inputs accordingly to optimize decision making. Similar types of automated information systems could be implemented in a variety of other professional contexts such as law enforcement, fire fighting, and emergency services.

Conclusions and Recommendations

Resilience is a term generally used to refer to the ability to overcome stress and maintain an effective level of appropriate behavior or performance when confronted by obstacles, setbacks, distractions, hostile conditions, or aversive stimuli. In this chapter, we have focused specifically on the possible effects of such external stressors on attention, memory, and JDM. To the extent that resilience can be learned, supported, or facilitated, strategies to improve cognitive resilience may offer potentially significant benefits for well-being and performance in a wide range of operational environments.

Observable effects of stress on attention, memory, and JDM are essentially alike. At low levels, stress facilitates cognitive task performance (e.g., recall, decision making). As stress increases, cognitive performance reaches an optimal level and additional resources can be mobilized in an effort to sustain optimal performance. Finally, excess stress causes performance degradation. This is a well-established and generally reliable pattern of effect. However, actual human performance under stress may vary depending on many number of individual differences, moderating or protective factors, and training or experience. Additional research is needed to develop interventions and strategies to sustain effective performance under positive stress states (facilitative stress, optimum stress, mobilization) and to improve performance by promoting resilience to negative effects of stress (degradation, choking, panic).

The objective of this chapter has been to review the essential effects of stress on cognition and to emphasize the need for additional research to determine how cognitive performance might be sustained or improved to overcome negative effects of stressors encountered in ordinary and extraordinary operational environments. The potential benefits of resilience research and development extend well beyond the military to include other high-performance occupations in aviation, public safety, law enforcement, and emergency services. Specific areas of applied concern that should be targeted include selection, assessment, measurement, training, and operational support.

Cognitive resilience research lacks in several areas. The first and perhaps most unsettling is the fact that there is little, if any, consensus concerning what cognitive resilience is and is not. Many related construct terms are used interchangeably, and resilience is poorly understood even among those most interested in its potential utility. We believe that this volume provides an initial binding of the concept of resilience to encourage and facilitate more focused research in the future.

Certainly, much more can be learned about the role of cognitive resilience in the areas of personnel selection, training, and operational support. So far, efforts to select nonresilient populations and to identify individuals least likely to succeed in various cognitively demanding tasks or critical professional roles have been relatively successful. However, we are as yet quite limited in our ability to select resilient individuals and those who might be trained to sustain effective cognitive performance under stress. The U.S. military and related operational organizations have always been dedicated to the development of effective training strategies and procedures. It is essential to test and evaluate systematically the effectiveness of military training to ensure its greatest possible benefit in preparing service members for a wide range of real-world operational duties, including combat. Additional improvement can be encouraged by emphasizing the need for ecological validity, computer-aided fidelity, and continued development of more realistically graduated or phased training models.

As a practical matter, it is important to meet the needs of military operators where they stand—on the battlefield, in aircraft, and on ships. We need to make careful study of current operational support systems to improve the ways in which we can augment operators' capabilities in specific operational environments. Specifically, we recommend investment in robust systems that are designed to accommodate and adapt to highly complex, dynamic environments. Likewise, there is a pressing need for targeted support of research in cognitive resilience as a subject matter that offers potential direct benefit to a broad variety of applied biobehavioral and technological concerns, including the need for improved operational effectiveness under stress and the continued development of state-of-the-art cognitive systems.

Finally, it is important to recognize that human cognitive capacities may be strained by the complexity of modern technological and operational systems in many sophisticated occupational environments. The successful use of technology depends ultimately on the extent to which human operators find it useable. Understanding that cognitive performance may otherwise suffer under stress, it is important to encourage system and human–machine interface designs that support efficient task prioritization, tools to enable task simplification, and options to support information and resource management.

References

Abela, J.R.Z. & Alessandro, D.U. (2002). Beck's cognitive theory of depression: a test of the diathesis-stress and causal mediation components. *British Journal of Clinical Psychology, 41,* 111–128.

Allport, D.A., Antonis, B. & Reynolds, P. (1972). On the division of attention: a disproof of the single-channel hypothesis. *Quarterly Journal of Experimental Psychology, 24,* 225–235.

Ashcraft, M.H. (2002). Math anxiety: personal, educational, and cognitive consequences. *Current Directions in Psychological Science, 11,* 181–185.

Ashcraft, M.H. & Kirk, E.P. (2001). The relationships among working memory, math anxiety, and performance. *Journal of Experimental Psychology: General, 130,* 224–237.

Atkinson, R.C. & Shiffrin, R.M. (1968). Human memory: a proposed system and its control processes. In: K.W. Spence & J.T. Spence (Eds.), *The Psychology of Learning and Motivation: Advances in Research and Theory* (Vol. 2). New York: Academic Press.

Baddeley, A.D. (1986). *Working Memory.* Oxford, U.K.: Clarendon Press.

Baddeley, A.D. (1992). Working memory. *Science, 255,* 556–559.

Badia, P. & Culbertson, S. (1970). Behavioral effects of signaled vs. unsignalled shock during escape training in the rat. *Journal of Comparative and Physiological Psychology, 72,* 216.

Bandura, A. (2001). Social cognitive theory: an agentic perspective. *Annual Reviews in Psychology, 52,* 1–26.

Baradell, J.G. & Klein, K. (1993). Relationship of life stress and body consciousness to hypervigilant decision making. *Journal of Personality and Social Psychology, 64*(2), 267–273.

Baranski, J.V., Gil, V., McLellan, T.M., Moroz, D., Buguet, A. & Radomski, M. (2002). Effects of modafinil on cognitive performance during 40 hr of sleep deprivation in a warm environment. *Military Psychology, 14*, 23–47.

Baron, R.S. (1986). Distraction-conflict theory: progress and problems. In: L. Berkowitz (Ed.), *Advances in Experimental Social Psychology* (pp. 1–40). New York: Academic Press.

Baum, A. & Paulus, P. (1987). Crowding. In: D. Stokols & I. Altman (Eds.), *Handbook of Environmental Psychology* (pp. 533–570). New York: John Wiley & Sons.

Beck, A.T. (1976). *Cognitive Therapy and the Emotional Disorders*. New York: International Universities Press.

Beilock, S.L. & Carr, T.H. (2001). On the fragility of skilled performance: what governs choking under pressure? *Journal of Experimental Psychology: General, 130*, 701–725.

Beilock, S.L. & Carr, T.H. (2005). When high-powered people fail: working memory and "choking under pressure" in math. *Psychological Science, 16*, 101–105.

Beilock, S.L., Carr, T.H., MacMahon C. & Starkes, J.L. (2002). When paying attention becomes counterproductive: impact of divided versus skill-focused attention on novice and experienced performance of sensorimotor skills. *Journal of Experimental Psychology: Applied, 8*, 6–16.

Beilock, S.L., Kulp, C.A., Holt, L.E. & Carr, T.H. (2004). More on the fragility of performance: choking under pressure in mathematical problem solving. *Journal of Experimental Psychology: General, 133*, 584–600.

Bell, P. & Greene, T. (1982). Thermal stress: physiological comfort, performance, and social effects of hot and cold environments. In: G.W. Evans (Ed.), *Environmental Stress*. New York: Cambridge University Press.

Ben Zur, H. & Breznitz, S.J. (1981). The effects of time pressure on risky choice behavior. *Acta Psychologica, 47*, 89–104.

Berntsen, D. (2002). Tunnel memories for autobiographical events: central details are remembered more frequently from shocking than from happy experiences. *Memory & Cognition, 30*, 1010–1020.

Bonanno, G.A., Field, N.P., Kovavecic, A. & Kaltman, S. (2002). Self-enhancement as a buffer against extreme adversity: civil war in Bosnia and traumatic loss in the United States. *Personality and Social Psychology Bulletin, 28*, 184–196.

Bourne, L.E. & Yaroush, R.A. (2003). *Stress and Cognition: a Cognitive Psychological Perspective*. Unpublished manuscript, NASA grant NAG2–1561.

Bower, G.H. (1981). Mood and memory. *American Psychologist, 36*, 129–148.

Bowers, C.A., Asberg, K., Milham, L.M., Burke, S., Priest, H. & Salas, E. (2002). Combat readiness and fatigue: laboratory investigation of teams. In: P. Hancock (Chair), *Combat Readiness and Fatigue*. Symposium presented at the 110th Annual Convention of the American Psychological Association, Chicago, IL.

Bowers, K. (1968). Pain, anxiety, and perceived control. *Journal of Clinical and Consulting Psychology, 32*, 295–303.

Brandimonte, M., Einstein, G.O. & McDaniel, M.A. (Eds.) (1996). *Prospective Memory: Theory and Applications*. Mahwah, NJ: Lawrence Erlbaum Associates, Inc.

Broadbent, D.E. (1971). *Decision and Stress*. London: Academic Press.

Broadbent, D.E. (1979). Human performance and noise. In: C.M. Harris (Ed.), *Handbook of Noise Control* (pp. 17.1–17.20). New York: McGraw-Hill.

Broadbent, D.E. (1958). *Perception and Communication*. London: Pergamon.

Broadbent, D.E. & Broadbent, M. (1988). Anxiety and attentional bias: state and trait. *Cognition & Emotion, 2*, 165–183.

Broder, A. (2000). Assessing the empirical validity of the "Take-the-Best" heuristic as a model of human probabilistic inference. *Journal of Experimental Psychology: Learning, Memory, and Cognition, 26*, 1332–1346.

Broder, A. (2003). Decision making with the "adaptive toolbox": influence of environmental structure, intelligence, and working memory load. *Journal of Experimental Psychology: Learning, Memory, and Cognition, 29*(4), 611–625.

Bundesen, C. (1990). A theory of visual attention. *Psychological Review, 97*, 523–547.

Burger, J.M. & Arkin, R. (1980). Prediction, control, and learned helplessness. *Journal of Personality and Social Psychology, 38*, 482–491.

Burke, W.P. (1980). *Development of predictors of performance under stress in jump-master training* (Research Report No. 1352). Ft. Benning, GA: U.S. Army Research Institute.

Bursill, A.E. (1958). The restriction of peripheral vision during exposure to hot and humid conditions. *Quarterly Journal of Experimental Psychology, 10*, 113–129.

Calvo, M.G. & Castillo, M.D. (2001). Selective interpretation in anxiety: uncertainty for threatening events. *Cognition & Emotion, 15*, 299–320.

Carver, C.S. & Scheier, M.F. (1981). *Attention and Self-regulation: A Control Theory Approach to Human Behavior*. New York: Springer Verlag.

Cesarone, B. (1999). *Resilience Guide: A Collection of Resources on Resilience in Children and Families*. Washington, D.C.: Office of Educational Research and Improvement (ED).

Chajut, E. & Algom, D. (2003). Selective attention improves under stress: implications for theories of social cognition. *Journal of Personality and Social Psychology, 85*(2), 231–248.

Champion, R.A. (1950). Studies of experimentally induced disturbance. *Australian Journal of Psychology, 2*, 90–99.

Chappelow, J.W. (1988). Causes of aircrew error in the Royal Airforce. In: Human Behaviour in High Stress Situations in Aerospace Operations. NATO AGAARD Conference Proceedings 458.

Cohen, E.L. (1952). The influence of varying degrees of psychological stress on problem-solving rigidity. *Journal of Abnormal and Social Psychology, 47*, 512–519.

Cohen, S. (1980). Aftereffects of stress on human performance and social behavior: a review of research and theory. *Psychological Bulletin, 88*, 82–108.

Combs, A.W. & Taylor, C. (1952). The effect of the perception of mild degrees of threat on performance. *Journal of Abnormal and Social Psychology, 47*, 420–424.

Comer, J.P. (1984). Home-school relationships as they affect the academic success of children. *Education and Urban Society, 16*(3), 322–337.

Cooke, N.J. (2005, July). Augmented team cognition. Paper presented at the annual meeting of the International Conference on Human-Computer Interaction (Augmented Cognition), Las Vegas, NV.

Cowan, N. (1999). An embedded-processes model of working memory. In: A. Miyake & P. Shah (Eds.), *Models of Working Memory*. Cambridge, U.K.: Cambridge University Press.

Davis, D.R. (1948). *Pilot error*. Air Ministry Publication A.P. 3139A. London: H.M. Stationary Office.

DeFrias, C.M., Dixon, R.A. & Backman, L. (2003). Use of memory compensation strategies is related to psychosocial and health indicators. *Journal of Gerontological Psychological Science, 58,* 12–22.

Doane, S.M., Woo Sohn, Y. & Jodlowski, M.T. (2004). Pilot ability to anticipate the consequences of flight actions as a function of expertise. *Human Factors, 46*(1), 92–103.

Doerner, J. & Pfeifer, E. (1993). Strategic thinking and stress. *Ergonomics, 36,* 1345–1360.

Dougherty, M.R.P. & Hunter, J. (2003). Probability judgment and subadditivity: the role of working memory capacity and constraining retrieval. *Memory & Cognition, 31*(6), 968–982.

Driskell, J.E., Mullen, B., Johnson, C., Hughes, S. & Batchelor, C. (1992). *Development of quantitative specifications for simulating the stress environment* (Report No. AL-TR-1991-0109). Wright-Patterson AFB, OH: Armstrong Laboratory.

Driskell, J.E. & Salas, E. (1996). *Stress and Human Performance.* Mahwah, NJ: Lawrence Erlbaum Associates, Inc.

Driskell, J.E., Salas, E. & Johnston, J. (1999). Does stress lead to a loss of team perspective? *Group Dynamics: Theory, Research, and Practice, 3*(4), 291–302.

Duckworth, K.L., Bargh, J.A., Gracia, M. & Chaiken, S. (2002). The automatic evaluation of novel stimuli. *Psychological Science, 13*(6), 513–519.

Durlach, B.N.I. & Mavor, A.S. (1995). *Virtual Reality: Scientific and Technological Challenges.* Washington, D.C.: National Academy Press.

Dutke, S. & Stoebber, J. (2001). Test anxiety, working memory, and cognitive performance. *Cognition & Emotion, 15,* 381–389.

Easterbrook, J.A. (1959). The effect of emotion on cue utilization and the organization of behavior. *Psychological Review, 66,* 187–201.

Einstein, G.O., McDaniel, M.A., Williford, C.L., Pagan, J.L. & Dismukes, R.K. (2003). Forgetting of intentions in demanding situations is rapid. *Journal of Experimental Psychology: Applied, 9,* 147–162.

Endler, N.S., Speer, R.L., Johnson, J.M. & Flett, G.L. (2001). General self efficacy and control in relation to anxiety and cognitive performance. *Current Psychology: Developmental, Learning, Personality, Social, 20,* 36–52.

Entin, E.E. & Serfaty, D. (1990). *Information Gathering and Decision Making Under Stress.* Burlington, MA: Alphatech, Inc. (NTIS/DTIC Accession #ADA218233).

Entin, E.E. & Serfaty, D. (1990). Information gathering and decision making under stress. NTIS HC A05/MF A01. Technical Report Number AD-A218233: AD-E501191: TR-454.

Entin, E.E., Serfaty, D. & Deckert, J.C. (1994). *Team Adaptation and Coordination Training* (TR-648-1). Burlington, MA: Alphatech, Inc.

Entin, E.E., Serfaty, D., Entin, J.K. & Deckert, J.C. (1993). *CHIPS: Coordination in Hierarchical Information Processing Structures* (TR-598). Burlington, MA: Alphatech, Inc.

Epstein, Y. (1982). Crowding stress and human behavior. In: G.W. Evans (Ed.), *Environmental Stress.* New York: Cambridge University Press.

Ericsson, K.A. & Kintsch, W. (1995). Long-term working memory. *Psychological Review, 102,* 211–245.

Evans, G.W. & Jacobs, S.V. (1982). Air pollution and human behavior. In: G.W. Evans (Ed.), *Environmental Stress*. New York: Cambridge University Press.

Florian, V., Mikulincer, M. & Taubman, O. (1995). Does hardiness contribute to mental health during a stressful real-life situation? The roles of appraisal and coping. *Journal of Personality and Social Psychology, 68,* 687–695.

Fowler, B., Prlic, H. & Brabant, M. (1994). Acute hypoxia fails to influence two aspects of short-term memory: implications for the source of cognitive deficits. *Aviation, Space, and Environmental Medicine, 65,* 641–645.

Future Force Warrior (n.d.). Retrieved September 24, 2004, from http://www.natick.army.mil//ffw/content.htm

Galinsky, T.L., Rosa, R.R., Warm, J.S. & Dember, W.N. (1993). Psychophysical determinants of stress in sustained attention. *Human Factors, 35,* 603–614.

Garmezy, N. (1991). Resilience and vulnerability to adverse developmental outcomes associated with poverty. *American Behavioral Scientist, 34,* 416–430.

Geer, J.H., Davison, G.C. & Gatchel, R.I. (1970). Reduction of stress in humans through nonveridical perceived control of aversive stimulation. *Journal of Personality and Social Psychology, 16,* 731–738.

Gigerenzer, G., Hoffrage, U. & Kleinbolting, H. (1991). Probabilistic mental models: a Brunswikian theory of confidence. *Psychological Review, 98,* 506–528.

Gigerenzer, G. & Selten, R. (2001). *Bounded Rationality: The Adaptive Toolbox.* Cambridge, MA: MIT Press.

Gilbertson, M.W., Paulus, L.A., Williston, S.K., Gurvits, T.V., Lasko, N.B., Pitman, R.K. & Orr, S.P. (2006). Neurocognitive function in monozygotic twins discordant for combat exposure: relationship to posttraumatic stress disorder. *Journal of Abnormal Psychology. 115,* 484–495.

Girolamo, H.J. (2005, July). Augmented cognition for warfighters; a beta test for future applications. Paper presented to the 11th Annual HCI Human Computer Interaction International Conference, Las Vegas, NV.

Gomes, L.M.P., Martinho-Pimenta, A.J.F. & Castelo-Branco, N.A.A. (1999). Effects of occupational exposure to low frequency noise on cognition. *Aviation, Space, and Environmental Medicine, 70,* A115–A118.

Gopher, D. (1992). The skill of attention control: acquisition and execution of attention strategies. In: S. Kornblum & D. Meyer (Eds.), *Attention and Performance XIV: Synergies in Experimental Psychology, Artificial Intelligence, and Cognitive Neuroscience.* Cambridge, MA: MIT Press.

Gopher, D., Weil, M. & Bareket, T. (1994). Transfer of skill from a computer game trainer to flight. *Human Factors, 36*(3), 387–405.

Hancock, P.A. (2002, April). A program of research on stress and performance. Paper presented at U.S. Army Research Office symposium, Life Sciences: The universal language (from microbe to man).

Hancock, P.A. & Desmond, P.A. (Eds.) (2001). *Stress, Workload, and Fatigue.* Mahwah, NJ: Lawrence Erlbaum Associates, Inc.

Hancock, P.A. & Warm, J.S. (1989). A dynamic model of stress and sustained attention. *Human Factors, 31,* 519–537.

Healy, A.F. & Bourne, L.E., Jr. (2005). *Training to minimize the decay of knowledge and skills* (Final Report to the National Science Foundation, REC-0335674).

Hockey, G.R.J. (1997). Compensatory control in the regulation of human performance under stress and high workload: a cognitive-energetical framework. *Biological Psychology, 45,* 73–93.

Hockey, G.R.J. (1970). Effect of loud noise on attentional selectivity. *Quarterly Journal of Experimental Psychology, 22,* 28–36.

Hockey, G.R.J. (1978). Effects of noise on human work efficiency. In: D. May (Ed.), *Handbook of Noise Assessment.* New York: Van Nostrand Reinhold.

Hockey, G.R.J. (1983). *Stress and Human Performance.* Chichester, U.K.: John Wiley & Sons.

Hockey, G.R.J. & Hamilton, P. (1970). Arousal and information selection in short-term memory. *Nature, 226,* 866–867.

Horrey, W.J., Wickens, C.D. & Consalus, K.P. (2006). Modeling drivers visual attention allocation while interacting with in-vehicle technologies. *Journal of Experimental Psychology: Applied, 12,* 67–78.

Houston, B.K. (1972). Control over stress, locus of control, and response to stress. *Journal of Personality and Social Psychology, 21,* 249–255.

Hovanitz, C.A., Chin, K. & Warm, J.S. (1989). Complexities in life stress-dysfunction relationships: a case in point—tension headache. *Journal of Behavioral Medicine, 12,* 55–75.

Hughes, P.K. & Cole, B.L. (1986). What attracts attention when driving? *Ergonomics, 29*(3), 377–391.

Hutton, R.J.B., Thordsen, M. & Mogford, R. (1997). Recognition primed decision model in air traffic controller error analysis. In: R.S. Jensen & L.A. Rakovan (Eds.), *Proceedings of the Ninth International Symposium on Aviation Psychology* (pp. 721–726). Columbus, OH: Ohio State University.

James, W. (1890). *The Principles of Psychology.* New York: Holt.

Janis, I. (1983). The patient as decision maker. In: D. Gentry (Ed.), *Handbook of Behavioral Medicine.* New York: Guilford.

Janis, I., Defares P. & Grossman, P. (1983). Hypervigilant reactions to threat. In H. Selye (Ed.), *Selye's Guide to Stress Research* (Vol. 3) (pp. 1–42). New York: Van Nostrand Reinhold.

Janis, I. & Mann, L. (1977). *Decision Making.* New York: Free Press.

Johnson, M.K., Hashtroudi, S. & Lindsay, D.S. (1993). Source monitoring. *Psychological Bulletin, 114,* 3–28.

Kahneman, D. (1973). *Attention and Effort.* Englewood Cliffs, NJ: Prentice Hall.

Katz, L. & Epstein, S. (1991). Constructive thinking and coping with laboratory induced stress. *Journal of Personality and Social Psychology, 61,* 789–800.

Keinan, G. (1987). Decision making under stress: scanning of alternatives under controllable and uncontrollable threats. *Journal of Personality and Social Psychology, 52,* 639–644.

Keinan, G., Friedland, N. & Sarig-Naor, V. (1990). Training for task performance under stress: the effectiveness of phased training methods. *Journal of Applied Social Psychology, 20,* 1514–1529.

King, D.W., King, L.A., Foy, D.W., Keane, T.M. & Fairbanks, J.A. (1999). Posttraumatic stress disorder in a national sample of female and male Vietnam veterans: risk factors, war-zone stressors, and resilience-recovery variables. *Journal of Abnormal Psychology, 108,* 164–170.

Kinsbourne, M. & Hicks, R.E. (1978). Functional cerebral space: a model for over-flow, transfer and interference effects in human performance. A tutorial review. In J. Requin (Ed.), *Attention and Performance VII* (pp. 345–362). Hillsdale, NJ: Lawrence Erlbaum.

Kjellberg, A. (1990). Subjective, behavioral, and psychophysiological effects of noise. *Scandinavian Journal of Work, Environment & Health, 16*, 29–38.

Klein, G.A. (1989). Recognition-primed decision (RPD). In: W.B. Rouse (Ed.), *Advances in Manmachine Systems* (pp. 47–92). Greenwich, CT: JAI.

Klein, G.A. & Klinger, D. (1991). Naturalistic decision-making. *CSERIAC Gateway, 2*, 1–4.

Klein, G.A. & Thordsen, M.L. (1991). Representing cockpit crew decision making. In: R.S. Jensen & L.A. Rakovan (Eds.), *Proceedings of the Sixth International Symposium on Aviation Psychology* (pp. 1026–1031). Columbus, OH: Ohio State University.

Kobasa, S.C. (1979). Stressful life events, personality and health: an enquiry into hardiness. *Journal of Personality and Social Psychology, 37*(1), 1–11.

Kobasa, S.C. (1982). The hardy personality: toward a social psychology of stress and health. In: G.S. Sanders & J. Suls (Eds.), *Social Psychology of Health and Illness*. Hillsdale, NJ: Lawrence Erlbaum Associates, Inc.

Kobasa, S.C. & Puccetti, M.C. (1983). Personality and social resources in stress resistance. *Journal of Personality and Social Psychology, 45*(4), 839–850.

Kornovich, W. (1992). Cockpit stress. *Flying Safety*, 20–23.

Kumpfer, K.L. (1999). Factors and processes contributing to resilience: the resilience framework. In: M.D. Glantz & J.L. Johnson (Eds.), *Resilience and Development: Positive Life Adaptations* (pp. 179–224). New York: Plenum.

Langewiesche, W. (1998). *Inside the Sky: A Meditation on Flight*. New York: Pantheon Books.

Larsen, J.D. & Baddeley, A. (2003). Disruption of verbal STM by irrelevant speech, articulatory suppression, and manual tapping: do they have a common source. *Quarterly Journal of Experimental Psychology A: Human Experimental Psychology, 56A*, 1249–1268.

Lazarus, R.S. (1966). *Psychological Stress and the Coping Process*. New York: McGraw-Hill.

Lazarus, R.S. (1990). Theory based stress measurement. *Psychological Inquiry, 1*, 3–13.

Lazarus, R.S. & Folkman, S. (1984). *Stress, Appraisal and Coping*. New York: Springer.

Lehner, P., Seyed-Solorforough, M., O'Connor, M.F., Sak, S. & Mullin, T. (1997). Cognitive biases and time stress in team decision making. *IEEE Transactions on Systems, Man, and Cybernetics Part A: Systems and Humans, 27*, 698–703.

Li, G., Baker, S.P., Lamb, M.W., Grabowski, J.G. & Rebok, G.W. (2001). Factors associated with pilot error in aviation crashes. *Aviation, Space, and Environmental Medicine, 72*, 52–58.

Logan, G.D. & Klapp, S.T. (1991). Automatizing alphabet arithmetic: I. Is extended practice necessary to produce automaticity? *Journal of Experimental Psychology: Learning, Memory, and Cognition, 17*, 179–195.

Luthar, S.S., Cicchetti, D. & Becker, B. (2000). The construct of resilience: a critical evaluation and guidelines for future work. *Child Development, 71*, 543–562.

MacDonald, R.R. & Lubac, S. (1982). *Parachuting Stress and Performance* (memorandum 82m511). Farnsborough, U.K.: Army Personnel Research Establishment.

Mackinnon, A., Christensen, H., Hofer, S.M., Korten, A.E. & Jorm, A.F. (2003). Use it and still lose it? The association between activity and cognitive performance established using latent growth techniques in a community sample. *Aging Neuropsychology and Cognition, 10*(3), 215–229.

Mackworth, N.H. (1948). The breakdown of vigilance during prolonged visual search. *Quarterly Journal of Experimental Psychology, 1*, 6–21.

MacLeod, C. & Mathews, A. (1988). Anxiety and the allocation of attention to threat. *Quarterly Journal of Experimental Psychology, 40*, 653–670.

Mandler, G. (1979). Thought processes, consciousness, and stress. In: V. Hamilton & D.M. Warburton (Eds.), *Human Stress and Cognition: An Information Processing Approach* (pp. 179–201). New York: John Wiley & Sons.

Matthews, G. (1997). Extraversion, emotion, and performance: a cognitive-adaptive model. In: G. Matthews (Ed.), *Cognitive Science Perspectives on Personality and Emotion* (pp. 399–442). Amsterdam: Elsevier.

Matthews, G. & Desmond, P.A. (1995). Stress as a factor in the design of in-car driving enhancement systems. *Le Travail Humain, 58*, 109–129.

Matthews, G., Emo, A.K., Funke, G., Zeidner, M., Roberts, R.D., Costa, P.T., Jr. & Schulze, R. (2006). Emotional intelligence, personality, and task-induced stress. *Journal of Experimental Psychology: Applied, 12*, 96–107.

Matthews, G., Sparkes, T.J. & Bygrave, H.M. (1996). Attentional overload, stress, and simulated driving performance. *Human Performance, 9*, 77–101.

McGrath, J.E. (1976). Stress and behavior in organizations. In: M.D. Dunnette (Ed.), *Handbook of Industrial and Organizational Psychology* (pp. 1351–1395). Chicago, IL: Rand McNally.

Metzger, U. & Parasuraman, R. (2001). The role of the air traffic controller in future air traffic management: an empirical study of active control versus passive monitoring. *Human Factors, 43*, 519–528.

Miyake, A. & Shah, P. (Eds.) (1999a). *Models of Working Memory*. Cambridge, U.K.: Cambridge University Press.

Miyake, A. & Shah, P. (1999b). Toward unified theories of working memory. In: Miyake, A. & Shah, P. (Eds.), *Models of Working Memory* (pp. 442–481). Cambridge, U.K.: Cambridge University Press.

Mogg, K., Bradley, B.P. & Hallowell, N. (1994). Attentional bias to threat: roles of trait anxiety, stressful events, and awareness. *Quarterly Journal of Experimental Psychology: Human Experimental Psychology, 47*, 841–864.

Monat, A., Averill, J.R. & Lazarus, R.S. (1972). Anticipatory stress and coping reactions under various conditions of uncertainty. *Journal of Personality and Social Psychology, 24*, 237–253.

Murata, A. (2004). Foveal task complexity and visual funneling. *Human Factors, 46*(1), 135–141.

National Research Council (1999). *Funding a Revolution: Government Support for Computing Research* (pp. 226–249). Washington, D.C.: National Academy Press.

Neath, I., Farley, L.A. & Surprenant, A.M. (2003). Directly assessing the relationship between irrelevant speech and articulatory suppression. *Quarterly Journal of Experimental Psychology A: Human Experimental Psychology, 56A*, 1269–1278.

Nicholson, D., Lackey, S., Arnold, R. & Scott, K. (2005, July). Augmented cognition technologies applied to training. Paper presented at the annual meeting of the International Conference on Human-Computer Interaction (Augmented Cognition), Las Vegas, NV.

Norman, D.A. & Bobrow, D.G. (1975). On data-limited and resource-limited processes. *Cognitive Psychology, 7,* 44–64.

Norman, D.A. & Bobrow, D.G. (1976). On the analysis of performance operating characteristics. *Psychological Review, 83,* 508–510.

Nowack, K.M. (1989). Coping style, cognitive hardiness, and health status. *Journal of Behavioural Medicine, 12*(2), 145–158.

O'Neal, M.R. (1999). Measuring resilience. Paper presented at the annual meeting of the Mid-South Educational Research Association. Point Clear, AL.

Orasanu, J.M. (1990). *Shared mental models and crew decision making* (CSL Report No. 46). Princeton, NJ: Princeton University, Cognitive Science Laboratory.

Pamperin, K.L. & Wickens, C.D. (1987). The effects of modality and stress across task type on human performance. *Human Factors Society 31st Annual Meeting.* Santa Monica, CA: Human Factors Society.

Parker, J.F., Bahrick, L.E., Fivush, R. & Johnson, P. (2006). The impact of stress on mothers' memory of a natural disaster. *Journal of Experimental Psychology: Applied, 12,* 142–154.

Pengilly, J.W. & Dowd, E.T. (2000). Hardiness and social support as moderators of stress. *Journal of Clinical Psychology, 56*(6), 813–820.

Pepler, R.D. (1958). Warmth and performance: an investigation in the tropics. *Ergonomics, 2,* 63–68.

Pollock, S.E. (1989). The hardiness characteristic: a motivating factor in adaptation. *Advanced Nursing Science, 11,* 53–62.

Raby, M. & Wickens, C.D. (1994). Strategic workload management and decision biases in aviation. *The International Journal of Aviation Psychology, 4,* 211–240.

Reber, A.S. (1989). Implicit learning and tacit knowledge. *Journal of Experimental Psychology: General, 118,* 219–235.

Recarte, M.A. & Nunes, L.M. (2000). Effects of verbal and spatial imagery task on eye fixations while driving. *Journal of Experimental Psychology: Applied, 6,* 31–43.

Recarte, M.A. & Nunes, L.M. (2003). Mental workload while driving: effects on visual search, discrimination, and decision making. *Journal of Experimental Psychology: Applied, 9*(2), 119–137.

Renge, K. (1980). The effects of driving experience on a driver's visual attention. An analysis of objects looked at: using the "verbal report" method. *International Association of Traffic Safety Sciences Research, 4,* 95–106.

Rhodewalt, F. & Zone, J.B. (1989). Appraisal of life change, depression, and illness in hardy and non-hardy women. *Journal of Personality and Social Psychology, 56*(1), 81–88.

Robbins, T.W. (2005). Controlling stress: how the brain protects itself from depression. *Nature Neuroscience, 8*(3), 261–262.

Robinson, M.S. & Alloy, L.B. (2003). Negative cognitive styles and stress-reactive rumination interact to predict depression: a prospective study. *Cognitive Therapy and Research, 27*(3), 275–291.

Rothstein, H.G. & Markowitz, L.M. (1982, May). The effect of time on a decision strategy. Paper presented at the meeting of the Midwestern Psychological Association, Minneapolis, MN.

Rotter, J.B. (1954). *Social Learning and Clinical Psychology*. Englewood Cliffs, NJ: Prentice Hall.

Rotton, J., Olszewski, D.A., Charleton, M.E. & Soler, E. (1978). Loud speech, conglomerate noise, and behavioral aftereffects. *Journal of Applied Psychology, 63*, 360–365.

Salas, E.M., Driskell, J.E. & Hughes, S. (1996). Introduction: the study of stress and human performance. In: J.E. Driskell & E. Salas (Eds.), *Stress and Human Performance* (pp. 1–46). Hillsdale, NJ: Lawrence Erlbaum Associates, Inc.

Samel, A., Wegmann, H., Vejvoda, M., Drescher, J., Gundel, A., Manzey, D. & Wensel, J. (1997). Two crew operations: stress and fatigue during long haul flights. *Aviation, Space, and Environmental Medicine, 68*, 679–687.

Scerbo, M.W. (2001). Stress, workload, and boredom in vigilance: a problem and an answer. In: P.A. Hancock & P.A. Desmond (Eds.), *Stress, Workload, and Fatigue*. Mahwah, NJ: Lawrence Erlbaum Associates, Inc.

Schacter, D.L. (1987). Implicit memory: history and current status. *Journal of Experimental Psychology: Learning, Memory, and Cognition, 13*, 501–518.

Schacter, D. (1989). Memory. In: M.I. Posner (Ed.), *Foundations of Cognitive Science* (pp. 683–725). Cambridge, MA: MIT Press.

Schmorrow, D.D. (Ed.) (2005). *Foundations of Augmented Cognition*. Mahwah, NJ: Lawrence Erlbaum Associates, Inc.

Schmorrow, D.D. (in press). Why virtual? In: J. Cohn & A. Bolton (Eds.), *Special Issue on Optimizing Virtual Training Systems in Theoretical Issues of Ergonomics Science*.

Schmorrow, D., Kruse, A., Reeves, L. & Bolton, A.E. (2007). Augmented cognition in HCI: 21st century adaptive system science and technology. In: A. Sears & J. Jacko (Eds.), *The Human-Computer Interaction Handbook: Fundamentals, Evolving Technologies, and Emerging Applications* (2nd Edition). USA: CRC Press.

Seeman, T.E., Lusignolo, T., Berkman, L. & Albert, M. (2001). Social environment characteristics and patterns of cognitive aging: MacArthur studies of successful aging. *Health Psychology, 20*, 243–255.

Seligman, M.E.P. (1998). *Learned Optimism*. New York: Knopf.

Seligman, M.E.P. & Csikszentmihalyi, M. (2000). Positive psychology: an introduction. *American Psychologist, 55*, 5–14.

Serfaty, D., Entin, E.E. & Johnston, J.H. (1998). Team coordination training. In: J.A. Cannon-Bowers & E. Salas (Eds.), *Making Decisions Under Stress*. Washington, D.C.: American Psychological Association.

Shafto, P. & Coley, J.D. (2003). Development of categorization and reasoning in the natural world: novices to experts, naïve to similarity to ecological knowledge. *Journal of Experimental Psychology: Learning, Memory, and Cognition, 29*(4), 641–649.

Shiffrin, R.M. & Schneider, W. (1977). Controlled and automatic human information processing: II. Perceptual learning, automatic attending, and a general theory. *Psychological Review, 84*, 127–190.

Sinclair, R.C. & Mark, M.M. (1995). The effects of mood state on judgmental accuracy: processing strategy as a mechanism. *Cognition & Emotion, 9*(5), 417–438.

Skinner, N. & Brewer, N. (2002). The dynamics of threat and challenge appraisals prior to stressful achievement events. *Journal of Social and Personality Psychology, 83*, 678–692.

Soetens, E., Hueting, J. & Wauters, F. (1992). Traces of fatigue in an attention task. *Bulletin of the Psychonomic Society, 30*, 97–100.

Sokolov, E.N. (1975). The neuronal mechanisms of the orienting reflex. In: E.N. Sokolov & O.S. Vinogradova (Eds.), *Neuronal Mechanisms of the Orienting Reflex* (pp. 217–235). New York: John Wiley & Sons.

Speier, C., Valacich, J.S. & Vessey, I. (1999). The influence of task interruption on individual decision making: an information overload perspective. *Decision Sciences, 30*(2), 337–360.

Sperandio, J.C. (1971). Variations of operator's strategies and regulating effects on workload. *Ergonomics, 14*, 571–577.

Staal, M.A. (2004). *Stress, Cognition, and Human Performance: A Literature Review and Conceptual Framework* (NASA Technical Memorandum 212824). Moffett Field, CA: NASA Ames Research Center.

Staw, R.M., Sandelands, L.E. & Dutton, J.E. (1981). Threat-rigidity effects in organizational behavior: a multi-level analysis. *Administrative Science Quarterly, 26*, 501–524.

Stokes, A.F. (1995). Sources of stress-resistant performance in aeronautical decision making: the role of knowledge representation and trait anxiety. *Proceedings of the 39th Human Factors and Ergonomics Society Annual Meeting*, Vol. 2 (pp. 887–890). Santa Monica, CA: Human Factors Society.

Stokes, A.F., Kemper, K.L. & Marsh, R. (1992). *Time-stressed flight decision making: a study of expert and novice aviators* (Technical Report ARL-93-1/INEL-93-1). Urbana-Champaign, IL: Aviation Research Laboratory, University of Illinois.

Stokes, A.F. & Kite, K. (1994). *Flight Stress: Stress, Fatigue, and Performance in Aviation*. Burlington, VT: Ashgate.

Stokes, A.F., Wickens, C. & Kite, K. (1990). *Display Technology: Human Factors Concepts*. Warrendale, PA: Society of Automotive Engineers.

Strayer, D.L. & Drews, F.A. (2004). Profiles in driver distraction: effects of cell phone conversations on younger and older drivers. *Human Factors, 46*, 640–649.

Strayer, D.L., Drews, F.A. & Johnston, W.A. (2003). Cell-phone induced failures of visual attention during simulated driving. *Journal of Experimental Psychology: Applied, 9*, 23–32.

Streufert, S. & Streufert, S.C. (1981). *Stress and information search in complex decision making: Effects of load and time urgency* (Technical Report No. 4). Arlington, VA: Office of Naval Research.

Suzuki, T., Nakamura, Y. & Ogasawara, T. (1966). Intrinsic properties of driver attentiveness. *The Expressway and the Automobile, 9*, 24–29.

Szpiler, J.A. & Epstein, S. (1976). Availability of an avoidance response as related to autonomic arousal. *Journal of Abnormal Psychology, 85*, 73–82.

Taynor, J., Crandell, B. & Wiggins, S. (1987). *The reliability of the critical decision method* (Technical Report Contract MDA903-86-C-0170, U.S. Army Research Institute). Fairborn, OH: Klein Associates, Inc.

Thompson, L.A., Williams, K.L., L'Esperance, P.R. & Cornelius, J. (2001). Context-dependent memory under stressful conditions: the case of skydiving. *Human Factors, 43,* 611–619.

Van Galen, G.P. & van Huygevoort, M. (2000). Error, stress and the role of neuromotor noise in space oriented behaviour. *Biological Psychology, 51,* 151–171.

Van Gemmert, A.W.A. & Van Galen, G.P. (1997). Stress, neuromotor noise, and human performance: a theoretical perspective. *Journal of Experimental Psychology: Human Perception and Performance, 23,* 1299–1313.

Van Overschelde, J.P. & Healy, A.F. (2001). Learning of nondomain facts in high- and low-knowledge domains. *Journal of Experimental Psychology: Learning, Memory, and Cognition, 27,* 1160–1171.

Ververs, P.M., Whitlow, S.D., Dorneich, M.C., Mathon, S. & Sampson, J.B. (2005, July). AugCogifying the army's future warfighter. Paper presented at the 11th Annual HCI Human Computer Interaction International Conference, Las Vegas, NV.

Vroom, V. (1964). *Work and Motivation.* New York: John Wiley & Sons.

Walton, R.E. & McKersie, R.B. (1965). *A Behavioral Theory of Labor Negotiation: An Analysis of a Social Interaction System.* New York: McGraw-Hill.

Wegner, D.M. (1994). Ironic processes of mental control. *Psychological Review, 101,* 34–52.

Weinberg, J. & Levine, S. (1980). Psychobiology of coping in animals: the effects of predictability. In: S. Levine & H. Ursin (Eds.), *Coping and Health* (NATO Conference Series III: Human factors). New York: Plenum Press.

Wenzlaff, R.M. & Wegner, D.M. (2000). Thought suppression. *Annual Review of Psychology, 51,* 59–91.

Westman, M. (1990). The relationship between stress and performance: the moderating effect of hardiness. *Human Performance, 3*(3), 141–155.

Wickens, C.D. (1984). Processing resources in attention. In: R. Parasuraman & D.R. Davies (Eds.), *Varieties of Attention* (pp. 63–101). New York: Academic Press.

Wickens, C.D., Stokes, A., Barnett, B. & Hyman, F. (1991). The effects of stress on pilot judgment in a MIDIS simulator. In: O. Svenson & A.J. Maule (Eds.), *Time Pressure and Stress in Human Judgment and Decision Making* (pp. 271–292). New York: Plenum Press.

Wiggins, M. & O'Hare, D. (1995). Expertise in aeronautical weather-related decision making: a cross-sectional analysis of general aviation pilots. *Journal of Experimental Psychology: Applied, 1*(4), 305–320.

Wilkinson, R.T. (1964). Effects of up to 60 hours' sleep deprivation on different types of work. *Ergonomics, 7,* 175–186.

Williams, H.L., Lubin, A. & Goodnow, J.J. (1959). Impaired performance with acute sleep loss. *Psychological Monographs, 73*(14), 1–26.

Williams, J.M., Tonymon, P. & Anderson, M.B. (1990). Effects of life-event stress on anxiety and peripheral narrowing. *Behavioral Medicine,* 174–184.

Williams, J.M.G., Watts, F.N., MacLeod, C. & Mathews, A. (1988). *Cognitive Psychology and Emotional Disorders.* Chichester, U.K.: John Wiley & Sons.

Williams, P.G., Wiebe, D.J. & Smith, T.W. (1992). Coping processes as mediators of the relationship between hardiness and health. *Journal of Behavioral Medicine, 15*, 237–255.

Wilson, R.S., deLeon, M.C.F., Barnes, L.L., Schneider, J.A., Bienias, J.L., Evans, D.A. & Bennett, D.A. (2002). Participation in cognitively stimulating activites and risk of incident Alzheimer disease. *Journal of the American Medical Association, 287*, 742–748.

Winograd, E. (1988). Some observations on prospective remembering. In: M.M. Gruneberg, P.E. Morris & R.N. Sykes (Eds.), *Practical Aspects of Memory: Current Research and Issues* (Vol. 1) (pp. 348–353). Chichester, U.K.: John Wiley & Sons.

Wofford, J.C. (2001). Cognitive-affective stress response effects of individual stress propensity on physiological and psychological indicators of strain. *Psychological Reports, 88*, 768–784.

Wofford, J.C. & Goodwin, V.L. (2002). The linkages of cognitive processes, stress propensity, affect, and strain: experimental test of a cognitive model of stress response. *Personality and Individual Differences, 32*, 1413–1430.

Wofford, J.C., Goodwin, V.L. & Daly, P.S. (1999). Cognitive-affective stress propensity: a field study. *Journal of Organizational Behavior, 20*, 687–707.

Wright, P. (1974). The harassed decision maker: time pressures, distractions, and the use of evidence. *Journal of Applied Psychology, 59*, 555–561.

Yamamoto, T. (1984). Human problem solving in a maze using computer graphics under an imaginary condition of "fire." *Japanese Journal of Psychology, 55*, 43–47.

Yerkes, R.M. & Dodson, J.D. (1908). The relation of strength of stimulus to rapidity of habit-formation. *Journal of Comparative and Physiological Psychology, 18*, 459–482.

Zakay, D. & Wooler, S. (1984). Time pressure, training and decision effectiveness. *Ergonomics, 27*, 273–284.

Zakowski, S.G., Hall, M.H., Cousino-Klein, H. & Baum, A. (2001). Appraised control, coping, and stress in a community sample: a test of the goodness-of-fit hypothesis. *Annals of Behavioral Medicine, 23*, 158–165.

Zbrodoff, N.J. & Logan, G.D. (1986). On the autonomy of mental processes: a case study of arithmetic. *Journal of Experimental Psychology: General, 115*, 118–130.

Zhang, K. & Wickens, C.D. (1990). Effects of noise and workload on performance with object displays versus a separated display. *Proceedings of the Human Factors Society 34th Annual Meeting.* Santa Monica, CA: Human Factors Society.

The Impact of Social Structural Conditions on Psychological Resilience to Stress

11

DAVID E. ROHALL
Western Illinois University

JAMES A. MARTIN
Bryn Mawr College

Contents

The study of stress and resilience evolves from a long and rich history of scientific inquiry into the nature and causes of nonphysical phenomena considered as possible causes of disease and behavioral dysfunction. Interest in the relationship between social structural conditions and stress dates back at least to the nineteenth century, when George Beard and others began to examine the role of society as a contributor to mental illness (Cooper & Dewe, 2004). Traditionally, social structure is defined as enduring patterns of behavior among groups, organizations, or society as a whole (Giddens, 1984). The resulting conditions that are derived from these patterns of behavior can range in scope from social relationships among members of a group or organization—including communities of people—to larger societal conditions that are reflected in outcome trends such as unemployment and poverty. The important point here is that relationships and events that occur regularly as a result of enduring group behavioral patterns typically manifest themselves as "conditions" in and around the daily lives of individuals.

Social psychologists apply this understanding of social structure to the study of resilience by examining the various ways in which social structure may affect relationships between life events or conditions and a broad spectrum of behavior and associated life outcomes. There are at least three ways in which social structure can influence these relationships. First, relationships with family, friends, and other associates may act as a direct source of stress in our lives. Second, social conditions may influence the way we experience and manage stressful events or conditions and thus serve indirectly to alleviate or exacerbate difficulties. Finally, social conditions may influence the manner in which we construct perceived meanings and interpretations of stressful events or conditions (Link & Phelan, 1995; Pearlin, 1989; Pearlin, Menaghan, Lieberman & Mullan, 1981).

Military service provides a unique context for consideration of how structural conditions influence individuals' ability to manage stress. Individuals who serve in the military are subject to chronic stress (e.g., long and demanding workdays and challenging training activities) as well as acute and potentially traumatic stress associated with military deployments and combat exposure (see Moelker & Kloet, 2003; Rohall, Segal & Segal, 1999; Segal & Harris, 1993). In addition, active duty military personnel and their families typically live on or adjacent to military bases, where specific social structural conditions may alleviate or exacerbate the stresses of military duty and daily life.

The goal of this chapter is to apply research and theory concerning the influence of social structural variables on resilience to the context of military service. The first section of this chapter reviews major perspectives on the relationship between social conditions and reactions to stress with emphasis on the nature and context of duty and daily life in the military. The subsequent section applies this literature to the study of stress and resilience using data from the 2003 Air Force Community Survey (Spera, Kunz, Meiman, Jones & Whitworth, 2003) to replicate these findings.

Theoretical Perspectives on Social Conditions and Resilience to Stress

A number of stress-processing models have been introduced to explain variations in resilience, which we define here as the ability to respond successfully to and manage stressful life events and conditions. One of such earliest models is Reuben Hill's ABC-X model (see Hill, 1958; Lavee, McCubbin & Patterson, 1985). Being used to portray relationships among stressful events ("A"), resources ("B"), and perceptions ("C"), the ABC-X and double ABC-X models have been applied to predict individual responses in military as well as civilian contexts. Here, resources ("B") refer to materials and people who may be accessed to alleviate difficulties, and perception ("C") refers to event definition or the extent to which it is seen as a problem. The final aspect of the model, "X," refers to the ultimate impact of an event, which is usually measured in terms of a traditional mental health outcome such as depression, anxiety, or "distress." For the purpose of the ABC-X model, resilience is measured in terms of its associated mental health outcome ("X"). Pearlin follows on the ABC-X model by outlining specific ways by which social conditions influence responses to stressful life events (Pearlin, 1989; Pearlin et al., 1981). Pearlin's "stress process" model includes four sets of variables (stressors, outcomes, mediators, and moderators or resources) and background characteristics (see Figure 11.1). In this framework, stressors include chronic stressors that may include daily hassles (e.g., heavy highway traffic, chronic family arguments) and acute stressors (e.g., the death of a loved one; Serido, Almeida & Wethington, 2004; Wheaton, 1999; throughout this chapter, we refer to both types of stressors more simply as "life events"). Resources include social (external) and personal (internal) resources that are thought to moderate or mediate the impact of life events (Aneshensel, 1992). Social resources include potential (accessible) as well as actual social support (e.g., trusted friends, loved ones, coworkers). These resources may also include larger community conditions, which will be addressed in more detail later in this chapter. Personal resources include personality characteristics such as self-efficacy, self-esteem, and self-image (see also Westphal, Bonnano & Bartone, this volume). These and other characteristics influence the manner

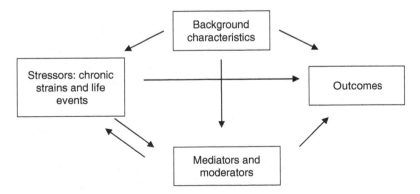

Figure 11.1 The stress process. (Adapted from Pearlin, L.I., *J. Health Soc. Behav.*, 30, 241–256, 1989. With permission.)

in which individuals manage or interpret life events. Finally, background characteristics are demographic and socioeconomic variables that can directly affect stress levels and exposure to life events. For example, individuals who get more income are typically exposed to fewer negative life events than their low-income counterparts (Lantz, House, Mero & Williams, 2005).

In the context of the stress process model, resilient individuals are those who are able to make use of the resources at their disposal and report or demonstrate fewer negative outcomes. The effects of negative life events and conditions can be studied using a variety of outcome measures including health (Lantz et al., 2005; Treharne, Lyons & Tupling, 2001), depression (Taylor & Turner, 2002), and mortality (Lantz et al., 2005). These studies generally show a negative relationship between life events or conditions and subsequent outcomes. That is, life events and conditions that cause stress are associated with poorer health and higher levels of depression and mortality. Some of the basic tenets of the stress-processing approach have been applied to the military context. For example, Elder and Clipp (1988, 1989) show that exposure to heavy combat (life event) has a negative impact on mental health. However, these effects tend to weaken over time and are reduced by exposure to supportive social resources (relationships with fellow service members and spouses). Ultimately, mastery of these experiences may help military members to improve their coping skills and thus enhance their resilience to other stressful life events and conditions.

Social Structure and the Stress Process

The stress process model is a useful paradigm to examine the role of social structural conditions on mental health outcome. Traditionally, this model has provided support for the notion that social support resources help to moderate negative effects of stress on psychological well-being (e.g., distress). In a study of psychological distress after exposure to natural disasters (Hurricanes Hugo and Andrew), Norris and Kaniasty (1996) found that even just the perception of available social support helped to reduce the long-term effects of disaster. Simply knowing that one has access to larger support networks of other people may be enough to buffer against the negative effects of certain stressors (Treharne et al., 2001). Hence, under this schema, individuals who have or perceive a greater reservoir of social support will tend to suffer fewer negative effects when they are exposed to stressful life events and conditions.

More recent versions of the stress process model (see Pearlin, 1999) directly incorporate the idea of structural conditions but do not clearly define social structure or its role in the stress process. Earlier, we defined social structure in terms of regular patterns of behavior in a given social context.

In other words, structural conditions exist in terms of interactions (patterns of behavior) as well as context (consideration of place). Studies of living conditions and their relationships to specific outcomes indicate that lack of infrastructure, isolation, high unemployment rates, and high crime rates exert direct and negative effects on distress levels (Amato & Zuo, 1992; Aneshensel & Sucoff, 1996; Dooley, Catalano & Rook, 1988; Iverson & Maguire, 2000). These same conditions may also affect individuals' ability to manage stressful life events, thus serving to exacerbate or moderate the effects of such experiences (Robert, 1998; Rohall, Booth, Spera, Martin & Whitworth, 2005). For example, living in a stable neighborhood (e.g., low crime and poverty levels) can help to buffer the negative effects of stress on health (Boardman, 2004). In a similar manner, researchers have also addressed internal perceptions of structural conditions on outcomes. For example, individuals who perceive their neighborhoods to be dangerous experience more symptoms of depression and anxiety, while those who perceive stability and social cohesion experience fewer such disorders (Aneshensel & Sucoff, 1996). In the next section, we review research that examines the effects of both real and perceived social contexts.

Neighborhood Contexts

In sociology, the "proximity principle" posits that we are affected by social structure through our immediate social environments (House, 1992). Neighborhood conditions can be a direct source of stress or a context in which one can access resources as needed to manage stress. When individuals who live in poor or isolated areas are confronted by stressful or traumatic life events, the potential negative effects of stress may be exacerbated by poor living conditions or by a shortage of helpful resources (Linsky & Strauss, 1986).

Neighborhood studies typically measure community conditions in the form of disorder, disadvantage, or instability. Neighborhood disorder refers to poor physical conditions (e.g., broken windows, abandoned buildings, garbage) or persistently high levels of criminal or antisocial behavior such as vandalism, drug use, and theft. Disadvantaged neighborhoods are those affected by high unemployment rates and considerable poverty. Neighborhood disorder and disadvantage are closely related in that disadvantage often leads to disorder (Ross, 2000). Finally, neighborhood instability refers to a high level of turnover among residents, which makes it difficult to develop or sustain a consistent context of social support.

A challenge involved in neighborhood studies is that it can be difficult to determine boundaries to define where one neighborhood ends and another one begins. Census tracts can be used to address this problem. For example, census tract data from the 1995 Detroit Area Study were used to delineate "neighborhoods" and to establish neighborhood disadvantage based upon percentages of respondents living below the poverty line, percentage of female-headed households, male unemployment rate, and percentage of families receiving public assistance (Boardman, Finch, Ellison, Williams & Jackson, 2001; Sampson, Moreneoff & Gannon-Rowley, 2002).

A number of studies have demonstrated that neighborhood disorder and disadvantage exert a negative impact upon physical health and mental health (Hill, Ross & Angel, 2005; Ross & Mirowsky, 2001). Boardman et al. (2001) found that neighborhood disadvantage (defined as a higher percentage of poor residents and single mothers) is associated with higher levels of distress and drug use. Neighborhood disadvantage has also been linked to depression (Ross, 2000). Similar findings have been reported in dozens of other studies (see review by Sampson et al., 2002).

Although it is clear that poor community conditions can lead to distress, the precise mechanism(s) that mediates such effects or, conversely, how better community conditions might promote resilience, are not yet clear. The presence or absence of real or perceived social support and resources likely plays a role at the individual level. As previously discussed in this chapter, social support can exert a positive impact on individual resilience to stress. Schieman (2005) has observed that neighborhood disadvantage is negatively associated with social support in areas with low stability (i.e., high residential turnover). Hence, to the extent that specific neighborhood conditions tend to promote or hinder social support, they may also exert an indirect positive or negative effect on residents' resilience to stress.

Perceptions of Structural Conditions

In addition to studying the actual structural and socioeconomic conditions that characterize different neighborhoods, researchers must consider residents' perceptions of the conditions in which they live. Research generally shows that perceptions of structural conditions also contribute to psychological distress, above and beyond the effects of actual conditions. For example, Ross (2000) found that low-subjective perceptions of neighborhood disorder significantly reduced the effects of actual neighborhood disadvantage on depression. In another study, Aneshensel and Sucoff (1996) found that individuals living in poor neighborhoods (actual conditions) also perceived greater "ambient hazards," such as crime, violence, and drug use, than people living in better neighborhoods; in this case, the effects of actual neighborhood conditions were mediated by perceptions of those conditions, ultimately leading to distress in the form of depression, anxiety, and conduct disorder. Finally, Downey and Van Willigen (2005) identified both direct and indirect effects of neighborhood conditions on well-being. Specifically, residential proximity to industrial activity associated with the release of toxins (measured in terms of the toxic release inventory) had a negative impact on mental health (depression, anxiety, and conduct disorder). However, some of the effects of actual living conditions were mediated by perceptions of neighborhood disorder. That is, living in a bad area (actual conditions) produced perceptions of neighborhood disorder, which led in turn to reduction in well-being.

The Military Base as Neighborhood

We conceptualize the military base as a comparative "neighborhood" for military personnel. We acknowledge, however, that this formulation of "neighborhood" is somewhat more complicated because military personnel and their families are typically engaged simultaneously in various aspects of both the military and the civilian communities in which they live and serve. Military installations exist within the context of larger surrounding communities, the circumstances and challenges of which extend to service members and their families. However, military installations provide a unique "neighborhood" context to the extent that they provide an abundance of support programs (e.g., counseling, health care, recreation, childcare) specifically designed to help manage various stresses associated with military life and service. In addition, military spouses and families are often well-organized to provide a reliable and proactive network of social support to one another.

A number of studies have examined the role of the military installation in society. In general, the U.S. military installations tend to have positive effects on surrounding community economic conditions (Hicks & Raney, 2003; Hooks, 2003). However, it is important to note that the presence of a military installation may have specific negative consequences as well. For example, a significant military presence can introduce a contextual disadvantage for women in the paid civilian labor force (Booth, 2003; Booth, Falk, Segal & Segal, 2000). Because women are underrepresented in the military labor force, the presence of a military installation can lead to an oversupply of women (e.g., military spouses) seeking employment in the local civilian labor force. This employment seeking can be particularly problematic in communities where employment opportunities are already limited.

Very little research has examined the impact of military "neighborhood" programs and conditions on vulnerability or resilience to stress *per se*. Orthner (2002) observed that nonmilitary spouses of Army service members are generally satisfied with installation conditions and services, and those who use those services report higher levels of adjustment to military life (e.g., deployment, separation). However, Orthner's study did not include military personnel or resilience *per se*. Rohall (2005) found that military personnel and their families are very concerned with the living conditions on and around military bases and especially with issues of neighborhood disorder and disadvantage. However, this study did not address the potential moderating effects of base conditions on distress.

Community Capacity

In recent years, theory and research has begun to emerge to address the question of how perceptions of community conditions can affect individual well-being. Much of this work has been done in the context of military life, perceptions of immediate military community (relationships, services, etc.), and the well-being of service members and their families. The "community capacity" model relates perceived (versus actual) community structural conditions and individual level (Bowen, Martin, Mancini & Nelson, 2001). Specifically, community capacity refers to the degree to which people in the community demonstrate (a) a sense of shared responsibility for the general welfare of the community and its individual members and (b) collective competence by taking advantage of opportunities for addressing community needs and confronting situations that threaten the safety and well-being of community members. Observable results are essential to this model, which is anchored by the presumption that responsibility and competence are manifested by action.

As an aspect of social organization, community capacity describes a set of process elements that leads to observable change in the form of manifest behavior. In this regard, community capacity is a dynamic and multidimensional construct. Although the community capacity is based on a subjective assessment of demonstrated behavior by community members, it can be seen as an additional structural resource to support the management of stress (Mancini, Bowen & Martin, 2005).

The conditions and relationships proposed to support community capacity are illustrated in Figure 11.2. In this framework, social structure exists in terms of available networks, interactions between networks, and the behavior-based development of trust among community members. These aspects manifest behaviorally as "shared responsibility" (for the welfare of the community and its members) and as "collective competence" or efficacy (management of challenges or threats to community well-being; Bowen, Martin, Mancini & Nelson, 2000). Finally, behavioral manifestations are proposed to be directly related to outcomes such as safety, health and well-being, family adaptation, military preparedness, and community satisfaction (Bowen et al., 2000).

In a study of community life across nine U.S. Air Force installations, Bowen et al. (2001) found community capacity to be a significant predictor of how residents felt about psychological connection to their community as measured by the overall "sense of community" among military respondents.

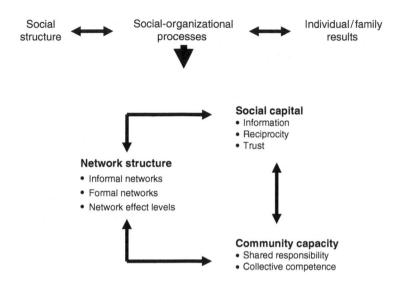

Figure 11.2 Linking social structural conditions to individual outcomes with community capacity. (Adapted from Mancini et al., 2006. With permission.)

Specifically, military personnel who perceived their fellow community members working together to meet community common needs also reported a greater sense of community among community members. Sense of community and community capacity did not vary by gender, residence location (i.e., on or off the military installation), or time spent within the community.

Bowen and his colleagues (2000) (see also Mancini, Martin & Bowen, 2003) propose that the effect of community capacity is similar to that of personal social support in times of need. In this sense, community capacity serves as part of a larger web of available support. In addition to formal services, such as health care and recreation facilities, service members must rely upon one another—other community members and families—to address and resolve community and personal problems. In this sense, the demonstrated behavior of community residents on military installations (and by extension, in the surrounding local community) represents a form of social capital that can be used as a resource to manage or alleviate stress.

Although the effects of actual military base community conditions have been studied, it is not yet clear how or if actual conditions on military installations affect the well-being of service members themselves. Using data from a survey (1999–2000) of 709 spouses of soldiers serving in the active, reserve, and National Guard components of the U.S. Army, Burrell, Durand, and Fortado (2003) considered the relationship of base conditions to well-being and retention preferences among military spouses. Burrell et al. found a direct relationship between community integration (i.e., likeliness to use and actual use of formal and informal installation support) and retention preferences but observed no relationship between community integration and emotional well-being. McClure and Broughton (2000) identified a similar relationship between community cohesion and retention but did not address the question of well-being. Both of these studies addressed community conditions as an independent variable, but neither considered community conditions as a resource for the mitigation of stress.

In the next section, we describe an effort to study community capacity as a possible contributor to resilience. Here, community conditions, including community capacity, are not conceived as a direct contributor to well-being but rather as a potential moderator of the effects of stressful life events. Burrell and colleagues (2003) posit a similar perspective, suggesting that while community conditions may not be relevant to well-being generally, they may be relevant to well-being specifically during times of need.

Community Capacity and Resilience

For the purpose of this study, we conceived of the military installation (base) as a neighborhood in which service members and their families are differentially exposed to sources of structural stress or support available both on and around the military base itself. We examined the impact of perceptions concerning base (neighborhood) conditions on resilience to stress by assessing the moderating effects of those perceptions on the relationship between exposure to stress and depression. To the extent that levels of depression changed in relation to perceived conditions, those conditions (perceived resources or stressors) were identified as contributors to stress resilience or vulnerability.

We predicted generally that perceived sources of stress (neighborhood disadvantage) would exert a direct and negative effect on depression (i.e., higher levels of depression) among base residents. Conversely, we predicted that perceived structural supports (i.e., levels of community capacity and self-efficacy) would exert a direct and positive effect on depression (i.e., less depression). Finally, we predicted that community capacity and self-efficacy would exert a moderating effect on the relationship between work-related stress and depression.

Methods

Data for this project were gathered from the 2003 Air Force Community Survey (Spera et al., 2003), which was conducted as a web-based survey of Air Force personnel, reserve components, and their spouses. A total of 67,200 respondents completed one of three separate surveys that had been constructed for survey participants in each group. (Separate surveys were necessary to recognize the qualitatively different experiences of active versus reserve service members and service members versus their spouses.) Here, we limit our analysis to data gathered from active duty personnel respondents who were married and stationed within the continental United States ($N = 17,608$).

Depression. We employed the survey's measure of depression, a seven-item version of the CES-D scale in which respondents had been asked to address their experience of symptoms common to depression, for example, "you just could not get going," "had trouble getting to sleep or staying asleep," and "felt sad." Numeric responses to these items ranged from 1 (5–7 days) to 4 (None). Scores were reverse coded such that higher scores indicated higher levels of depression. This scale produced a Cronbach's alpha coefficient of .85 with a mean of 1.4 and a standard deviation of 0.49 (Table 11.1).

Work-related stress. A primary independent variable of interest was work-related stress, identified on the basis of an index of work-related stressors. Respondents were asked in the survey whether or not they had experienced 11 different types of work stressors including "working weekends," "swing shifts," "midnight shifts," "worked while on scheduled leave," or "brought work home." The average number of stressors affirmed was 4.6 with a standard deviation of 2.7.

Community capacity. We considered community capacity as a resource condition, and we measured it on the basis of perceived shared responsibility and community self-efficacy. In the first case, we combined responses to

Table 11.1 Distribution of Model Variables

	N	Minimum	Maximum	Mean	Standard Deviation
Work stress	16,935	0.00	11.00	4.6115	2.73283
Depression	16,068	1.00	4.00	1.3697	0.49239
Community capacity	—	—	—	—	—
Shared responsibility	14,587	1.00	6.00	4.4472	0.90315
Self-efficacy	14,641	1.00	6.00	4.6599	0.93666
Concerns over base safety	15,848	1.00	6.00	1.8780	0.68291
Control variables	—	—	—	—	—
Number of years on base	15,071	1.00	6.00	2.4168	0.85441
Live on or off base (1 = on base)	17,606	0.00	1.00	0.3714	0.48319
Gender (1 = female)	17,608	0.00	1.00	0.1962	0.39715
Rank	17,597	1.00	5.00	2.6222	1.27816

three survey items in which respondents had been asked the degree to which they agreed with the following statements:

Active duty members join together to solve problems that threaten the safety and well-being of members and families assigned to this base.

Active duty members look after and show concern for members and families assigned to this base.

Active duty members take advantage of opportunities to address the support needs of members and families assigned to this base.

Responses ranged from 1 ("strongly agree") to 6 ("strongly disagree") but were recoded such that higher scores reflect higher levels of perceived shared responsibility. These items were combined into a single scale measure of shared responsibility, producing a Cronbach's alpha coefficient of .92 with a mean of 4.45 and a standard deviation of 0.90.

The second measure of community capacity was described as community self-efficacy. Three survey items were included in this composite scale:

People like me can have an impact on making the on-base community a better place to live and work.

People like me can have an impact on making the civilian community surrounding the base a better place to live and work.

People like me can make a positive difference in the lives of other people assigned to this Air Force base.

Responses again ranged from 1 ("strongly agree") to 6 ("strongly disagree") but were recoded such that higher scores reflected higher levels of perceived efficacy. These items were then combined into a single scale measure of community self-efficacy, producing a Cronbach's alpha coefficient of .89 with a mean of 4.66 and a standard deviation of 0.94.

Neighborhood disadvantage. Finally, we included a measure of (perceived) neighborhood disadvantage by combining four survey items into a single scale measurement of respondents' perceptions of safety, crime, and violence in their immediate neighborhood, on the Air Force base, and in the surrounding civilian area. Item responses ranged from 1 ("very safe") to 6 ("very unsafe"). Our combined scale produced a Cronbach's alpha coefficient of .81, with a mean of 1.88 and a standard deviation of 0.68.

Demographic variables. Additional variables that may influence real or perceived quality of life include marital status, income, and other background characteristics (Bowen et al., 2001). Our sample included only those survey respondents who were married and were active duty service members. Our analysis considered and addressed the period of time (in years) respondents had spent serving at the current military installation as well as their on-base versus off-base residential status. We controlled for respondent gender and rank to avoid the known independent effects of these variables on depression (Kessler & McLeod, 1984; Pearlin, 1989; Pearlin et al., 1981).

Results

Our analyses examined the direct and moderating effects of perceived community conditions on the relationship between work-related stress and depression. Here, we found a small negative effect ($b = .13, p < .001$). Controlling for respondent rank and gender, larger numbers of work-related stressors were associated with increased levels of depression (Table 11.2, Model 1). We also observed that service members who had served longer periods of time on base reported somewhat lower levels of depression ($b = -.03, p < .01$).

As predicted, respondents' concerns about base and community safety were positively related to depression. Specifically, greater concerns about crime and violence on and around the base were associated with higher levels of depression ($b = .16, p < .01$) (Table 11.2, Model 2).

Also as predicted, both measures of community capacity (shared responsibility and community self-efficacy) were negatively related to depression levels ($b = -.14, p < .01$ for both measures) (Table 11.1, Model 3). That is, a stronger sense of community was associated with less depression among the respondents included in our sample. We also observed small moderating effects of perceived neighborhood disadvantage and community capacity on the impact of work-related stress. When we included perceived disadvantage in our model, the impact of work-related stress on depression was reduced by 8%. When we included community capacity and community self-efficacy into the model, the effect of work-related stress on depression was reduced by 15%. When both moderating factors were included in the model, their combined effect was a 23% reduction of the impact of work-related stress on

Table 11.2 Standardized Beta Coefficients for Ordinary Least Squares Regression Depression Regressed on Base Conditions and Community Capacity

Independent Variables	Model 1	Model 2	Model 3	Model 4
Work stress	.13**	.12**	.11**	.10**
Concerns over base safety	—	.16**	—	.09**
Community shared responsibility	—	—	−.14**	−.12**
Community self-efficacy	—	—	−.14**	−.12**
Time on base	−.03**	−.02*	−.03**	−.03**
Live on or off base (1 = on base)	−.01	.00	−.02**	−.01
Gender (1 = female)	.09**	.09**	.09**	.09**
Rank	−.15**	−.12**	−.12**	−.11**
Adjusted R^2	.05	.07	.10	.11

* $p < .05$, ** $p < .01$.

depression. Hence, it appears that positive perceptions of social structural and community conditions may help to reduce the risk of depression associated with work-related stress among Air Force personnel.

Discussion

The analyses and results presented here serve to demonstrate direct and moderating effects of community capacity and thus help to illustrate the usefulness of the construct of community capacity itself. These findings fit well with the civilian literature on neighborhood contexts as reviewed earlier in this chapter, providing additional evidence that poor structural conditions—real or perceived—can exert a direct and negative effect on individuals who reside in affected areas (e.g., Aneshensel & Sucoff, 1996; Sampson et al., 2002). This evidence helps to extend the civilian research literature to the unique context of military life and service. Although military personnel often experience multiple opportunities and extended assignments of "place" in which they may live with, work with, and identify others, the military base itself provides a fairly well-defined local "neighborhood" within which service members must contend with specific social and structural conditions (Sampson et al., 2002). It is interesting to note that our own analyses demonstrated no effect of residence status (on-base versus off-base) on depression, nor did it impact the relationship between work-related stress and depression. However, respondents who had lived in residence on or around their respective military installations for longer periods of time were somewhat less likely to be negatively affected by work-related stress.

We acknowledge that the study we report here was limited in a number of ways. We limit our observations to the effects of community capacity, which turns upon respondents' perceptions of community conditions. We did not address the question of to what extent perceived conditions were indicative of actual conditions on each of the 64 military bases included in our analysis. Hence, there remains a need to address how actual social structural and community conditions might influence risk or resilience to stress among military personnel. Research based on data from a Russian military sample suggests that access to major urban centers may make it easier for military personnel to manage the stress of military life (Rohall, 2003). Future studies of this type should clearly address specific conditions on the installation (the "neighborhood") itself as well as in surrounding communities. For example, it would be useful to compare and validate perceived community safety against actual data concerning community crime and unemployment rates.

To support this objective, we recommend the development of databases that provide researchers an opportunity to perform advanced, multilevel statistical analyses of individual and group data. Such a database should include perceived (subjectively rated) as well as objective measures of social structural conditions on and around military installations. Although the unique nature of military service sometimes makes it difficult to extend research and theory from the civilian sector directly to the military context, additional research with careful attention to similarities and differences can provide insight into the processes by which specific real and perceived social structural conditions affect individual and group resilience to stress. Most service members and their families are assigned to specific geographic areas for limited (2–3-year) periods of time. Frequent relocation of this sort is unusual in the context of civilian life, and thus the military context provides a unique opportunity to study the direct immediate, short-term, and variable impact of conditions at different military installations and after transfers to installations where conditions are recognized to be especially challenging or supportive. In this case, studies conducted in the military context may be informative to the development of research and theory as pertains to civilian neighborhood and community conditions.

Of course, it must be recognized that the type of research we suggest here would necessitate longitudinal analyses of large samples. However, we propose that the results of such an effort would be well worth the investment, given the potential informative benefit to civilian and military science as well as to the informed development of base support services, infrastructure, and placement. Finally, of most direct relevance to this chapter and volume, it would be extremely useful to better understand the potential impact of social structural conditions on resilience processes and outcomes.

References

Amato, P.R. & Zuo, J. (1992). Rural poverty, urban poverty, and psychological well-being. *The Sociological Quarterly, 33,* 229–240.

Aneshensel, C.S. (1992). Social stress: theory and research. *Annual Review of Sociology, 18,* 15–38.

Aneshensel, C.S. & Sucoff, C.A. (1996). The neighborhood context of adolescent mental health. *Journal of Health and Social Behavior, 37,* 293–310.

Boardman, J. (2004). Stress and physical health: the role of neighborhoods as mediating and moderating mechanisms. *Social Science & Medicine, 58,* 2471–2483.

Boardman, J., Finch, B.K., Ellison, C.G., Williams, D.R. & Jackson, J.S. (2001). Neighborhood disadvantage, stress, and drug use among adults. *Journal of Health and Social Behavior, 42,* 151–165.

Booth, B. (2003). Contextual effects of military presence on women's earnings. *Armed Forces & Society, 30,* 25–52.

Booth, B., Falk, W.W., Segal, D.R. & Segal, M.W. (2000). The impact of military presence in local labor markets on employment of women. *Gender and Society, 14,* 318–322.

Bowen, G.L., Martin, J.A., Mancini, J.A. & Nelson, J.P. (2001). Civic engagement and sense of community in the military. *Journal of Community Practice, 9*, 71–93.

Bowen, G.L., Martin, J.A., Mancini, J.A. & Nelson, J.P. (2000). Community capacity: antecedents and consequences. *Journal of Community Practice, 8*, 1–21.

Burrell, L., Durand, D.B. & Fortado, J. (2003). Military community integration and its effects on well-being and retention. *Armed Forces & Society, 30*, 7–24.

Cooper, C.L. & Dewe, P. (2004). *Stress: A Brief History*. Malden, MA: Blackwell Publishing.

Dooley, D., Catalano, R. & Rook, K.S. (1988). Personal and aggregate unemployment and psychological symptoms. *Journal of Social Issues, 44*, 107–123.

Downey, L. & Van Willigen, M. (2005). Environmental stressors: the mental health impacts of living near industrial activity. *Journal of Health and Social Behavior, 3*, 289–305.

Elder, G.H. & Clipp, E.C. (1989). Combat experience and emotional health: impairment and resilience in later life. *Journal of Personality, 57*, 311–341.

Elder, G.H. & Clipp, E.C. (1988). Wartime losses and social bonding: influences across 40 years in men's lives. *Psychiatry, 51*, 177–197.

Giddens, A. (1984). *The Constitution of Society*. Berkeley, NJ/Los Angeles, CA: University of California Press.

Hicks, L. & Raney, C. (2003). The social impact of military growth in St. Mary's County, Maryland, 1940–1995. *Armed Forces & Society, 29*, 353–371.

Hill, R. (1958). Social stress and the family. *Social Casework, 39*, 139–150.

Hill, T.D., Ross, C.E. & Angel, R.J. (2005). Neighborhood disorder, psychological distress, and health. *Journal of Health and Social Behavior, 46*, 170–186.

Hooks, G. (2003). Military and civilian dimensions of America's regional policy, 1972–1994. *Armed Forces & Society, 29*, 227–251.

House, J.S. (1992). Social structure and personality. In: M. Rosenberg & R.H. Turner (Eds), *Social Psychology: Sociological Perspectives* (pp. 525–561). New Brunswick, NJ: London: Transaction Publishers.

Iverson, R. & Maguire, C. (2000). The relationship between job and life satisfaction: evidence from a remote mining community. *Human Relations, 53*, 807–839.

Kessler, R.C. & McLeod, J.D. (1984). Sex differences in vulnerability to undesirable life events. *American Sociological Review, 49*, 620–631.

Lantz, P.M., House, J.S., Mero, R.P. & Williams, D.R. (2005). Stress, life events, and socioeconomic disparities in health: results from the Americans' changing lives study. *Journal of Health and Social Behavior, 3*, 274–288.

Lavee, Y., McCubbin, H.I. & Patterson, J.M. (1985). The double ABC-X model of family stress and adaptation: an empirical test by analysis of structural equations with latent variables. *Journal of Marriage and the Family, 47*, 811–825.

Link, B.G. & Phelan, J. (1995). Social conditions as fundamental causes of disease. *Journal of Health and Social Behavior*, extra issue, 80–94.

Linsky, A.S. & Straus, M. (1986). *Social Stress in the United States: Links to Regional Patterns in Crime and Illness*. Dover, MA: Auburn House Publishing Company.

Mancini, J.A., Bowen, G.L. & Martin, J.A. (2005). Community social organization: a conceptual linchpin in examining families in the context of communities. *Family Relations, 54*, 570–582.

Mancini, J.A., Martin, J.A. & Bowen, G.L. (2003). Community capacity. In: T. Gullotta & M. Bloom (Eds), *Encyclopedia of Primary Prevention and Health Promotion* (pp. 319–330). New York: Kluwer Academic/Plenum Publishers.

McClure, P. & Broughton, W. (2000). Measuring the cohesion of military communities. *Armed Forces & Society, 26*, 473–487.

Moelker, R. & Kloet, I. (2003). Military families and the armed forces: A two-sided affair? In: G.C. Caforio (Ed), *Handbook of the Sociology of the Military* (pp. 201–224). New York: Kluwer.

Norris, F.H. & Kaniasty, K. (1996). Received and perceived social support in times of stress: a test of the social support deterioration deterrence model. *Journal of Personality and Social Psychology, 71*, 498–511.

Orthner, D.K. (2002). MWR and Adjustment among Army Non-Military Spouses. Report. University of North Carolina at Chapel Hill.

Pearlin, L.I. (1989). The sociological study of stress. *Journal of Health and Social Behavior, 30*, 241–256.

Pearlin, L.I. (1999). The stress process revisited: reflections on concepts and their interrelationships. In: C.S. Aneshensel & J.C. Phelan (Eds), *Handbook on the Sociology of Mental Health* (pp. 395–415). New York: Springer.

Pearlin, L.I., Menaghan, E., Lieberman, M.A. & Mullan, J.T. (1981). The social stress process. *Journal of Health and Social Behavior, 22*, 337–356.

Robert, S.A. (1998). Community-level socioeconomic status effects on adult health. *Journal of Health and Social Behavior, 39*, 8–37.

Rohall, D.E. (2003). Macro- and micro-social conditions affecting individual sense of mattering during a period of downsizing. *Current Research in Social Psychology, 9*, 1–17.

Rohall, D.E. (2005). Making a base into a home: a qualitative study of the base and local-area conditions most important to military families. Paper presented at the American Sociological Association Meeting in Philadelphia, PA, August 13–16.

Rohall, D.E., Booth, B., Spera, C., Martin, J.A. & Whitworth, J. (2005). Linking base conditions and quality of life: an exploratory study of air-force installations. Paper presented at the Inter-University Seminar on Armed Forces and Society Bi-Annual Conference, Chicago, IL, October 21–23.

Rohall, D.E., Segal, M.W. & Segal, D.R. (1999). Examining the importance of organizational supports on family adjustment to army life in a period of increasing separation. *Journal of Political and Military Sociology, 27*, 49–65.

Ross, C.E. (2000). Neighborhood disadvantage and adult depression. *Journal of Health and Social Behavior, 41*, 177–187.

Ross, C.E. & Mirowsky, J. (2001). Neighborhood disadvantage, disorder, and health. *Journal of Health and Social Behavior, 42*, 258–276.

Sampson, R.J., Moreneoff, J.D. & Gannon-Rowley, T. (2002). Assessing "neighborhood effects": social processes and new directions in research. *Annual Review of Sociology, 28*, 443–478.

Schieman, S. (2005). Residential stability and the social impact of neighborhood disadvantage: a study of gender- and race-contingent effects. *Social Forces, 83*, 1031–1064.

Segal, M.W. & Harris, J.J. (1993). What We Know About Army Families. Special Report 21. U.S. Army Research Institute for the Behavioral and Social Sciences.

Serido, J., Almeida, D.M. & Wethington, E. (2004). Chronic stressors and daily has-
    sles: unique and interactive relationships with psychological distress. *Journal
    of Health and Social Behavior, 45*, 17–33.
Spera, C., Kunz, J., Meiman, E., Jones, F. & Whitworth, J. (2003). *The 2003 Commu-
    nity Assessment*. Fairfax, VA: Caliber Associates, Inc.
Taylor, J. & Turner, R.J. (2002). Perceived discrimination, social stress, and depres-
    sion in the transition from adulthood: racial contrasts. *Social Psychology
    Quarterly, 65*, 213–225.
Treharne, G.J., Lyons, A.C. & Tupling, R.E. (2001). The effects of optimism,
    pessimism, social support, and mood on the lagged relationship between daily
    stress and symptoms. *Current Research in Social Psychology, 7*, 60–81.
Wheaton, B. (1999). Social stress. In: C.S. Aneshensel & J.C. Phelan (Eds), *Handbook
    of the Sociology of Mental Health* (pp. 277–300). New York: Kluwer.

Section IV

**Resilience as an Empirical
and Operational Priority**

Resilience: Toward the State of the Possible

12

VICTORIA TEPE

Survivability/Vulnerability Information Analysis Center (SURVIAC)

BRIAN J. LUKEY

U.S. Army Medical Research and Materiel Command

Contents

Three decades ago, researchers who pioneered the study of resilience were concerned specifically with its relevance to the etiology of psychopathology in children (Garmezy, 1971, 1974; Garmezy & Streitman, 1974). Today, resilience occupies the attention of investigators and theorists whose concerns span a broad array of scientific endeavors ranging from genetic epidemiology to sociology. The multidisciplinary scope of this volume reflects broad recognition of the need for meaningful progress toward an improved understanding of resilience.

Contributors to this book have brought to bear an appropriately diverse variety of biobehavioral interests and methodological perspectives. They recognize that resilience research is challenged by the apparently stubborn relevance of individual differences but are nonetheless hopeful that resilience will eventually be understood as a valid and useful construct basis for the prediction, prevention, and treatment of stress-related disorders. To that end, these authors offer specific guidance for future research and development. Of particular interest here are recommendations that emerge as recurrent themes throughout the volume across disciplinary divides. Here, we explore these and related issues that we believe are important to robust and coordinated progress in this area. We conclude by identifying specific objectives for clinical practice and military application.

Definition, Methodology, and Measurement

Resilience research is motivated generally by the recognition of the need to move beyond the study of risk and to identify and elucidate protective factors that tend to militate against the development of stress-related disorders. Since resilience is an inferred phenomenon, resilience researchers must confront a host of conceptual hurdles and methodological obstacles (see discussions by Luthar & Cushing, 1999; Luthar & Zelazo, 2003). Nonetheless, authors in this volume and elsewhere are optimistic that there is promise in the study of resilience and have called for more basic research in this area. In particular, researchers are challenged to define and measure resilience in terms of its essential (necessary and sufficient) aspects and to explicate the mechanisms and interactions by which those aspects exert their effects.

To the extent that some adult resilience research paradigms might involve retrospective analysis of potentially relevant childhood experiences (e.g., abuse, neglect, poverty), investigators should carefully consider the existing body of research pertaining to stress and resilience in children (e.g., Glantz & Johnson, 1999; Luthar, 2003). Although it is interesting and probably worthwhile to identify potentially relevant factors of early life experience, it is also important for researchers who are concerned primarily with resilience in adults to remember that effects of stress on children may be even less predictable. Findings drawn from child development and developmental psychopathology increasingly tend to support a transactional framework (e.g., Kumpfer, 1999) in which resilience is viewed not as a capacity or an outcome, but rather as a dynamic process of negotiation between self and environment. There is also evidence to suggest that resilience may be at least partly heritable (see Kim-Cohen, Moffitt, Caspi & Taylor, 2004; Rutter, 2003). Thus, in childhood, resilience processes necessarily occur against the complex backdrop of other significant developmental processes, capacities, and tendencies whose effects may or may not be conducive to stress adaptation at a given time or in a given circumstance. The impact of childhood experiences may be constrained, exaggerated, or rendered moot by factors and forces that influence a child's ability to recognize, consider, or respond to stress.

Given that the construct of resilience is not yet well-defined, efforts to explain its basis should avoid resting entirely upon other psychosocial constructs (e.g., hardiness, thriving) whose predictive value is also not yet established. Rather, there is an obvious need for more precise definition and greater predictive validity. At present, it seems that the most conservative and promising path toward defining resilience is to explore its basis in terms of well-established neurobiological, physiological, and genetic processes and systems. This approach lends the validity and explanatory power of an extensive, interdisciplinary, and generally accessible body of biobehavioral literature on the subjects of stress response, stress adaptation, and stress control or stress plasticity (e.g., Amat, Paul, Zarza, Watkins & Maier, 2006; Yehuda & McEwen, 2004).

In recent years, several authors have addressed resilience specifically in terms of its biological and genetic underpinnings (Charney, 2004; Cicchetti & Blender, 2004; Curtis & Cicchetti, 2003; Curtis & Nelson, 2003; Rutter, 2003; Southwick, Vythilingam & Charney, 2005). Contributors to the current volume have considered resilience in specific relationship to biological, physiological, and genetic mechanisms of stress adaptation (Southwick, Ozbay, Charney & McEwen, Chapter 5), stress anticipation and recovery (Waugh, Tugade & Fredrickson, Chapter 6), survival in extreme environments (Friedl & Penetar, Chapter 7), and predisposition to stress-related disorders (Baker, Risbrough & Schork, Chapter 8). All of these chapters are helpful because they support the conceptual refinement of resilience as a construct whose biological basis is empirically observable within the larger framework of physical reactivity to stress. Efforts to elucidate the biological basis of resilience also encourage the formulation of new testable hypotheses and lay essential groundwork for the validation of interventions that may be conceived specifically to promote resilience or reduce susceptibility to stress.

Resilience researchers are in general agreement concerning the need for additional basic research to identify individual attributes, characteristics, and differences that directly, indirectly, or interactively predispose people to resilient behavior. We concur but emphasize that progress toward this goal may be artificially limited by reliance upon nomothetic (group-based) experimental methodologies, which relegate the "noise" of individual differences to statistical error. Group-based analyses are insufficient to rule out the involvement of alternative forces at the individual level. Others have argued persuasively for the use of idiographic and combined methodologies to assess relationships between individual attributes and differences in ability or behavior (e.g., Kosslyn et al., 2002; Ness & Tepe, 2004; Silverstein, 1988). In particular, Kosslyn et al. (2002) observed the effectiveness of combining nomothetic and idiographic analyses to study the involvement of neurophysiological systems and processes essential to the stress response. Recently, Yehuda, Flory, Southwick, and Charney (2006) have argued the need for an individual differences approach to the biobehavioral basis of resilience. Resilience researchers are well-advised to incorporate idiographic analyses as part of the overall effort to develop a "phenotype" or comprehensive taxonomy of resilient individual variables and attributes.

Difficulties and issues involved in the measurement of resilience have been discussed in detail elsewhere (Luthar & Cushing, 1999; Windle, 1999).

Rather than trying to measure resilience directly, many researchers opt instead to assess its variance indirectly as a function of other phenomena (e.g., hardiness), clinical outcomes (e.g., depression, posttraumatic stress disorder [PTSD]), or behavioral measures (e.g., academic performance). A number of resilience measurement scales and instruments have emerged to support research and clinical practice with children, adolescents, and adults (Baruth & Carroll, 2002; Brady, 2005; Connor & Davidson, 2003; Friborg, Hjemdal, Rosenvinge & Martinussen, 2003; Osman et al., 2004; Wagnild & Young, 1993; see also reviews by Ahern, Kiehl, Sole & Byers, 2006; Wald, Taylor, Asmundson, Lang & Stapleton, 2006). In addition, military scientists have developed the deployment risk and resilience inventory (DRRI), which is a collection of scales selected to assess specific risk and resilience factors (e.g., early life experience, social support, previous combat exposure) that have demonstrated relevance to the long-term well-being of combat veterans (King, King & Vogt, 2003; King, King, Vogt, Knight & Samper, 2006). Currently used primarily as a research instrument, the DRRI can also be used as an exploratory tool in clinical therapeutic settings.

Where possible, psychosocial instruments such as those described above should be expanded to integrate biomarkers, health measures, and physical lifestyle factors with demonstrated relevance to resilience. For example, contributors to this volume have identified cardiovascular reactivity, blood pressure, and salivary cortisol as potentially informative indirect but objective indices of psychological orientation to, anticipation of, and general responsiveness to stress. Measures of this type are easily accessible and provide a valuable basis for the validation of inventories that are otherwise based entirely on self-report.

Positive effects of mild to moderate stress on human performance may be an essential manifestation of resilience to otherwise potentially negative effects of stress. There is an opportunity here for additional study of resilience specifically in terms of its relationship to positive stress states (e.g., Staal, Bolton, Yaroush & Bourne, Chapter 10). In this context, it is reasonable to view resilience as a process whose effects should be conceived and measured along a continuum of outcome variables on specific (e.g., cognitive) tasks of interest. Studies of this sort can also be enhanced through the use of brain imaging and physiological data to document-related changes in cortical and sympathetic nervous system activity.

Social psychologists have observed that individual resilience to stress, including everyday stresses and job-related stress, may be influenced in part by the proximal social structural conditions in which people live. They emphasize the importance of neighborhood stability (Boardman, 2004) and "community capacity" (Bowen, Martin, Mancini & Nelson, 2000). These and related concerns have been studied in the specific context of military life and service (Bowen, Mancini, Martin, Ware & Nelson, 2003) where level of community participation predicts a stronger "sense of community" (Bowen, Martin, Mancini & Nelson, 2001), which in turn is associated with lower incidence of depression (Rohall & Martin, Chapter 11). A shortcoming of research done to date is its emphasis on subjective/perceived (versus objective/actual) community conditions. Thus, there is a need for additional research to determine how actual neighborhood/installation and community conditions (including location and access to support services) influence vulnerability to stress among service members and their families. Findings from studies in this area should be utilized to inform priorities for the planning, location, and design of military installations.

Application and Intervention

Previous authors have addressed the application of resilience as a basis for clinical intervention in the context of child development and family relations (e.g., Benard, 1999; Walsh, 2002; Werner & Johnson, 1999). Looking to the future, contributors to the current volume also see resilience as a potential knowledge base for application and intervention in adult populations, with particular attention to those who serve in the military. The hope is that resilience may serve a variety of needs, including screening and assessment, training, planning, operational support, and mental health services.

With continuing emphasis on the need for basic research to clarify essential factors of resilience, it may eventually become possible to assess the capacity of individuals for resilience. The goal would be to identify "resilient" and "nonresilient" (at-risk) individuals for the purpose of assignment, intervention, and training. Authors in this volume have explicitly recognized the need for real-world applications, for example, in human resources and in the military. To this end, we recommend that continued development and validation of instruments, such as the DRRI, should recognize and begin to include relevant biomarkers (e.g., cardiovascular reactivity, cortisol response and recovery), physical fitness indices, and measurable responses to anticipated stress as predictive of subsequent responsiveness to actual stress.

In general, military training implicitly recognizes the need to enhance overall physical and psychological capacities and endurance in preparation for the demands of combat. The specific objective of training war fighters to cope with and manage stress is addressed through stress exposure training (SET; Johnston & Cannon-Bowers, 1996) and stress inoculation training (SIT; Meichenbaum & Cameron, 1983). Others have addressed the need for greater emphasis on a cognitive–behavioral paradigm for mental readiness training (Thompson & McCreary, 2006). Virtual reality paradigms have been used with some success therapeutically (e.g., Difede & Hoffman, 2002; Rothbaum, Hodges, Ready, Graap & Alarcon, 2001) to train decision making under stress (Tichon, Wallis & Mildred, 2006) and, most recently, as a means to inoculate against traumatic effects of future stressors (Wiederhold & Wiederhold, 2006). Very recently, NATO has prereleased a new guide based on the international and interdisciplinary effort of mental health experts from 19 nations to assist military leaders in dealing with stress and the need for psychological support among military personnel (NATO Research and Technology Organisation, 2007). The NATO guide identifies resilience as an essential attribute of overall "psychological fitness" and observes that while individual military personnel are largely responsible for their own psychological fitness, military leaders establish the conditions (training, motivation, and morale) that promote this focus.

Several studies have provided empirical support for the effectiveness of programs designed to train or develop resilience *per se* (Sadow & Hopkins, 1993; van Breda, 1999; Waite & Richardson, 2004). The basic research literature suggests several areas where it may be helpful to develop specific skills or aspects of resilience, including self-enhancement and positive emotions (Luthans, Vogelgesang & Lester, 2006), perceived control and confidence (Amat et al., 2006; Davidson et al., 2005), optimism (Gillham & Reivich, 2004; Gillham, Reivich, Jaycox & Seligman, 1995), and hardiness (Maddi, Kahn & Maddi, 1998). Certainly, there is a need for more research in this area, beginning with a comprehensive review and analysis of currently available experimental, occupational, and therapeutic resilience training techniques. In the interim, it is reasonable to facilitate self-help through basic education. Organizations such as the American Psychological Association (APA, 2004) and the American Academy of Pediatrics (AAP; Ginsburg & Jablow, 2006) offer accessible, scientifically grounded information to laypersons who seek to build their individual resilience to stress and trauma. Basic education on aspects of resilience should not be overlooked as a potentially valuable strategy for military officers, team leaders, and mental health practitioners (including combat stress control personnel) who can actively promote resilience in others.

Findings from resilience research may be useful to inform the design and development of occupational and operational support systems to maximize information management and task performance under stress. Current interest in "augmented cognition" (e.g., Schmorrow, Kruse, Reeves & Bolton, 2007; Schmorrow, Stanney, Wilson & Young, 2004) brings attention to the need for interdisciplinary perspective on human information processing. Objectives in this area emphasize the need for strategies that can improve cognitive task and multitask performance by supporting task prioritization, resource maximization, and task management simplification. In each case, resilience is implied by the goal to reduce negative impact of stress on performance outcome. Thus, there is an opportunity to consider and integrate findings that address cognitive performance as relates to stress adaptation (e.g., Manzey,

Lorenz & Poljakov, 1998; Manzey, Lorenz, Schiewe, Finell & Thiele, 1995), and there is a clear and compelling need for additional research in this area.

Conclusion

Despite its elusiveness, resilience offers a valuable basis for insight into the generally durable character of the human mind, spirit, and body. Definitional struggles may be due in no small part to the inherently multidisciplinary attractiveness of resilience. As a still poorly defined empirical construct, resilience may force researchers from different disciplinary traditions to reckon with divergent and sometimes contradictory methodological habits and theoretical priorities. More generally as an organizing construct, resilience promotes an orientation to positive outcome, which in the context of traditional health models is conceived vaguely for now as the absence of negative outcome. Continued efforts to define and understand resilience must encourage new ways of thinking about human psychology and health and should emphasize the importance of interactivity between physical and nonphysical processes and systems.

We hope that the current volume serves not only to document the current state of the art in adult resilience research but also to inspire new progress in the form of much-needed research and practical development. The ultimate goal of all such work should be to generate predictive models based on measurable indices and outcomes. As a military scientific priority, resilience may offer practical benefits in essential areas of concern, such as personnel health protection and readiness, first-term attrition, effects of chronic stress, PTSD, risk management, technology-related stress, costs associated with mental health intervention, and specific problems, such as sleep deprivation and nutrition/weight management, which are commonly associated with prolonged deployments or personnel tempo (PERSTEMPO). Analogous concerns can be found in a variety of civilian and occupational settings outside the military. Thus, it is essential that civilian and military researchers recognize the need to coordinate and share their knowledge across multiple domains of interest.

References

Ahern, N.R., Kiehl, E.M., Sole, M.L. & Byers, J. (2006). A review of instruments measuring resilience. *Issues in Comprehensive Pediatric Nursing, 29,* 103–125.

Amat, J., Paul, E., Zarza, C., Watkins, L.R. & Maier, S.F. (2006). Previous experience with behavioral control over stress blocks the behavioral and dorsal raphe nucleus activating effects of later uncontrollable stress: Role of the ventral medial prefrontal cortex. *The Journal of Neuroscience, 26,* 13264–13272.

American Psychological Association (2004). *The Road to Resilience.* Washington, D.C.: The American Psychological Association. http://helping.apa.org

Baker, D.G., Risbrough, V.B. & Schork, N.J. (2007). Posttraumatic stress disorder: Genetic and environmental risk factors. In B. Lukey & V. Tepe (Eds.), *Biobehavioral Resilience to Stress*. London: Taylor & Francis.

Baruth, K.E. & Carroll, J.J. (2002). A formal assessment of resilience: The Baruth protective factors inventory. *Journal of Individual Psychology, 58*, 235–244.

Benard, B. (1999). Applications of resilience: Possibilities and promise. In M. Glantz & J. Johnson (Eds.), *Resilience and Development: Positive Life Adaptations* (pp. 269–277). New York: Plenum Press.

Boardman, J. (2004). Stress and physical health: The role of neighborhoods as mediating and moderating mechanisms. *Social Science and Medicine, 58*, 2471–2483.

Bowen, G.L., Mancini, J.A., Martin, J.A., Ware, W.B. & Nelson, J.P. (2003). Promoting the adaptation of military families: An empirical test of a community practice model. *Family Relations, 52*, 33–35.

Bowen, G.L., Martin, J.A., Mancini, J.A. & Nelson, J.P. (2001). Civic engagement and sense of community in the military. *Journal of Community Practice, 9*, 71–93.

Bowen, G.L., Martin, J.A., Mancini, J.A. & Nelson, J.P. (2000). Community capacity: Antecedents and consequences. *Journal of Community Practice, 8*, 1–21.

Brady, R.P. (2005). *Youth Risk and Resilience Inventory (YRRI)*. Indianapolis, IN: JIST Life.

Charney, D.S. (2004). Psychobiological mechanisms of resilience and vulnerability: Implications for successful adaptation to extreme stress. *American Journal of Psychiatry, 161*, 195–216.

Cicchetti, D. & Blender, J.A. (2004). A multiple-levels-of-analysis approach to the study of developmental processes in maltreated children. *Proceedings of the National Academy of Sciences, 101*, 17325–17326.

Connor, K.M. & Davidson, J.R.T. (2003). Development of a new resilience scale: The Connor-Davidson resilience scale (CD-RISC). *Depression and Anxiety, 18*, 76–82.

Curtis, W.J. & Cicchetti, D. (2003). Moving research on resilience into the 21st century: Theoretical and methodological considerations in examining biological contributors to resilience. *Development and Psychopathology, 15*, 773–810.

Curtis, W.J. & Nelson, C.A. (2003). Toward building a better brain: Neurobehavioral outcomes, mechanisms, and processes of environmental enrichment. In S.S. Luthar (Ed.), *Resilience and Vulnerability: Adaptation in the Context of Childhood Adversities* (pp. 463–488). New York: Cambridge University Press.

Davidson, J.R., Payne, V.M., Connor, K.M., Foa, E.B., Rothbaum, B.O., Hertzberg, M.A. & Weisler, R.H. (2005). Trauma, resilience, and saliostasis: Effects of treatment in post-traumatic stress disorder. *International Clinical Psychopharmacology, 20*, 43–48.

Difede, J. & Hoffman, H.G. (2002). Virtual reality exposure therapy for World Trade Center post-traumatic stress disorder: A case report. *Cyberpsychology and Behavior, 5*, 529–535.

Friborg, O., Hjemdal, O., Rosenvinge, J.H. & Martinussen, M. (2003). A new rating scale for adult resilience: What are the central protective resources behind healthy adjustment? *International Journal of Methods in Psychiatric Research, 12*, 65–76.

Friedl, K.E. & Penetar, D.M. (2007). Resilience and survival in extreme environments. In B. Lukey & V. Tepe (Eds.), *Biobehavioral Resilience to Stress*. London: Taylor & Francis.

Garmezy, N. (1974). Children at risk: The search for antecedents of schizophrenia. *Schizophrenia Bulletin, 8,* 14–90.

Garmezy, N. (1971). Vulnerability research and the issue of primary prevention. *American Journal of Orthopsychiatry, 41,* 101–116.

Garmezy, N. & Streitman, S. (1974). Children at risk: Conceptual models and research methods. *Schizophrenia Bulletin, 9,* 55–125.

Gillham, J.E. & Reivich, K.J. (2004). Cultivating optimism in childhood and adolescence. *The Annals of the American Academy of Political and Social Science, 591,* 146–163.

Gillham, J.E., Reivich, K.J., Jaycox, L.H. & Seligman, M.E.P. (1995). Prevention of depressive symptoms in schoolchildren: Two-year follow-up. *Psychological Science, 6,* 343–351.

Ginsburg, K.R. & Jablow, M.M. (2006). *A Parent's Guide to Building Resilience in Children and Teens: Giving Your Child Roots and Wings.* Elk Grove Village, IL: American Academy of Pediatrics.

Glantz, M.D. & Johnson, J.L. (Eds.) (1999). *Resilience and Development: Positive Life Adaptations.* New York: Kluwer Academic/Plenum Publishers.

Johnston, J.H. & Cannon-Bowers, J.A. (1996). Training for stress exposure. In J.A. Driskell & E. Salas (Eds.), *Stress and Human Performance* (pp. 223–256). Mahwah, NJ: Lawrence Erlbaum Associates.

Kim-Cohen, J., Moffitt, T.E., Caspi, A. & Taylor, A. (2004). Genetic and environmental processes in young children's resilience and vulnerability to socioeconomic deprivation. *Child Development, 75,* 651–668.

King, D.W., King, L.A. & Vogt, D.S. (2003). *Manual for the Deployment Risk and Resilience Inventory (DRRI): A Collection of Scales for Studying Deployment-Related Experiences in Military Veterans.* Boston, MA: National Center for PTSD.

King, L.A., King, D.W., Vogt, D.S., Knight, J.A. & Samper, R.E. (2006). Deployment risk and resilience inventory: A collection of measures for studying deployment-related experiences of military personnel and veterans. *Military Psychology, 18*(2), 89–120.

Kosslyn, S.M., Cacioppo, J.T., Dvidson, R.J., Hugdahl, K., Lovallo, W.R., Spiegel, D. & Rose, R. (2002). Bridging psychology and biology: the analysis of individuals in groups. *American Psychologist, 57*(5), 341–351.

Kumpfer, K.L. (1999). Factors and processes contributing to resilience: The resilience framework. In M. Glantz & J. Johnson (Eds.), *Resilience and Development: Positive Life Adaptations* (pp. 179–224). New York: Plenum Press.

Luthans, F., Vogelgesang, G.R. & Lester, P.B. (2006). Developing the psychological capital of resiliency. *Human Resources Development Review, 5,* 25–44.

Luthar, S.S. (Ed.) (2003). *Resilience and Vulnerability: Adaptation in the Context of Childhood Adversities.* New York: Cambridge University Press.

Luthar, S.S. & Cushing, G. (1999). Measurement issues in the empirical study of resilience: An overview. In M. Glantz & J. Johnson (Eds.), *Resilience and Development: Positive Life Adaptations* (pp. 129–160). New York: Plenum Press.

Luthar, S.S. & Zelazo, L.B. (2003). Research on resilience: An integrative review. In S.S. Luthar (Ed.), *Resilience and Vulnerability: Adaptation in the Context of Childhood Adversities* (pp. 510–549). New York: Cambridge University Press.

Maddi, S.R., Kahn, S. & Maddi, L.K. (1998). The effectiveness of hardiness training. *Journal of Consulting Psychology, 50,* 78–86.

Manzey, D., Lorenz, B. & Poljakov, V. (1998). Mental performance in extreme environments: Results from a performance monitoring study during a 438-day spaceflight. *Ergonomics, 41,* 537–559.

Manzey, D., Lorenz, B., Schiewe, A., Finell, G. & Thiele, G. (1995). Dual-task performance in space: Results from a single-case study during a short-term space mission. *Human Factors, 37,* 667–681.

Meichenbaum, D. & Cameron, R. (1983). Stress inoculation training: Toward a general paradigm for training coping skills. In D. Meichenbaum & M.E. Jeremko (Eds.), *Stress Reduction and Prevention* (pp. 115–154). New York: Plenum Press.

NATO Research and Technology Organisation (2007). *A Leader's Guide to Psychological Support Across the Deployment Cycle* (RTO-TR-HFM-081). Retrieved 26 April 2007, from the NATO RTO website: http://www.rta.nato.int/pubs/rdp.asp?RDP=RTO-TR-HFM-081.

Ness, J.W. & Tepe, V. (2004). Theoretical assumptions and scientific architecture. In J.W. Ness, V. Tepe & D.R. Ritzer (Eds.), *The Science and Simulation of Human Performance* (pp. 127–155). Amsterdam: Elsevier.

Osman, A., Gutierrez, P.M., Muehlenkamp, J.J., Dix-Richardson, F., Barrios, F.X. & Kopper, B.A. (2005). Suicide resilience inventory-25: Development and preliminary psychometric properties. *Psychological Reports, 94,* 1349–1360.

Osman, A., Gutierrez, P.M., Muehlenkamp, J.J., Dix-Richardson, F., Barrios, F.X. & Kopper, B.A. (2004). Suicide Resilience Inventory – 25: development and preliminary psychometric properties. *Psychological Reports, 94,* 1349–1360.

Rohall, D.E. & Martin, J. (2007). The impact of social structural conditions on psychological resilience to stress. In B. Lukey & V. Tepe (Eds.), *Biobehavioral Resilience to Stress.* London: Taylor & Francis.

Rothbaum, B.O., Hodges, L., Ready, D., Graap, K. & Alarcon, R.D. (2001). Virtual reality exposure therapy for Vietnam veterans with posttraumatic stress disorder. *Journal of Clinical Psychiatry, 70,* 428–432.

Rutter, M. (2003). Genetic influences on risk and protection: Implications for understanding resilience. In S.S. Luthar (Ed.), *Resilience and Vulnerability: Adaptation in the Context of Childhood Adversities* (pp. 489–509). New York: Cambridge University Press.

Sadow, D.C. & Hopkins, B. (1993). Resiliency training and empowerment among homeless, substance abusing veterans. *Research Communications in Psychology, Psychiatry and Behavior, 18,* 121–134.

Schmorrow, D., Kruse, A., Reeves, L. & Bolton, A.E. (2007). Augmented cognition in HCI: 21st century adaptive system science and technology. In A. Sears & J. Jacko (Eds.), *The Human-Computer Interaction Handbook: Fundamentals, Evolving Technologies, and Emerging Applications* (2nd Edition). USA: CRC Press.

Schmorrow, D., Stanney, K.M., Wilson, G. & Young, P. (2004). Augmented cognition in human–system interaction. In G. Salvendy (Ed.), *Handbook of Human Factors and Ergonomics* (3rd edition). New York: John Wiley.

Silverstein, A. (1988). An Aristotelian resolution of the idiographic versus nomothetic tension. *American Psychologist, 43,* 425–430.

Southwick, S., Ozbay, F., Charney, D.S. & McEwen, B.S. (2007). Adaptation to stress and psychobiological mechanisms of resilience. In B. Lukey & V. Tepe (Eds.), *Biobehavioral Resilience to Stress*. London: Taylor & Francis.

Southwick, S., Vythilingam, M. & Charney, D.S. (2005). The psychobiology of depression and resilience to stress: Implications for prevention and treatment. *Annual Review of Clinical Psychology, 1,* 255–291.

Staal, M.A., Bolton, A.E., Yaroush, R.A. & Bourne, L.E. (2007). Cognitive performance and resilience to stress. In B. Lukey & V. Tepe (Eds.), *Biobehavioral Resilience to Stress*. London: Taylor & Francis.

Thompson, M.M. & McCreary, D.R. (2006). Enhancing mental readiness in military personnel. In T.W. Britt, A. Adler & C.A. Castro (Series Eds.) and A. Adler, T.W. Britt & C.A. Castro (Volume Eds.), *Military Life: The Psychology of Serving in Peace and Combat: Vol. 2. Operational Demands and Adjustment* (pp. 54–79). New York: Praeger Press.

Tichon, J., Wallis, G. & Mildred, T. (2006). Virtual training environments to improve train driver's crisis decision-making. *Proceedings of Simtect,* Melbourne. 29 May–1 Jun, Melbourne, Australia.

Van Breda, A. (1999). Developing resilience to routine separations: An occupational social work intervention. *Families in Society, 80,* 597–605.

Wagnild, G.M. & Young, H.M. (1993). Development and psychometric evaluation of the resilience scale. *Journal of Nursing Measurement, 1,* 165–178.

Waite, P.J. & Richardson, G.E. (2004). Determining the efficacy of resilience training in the worksite. *The Journal of Allied Health, 33,* 178–183.

Wald, J., Taylor, S., Asmundson, G.J.G., Lang, K.L. & Stapleton, J. (2006). *Literature Review of Concepts: Psychological Resiliency*. (DR 2006-073). Toronto, Canada: DRDC Toronto. http://pubs.drdc.gc.ca/inbasket/CEBsupport.060410_1000. toronto_cr_2006_073.pdf

Walsh, F. (2002). A family resilience framework: Innovative practice applications. *Family Relations, 51,* 130–137.

Waugh, C., Tugade, M. & Fredrickson, B. (2007). Psychophysiology of resilience to stress. In B. Lukey & V. Tepe (Eds.), *Biobehavioral Resilience to Stress*. London: Taylor & Francis.

Werner, E.E. & Johnson, J.L. (1999). Can we apply resilience? In M. Glantz & J. Johnson (Eds.), *Resilience and Development: Positive Life Adaptations* (pp. 259–268). New York: Plenum Press.

Wiederhold, B.K. & Wiederhold, M.D. (2006). Virtual reality as a tool in early intervention. In *Human Dimensions in Military Operations—Military Leaders' Strategies for Addressing Stress and Psychological Support* (pp. 45-1–45-8). Meeting Proceedings RTO-MP-HFM-134, Paper 34. Neuilly-sur-Seine, France: RTO.

Windle, M. (1999). Critical conceptual and measurement issues in the study of resilience. In M. Glantz & J. Johnson (Eds.), *Resilience and Development: Positive Life Adaptations* (pp. 161–176). New York: Plenum Press.

Yehuda, R., Flory, J.D., Southwick, S. & Charney, D.S. (2006). Developing an agenda for translational studies of resilience and vulnerability following trauma exposure. *Annals of the New York Academy of Sciences, 1071,* 379–396.

Yehuda, R. & McEwen, B. (Eds.) (2004). *Biobehavioral Stress Response: Protective and Damaging Effects*. New York: The New York Academy of Sciences.

Index

9 780367 864866